THE
U.S.-SINGAPORE
FREE TRADE
AGREEMENT

The **Institute of Southeast Asian Studies (ISEAS)** was established as an autonomous organization in 1968. It is a regional centre dedicated to the study of socio-political, security and economic trends and developments in Southeast Asia and its wider geostrategic and economic environment.

The Institute's research programmes are the Regional Economic Studies (RES, including ASEAN and APEC), Regional Strategic and Political Studies (RSPS), and Regional Social and Cultural Studies (RSCS).

ISEAS Publishing, an established academic press, has issued more than 2,000 books and journals. It is the largest scholarly publisher of research about Southeast Asia from within the region. ISEAS Publications works with many other academic and trade publishers and distributors to disseminate important research and analyses from and about Southeast Asia to the rest of the world.

THE
U.S.-SINGAPORE FREE TRADE AGREEMENT

AN AMERICAN PERSPECTIVE ON POWER, TRADE, AND SECURITY IN THE ASIA PACIFIC

EUL-SOO PANG

ISEAS

INSTITUTE OF SOUTHEAST ASIAN STUDIES

Singapore

First published in Singapore in 2011 by
ISEAS Publishing
Institute of Southeast Asian Studies
30 Heng Mui Keng Terrace
Pasir Panjang
Singapore 119614

E-mail: publish@iseas.edu.sg
Website: http://bookshop.iseas.edu.sg

The responsibility for facts and opinions in this publication rests exclusively with the author and his interpretations do not necessarily reflect the views or the policy of the publishers or their supporters.

ISEAS Library Cataloguing-in-Publication Data

Pang, Eul-Soo.
    The U.S.-Singapore Free Trade Agreement: an American perspective on power, trade, and security in the Asia Pacific.
  1.   Free trade—United States.
  2.   Free trade—Singapore.
  3.   United States—Commerce—Singapore.
  4.   Singapore—Commerce—United States.
  5.   United States—Commercial policy.
  6.   Regionalism—Asia.
  I.   Title.
HF1756 P19   2011

ISBN 978-981-4311-99-1 (soft cover)
ISBN 978-981-4311-00-2 (e-book PDF)

Typeset by Superskill Graphics Pte Ltd
Printed in Singapore by

To Ruth Peake Jarnagin

Contents

List of Tables

Foreword

In 2004, my colleague Chang Li Lin and I edited a book entitled, *The United States-Singapore Free Trade Agreement: Highlights and Insights*. The contributors included key members of the Singapore negotiating team, as well as essays by the leader of the U.S. Delegation, the then U.S. ambassador to Singapore and a member of the U.S. Chamber of Commerce. It is an official and insiders' account. I wanted to record, while the memory was fresh, our common experiences in negotiating this remarkable bilateral trade agreement.

Now, Dr Eul-Soo Pang, a Korean-American scholar and visiting professorial fellow at the Institute of Southeast Asian Studies (ISEAS) in Singapore has written a book from an outsider's and American perspective, drawing principally on published and unpublished U.S. government documents, especially from the U.S. Congress, the United States Trade Representative Office, the International Trade Commission, the U.S. Chamber of Commerce, the American Federation of Labor and Congress of Industrial Organization (AFL-CIO), American Chamber of Commerce (AmCham) in Singapore, and corporations, as well as NGOs, all key players in the making of free trade agreements in the American system.

The most interesting part of Pang's book is how complex the American system of decision making was for the USSFTA. By law, the president is required to create twenty-eight national committees from agriculture to business, environment, financial services, labour, and everything in between. Corporate and citizen inputs must be solicited through timely announcements in the *Federal Register*. Based on data from public and private sources, Pang has shown in detail how these committees, corporations, NGOs, and individual citizens have supported or opposed aspects of the USSFTA's provisions.

The book also covers annual reviews. It reveals a host of issues that we, the negotiators, did not anticipate. One example is the case of polycarbonate trade. The USSFTA has created a situation in which the U.S. government was called upon to protect a German firm's market share in the United States, which was seriously challenged by a Japanese manufacturer residing in Singapore. Indeed, globalization has created strange bedfellows. Neither Japan nor Germany has FTAs with the United States. Singapore has an FTA with Japan and is negotiating one with the European Union.

Aside from a series of vignettes that Pang has used to reinforce the thesis of the book, his conclusion is compelling: FTAs are not about trade, but in the case of the USSFTA — between two high income countries — it is more about financial market access, tightening intellectual property rights, e-commerce, capital controls, binational licensing of professionals, government monopolies, bidding for government procurement projects, stronger IPR laws, introducing more up-to-date competition law and practices, and even visas for Singaporeans planning to work in the United States. Furthermore, underneath all these "WTO-plus" issues that we have built into the USSFTA, Singapore and the United States have managed to strengthen their existing security ties, which Pang sees as deeply embedded in the trade and investment relationship.

In hindsight, then Prime Minister Goh Chok Tong made a timely and prescient decision to start the FTA negotiations with the United States in 2000. At the time, the prospects for a single global market seemed low, as Doha in 2001 and Cancún in 2003 have confirmed. Just emerging from the devastating financial crisis of 1997–98, the ASEAN Free Trade Area also seemed to be moving at a more sluggish pace than we would have liked. The intra-NAFTA trade was maxing out. It seemed opportunities lay as much outside each other's RTAs (regional trade agreements) as inside. This common frustration was shared by Prime Minister Goh and President Bill Clinton. They agreed to start the process of the USSFTA during a midnight golf game in Brunei. I was contacted the next day to lead the Singaporean FTA delegation. At the time I was teaching in China.

Those willing to create more trading and investment opportunities should not put all their eggs in a single WTO basket. Those willing to move faster should be allowed to move ahead. Although President Clinton did not have the "fast-track" authorization from Congress — Congress had rejected his request twice and Clinton became the only post-Second World War president without one — we were willing to take the chance. According to Pang's research, between 1890 and 2002, the Americans had eight trade promotion acts, or fast tracks. We began to negotiate with the Americans in December 2000, and by late summer of 2002, President Bush was granted a fast-track authority, or the Trade Promotion Act of August 2002. It required a stream of consultations.

As it turned out, the USTR (US Trade Representative) and his representatives consulted and briefed senators, congressmen, and their staffers no fewer than 1,605 times on ongoing negotiations! Furthermore, soon after the USSFTA was signed, President Bush, obviously motivated by the desire to build more post-9/11 security partnerships, instituted pre-FTA qualifications screening for future partners that the National Security Council and National Economic Council were asked to vet. Given all these constraints and bureaucratic hurdles in the American system, our timing was perfect!

A 2006 IMF study shows — cited in the book — that for the past twenty years, all the countries that have had good economic growth rates are the ones that opened their markets unilaterally, or through FTAs or RTAs, to the outside world. In the process, they were also able to reduce mass poverty by 2 per cent per annum, and this was a boon to poor countries. The same study has also shown that 70 per cent of all trade barriers that developing countries face today are coming from the South. The World Bank has discouraged South-South FTAs and RTAs for this reason. This is, however, a mistaken view as the success of the ASEAN Free Trade Agreement has demonstrated.

The USSFTA is unique in several ways. First, it is the first Asian-U.S. free trade agreement, and Singapore was delighted to play the role of leader for the region. Second, the FTA is between two advanced economies, and as such, it covers more than trade in goods. Third, the engagement of the United States in the region has been the big concern of our government, and the USSFTA has helped to anchor America in the region and allowed it to deepen its economic roots throughout the region. In addition to the $44 billion two-way trade in 2008, we hosted $106 billion of American FDI, according to the U.S. Department of Commerce. This is the largest in the region, more than what the Americans have invested in Australia, Japan, or China. Fourth, in spite of some concerns shown by our neighbors about bilateral FTAs as "backdoors" to ASEAN, we have been able to include parts of Indonesia (Bintan and Batam) in our access to the American market. Roughly 270 categories of products made by our companies on those two islands can enter the American market with a "Made in Singapore" label. This is a positive and salutary backdoor for our neighbour.

Finally, the Obama administration is responding to our wish. The Trans-Pacific Partnership negotiations, so far having completed three rounds, have to deal with a series of overlapping and even conflicting terms of agreements because the majority of the negotiating parties have bilateral FTAs with each other. At the third round in Peru, a consensus emerged: adopt the highest "gold standards" for trade, investment, environment, and labour. That means the USSFTA in effect.

So far, in addition to the original members of the group (Brunei, Chile, New Zealand, and Singapore), I am happy to say that we have been able to persuade the United States, Vietnam, Peru, and Australia to join us. In August 2010, Malaysia decided to participate. In September, the Philippines expressed its interest. Japan has also expressed interest. China, South Korea, and Canada are said to be looking into joining. When the APEC Summit meets in Honolulu, in November 2011, I am told that the negotiating parties of the Trans-Pacific Partnership (TPP) hope to complete their work. This will be a sea change for the region. The Bogor agreement was non-binding, and APEC has no formal commitment to create a single super-regional market. The TPP may be the answer. We should not take all the credit for it, but Pang will readily agree that Singapore and its USSFTA have played an indispensable role for the expansion of economic integration throughout the Asia Pacific, now including South America.

In this broad panoply of comprehensive bilateral FTAs, partial scope agreements, multilateral regional trade areas, and economic integration partnerships, Pang's book adds much to the understanding of the intricacies of international political economy. Trade is not just about trade. In Singapore's case, it is about expanding our political and economic space. What Singapore has been pursuing — trading partnerships — is not unique. What is unique is how we fashion our relationships. It is the breadth and depth that count. The book is full of new information, not readily available in this region, useful in-depth look at the complex American system of trade decision making, and new ideas for international political economy of trade and security.

Tommy Koh
Ambassador-at-Large, Ministry of Foreign Affairs, Singapore and
Chief Negotiator for the USSFTA
November 2010

Message

The linkage between trade and development has constituted a cornerstone theme for ISEAS research, seminars, workshops, and conference agendas for decades now. Dedicated to the study of large regional economic, sociopolitical, security, and geostrategic issues, the Institute has pursued multidisciplinary approaches to public policy analysis and policymaking. We have scholars in residence from all over the world, and their professional, academic, and intellectual backgrounds are so diverse that they reflect well the currents of globalization and regionalization that Southeast Asia and its close and distant neighbours have been experiencing for the past decades. Over the years, we have come to realize that such policy-focused issues as trade and development must be viewed and analysed from diverse disciplinary perspectives, not just from the single angle of economics, because the consequences of trade are far reaching, often impacting the domestic polity, society, culture, and even daily habits of peoples. By adopting this view, the Institute has produced more balanced and nuanced policy analysis and policy recommendations. We have established various programmes ranging from looking at religion and culture (the Nalanda-Sriwijaya Centre) to linking law, diplomacy, history, sociology, and business economics (the ASEAN Studies Centre and the Singapore APEC Study Centre). Their research output has considerably enhanced the current state of knowledge on how policy is made, how it could be made better, and how it contributes to development.

Professor Pang is a historian who has been working on trade and development issues from the perspective of international political economy. His book examines free trade agreement (FTA) issues, linking them to their broader development contexts. Political economy approaches can go far in explaining how FTAs can be used to enhance political, cultural, and even security cooperation while promoting domestic policy reforms for trade partners. As a Latin American specialist, Professor Pang brings to the book both historical and comparative regional perspectives. I believe the book will be useful to the academic and policy communities because it bridges theories and policymaking, especially in the context of the U.S. politics of trade, its foreign policy objectives toward Southeast Asia, and its increasing trade and security partnership with Singapore. The book's focus on how American policymakers view FTAs and how this has contributed to bilateral relations between Singapore and the United States is a unique contribution to the scholarly literature as well as a readable treatise on the subject for the informed layperson.

K. Kesavapany
Director
Institute of Southeast Asian Studies

Preface

The aetiology of this book has an interesting history. In the summer of 2000, I met Ambassador K. Kesavapany ("Pany" to his friends), then high commissioner of Singapore to Malaysia and now director of the Institute of Southeast Asian Studies in Singapore. At the time, I held a joint appointment as a Fulbright Visiting Professor to the Universiti Kebangsaan Malaysia and the Institute of Diplomacy and Foreign Relations (IDFR), then a department at the Prime Minister's Office. My relationship with IDFR grew to be an eight-year summer stint from 2000 to 2007. I often stopped over in Singapore to visit with Ambassador Pany on my way home from Kuala Lumpur. During one of my stopovers, Pany told me that he had been appointed chief negotiator to lead the Singapore-Korea Free Trade Agreement negotiation. Then, he said, "FTA is not about trade; it is about political relationships; it is about finances; and it is about locking in or launching domestic reform." He also assured me that an FTA cannot hurt its neighbours, as some in Southeast Asia had feared that the Singapore-Korea FTA could serve as a "backdoor" for Korea into the ASEAN market. The ambassador published several articles in the Malaysian and Singaporean newspapers explaining why FTAs would help all of ASEAN, not just the signatories. The idea intrigued me, so I began to read about free trade in general and the U.S.–Singapore Free Trade Area (USSFTA) in particular. In the process, I discovered that there was no academic literature on the USSFTA. Here was my new research agenda.

I decided to tackle the project by testing Pany's ideas. The result was the publication of my 2007 article entitled, "Embedding Security in Free Trade: The Case of the U.S.-Singapore Free Trade Agreement". Soon after that, I had an opportunity to present a paper at a workshop at the University of Southern California and was able to "compare notes" to see how political scientists handled the subject. My perspective as a historian was quite different from those who populated the workshop. As a Latin Americanist, I was a novice in the field of Asian studies, but I could at least bring a comparative viewpoint to bear. In 2008 and 2009, Ambassador Pany gave me a summer fellowship at the Institute of Southeast Asian Studies, where I began to deepen my understanding of Singapore's political economy and started writing this book. What follows in these chapters are the findings of my research, which confirm what Ambassador Pany has said: FTA is not about trade, especially not about merchandise trade. Rather, it is about a far more complex set of international relationships that are as much about security and development as anything else.

I chose to write this book from an American scholar's perspective because in 2004 the Singaporean negotiating team produced a fine piece of work on the subject from their frame of reference. Thus, I decided to rely on U.S. government sources as the principal set of data (Congress seemed keenly interested in the topic), complemented by scholarly works, newspaper articles, and the publications of various Asian and multilateral organizations.

Finally, I must mention that this book is not a quantitative economic study; nor is it political science. Rather, it is a work by a historian interested in international political economy (IPE) issues and the comparative history of trade and development. But unlike traditional historical monographs, the book does not dwell on details, facts, and dates. Instead, I provide historical analysis based on empirical data. In the process, I have sought to test whether many IPE theories and assumptions on FTAs are valid for the subject. As the reader will discover, while these theories and assumptions go a long way towards framing big questions, they fall short of capturing the real motivations, and explaining the objectives behind the crafting of free trade agreements. In the book, I suggest some ways in which the theories can be fine-tuned with case studies such as this one.

Acknowledgements

This is my first book on East Asia, or more specifically, Southeast Asia. As a Latin American historian, I needed guiding hands from Asian, North American, Latin American, and European friends and strangers to gather data and acquire the proper perspectives for the book. Ambassadors K. Kesavapany and Tommy Koh shared their personal views as Singapore's chief negotiators for free trade agreements (FTAs) with South Korea and with the United States, respectively. Thank you, Pany and Tommy.

At the Institute of Southeast Asian Studies (ISEAS), I got to know several retired ambassadors, development bankers, and academics from the region. They shared their views and insights on FTAs. Ambassador Keng Jin Tan, Ambassador Rod Severino, Dr Omkar Shrestha and Mark Hong (my Gang of Four) made me an honorary member of their lunch club. They shared with me their perspectives and personal experiences. Also at ISEAS, the administrative staff and librarians merit my thanks for the strong support they gave me.

My special thanks must go to Alan Colegrove (a former U.S. naval aviator) and Jim Tietjen. I met Alan in Kuala Lumpur in 2000 when he was selling Boeing aircraft in Southeast Asia. Alan shared with me his contacts in Singapore, which included an introduction to Jim Tietjen, former U.S. Air Force attaché at the U.S. Embassy in Singapore. Jim and his wife Valerie have been a constant source of encouragement and friendship. Singaporean ministry officials also helped me, but will remain anonymous at their request.

I also thank Ambassador Dr Yusof Ahmad and his wife, Niki, Dr Zakkybaby, Dr James Jesudason, Phil Overmyer, Emily Dunivant, Derek Loh, Dom LaVine, Jasmine Ng, Dr Debrah Kay Elms, Dr Helen Nesadurai, Dr Johan Saravanamuttu, Paulo de Miranda, Dr Razeen Sally, Dr Christopher Dent, Dr Kogi, Delfina, Shiruzimath, Begum, Suriani,

Razief, Mano, Nazcov, Amer, Aniza, Nasrul, Farizal, Sadik, Ganesh, James Ng, Halim Saad, David Ong, Dana Simmons, Katherine Emmanuel, and Philippe and Cynthia Dunoyer. Philippe is a former CEO of Total-America and taught an IPE honors seminar with me at Colorado School of Mines for nine years. He has shared his practical experience as an IPE practitioner in the petroleum business in the Middle East, North Africa, Europe, and the United States. I have learned much from him. At the Colorado School of Mines, I owe much to my students and staff. Tom Bonnie, Jentry Mitchell, An (Ethan) Ngo, and Kurtis Griess helped me collect data. In my IPE seminars, Jeremy Sauer, Chris Kretchman, Gemma Lockhart, Ikram al-Yacoub, Khan Vu, Jill Savage, Joby Rittenhouse, LeVell Hill, and others shared their views on FTAs and East Asia. Connie Warren and Janelle Duke also gave me invaluable staff support. Also, I thank the anonymous external reviewers who made constructive suggestions on how to improve the book.

Finally, I would like to thank my wife, Laura, who is a fine Latin American historian and my former boss at Mines. She has helped me with new ideas, made invaluable suggestions for structuring the book, and given me constant encouragement in completing it. My sons, Alex and Steve, have been enthusiastic about the project. And Ruth Peake Jarnagin, my mother-in-law, has shown an insatiable curiosity about this book, which I am dedicating to her.

Eul-Soo Pang
Singapore
15 March 2011

Introduction

This book presents an American perspective on how the United States views free trade agreements (FTAs) in general, and, specifically, how the government, business sectors, organized labour, NGOs, and civil society groups interacted among themselves and chose to respond to the making of the United States-Singapore Free Trade Agreement (USSFTA). Singapore's negotiator, Ambassador Tommy Koh, and his negotiating team produced an informative book in 2004 that has captured succinctly the Singaporean perspectives. Dozens of economists, international relations specialists, and political scientists have written about the positive and negative economic consequences of free trade agreements. Hence, I chose to focus on the little explored aspect of American domestic political economy dimensions in the making of the USSFTA, given the complex processes the Clinton and Bush administrations underwent to obtain congressional approval for it.

The United States has seventeen working FTAs. Between 2002 and 2007, the Bush administration signed eighteen FTAs. The U.S. Congress has approved fifteen while three are pending (South Korea, Panama, and Colombia). With this record, George W. Bush has emerged with the most number of bilateral and multilateral FTAs brought into effect by any president during his two terms, a remarkable accomplishment considering the cumbersome and divisive nature of the American political system. But what history will remember most is that Bush's FTAs were *less* about economics and *more* about consolidating the political and security objectives of the United States and its partners.

The tedious procedure for negotiation and congressional approval required the United States Trade Representative (USTR) and his associates to consult the Congress 1,605 times for the eighteen negotiated FTAs (an average of ninety consultations with congressional leaders and staffers for each FTA), in addition to endless meetings, documents and e-mail exchanges, and teleconferences at the executive branch's interagency and interdepartmental levels. In addition, there was a plethora of unsolicited input from private business sectors along with labour, human rights, religious, and environmental groups, with real and perceived stakes in trade and post-FTA annual reviews. Congressional hearings in both houses on FTAs were numerous as well and questioned subject matter specialists for the pros and cons of the USSFTA.

Equally intriguing but largely hidden was how the free trade agreement between the world's largest economy and the Asian Venice could impact the security landscape of the Asia Pacific as well as Southeast Asia. The American GDP was at least 100 times Singapore's during the negotiations, but the U.S. ratio of GDP to trade was less than 20 per cent; Singapore's represented at least 350 per cent its domestic output. Like the Mediterranean trading state of yore, Singapore has the power, vision, means, and courage to influence both the great powers and its neighbours. In many ways, Singapore, like Venice, has more clout than a Byzantium in shaping the regional economic and security environment. Down the road, it will play an indispensable role in persuading the great powers from East Asia and beyond to embrace a constructive role in the now budding Asia Pacific economic and security architecture.

Specifically, at the USSFTA signing ceremony at the White House, President George W. Bush, his U.S. trade representative, and others emphasized how the FTA was a logical sequel to the existing security relationship that had been steadily growing since the early 1990s between Singapore and the United States. The response from Prime Minister Goh Chok Tong and his colleagues was no less emphatic about the link between trade and security. Singapore has no formal alliance with Washington and probably never will. But it has greater clout in shaping and reshaping America's strategy towards East Asia than some formal allies of the United States in the region. In this context, I have reviewed and explored the pros and cons of embedding security into trade relationships. The convergence of these two spheres persisted as the cornerstone of the Bush administration's free trade and global war on terrorism strategy, and President Barack Obama has not discarded it as of his second year in office.

On 14 December 2009, the president notified Congress that the United States would commence multiparty negotiations to become a member of the Trans-Pacific Partnership, a four-country economic and trade integration agreement among Singapore, Brunei, Chile, and New Zealand. Soon, Vietnam, Australia, and Peru decided to join the negotiations. The first round of the meeting was held in Sydney, Australia on 15 March 2010. The second and third rounds were held in San Francisco in June, and Lima in August, respectively. Thus, Obama has taken the Asia Pacific economic integration to the next level. Others in the region are watching. In the Pacific, the United States has bilateral FTAs with Australia, Chile, Singapore, Mexico, Canada, five central American states, and Peru. The FTA with Korea as of March 2011 has yet to receive congressional approval. Washington has been receptive to overtures from Vietnam and New Zealand about potential bilateral FTAs as well. For too long, the core of American foreign policy towards East Asia has been focused on security, and Obama has launched serious efforts to push trade and economic ties with America's Asian allies and partners. If successful, these efforts will balance Cold War-era U.S. preoccupations with security nicely and can even enhance its overall position as a major Pacific power for decades to come.

Singapore was the first Asian country to sign an FTA with the United States and remains the only Asian country with an FTA *in force*. In the Asia Pacific of some sixty sovereign states, Singapore is one of two FTA partners with the United States — Australia being the other. For Singapore, this convergence offers a unique opportunity to reinforce its foreign policy tradition of opening to the world, but guarding itself from an uncertain regional security environment. It also sends a strong message to its neighbours that the city state is *no* beachhead of China. By engaging the United States in Southeast Asia and tapping into America's military technology and strengthening interoperability, Singapore has emerged as the region's formidable military power. Even before Manila refused to renew base rights for the American navy at Subic Bay and for the air force at Clark Field in 1991, the United States had already been exploring the possibility of access to Singapore's facilities. When the Philippine Senate failed to approve the renewal contract, the Singapore Government stepped forward, at no one's prodding, to offer the homeless American military access rights to its Changi and Paya Lebar facilities, at great risk of irking its northern and southern neighbours. Interestingly enough, the Singapore model ("places, not bases") has given a new dimension to the structure of America's twenty-first century Pacific strategy, in which having permanent bases may not be necessary to remain relevant in the Pacific Century, but having permanent staging grounds for economic interests will be.

Aside from the obvious economic gains that Singapore now has with full, unencumbered access to the world's largest economy and its largest hinterland, the city state has made several domestic political gains from the FTA. Singapore moved swiftly to improve its competitiveness by implementing a host of reforms such as in the Competition Act of 2004, which spells out better enforcement procedures for business activities. The government has also strengthened the oversight of intellectual property rights. Doing so has attracted a slew of American and non-American multinational companies in the pharmaceutical, biotechnological, and digital sectors. Also Singapore has granted greater market space for more American banks to introduce full banking services for Singapore's citizens; it has opened up e-commerce; it has allowed cross-professional licensing (beginning with lawyers and engineers); and it has secured 4,500 business visas for Singaporeans to work in the United States *per annum*.

On the American side, there were few domestic gains, but the FTA debate brought to the surface a sharper partisanship in political discourse and worsened labour-business relations. In the process, the American system of open government proved starkly to be less efficient and even less competitive when it comes to dealing with such global issues as FTAs. But the participation of civil society on the American side was notable, and Congress, the USTR, and various agencies of the executive branch of the government went out of their way to involve non-state actors. The use of e-mail and the Internet made this broader discussion possible. On its own, the Singapore Government solicited views on the FTA from American firms and influential individuals in the city. All in all, the agreement received a fair review from all parties concerned in Singapore and the United States. The process turned out to be transparent and society-wide. As a result, it produced the most comprehensive ("WTO plus") and "gold standard" FTA in American history.

The World Bank, the International Monetary Fund, and the World Trade Organization have argued that trade contributes to growth and that the more free trade there is, the faster growth will be. It may be an advocate's tinted view, but there is much truth in it. Seen strictly from the economic standpoint of the United States, FTAs in general offer few benefits. U.S. government-sponsored studies, as well as academic researches on trade, have been unanimous in their verdict that the benefits from free trade to the American economy of US$12 trillion (at the time of the USSFTA negotiations) would be 4.5 per cent of GDP, or US$497 billion, *in the unlikely scenario of the entire world unilaterally removing all tariff and non-tariff barriers to American merchandise and services*. A study by the University of Michigan estimated that under the most optimistic scenario, the USFFTA would add, at most, US$17.5 billion to the American GDP per year. FTAs with

Australia could mean an additional US$14 billion, Korea US$30 billion, Chile US$4.4 billion, and the entire four Central American countries, plus the Dominican Republic, US$17.3 billion, less than that with Singapore. On the other hand, Prime Minister Goh stated that the USSFTA could raise Singapore's GDP by as much as 2 per cent per year. The FTA offers both economic and security benefits to the city state. But the jury is still out. As for the United States, none of these econometric predictions has been realized.

The negotiations for the agreement took eleven rounds (a year plus a few days, from late December 2000 to January 2002) and involved American 139 issue specialists from a dozen or so U.S. Government agencies. It cost American taxpayers US$172,000. Australia, with a GDP several times larger than Singapore's, took five fewer American specialists to negotiate. The largest number of the American participants came from the Department of Agriculture. This is not surprising, given that the two most senior senators of the Finance Committee (empowered to oversee trade issues) were from agricultural states. The Treasury also had sixteen staffers involved in the FTA negotiation, indicating that the financial services market opening of Singapore — reform, deregulation, and liberalization — was of the utmost interest to the United States, not manufacture trade. In 2008, the top three hosts of America's investment in the Asia Pacific were Singapore, Australia, and Japan, in that descending order. The city state hosts the largest amount of American investment: the 2008 year-end total investment stock was US$106 billion, followed by Australia (US$89 billion), and Japan trailing in third place (US$79 billion). Hong Kong ranked fourth (US$51 billion) and China was a distant fifth, hosting US$46 billion of U.S. investment in the Asia Pacific.

On trade of manufactures, the United States agreed to give a "Made in Singapore" status to medical instruments and informatics products that Singapore's firms make in Indonesia's Bintan and Batam islands. This provision of an "integrated sourcing initiative" (in a trade specialist's jargon) was unprecedented and validated Singapore's offshore production strategy. Indonesia now has access to the world's largest market through a "backdoor" (Singapore) even though it has not signed an FTA with Washington. Singapore has brought the benefits of the FTA to its neighbour. America's offshore production in the Mexican and Honduran *maquiladoras* was not included, however: the United States did not insist on *quid pro quo* and Singapore did not volunteer to reciprocate.

The emphasis on increasing American agricultural exports certainly complemented Bush's re-election strategy of wooing Mid-Western, Western, and Southern states well. The two top ranking senators of the Finance Committee came from agricultural and ranching states — Iowa (Republican Senator Chuck Grassley) and Montana (Democratic Senator Max Baucus). Singapore, with no commercial scale agriculture, has been an enthusiastic importer of American agricultural products. U.S. Department of Agriculture specialists unreservedly endorsed the FTA.

In the House, the leadership was equally supportive of the FTA. The chairman of a trade supervising subcommittee of the House Ways and Means Committee came from Chicago (Republican Congressman Phil Crane), where the chewing gum maker (Wriggley) has been a prominent civic leader and political voice for over a century. Crane wanted Singapore to lift the existing ban on the use of chewing gum. Ambassador Tommy Koh mentioned to me that the chewing gum issue could have been the deal breaker, appearing in the last hour of the negotiation. Both sides compromised, however: Singapore classified chewing gum as a therapeutic product that a dentist could prescribe to patients; thus, technically, the ban on the sale of chewing gum was removed. But the average person still cannot buy Big Red at a supermarket or a 7-Eleven in Singapore. These were some of the vagaries of American democracy in crafting the final version of the FTA, illustrating that a handful of powerful senators and congressmen can hold up interstate negotiations and can make or break international treaties.

In March 2010, the Congressional Research Service (CRS) reported an interesting titbit about Singapore's chewing gum imports. In 2005 (the second year of the FTA), Singapore imported US$1,298 worth of American chewing gum, and the following year, it spent US$246 for the American imports! In 2009, according to the congressional report, "none came from the United States". Indonesia exported US$627,016 worth of chewing gum and South Korea reported US$112,907 in its gum exports. The congressional researchers added an intriguing footnote: "CRS attempted to obtain export data from a major U.S. chewing gum company, but it declined to cooperate. Likewise, the International Chewing Gum Association [sic] would not provide CRS with data on exports to Singapore." This book has sought to analyse the extent of the power that a single House or Senate member can wield in the American system of government, but has little or no consequences for the big picture.

The American and Singaporean negotiators launched their first round of talks in Washington in mid-December 2000. Then, they agreed to hold subsequent meetings in London — not only a neutral ground, but less costly and time-consuming for travel to for both sides. If one looks at the ratio between the total two-way trade value, the expenses incurred for negotiators' trips and lodgings, and the comprehensiveness of the agreement (twenty-one chapters covering issues that the WTO has not addressed or does not dare to address, such as capital controls, e-commerce, worker migration, work visas, and competition law), the USSFTA was the least expensive and most comprehensive product that the USTR has ever successfully concluded: US$273 million per American specialist (dividing US$38 billion in bilateral trade value by the 139 issue specialists). Singapore came out even better; it fielded only fifty-three specialists for the negotiation.

There were several reasons and motives for the United States and Singapore to go for a bilateral FTA. Both were frustrated by the snail-paced progress being made in WTO-led multilateral trade liberalization, as subsequently confirmed by the stalemate of the Doha Round (2001) and the collapse of the Cancún Round (2003). The ASEAN Free Trade Area (AFTA) was fashioned in 1991. As the largest player in the intra-AFTA trade, Singapore became impatient with the equally slow pace of the financial market opening. Malaysia and Indonesia were unwilling to move any faster. The intra-ASEAN trade ratio has been stuck in the low twenties percentile ever since, reaching a peak of 25 per cent only once. By contrast, the intraregional ratio is 73 per cent for the European Union, and 50 per cent for the North American Free Trade Agreement (NAFTA). For the United States, the effect of NAFTA, comprising Canada, Mexico and the United States, has not been as magnanimous as what had been anticipated in terms of creating jobs and expanding U.S. exports to northern and southern neighbours. Mexico did overtake Japan as America's second largest trading partner, but that was not enough to fuel America's growth. Canada continues to hold the pre-NAFTA position of number one. In Singapore's case, the American agricultural sector fared better than labour-intensive manufacturing.

Thus, North American trade regionalism was, to use an American expression, "maxing out". Bill Clinton needed more ways to expand U.S. trade, especially in his twilight years in office when he was engulfed by a sex scandal, and rising tides of partisan rancour and media criticism.

The negotiation in building a thirty-four-country Free Trade Area of the Americas (FTAA) was going badly, as Brazil, Argentina, and Venezuela were determined to derail Clinton's dream of trade integration "from Alaska to Tierra del Fuego". Neither Singapore nor the United States was willing to leave the future of their trade policy to groups of obstructionist countries. It was the position of the American Government that those unwilling to liberalize trade regimes further should be ignored and left behind. The willing should rally and move forward. The leaders of the two countries shared this view and chose to forge ahead with a bilateral approach. It took one midnight golf game in Brunei between President Clinton and Prime Minister Goh for agreement to be reached on launching negotiations for the bilateral FTA.

If the bilateral FTAs were all about trade, one could argue that the logic of the Bush administration's and his predecessor's emphasis on focusing on small countries made little sense. In 2008, a little over half the world's trade takes place within 211 regional free trade areas and bilateral FTAs. That year, 44 per cent of the American trade was conducted with FTA partners and those *in negotiation* for FTAs; 56 per cent of the U.S. trade was with non-FTA partners — the three largest *non-FTA* partners being China, Japan, and the European Union. Over half of America's annual trade deficit has been incurred with those three entities. Also, the United States offers 131 developing countries one-way FTAs (preferential trade terms) for their economic growth and overall development. Cambodia and Bangladesh, for instance, enjoy preferential tariffs in their textile and apparel exports to the United States, but are not required to, and do not, reciprocate for similar American products. Therefore, the American FTAs are not about trade.

The foreign trade of the United States in 2008 came close to US$3 trillion. But it has been running a trade deficit since 1970, every year *non-stop*, except in 1973 and 1975. The American trade deficit in 1980 was US$100 billion; by 2003, it had surpassed the US$500 billion milestone, soaring to US$838.3 billion by 2006, the largest in history. In 2007, the deficit came down slightly to US$819.4 billion, thanks to a cheaper dollar and increased exports. The American deficit against China, Japan, and the European Union *combined* came to a whopping US$446 billion, or 55 per cent of the total. If the aim of free trade agreements is to eliminate or reduce the deficit, the Unites States should pursue FTAs with the European Union, Japan, and China, but to date it has not done so.

Furthermore, to prepare for better negotiation results, the United States has spent billions of dollars for small prospective FTA partners to upgrade their negotiating capacity and build up their trade-related infrastructure and bureaucracies. The U.S. Government invested US$47 million to improve the bargaining skills of four Central American countries and another US$40 million for a single country: Morocco. The Southern African Customs Union began to negotiate with the United States after receiving US$2 million for capacity building, and then both sides agreed to suspend negotiations. The African side was still ill prepared to deal with comprehensive FTA negotiations. Compared with these experiences, the Singapore case was an inexpensive and felicitous one. Taking all these factors into account, I argue that the American FTAs are more about advancing political objectives than attaining economic gains. The United States has used FTAs to push domestic reforms for its developing country partners, as well as to consolidate or "lock in" their democratic achievements thus far. Morocco, Jordan, Bahrain, Oman, the Central American countries, the Dominican Republic, Peru, and Chile are all examples. One might add Korea, Colombia, and Panama to the list. But with developed countries such as Australia and Singapore, there are other motives that this book will delve into in the coming chapters.

The book is organized into six chapters and a conclusion. Chapter 1 provides a historical overview of the role of trade and globalization in America, Singapore's economic growth and development, and both countries' objective of building overarching regional peace and stability. Chapter 2 deals with the making of the USSFTA against the backdrop of each party's motives to pursue bilateralism. Chapter 3 examines American trade practices and their impact on American thinking about how to forge the best trade policy, especially the political use of "fast track", including the 2002 Trade Promotion Act.

Chapter 4 explores the nuances of stand-alone economic regionalism and security regionalism, assessing the strengths and weaknesses of the convergence approach of merging the two realms, or embedding one into the other. Asia has practised the divergence approach, or separating, or delinking the two, while the United States has been the strongest advocate of convergence. Chapter 5 examines the harmful consequences of lobbying the U.S. Congress and a coterie of trade-related executive branch agencies. Chapter 6 traces the evolution of American foreign economic and security policy towards Northeast Asia and Southeast Asia, especially in terms of weighing Asia's preferences and America's choices since the 1990s, a proper examination which merits a book-length treatment in itself.

The Conclusion sums up the highlights of the book and provides a prognostication of what lies ahead for the region in a world of convergence as opposed to a world of divergence. The rapidly shifting world geopolitical and geo-economic weight from the Atlantic-Pacific nexus to the now emerging Pacific-Indian Ocean system can create a brave new world, and these changes will redefine America's security and economic interests in the region. For the coming decades at least, the United States should play the vital role of being an important link in the chain, if not occupying systemic centrality, in both the Atlantic-Pacific as well as the Pacific-Indian system. America's central role in the Atlantic-Pacific and Pacific-Indian duality is the challenge that Obama and his successors need to address. Within it, FTAs will continue to remain an important foundation piece for the making of Asia-Pacific material prosperity and a stable security landscape for the coming decades.

1

On the Crest of Trade and Globalization: Singapore and America

Since our neighbours were out to reduce their ties with us, we had to link up with the developed world — America, Europe, and Japan — and attract their manufacturers to produce in Singapore and export their products to the developed countries.

Lee Kuan Yew, *From Third World to First:*
The Singapore Story: 1965–2000

1.1 AMERICAN VIEWS ON TRADE GAINS AND LOSSES

Trade has been a positive factor in America's growth throughout its history and has been viewed as a driver for the expansions and contractions of the general economy. However, given the enormous size of the U.S. economy (US$14 trillion in gross domestic product [GDP] in 2007), economists have also argued that international trade *alone* does not affect the future of the American economy (CRS 2007b, pp. 9–12). It is known that once launched, free trade generates short-term, one-time static gains for partners. However, in order to turn the short-term gains into long-term, dynamic prosperity, the partners must invest in education, build modern infrastructure, attract fresh foreign capital and technology, discard unproductive plants in favour of new ones, adopt a host of policies to improve competitiveness, and introduce domestic reforms to realign the country with the practices of a globalized world economy (USITC 1993). Without these additional reforms, human capital, and infrastructure, there can be no dynamic long-term gains to be had from free trade.

There are three standard trade impact models: gravity, partial equilibrium, and computable general equilibrium. Of these, the most frequently cited is the third one, known as "the Michigan model" (D. Brown, Deardorff and Stern 2002). One *assumption* built into this model is that with a 33 per cent reduction of tariffs in agricultural, manufacturing, and service products (had the Doha Round succeeded), the benefits to the United States would have been US$164 billion, or a 1.5 per cent gain in GDP. If the world would *unilaterally* remove all tariffs, the gains could be as high as US$497 billion, or 4.5 per cent. Also, a U.S. government report asserts that with worldwide free trade, the effect on job creation would be small: agriculture would increase jobs, but workers in textiles and apparel, the retail trade, and some service sectors would lose their jobs (CRS 2007b, pp. 13–16). Thus the overall benefits of free trade for the United States would be small. If this assumption is true, it raises an important question: if the projected gains from free trade are relatively insignificant economically, why has the U.S. government pursued free trade agreements (FTAs) around the world so vigorously?

On regional and bilateral levels, the economic benefits to the United States seem even smaller. The Singapore FTA was estimated to generate US$17.5 billion per year in additional revenue for the American economy while the Chile FTA would produce US$4.41 billion. Free trade with Australia is projected to generate US$19.39 billion, the Korea FTA US$30.1 billion, and the Morocco FTA US$5.97 billion. The five-country Central America — Dominican Republic — United States of America Free Trade Agreement (CAFTA-DR) is expected to add US$17.26 billion, slightly less than that with Singapore. Ironically, an FTA with the ten country members of the Association of Southeast Asian Nations (ASEAN-10) would generate US$12.98 billion, less than the single FTA with Singapore (see Table 1.1). If bilateral FTAs generate small gains, why has the U.S. government pursued trade liberalization strategies on multilateral and regional levels as well? There has been no shared common perspective on trade among large American firms, labour unions, small and medium businesses, environmental groups, or other special interest and non-

TABLE 1.1
Economic Gains of FTAs to the United States, Estimated in 2002
(US$ billion)

APEC FTA	ASEAN FTA	FTAA	Chile FTA	Singapore FTA	Korea FTA	SACU FTA	CAFTA	Australia FTA	Morocco FTA
$244.25	$12.98	$67.59	$4.41	$17.5	$30.1	$12.61	$17.26	$19.39	$5.97

Source: CRS 2007b, p. 15.

governmental organization entities. Often, these groups seek to influence Congress and the president to take their position as the official policy for international trade and bilateral trade agreements. For the most part, this lobbying has been counterproductive for the country and has often created rancour among the players, but it has also produced gains for particular industries. In the United States, it is politics rather than the economic stakes that has played the greater role in free trade decisions, as this book will clearly demonstrate.

1.2 AMERICA'S RECENT TRADE PERFORMANCE

In 2007, the total U.S. trade deficit in goods reached its second highest level in history: US$819.4 billion. The year before, the United States exported over US$1 trillion in goods and services for the first time in its history, but also racked up its largest trade deficit ever: US$838.3 billion (CRS 2008h, p. 9). By contrast, all of the United States' major security allies and trading partners have been generating trade surpluses: the European Union, US$107.2 billion; Canada, US$68.2 billion; Mexico, US$74.6 billion; and the four recently industrialized countries in Asia, known as the Four Tigers (South Korea, Singapore, Taiwan, and Hong Kong), a combined US$3.9 billion. Since 1990, the U.S. trade deficit in merchandise with the Four Tigers has been decreasing while it has been increasing with China, from US$10.4 billion in 1990 to US$256.2 billion in 2007, representing 35.3 per cent of all U.S. imports and a full third (32.2 per cent) of the entire American trade deficit (CRS 2008h, pp. 27–28). In fact, Singapore and Hong Kong, the two most advanced service economies of the four, ran a trade deficit in merchandise against the United States of US$7.9 billion and US$13.1 billion, respectively (CRS 2008h, p. 18). American exports

to the world amounted to US$1,162.5 billion, while its imports were
US$1,957 billion, for a total trade of US$3,119.5 billion, or an 8 per cent
increase from the previous year's US$2,884 billion. In services, the United
States was running a surplus of US$119.1 billion based on exports of
US$497.2 billion versus imports of US$378.1 billion (CRS 2008*h*, p. 1). Over
half of U.S. service exports go to Europe. In short, the United States does
better trading with developed than developing countries (see Table 1.2).

TABLE 1.2
U.S. Trade: Balance of Payment Basis: Exports and Imports, 1982–2007
(US$ billion)

Year	Exports	Imports	Trade Balance
1982	$211.2	$247.6	–$36.4
1984	$218.9	$332.4	–$112.5
1986	$223.3	$368.4	–$145.1
1988	$320.2	$447.2	–$127.0
1990	$387.4	$498.4	–$110.0
1992	$439.6	$536.5	–$96.9
1994	$502.9	$668.7	–$165.8
1996	$612.1	$803.1	–$191.0
1998	$670.4	$917.1	–$246.7
2000	$772.0	$1,224.4	–$452.4
2001	$718.7	$1,145.9	–$427.2
2002	$681.8	$1,164.7	–$482.9
2003	$713.1	$1,260.7	–$547.6
2004	$807.5	$1,447.1	–$669.6
2005	$894.6	$1,681.8	–$787.2
2006	$1,023.1	$1,861.4	–$838.3
2007	$1,148.5	$1,967.9	–$819.4

Source: CRS 2008*h*, p. 9.

There are two hidden but related issues in this trade picture. One is
the exports of U.S.-based affiliates operating overseas back to the United
States. The value of that trade went from US$39.3 billion in 1982 to
US$209.1 billion in 2004, constituting 15 per cent of all American imports,
and has remained consistently at the same level ever since. The other is
that foreign corporations operating in the United States account for 64 per
cent of all imports (CRS 2008*h*, p. 24). The share of the American affiliates

in a given Asian country's export varies widely, ranging from 40 per cent for Singapore to less than 1 per cent for Korea. What this means is that the income generated abroad by U.S. foreign direct investment (FDI) can be seen as essentially offsetting the U.S. trade deficit. The United States strategy has been to invest more in manufacturing economies from which American firms export their products back to the United States. This approach should garner greater parts of the trading partners' surplus in favour of U.S. FDI income. However, this strategy has not worked as planned.

This point can be illustrated by examining the statistics associated with U.S. FDI around the world in 2007, which generated US$81.7 billion in income. In the European Union and Canada, U.S. multinational companies (MNCs) earned US$39.6 billion and US$18.1 billion, respectively, that year. In Japan, U.S. MNCs incurred a US$41.2 billion deficit in corporate income because Japan's FDI in the United States generated a greater amount. However, if one adds the income from stocks and bonds, the balance of the current account changes. Japan and China held US$581 billion and US$477 billion, respectively, in U.S. treasuries alone at the end of 2007 (CRS 2008*h*, p. 6). Looking at the combined picture of trade in 2007 in merchandise and services, income from investment, and returns on the government bonds and private stocks, the American deficit with Asia (US$445 billion) was roughly eleven times that with the European Union (US$42.4 billion) (CRS 2008*h*, p. 21). U.S. merchandise deficits are often reduced by investment income (MNC affiliates sales) as well as trade surplus in services.

It is clear from U.S. trade statistics that the country cannot compete in manufacturing against cheap labour countries, but it is competitive in high-tech products and services. This has led some to argue that America must move away from trade in goods and instead further open up the domestic markets of its trading partners for American FDI in manufacturing and service industries (Quinlan 2000; Quinlan and Chandler 2001, pp. 87–97). This is the reason American trade negotiators have pushed for the opening of investment and service markets in all FTAs since the Trade Promotion Act (TPA) of 2002. But at present, the United States has not been successful in pursuing these two goals with its largest deficit-producing trade partners — China, Japan, and the European Union — which have shown no interest in signing FTAs with the United States. From a purely economic standpoint, there are two major flaws in America's current FTA strategy: (1) most U.S. FTAs are with small countries, or countries with which the United States has insignificant trade relations, and are thus *politically*, not economically, motivated; and (2) Washington has made no serious advances in negotiating with its large trading partners to correct existing trade imbalances. This state of affairs could lead to hostile diplomatic relations and, in the case of China, has already caused economic conflicts between the two countries.

1.3 THE UNITED STATES GOES FOR FTAs

As of August 2009, the United States had seventeen FTAs in force. The value of the trade with the FTA partners reached 44 per cent of total U.S. trade. Under the Bush administration, the United States signed eighteen FTAs, but Congress approved only fifteen, with three (South Korea, Panama, and Colombia) still awaiting approval or disapproval. If one leaves Canada and Mexico (two pre-2002 TPA partners) out of the equation, the total ratio of the fifteen FTAs in force declines to 16 per cent of the total value of U.S. trade. This means that over half (56 per cent) of America's trade is with non-FTA partners (USGAO 2007c). Thus, critics have argued that the United States should stop focusing on trade negotiations with small economies but instead go for the big ones. If one motivation in pursuing FTAs is to reduce or eliminate trade deficits, then the United States needs agreements with China, Japan, and the European Union. In the case of Canada and Mexico, two of the top ten deficit-causing partners, their membership in the North American Free Trade Agreement (NAFTA) has helped American agriculture, but not manufacturing (CRS 1997; CRS 2002b; CRS 2009a). The U.S. trade deficit with Canada was US$68 billion and with Mexico, US$75 billion, or a combined total of US$143 billion in 2007. Of the top ten countries with which the United States ran trade deficits in 2007, three were oil exporters (Nigeria, US$30 billion; Venezuela, US$30 billion; and Saudi Arabia, US$25 billion); four were developed economies (Japan, US$83 billion; Canada, US$68 billion; Germany, US$45 billion; and Ireland, US$21 billion), and three were highly developed manufacturing economies of labour intensive goods (China, US$256 billion; Malaysia, US$21 billion; and Mexico, $75 billion) (CRS 2008h, p. 17).

In 2007, the United States generated trade surpluses with the following countries: Singapore (US$8 billion), Belgium (US$10 billion), UAE (US$10 billion), Australia (US$10 billion), Hong Kong (US$13 billion), and the Netherlands (US$15 billion). The United States has FTAs in force with Canada, Mexico, and Korea (awaiting Congressional approval) in the deficit column, and in force with Singapore, Australia, and the UAE (in negotiations) in the surplus column. It is hard to draw any conclusions from these cases. In fact, one could argue that past and current trade with large economies has not helped reduce deficits while it has done so with smaller economies, when FTAs are signed. But this is a simplistic generalization. In the case of NAFTA, an FTA did not help reduce the deficits. What, then, was the motivation for Clinton and Bush to sign a host of preferential trade agreements with small countries?

1.4 FTA STRATEGIES UNDER CLINTON AND BUSH

The United States began to firm up its FTA strategies under the Clinton and Bush administrations. There were no specific procedures for pursuing FTAs during the Clinton years, but by the time Bush received the trade promotion authority in 2002, a specific set of guidelines for how FTAs should be negotiated had emerged: the United States should (1) pursue comprehensive FTAs (that is, the elimination of tariffs on 80 per cent or more for bilaterally traded goods and services, in accordance with World Trade Organization rules); (2) pursue a three-pronged FTA strategy by targeting multilateral, regional, and bilateral levels of agreements; (3) give priority to agriculture and service sector-driven FTAs, not manufacturing-driven FTAs; (4) build permanent protection into FTAs for certain products such as sugar for American producers and fresh onions for Costa Rica and Panama; (5) provide longer transition periods for phasing out existing tariffs of up to twenty-three years in the case of apples in Korea, twenty years for rice in Panama, and nineteen years for rice in Colombia; and (6) exclude altogether sensitive items such as rice in the Korean FTA (CRS 2009a, pp. 4–14).

The U.S. FTA strategy has been consistent in maintaining a minimum of 80 per cent or higher for duty free trade in its negotiations, but the remainder of the TPA guidelines (congressional mandate) is not in sync with what Washington has been preaching, namely, a belief in market economies and free trade. These anti-market practices are disturbing signs and one-way concessions are made for the sake of political convenience. Also, the United States has chosen a route for signing FTAs with small countries, not with large economies against which the United States has been running a bone-crushing trade deficit — US$446 billion against China, the European Union, and Japan combined, out of the total US$819 billion in 2007.

In fact, security and political objectives are far more important drivers of FTAs with the likes of Jordan, Singapore, Oman, Morocco, Israel, and Panama, a point that will be demonstrated later in this work. The desire to expand service markets (banking in particular) was one motivation for the USSFTA (U.S.-Singapore FTA); agricultural market access was the main driver for the KORUSFTA (Korea-U.S. FTA) (CRS 2009a, p. 11). Additionally, the United States has used FTA negotiations to instigate domestic reforms for its partners, as well as to lock in its current subsidy policy for itself (the sugar compensation programme, for instance). With Panama, the United States insisted on changes in labour and tax laws. Panama requires a minimum of forty workers to form a union and its tax haven practices have contributed to gross tax evasion. When negotiating the FTA with Panama, the United States wanted to see modifications to these policies. The United States has inserted its long-running sugar compensation programme in FTAs to pre-empt any and all domestic reforms. The Colombia Free Trade Agreement is most emphatic about this American protectionism (CRS 2009a, p. 9). These kinds of anti-free market practices have sheltered special interest groups and protected inefficient sectors in the American economy from foreign competition.

Furthermore, the content of some FTA negotiations have ended up reflecting an excessive emphasis on congressional district-level interests rather than national interests. For instance, all mention of rice was excluded from the KORUSFTA with the blessing of Senator Baucus of Montana (chair of the Finance Committee) and Senator Grassley of Iowa (the ranking Republican member of the Finance Committee) once Korea agreed to allow the sale of American beef (regardless of its age), a major product of both Montana and Iowa. One must wonder whether the interests of the major rice-producing states (Arkansas, California, Louisiana, Mississippi, Missouri, and Texas) were ever taken into account in the negotiations.

Another example comes from the U.S.-Singapore FTA. During those discussions, Representative Phil Crane pushed so hard for the inclusion of chewing gum in the list of products to be traded that it almost wrecked the negotiations. Crane was a Republican representing Chicago, home of the William Wriggley, Jr. Company, a major producer of chewing gum for more than a century and now a subsidiary of Mars, a major food manufacturer. Such deal breakers or potential deal breakers are often championed by a single representative or senator, or by a powerful lobbying group whom the U.S. Trade Representative (USTR) can ignore only at its own peril. In essence, and unlike Singapore's governing elites, American policymakers in Congress and the executive branch have lacked consistency in FTA negotiations, often driven by strong local rather than national interests. Often, the economic benefit is small, and in the chewing gum case, Singapore imported *no* chewing gum from the United States in 2009.

1.5 THE U.S. CONVERGENCE MODEL

In the twentieth century, it was Franklin Delano Roosevelt who laid the foundation for converging, or co-joining, U.S. foreign economic *and* security interests, although some argue that Woodrow Wilson enmeshed security concerns with international economic prosperity after the end of World War I. But Wilson's grand design for a League of Nations was never given a chance to work. Hence, it was Roosevelt and his advisers (Secretary of State Cordell Hull and Secretary of the Treasury Henry Morgenthau, Jr.) who refined trade strategy as the Second World War was under way as is clearly reflected in the Atlantic Charter of August 1941, signed by Roosevelt and Winston Churchill at Ship Harbour in Placentia Bay, Newfoundland (Frieden 2006, pp. 254–56). Specialists in international relations have often cited the charter as the document that forged together the two "English-speaking races" (Churchill's expression) in a common effort to defeat Hitler's Germany and to establish a peaceful world after the war. But the adoption of the charter set in motion the modern approach for merging free trade objectives with cooperative security arrangements. In fact, free trade was the main precondition for the Lend-Lease programme for Britain. More specifically, the two countries committed themselves to a post-war goal of eliminating "all forms of discriminatory treatment in international commerce, and to the reduction of tariff and other trade barriers" (Frieden 2006, p. 256).

The Atlantic Charter of 1941 culminated several years of efforts on the part of the Roosevelt administration to reverse protectionist trade policies adopted during the Great Depression when political and economic realities had encouraged Congress to turn inward by passing the Smoot-Hawley Tariff Act of 1930. Britain responded by organizing the Ottawa Free Trade Agreement of 1932 that granted preferential trade terms to the self-governing dominion and Britain (Bercuson and Herwig 2005, pp. 21, 28–29). This closed regionalism discriminated against American products.

Reeling against protectionist waves around the world, U.S. Secretary of State Cordell Hull and his deputy, Sumner Wells, became the champions of free trade. By 1934, Roosevelt had persuaded the isolationist Congress to pass the Reciprocal Trade Agreements Act, which granted the president the authority to negotiate tariff rates downward on a bilateral basis. Both Roosevelt and Hull served in the Wilson administration and believed that "unhampered trade dovetailed with peace" and equated "high tariffs, trade barriers, and unfair economic competition, with war" (Frieden 2006, p. 254). They were not alone. Secretary of the Treasury Henry Morgenthau, Jr. shared much of Roosevelt and Hull's world views. He too was of the opinion that economic conflicts between nations were the prime causes of war; hence, the elimination of war must begin with good economic relations among countries. In other words, the Wilsonian world view was to embed security into economic relations. One without the other cannot thrive. However, it was Roosevelt, not Wilson, who had the opportunity to put this tenet into action.

At Placentia Bay, Under Secretary of State Sumner Wells and his British counterpart, Sir Alexander Cadogan, held a series of acrimonious meetings to tie free trade to security collaboration. Hull was determined to link the Lend-Lease aid and future military collaboration with Britain to the abrogation of the Ottawa Agreement, thus committing post-war Britain to free trade (Bercuson and Herwig 2005, p. 29). Article Four of the Atlantic Charter specifically referred to granting "equal terms" in international trade to "all states, great or small, victor and vanquished" after the war (Davis 2000, p. 271). In 1944, the International Trade Organization (ITO) was established along with the International Bank for Reconstruction and Development (IBRD, later part of the World Bank) and the International Monetary Fund (IMF). As the Cold War was festering and the American fear of war with the Soviet Union was mounting, the U.S. Senate was in no mood to surrender economic sovereignty to an international entity. The Senate ratified the establishment of the IBRD and the IMF, but it failed to create the ITO. Instead, Congress went for the establishment of a massive development programme, the Marshall Plan, to save Europe and the world. Global free trade could wait.

What many students of the Second World War have failed to notice in terms of the international institutional changes wrought by the Atlantic Charter was the birth of the U.S. convergence policy linking security (the United Nations) and economic well-being (the Bretton Woods institutions).

Morgenthau articulated the convergence better than anyone. Four days after Pearl Harbor, he was ready to put the creation of the three Bretton Woods institutions into motion. In a House hearing, the treasury secretary testified that the security project (adopting the Lend-Lease plan) and the economic grand strategy (ending protectionism) went hand in hand, "as interdependent as the blades of a pair of scissors" (Nau 1990, p. 81). Isolationist Republicans believed that a peacetime large army would be sufficient to provide the best security for the country while the Democrats argued that the best security policy was to implement Point Three of Wilson's Fourteen Points, which states that open, free trade among nations could bring peace to the international system. It would also engender domestic economic prosperity, thus paving the way for "the firm establishment of a basis of friendship and confidence on which permanent peace could be built" (Nau 1990, p. 80).

The core of the Wilsonian ideal was to link the American war aims to a peaceful international system (McNamara and Blight 2001, pp. 3–15; Gaddis 1997, pp. 12–13). To this convergence, Roosevelt and his advisers added another dimension: internationalizing New Deal idealism. To them, humanity could never have the Four Freedoms (of speech, of worship, from want, and from fear) without economic and military security for all, not just for some. The absence of economic fear could not be achieved just by building a large peacetime military establishment. Instead, there had to be a worldwide economic system of interdependence, collaboration, and sustained reforms in trade and investment; without these, the commonly shared goals for prosperity and security would remain elusive, beyond the reach of human civilization. What has been buried in the dusty bin of history by scholars is the very notion of comprehensive security that today's International Relations (IR) and International Political Economy (IPE) specialists in East Asia now extol. Its real authors were Roosevelt, Hull, and Morgenthau.

If the concept of "stability" is defined as "the absence of serious military, economic, or political conflict among nation-states" (Ikenberry and Mastanduno 2001, p. 2), it is logical to argue that the interplay of international relations (focusing on war and diplomacy) and international political economy (focusing on the relationship *among* states and markets either on a bilateral, regional, or multilateral basis) must serve as the explanatory framework for analysing today's interstate relationships. It is also argued in this book that the economic universe and the security universe constantly interact with, and react to, each other in Asia where history, collective memory, and cultural differences precondition and shape state behaviour and market responses. This has also been the case in other regions of the world, including Europe and Latin America. Also, the seed of today's globalization in the Atlantic world was sowed in the aftermath of World War II under the aegis of the victorious United States. This was the first leg of world economic integration that Wilson and Roosevelt advocated.

There have been two extremes in the post-war foreign policy of the United States: (1) the economic and security convergence of the Marshall Plan and the Truman Doctrine; and (2) George W. Bush's modified version of the Reagan Doctrine, which unilaterally projects American military power to engender democracy and promote free markets globally. To the delight of extreme right-wing American politicians, the hegemony-prolonging Project for the New American Century became the philosophical foundation for Bush's foreign security policy. The U.S.-Singapore Free Trade Agreement is thus a piece of a larger foreign policy puzzle emerging from the seven decades of the evolution of American foreign economic and security policy from Roosevelt to Bush.

The American Century of Henry Luce that began during Truman's times was built on enlightened generosity, self-sacrifice, and transatlantic interdependence. It laid the foundation of post-war American political bipartisanism. The Marshall Plan is one example. The New American Century of George W. Bush sought to propagate the United States' selfish interests worldwide, maximizing profits for America's pro-oil and financial groups, fulfilling the agenda of the Christian Right, and enforcing the politically rapacious hegemonism worldwide. This was the core agenda of the Republican Party's neoconservative elites. This policy was the product of post-Reagan partisan extremism. These fundamental differences in U.S. foreign policy stances between the Democratic and Republican presidencies over the past seven decades must be recognized because the USSFTA, unlike the Marshall Plan, came into being when America's motivations were not noble and the president who led it was a dedicated partisan ideologue.

A short historical overview of the two extreme forms of foreign policy (the first from a Democratic administration and the second from a Republican administration) is in order when we keep in mind that free trade works better among prosperous partners. Beginning with the US$17 billion

Marshall Plan in 1948 and followed by the establishment of the North Atlantic Treaty Organization (NATO) in 1949, the United States envisioned that a united Europe would better serve the Atlantic security needs of stopping Stalin's expansive communism than a continent devastated by the war, fragmented, and poor. At the time, the appeal of the Soviet model was sweeping throughout war-torn Europe, with Italy and France tottering on the verge of electing communist regimes, a possibility that the United States wanted to avoid at all costs. The genius of the American grand strategy was to merge the security needs of the North Atlantic world with the deepening global economic interests of the United States. In the process, the plan would stop Soviet communism within the confines of Eastern Europe *and* would launch Western Europe's economic recovery, thus letting it get on with development (Behrman 2007, pp. 175–82).

These twin goals worked hand-in-hand for the next four-and-a-half decades until the fall of the Soviet Union in 1990. Meanwhile, the Marshall Plan set off the integration of Western Europe (today's core twelve of the European Union-27), while the external hegemon treated both former allies and enemies with equal generosity. In the first year of the Marshall Plan, 75 per cent of the aid went to three countries: the United Kingdom, France, and Italy. The first was in dire need to rebuild its economy, and a tranche of the aid brought 10,000 unemployed back to work in Birmingham, England alone (Behrman 2007, p. 108).

The integration of today's European Union owed much to the U.S. initiatives in the Marshall Plan and NATO. Countries were willing to give in to neighbours' demands, to scale down national autonomy in economic decision making, to eschew aggressive nationalism (especially in France and Germany), and to subordinate petty nationalistic squabbles to the group's common interest. In the process, Europe began to "pool sovereignty" from various countries to advance collective interests, thus rising above the confines of the Westphalian state. The NATO alliance played a major role in this integration wherein large and small countries were asked to cooperate and U.S. military leadership was a vital pacesetter. It should be remembered that ultra-nationalist de Gaulle pulled the French military out of the NATO command (no American should command the French military!), but the French cooperation in NATO operations was of utmost importance. Nevertheless, anti-Americanism has persisted within French foreign policy ever since. In August 2009, for instance, France agreed to sell a helicopter assault carrier to Russia, and the two countries will open negotiations for the co-production of three more carriers (Barry 2009).

After de Gaulle, Europe went farther and has successfully implemented a convergence model of merging its group economic interests with collective security exigencies by sacrificing national pride, setting aside petty jealousies, and forging a united vision. For over thirty years, the Franco-German rapprochement has set the political tone for European integration. It took nearly half a century from the establishment of the Marshall Plan of 1948 to the enlargement of the European Union in 2005, by which time twenty-five countries had come under one economic roof. Today, the European Union has twenty-seven members, Romania and Bulgaria being the latest to sign up. Few scholars have given credit to post-war Europe in terms of how well the once divided continent managed to continue working with Washington on the transatlantic alliance. Others underplay the contribution of the Marshall Plan, even while recognizing the U.S. effort to revitalize Europe in general terms (Moller 2008, p. xxix). The fact remains, however, that the convergence model of the North Atlantic alliance was a success because both America and Western Europe were willing to link their fates through the Marshall Plan and NATO.

No parallel effort could be put into effect in the Asia Pacific, because America did not have a willing Germany and a petulant but willing France in that region's two major powers, China and Japan. America's historical ties were commercial, not ancestral and kindred. And in the post-war period, East Asia (Northeast and Southeast Asia) has travelled a different road. The rise of "Red China" in December 1949 and the Korean War (1950–53) set a radically different tone for the economic development trajectory and security arrangements for East Asia. Much of American politics in the 1950s was focused on who lost Kuomintang-run China to the Maoist communists, how to contain Red China, and how to redraw the U.S. defence perimeter in Northeast Asia — all security-driven concerns.

One outcome of this political maelstrom in Washington was the rise of McCarthyism (an era of irrational political witch-hunting) at the same time that the Truman administration was willing to make peace with Maoist China. The media and Republicans in Congress vociferously attacked the Truman administration for losing Kuomintang China and his willingness to appease the Maoist regime. Hawkish generals such as Douglas A. MacArthur, the "American viceroy" in Japan, called for "unleashing Chiang Kai-Shek" and attacking Red China. He was not without supporters (Weintraub 2007, pp. 433–61). In this virulently anti-communist environment, Japan, China, and Thailand were the only sovereign countries without colonial domination, but none was prepared to lead East Asia. Asia had no indigenous Konrad Adenauer, Robert Schuman, Altiero Gaspari, or Jean Monet (founders of the convergence in Europe) to shape its future by tapping into America's goodwill, enormous material resources, and grand strategic vision.

A reconstructed and reformed Japan was the best security ally and first major proving ground to test whether the security bilateralism of the United States could hold. MacArthur's reforms laid the foundation for modern Japan: land distribution to small farmers, gender equality to universal education, access to democratic politics (Gordon 1997), abolition of the militarist *zaibatsu* system and replacing it with the *keiretsu*-driven firms, workers' rights, unionization, credible opposition parties, a bureaucracy-dominated executive branch, political stability forged by Yoshida Shigeru (prime minister during 1946–47 and 1948–54), and the Korean War boom. All these changes and events have served well in building a democratic Japan (Burks 1961, pp. 17–22, 108–10). Indeed, MacArthur's critics said that Japan was more inflicted by New Deal ideals and institutions than America itself. In 1952, Truman wisely appointed Republican John Foster Dulles to negotiate the San Francisco Treaty. Japan was restored to full sovereignty and signed an enduring security treaty with the United States. Successive American presidents since Harry Truman have sought to replicate this Japanese experiment throughout the region, with less success.

In the Asia Pacific, bilateral economic and security agreements, accords, and treaties were also signed with Australia, New Zealand, South Korea, the Philippines, Taiwan, and Thailand. The United States security relationship in Asia was to remain *bilateral* (Pempel 2006, pp. 1–33, esp. 7) and is likely to continue to be so for the next decade or two. The only trilateral security alliance treaty ever negotiated in the region was among the United States, Australia, and New Zealand (ANZUS) and went into effect in 1952 (Abramowitz and Bosworth 2006; Gaddis 1997, pp. 62–67). But by the mid-1980s, pacifist New Zealand blocked visits by the U.S. Navy's nuclear vessels, and the ANZUS treaty became dysfunctional. The Eisenhower administration put together the Southeast Asian Treaty Organization (SEATO) in 1954 as a "geostrategic Great Wall" to contain China and the Soviet Union from gaining influence in East Asia (Gaddis

1997, p. 169). Only two countries from Southeast Asia joined: Thailand and the Philippines. Others stayed out.

The first major test for SEATO came in the early 1960s, as the war in Vietnam was heating up. No member of SEATO, except the Philippines and Thailand, stepped forward to help the war effort. Pakistan, SEATO's western anchor and vital link to Middle Eastern security (culturally and geographically), stayed mum, choosing not to be involved. In short, multilateralism has not found a place in the Asia Pacific where anticommunism was no enduring glue as in Europe. The United States has never had an opportunity to engage East Asia in creating a convergence model, wherein economic development leads to regional security commitments on a multilateral scale and, in turn, engenders stability for the region, thereby fuelling more growth and development. Hence a virtuous circle never had a chance to be implemented. Instead, establishing a U.S. military presence in Asia and granting unrestricted access to the American market became Washington's strategy. In this context, FTAs are a continuation of bilaterally driven U.S. policy, albeit in a post-communist and globalization era.

1.6 TWO ASIAN MODELS OF DEVELOPMENT

Asia has viewed trade and globalization from a different prism. Both have been the roads to development. On the one extreme it has been argued that there is no consensus on what constitutes "development", while at the other end of the spectrum, development has been defined simply as "improvement in human well-being" (O'Brien and Williams 2004, pp. 254–62; Harrison 1985, p. 1). There is no doubt that ideology, international politics, and the timing of integrating a country into a globalized world play critical roles in how and when a country can develop. Scholars and practitioners of development accept the premise that development is the multifaceted process of improving people's lives in social, political, and economic arenas where they live, work, and from which they benefit.

While the term has moved away from the old economists' definition of measuring development solely in terms of quantitative growth in GNP, GDP, and per capita income (while ignoring the social, cultural, environmental, and even political aspects of development), there remains a pejorative insinuation that development is for the poor. Ireland, Portugal, Spain, southern Italy, and Greece in Western Europe were as poor and underdeveloped in the 1950s and 1960s as some many Asian and Latin

American countries, but these European countries have escaped supervision by such multilateral institutions as the World Bank and the IMF. Thus the notion of the "south", or better yet, the "global south", has referred to non-European countries with less-than-desirable living standards.

It has been said that diplomacy is the face that a nation wears to the world. Development has been seen as the ladder which a nation uses to climb to reach the apex of wealth, prosperity, and security, and therefore power. Unfortunately, the concept of development has been (mis)applied only to the poor, implying that the rich do not need development. Presumably, the rich are already *developed*. In the age of globalization since the mid-1960s (Sachs 1998, pp. 97–111), it has been pointed out that a poor nation could "develop" by importing capital, labour, technology, and other factors of production that globalization provides.

To do this, nations must open up, liberalize, and deregulate. Trade has become the vehicle for growth and development. But in order to benefit from trade, a country must concurrently invest in education, infrastructure, and public health, and even mobilize culture, geopolitical location, and history as constituent factors in development. In other words, development is a process, not something that hinges on a single factor, not something that must end at a particular time. Not having sufficient capital to install a factory is not an automatic barrier to development. Concomitantly, having bountiful natural resources is not a guarantee that development will occur. In a way, development is an art, for a country must find ways to combine what it has with what it has to import to become rich. Singapore is one example of this artful strategy.

Lee Kuan Yew discovered the right formula for Singapore's success: invite multinational corporations to the city state and start manufacturing products that they normally would produce at home. Then, the MNCs export their products to home countries while also marketing them throughout East Asia and around the world. Singapore contributed its geostrategic location, sound infrastructure, skilled labour force, pro-business environment, financial incentives for investors, export promotion benefits, and a clean government willing to partner with business (Lee 2000, p. 60). It worked. What others have not been able to replicate is Singapore's cohesive political will, high quality of the governing elite, and unilateral opening to the world.

Also unlike other countries, Singapore has not clashed with the neoliberal values that globalization has propagated. Today's IPE practitioners tend to highlight the role of the market in development and even reject "state-

centrism" as a viable approach to engendering development. Its concern with globalization is not state-centric, but rather market driven, focusing on the conduct of trade and flows of foreign direct investment (FDI) — that is, features of development that readily lend themselves to quantification. Meanwhile, the neoliberal tendencies of globalization have attracted the attention of Singapore's elites. The existing concepts and concerns of international relations are decidedly Westphalian and Western, focusing on the question of diplomacy and war, the twin policy responses available to the state (Phillips 2005, pp. 82–85). But IPE approaches diverge from IR's traditions. The role of market, ours and theirs, plays an important part in IPE approaches to development, its processes, and its consequences. Singapore's success to date can be better understood and appreciated through an IPE prism than an IR one.

There are examples of countries with neoliberal proclivities that have grown and developed *faster* in recent decades than those without. According to 2008 World Bank statistics, the Irish have come within shouting distance of catching up with the British in terms of average income (US$34,730 for each Irish citizen as opposed to US$40,560 for a Briton), and Norwegians now enjoy a higher level of income than their former Swedish masters (US$68,440 versus US$34,530) (WB 2008, pp. 14–16). This increase in living standards (gross national income per capita) is the direct result of development and has been driven by forces of globalization for the past three decades. In it, trade and investment have assumed primacy as drivers of the process. By contrast, no similar income convergence has occurred among the Japanese, Chinese, and Koreans and is not likely to occur for decades, if not a century. Each Japanese citizen is seven times richer than a Chinese (US$32,840 versus US$4,660), while a Korean is almost five times richer than a Chinese (US$22,990 versus US$4,660). The Japanese are also one-and-a-half times richer than the Koreans. Korea's goal of catching up with Japanese income is a realistic one which can be achieved within two to three decades.

In terms of the United Nations Development Programme's 2007 Human Development Index, Norway ranked second globally (with a score of 0.968 out of a perfect 1.000), Ireland fifth (0.959), Sweden sixth (0.956), and the United Kingdom sixteenth (0.946). In Northeast Asia, Japan ranked eighth (0.953), Korea twenty-sixth (right behind Singapore, with 0.921), and China eighty-first (0.777) out of the 177 countries assessed (UNDP 2007, pp. 229–32). This quality of life index is based on four different variables: life expectancy at birth; the adult literacy rate; the combined gross enrolment ratio for primary, secondary, and tertiary education; and GDP per capita.

If an academic had argued a mere two decades ago that Ireland, an underdeveloped country then, could become prosperous by maximizing the trade and investment opportunities offered by neoliberal globalization and would emerge as the fastest growing economy in the European Union, he/she would have been laughed out of the profession. But Eva Paus has done just that. She offers interesting empirical data to explain how this miracle has happened by comparing the results of Intel's investment in Costa Rica and Ireland. The latter reformed its education system, invested in infrastructure, and restructured public and private finances, while the former, Latin America's most developed social democracy, has failed to respond to the challenges of globalization (Paus 2005). The Irish now emphasize science and technology in their higher education, offering a free ride to all qualified students, while in Costa Rica, law and the humanities remain the most respected fields among the college crowd. Ireland has advanced while Costa Rica has lagged. Well before Intel showed up, Ireland had a free trade agreement with Britain, and Costa Rica had one with the other Central American countries. But it was Intel's investment that galvanized the development of the two countries, although Ireland outpaced Costa Rica, thanks to its deeper domestic reforms. Each country's existing FTAs played far lesser roles in the development process.

Globalization matters as long as a country's elites know how to respond to its challenges and take advantage of neoliberal opportunities that it has to offer. Some countries have succeeded in meeting this challenge while others have failed. Those who have taken advantage of globalization include Chile, Brazil, and Mexico in Latin America, and Korea, Japan, China, Singapore, Malaysia, and Thailand in East Asia. Why some countries have been able to pull themselves out of poverty while others have not is one focus of this book. Free trade, when put together correctly, along with prudent security ties built into it to safeguard prosperity already gained, has created new wealth (WB 2002). However, if a country has no mechanism for equitable income distribution in place, then no amount of economic growth and expansion will help. Extreme wealth gaps will occur, which in turn are likely to cause social instability, and even destroy the country. A comparative look at how domestic policies of countries have responded to globalization can shed further light on this view.

1.7 GHANA, MALAYSIA, AND KOREA

According to World Bank data, South Korea, Ghana, and Malaysia had similar per capita income in 1960, about US$60 per person. Korea was as poor as Ghana. The Nobel prize-winning Swedish economist, Gunnar Myrdal, used three volumes to predict that Asia would never emerge from its poverty and develop on par with the West, a culturally unrealizable goal (Myrdal 1968). We have since had the Asian miracle to disprove Myrdal's thesis (Emmott 2008, p. 44). In 1968, Ghana's GDP was US$1.6 billion, Korea's US$3.8 billion, and Malaysia's US$1.5 billion. Korea was about to enter two-and-a-half decades of military dictatorship; Malaysia was settling into its fourth year of independence under one-party authoritarian rule; and Ghana was in the throes of African socialism, the then faddish model of autarkic development then sweeping throughout Africa. All three pursued an inward-looking import substitution industrialization (ISI) policy, but Korea and Malaysia reversed their policy in the mid-1970s by embracing an export-promoting industrialization approach. Ghana under K. Nkrumah stayed the course with the closed ISI model. Three decades later, the results of these choices are astounding in terms of the differences in levels of economic performance.

Between 1971 and 2003, the population of Ghana grew 2.5 times (from 8.5 million to 21 million), while its GDP increased 3.2 times (from US$2.4 billion to US$7.6 billion) and its per capita income increased 1.2 times (from US$270 to US$320). For Malaysia, the population rose from 11 million to 24 million, or 2.4 times between the two dates. Its GDP went from US$4.5 billion to US$103 billion, or an astonishing twenty-threefold increase, and its per capita income rose from US$420 to US$3,880, or nine times expansion. Korea's population increased 1.4 times (from 35 million to 48 million) while its GDP experienced an almost incomprehensible sixty-onefold increase (from US$9.9 billion to US$605 billion) and its per capita income went from US$310 to US$12,030, a thirty-ninefold increase. Ghana and Malaysia experienced similar population increases, percentage-wise, but pursued two different development strategies: Ghana retained the closed ISI or African socialist model, while Malaysia switched to open export-promoting industrialization. As the data show, Malaysia grew faster by a wide margin. In fact, this simple computation shows that Korea has fared the best, followed by Malaysia, while Ghana has emerged as the laggard of the three. There is no doubt that the years from 1971 to 2003 were the most intense period of globalization in terms of trade expansion and cross-border flows of foreign direct investment. In 2003, total international trade (imports plus exports) in merchandise reached US$17.6 trillion, compared with US$7.1 trillion in 1990 (WB 2007) (see Table 1.3).

TABLE 1.3
GDP Growth: Ghana, Korea and Malaysia, 1960–2006
(US$ billion)

Year	Ghana	Korea	Malaysia
1960	$1.2	$3.8	$1.5
1980	$4.4	$64.0	$25.0
1990	$6.0	$253.0	$44.0
1995	$6.5	$517.0	$89.0
2006	$13.0	$888.0	$151.0

Source: WB 1998, table 4.2; WB 2008, table 4.2.

According to a United Nations Conference on Trade and Development (UNCTAD) publication, the world had 70,000 multinational corporations in 2004 with 690,000 affiliates. Together they invested US$625 billion, down from a high of US$2 trillion in 2000, followed by a decrease in FDI after 11 September 2001 (UNCTAD 2006, pp. 4–19). The 500 largest corporations by revenue boasted combined sales of US$18.9 trillion, with US$72.8 trillion in assets, US$8.8 trillion in equities, and US$1.2 trillion in profits by employing 50.5 million people the world over, or twice the population of Malaysia ("Global 500" 2005). By the din of these measures, the private sector economy was enormously effective, productive, and more profitable than public sector corporations, such as state-owned enterprises in Latin America and government-linked companies in East Asia. Globalization has created opportunities to benefit from, if countries were ready with a properly trained and skilled labour force, a sound education system, harmonious policy coordination between the *state* and the *market* on development strategies, and good governance practices such as the rule of law, efficient administrative institutions, and the creation of an environment favourable for the growth of private market institutions. If they were without these fundamentals, globalization has hurt them.

Globalization has irreversibly contributed to the rapid growth and development of some countries. This has clearly been the case for

Korea and Malaysia, but not for Ghana. Korea and Malaysia have been "globalizers", fully integrating themselves into the globalized or interlinked world economy. Ghana has resisted globalization. Ghanaians may blame globalization for their social, economic, and political woes, but the Koreans and Malaysians can be nothing but thankful for well timed and sequenced development policies and implementation, which all coincide precisely with the high tide of globalization. Ghana isolated itself, withdrawing into an autarkic cocoon of socialism that eventually brought stagnation to the country. Malaysia could have gone farther than it did, had it not been for its "Malay first" development strategy that restricted the economic activities of the Chinese, Indian, and foreign populations in the country.

Similarly, Korea could have surpassed Japan — its unfulfilled national dream — had it welcomed international capital and technology like Singapore did. Instead, Korea chose to build its own economic tools, the *chaebols*, often handpicked by the military in the name of national economic development and national security. Instead of scattering its scarce resources, the ruling elites of Korea chose to focus on a dozen or so conglomerates to pull the country's economic train. Korea was ready for globalization on its own terms. Malaysia sought to use it for the benefits of the Malays, excluding its minorities. Ghana never considered globalization to be a tool for development and growth; rather, its socialist upbringing, much like that of other socialist autarkic or closed political economies, pursued anti-globalization policies and ideals.

Many will attribute such differences in development to culture, history, inefficient government, and even evil foreign designs (Petras and Veltmeyer 2001; Petras 2003; Rosenberg 2000; Goldsmith 1994; Martin and Schumann 1997; Hertz 2001; Malone and Khong 2003). Naturally there are also benign views on the impact of globalization, globalism, and, in particular, the globalization of production. Alice Amsden of MIT argues that globalization laid the groundwork for developing countries ("the rest") to grow in the decades between 1950 and 1980. In East Asia, Japan, Korea, and Taiwan licensed or bought foreign technology, and then through "adaptive" processes, invented their own technologies (Amsden 2001, p. 14). The geographic dispersal of national production systems (production platforms of MNCs) throughout the world, *more than trade*, has accelerated regional economic integration. In Southeast Asia, the influx of MNCs and their production facilities have contributed to the region's economic boom, which in turn has compelled these countries to nurture peaceful, stable security environments (Brooks 2005, pp. 7–9). Whichever interpretation one chooses to subscribe to, Korea and Malaysia have done better than Ghana because the first two became global trading economies and knew how to take advantage of globalization and its opportunities.

1.8 THE STATE VS. THE MARKET IN DEVELOPMENT

Over the past three decades, the scholarship on development has witnessed a sea change. Two rival camps have emerged: neomercantilism and neoliberalism. "Neo", meaning "new" in Latin, tends to dominate the thinking about development since the 1980s, whether in a "mercantilist" or a "liberal" mode. Many "neos" today are former colonies and young independent states with little historical experience in industrialization. This is not to deny, as Amsden points out, that a manufacturing experience under colonization is relevant. In fact, this MIT political economist argues that those countries with a colonial history of manufacturing such as Korea, India, and Taiwan, performed better in their later development than countries without a colonial manufacturing history, such as Argentina, Brazil, Mexico, and Chile (Amsden 2001, pp 16–18). One might add Indonesia and Vietnam to this latter list as well. Amsden is not alone in identifying the value-adding phenomenon of colonial manufacturing. A Princeton academic also lays a similar claim to this thesis (Kohli 2004, pp. 27–36). Furthermore, Amsden advances an intriguing thesis about the rise of neoliberal globalization as the fault line for explaining the crises, woes, and stagnation of developing countries since 1980, and the rise to power of Margaret Thatcher in Britain and the election of Ronald Reagan in the United States.

Many of these post-1980 development problems were not of their own making (Yergin and Stanislaw 1998). Instead, neoliberal globalization must bear some of the blame (Amsden 2007, pp. 1–3). Thus, the jury is still out in terms of determining which of these divergent views more accurately explains the short history of neoliberal globalization, including the role played by its hidden clauses, small print, and shyster lawyers' tricks. Whatever the verdict, though, it is a fact that neoliberalism was foisted upon developing nations before being adopted domestically. For instance, the U.S. Treasury, at the instigation of Wall Street bankers and MNC executives, pressured developing countries to liberalize their trade practices, deregulate domestic markets, and privatize state-owned enterprises well before America opened its markets to foreign sugar, peanuts, rice, textile, steel, and cotton — much like Britain forced a free trade policy on the Ottoman Empire in the early nineteenth century before it was introduced at home. The eclipse of the state and the rise of the market spurred today's dominant neoliberal political trends and elected market-friendly governments to power in the 1980s and 1990s in the West.

Neoliberalism is defined herein as the *privatization* of state-owned assets in favour of market driven operations, state *deregulation* in the economy and society so as to welcome foreign investment, and greater *liberalization* of international trade in goods and services. Daniel Yergin and Joseph Stanislaw attribute the rise of neoliberalism to popular disenchantment with the socialist experiments in Britain and the New Deal-inspired creeping welfarism in the United States. As of the mid-twentieth century, both countries had strong statist intervention in the market (Yergin and Stanislaw 1998). Unlike others, Yergin and Stanislaw do not believe that neoliberal reforms were specifically designed for developing countries, as averred by the critics of the "Washington Consensus" of the late 1980s and 1990s. Rather, Yergin and Stanislaw view neoliberalism as the philosophical linchpin of the Margaret Thatcher and Ronald Reagan agendas for domestic reforms in the most developed countries.

As their policies began to bear fruit, developing countries sought to copy it, and the U.S. Treasury, the World Bank, and the IMF encouraged it. In her autobiography, Thatcher recites a litany of negative social, economic, and political consequences that stemmed from the British "cradle-to-grave" socialist system that plagued her country with "a centralizing, managerial, bureaucratic, interventionist style of government" (Thatcher 1993, p. 6). Nationalization (or state-ownership of key industries), the unchallengeable power of trade union bosses, and a self-promoting state bureaucracy all sapped British energy, competitiveness, and, eventually, productivity.

The role of the *state* drew the attention of the social scientists and economic planners soon after the end of World War II and continued for several decades beyond (Evans, Rueschemeyer, and Skocpol 1985). The Marshall Plan certainly would not have survived without a strong role of the state, as was also true for the post-war economic recovery of Japan, Germany, and the rest of Europe. The state-centric trend continued and became the linchpin of development, as embodied in the rise of the Asian Tigers (South Korea, Taiwan, Hong Kong, and Singapore) and in the "state-led" capitalist development of Mexico and Brazil (Gereffi and Wyman 1990; Wade 1990; Woo 1991; Kim 1997).

Raul Prebisch's import-substituting industrialization, also known as import substitution industrialization, became the most popular post-war development paradigm in Asia, Latin America, and Africa with varying degrees of direct state ownership and participation in the market. Instead of welcoming foreign corporations and their capital and technology, economic nationalism saw to it that restrictions were broad and sweeping in order either to keep MNCs out, or force them to relocate their production platforms to another country. Instead of welcoming foreign capital, Latin America, South Asia, and Africa preferred to fund state-owned and state-managed projects under the guise of joint ventures (Hirschman 1963; Hirschman 1971; Bates 2001, pp. 85–88). Mexico and Brazil were the first of Latin America's successful import-substituting industrialization cases that match the pace of Asian development. They were also the first two countries in Latin America to question the efficacy of the statist ISI model of development when, in September 1982, the prosperous Mexico was forced to declare a debt moratorium. By November 1982, Brazil had followed suit, unable to pay interest on some US$100 billion that the government of Brazil had borrowed from external bankers (Stallings and Kaufman 1989).

The Latin American model of development thus set off a debate, causing a crisis of confidence among global bankers in Latin America's ability to sustain its statist development and to service its mountain of debt. Then external pressure for change began to mount. In fact, it was the debt crisis that ushered in reform policies that have been deeply influenced by neoliberalism, thus transforming the continent and setting it on a growth path as of the early 1990s (Pang 2002). For a decade or more, neoliberalism in Latin America worked well. Chile, Mexico, and Brazil are today more open and market-driven economies than in the 1970s and 1980s and are among the most robust economies in the region.

1.9 JAPANESE-LED FLYING GEESE AND THE EAST ASIAN MIRACLE

The vaunted Flying Geese model was predicated on Japan's global trade ambitions and its vastly expanding investment in offshore production platforms scattered throughout Northeast and Southeast Asia. Japan was so convinced of the invincibility of its own state-driven model of economic development that it sought to institutionalize it throughout East Asia as part of its strategy to dominate East Asia. It paid for the publication of the World Bank's *The East Asian Miracle: Economic Growth and Public*

Policy (1993, written by staff of *The Economist*) to trumpet the success of those Asian countries that emulated the Japan, Inc. model. The Rising Sun had emerged as the lead goose and other Asian countries fell into the flying formation. Together they reached their destination of growth and development.

The book identified ten factors contributing to the East Asian economic miracle, which set the stage for subsequent discussions of development in the literature. It demonstrates that there are several avenues for economic development and societal prosperity *other than* the North-western European and North American model. James Fallows, the Washington editor of *The Atlantic* magazine, relocated his family to Japan for four years to study its secret recipe for success in the form of a modified Meiji development model. The core role of the state was key to the success of the East Asian miracle (Fallows 1994). Fallows was so impressed with the success of the Japanese model and its clone that he was as convinced as Lee Kuan Yew of America's decline as something permanent, not temporary.

In recent years, Francis Fukuyama has been similarly and deeply convinced that "Japanese-pioneered" Asian capitalism poses a threat and "a long term challenge to the Western liberal model" (Fukuyama 2006). Thus, between the late 1980s and the Asian financial crisis of 1997–98, East Asia was *the* economic showcase that the World Bank recommended other developing countries to follow. Perhaps Asian technocrats in the World Bank were easily intoxicated by the achievement of the miracle — more money poured into public education, rising living standards, galloping exports, and more foreign investment pouring into the region. All these trends for economic growth and development were presumed to be unshakeable and sustainable. Then, the sky caved in.

The Asian financial crisis of 1997–98 can be construed in two ways. First, it signaled the end of the *state-led* development model (Pang 2000). Second, it was argued by some that the entire crisis was manufactured by jealous Western countries that envied Asia's development and were determined to stop it, especially those Jewish financiers living in the United States. This take on the crisis was much touted by such nationalistic Asian leaders as Mahathir Mohamad of Malaysia (Mahathir 2000; Biers 1998). Although this view is not widely held among serious thinking Asians, I have occasionally run into academics in the region who persist in believing in this conspiracy theory. If the state and its leaders are ultimately credited with the economic success of a country and amply rewarded for their policy implementation, they must also be held accountable for policy flaws and subsequent market failures that brought about the crisis. Regime changes did take place in all crisis-inflicted countries except in Malaysia. This is one indication that those countries were at a maturing stage of political democracy.

Many observers pointed out that when the Mexican peso meltdown occurred in December 1994, the United States rushed in with a bale of dollars to save Mexico. When the financial crisis crippled Southeast Asia and Korea, the United States chose to sit this out, blaming the entire mess on the Asian way of doing business, which ranges from the cosy state-business ties to politically-driven "crony capitalism", corruption, and nepotism (Jomo 1998). The moral hazards served as an excuse for the United States not to rush to the rescue. In fact, the Clinton administration helped Korea, but left Thailand and Indonesia at the mercy of the IMF. Security considerations played a role here. Secretary of the Treasury Robert Rubin admitted in his biography that there had been an acrimonious division between the military and economic advisers in the Clinton administration on how to rescue Thailand. State and Defense leadership supported a direct bilateral U.S.-Thai solution by tapping into the Exchange Stabilization Fund — the same fund that had saved Mexico two years earlier — while Treasury opposed it. Rubin never explained the reasons for his opposition. Security concerns seemed to play an overarching role in the economic rescue plan (Rubin and Weisberg 2003, pp. 215–22). Thus the link or convergence between economic well-being and security mattered. South Korea was firmer in its security commitment to the United States than Thailand was. Also, the proximity of a hostile North Korea figured prominently in the Clinton administration's decision. Thailand, on the other hand, did not have a belligerent neighbour(s) threatening its security.

Also, the Clinton administration, with the support of the European Union and China, reacted sharply against the Japanese proposal for an Asian Monetary Fund (AMF) to deal with the crisis *on Asian terms* (Pang 2000). For reasons of their own, all three opposed the AMF plan. The United States and the European Union feared the weakening of the IMF, thereby endangering their own control over the global economy, while China objected because it was Japan's idea, fearing that the AMF might become pro-Japanese. Whatever the explanation that was put forward for the absence of a proactive American stance, U.S.-ASEAN relations were deteriorating. One example was the pre-crisis weakening of Asian support for the U.S.-backed Asia Pacific Economic Cooperation (APEC), which became almost dysfunctional, as China, Japan, and several Southeast Asian countries joined forces to block key U.S. proposals (Bergsten 1997; Ravenhill 2001; Feinberg 2003). When the 1997–98 crisis occurred, Clinton was in no mood to forget the Asian obstructionism in APEC and rush in with a truckload of money.

By December 1997, the Asian countries on their own and without U.S. support established a new mechanism for cooperation, ASEAN Plus Three (the ten members of ASEAN plus Japan, China, and South Korea). It was set up as the core political group for the region and excluded the United States. This arrangement has been the most prominent expression of Asian independence and has the potential to play havoc with U.S. strategies for its role in the region. The Chiang Mai swap scheme, which was devised to aid the thirteen countries in future crises, also excludes the United States. However, when the ASEAN Regional Forum was being put together in 1994, the Southeast Asians included the United States, probably against China's opposition, but at Japan's insistence. Some said Korea abstained. The United States overnight became the odd man out.

Thus, Asia's development strategy since 1997–98 has entered a new phase in which China and Japan have assumed a more important role and the United States has been relegated to a lesser role, each battling the other, inching further away from the Bretton Woods order that the United States and Europe have dominated. This seemingly innocuous development signalled an important change, however: the United States is to have no role in regional economic issues, while it is allowed to sit at the table of regional security. The division of labour that Japan has been advocating for decades is now institutionalized in the form of reserving economic matters for itself, while enjoying the security umbrella provided by the United States to balance out China. In hindsight, Clinton and Rubin committed a serious error in judgement, saving a penny then at the risk of spending millions now and in the future.

Obama's major challenge remains one of changing the region's perception of America and convincing Asians that they will be accorded respect. Within less than two years in office, his administration has implemented a proactive agenda to do just that as evidenced by the U.S. ascension to ASEAN's Treaty of Amity and Cooperation; frequent visits to the region by Secretary of State Hillary Clinton (six) and Secretary of Defense Robert Gates (five); the creation of the U.S.-ASEAN Summit (two meetings by September 2010); the reopening of defence ties with Indonesia;

a softened but clearer position towards Burma's junta; and a heightened profile of the United States as a willing Pacific neighbour to stand with small countries against China's claims in the East China Sea and South China Sea disputes. The question is: will America have the staying power to sustain this level of engagement?

1.10 NEOMERCANTILIST ASIA AND NEOLIBERAL AMERICA

The archetypical developmentalist state in East Asia has been Japan. Chalmers Johnson, Alice Amsden, Robert Wade, J.T. Pempel, Meredith Woo-Cumings, Ha Joon Chang, and others have recognized the centrality of the state in the early phase and intermediary "catch up" phase of Asia's development (Johnson 1995; Pempel 2005; Amsden 2001; Wade 1990; Woo 1991; H. Chang 2002). They have shown that the quality of bureaucracy that piloted institutions mattered. Japan, Korea, China, Singapore, and other countries select their civil servants by competitive examination. University education matters. The passport to a successful public service career in Japan's civil service is an education at the University of Tokyo; for Korea, Seoul National University; and for Singapore, the National University of Singapore. In the 1990s, the educational pedigree of the Top Ten bureaucrats in the Ministry of Finance in Korea is revealing: nine graduated from Seoul National University and the tenth one from Korea University (Amsden 2007, p. 141).

Over time, such elite recruiting will suffer from all the ills of inbreeding and its own defective gene pool. Perhaps the 1997–98 financial crisis was one such manifestation. However, the case of development in East Asia — especially China, Vietnam, and other latecomers — has demonstrated that a country's development is a matter of how to calibrate and harmonize its objectives with globalization opportunities. The cases of Ghana, Malaysia, and Korea exemplify how well the opportunities of globalization can produce positive results for a country's benefit. For the most part, earlier development analysts did not pay sufficient attention to the links between the statist model and the globalization environment. More typically, the older literature focuses on state responses or resistance to globalization.

Two of the strongest supporters of globalization and its attendant neoliberalism have argued that the developed countries must seek to reform their current trade and investment practices to favour developing countries more. Martin Wolf in his seminal work, *Why Globalization Works*, proposes that the world needs more globalization, not less. Globalization means the integration of economic activities across borders. There are no foreigners in globalization. More singularly, it was the trade in the nineteenth and twentieth centuries that integrated the world across borders. In half a century (1950–98), world output increased by 530 per cent (manufactures by 820 per cent), but merchandise exports outpaced production by 1,840 per cent and manufactures exported by 3,500 per cent (Wolf 2004, p. 112). The globalization that has uplifted 55 per cent of the world population from poverty has met the greatest resistance from "radical socialism", or "new millennium collectivism", and ethnocentric nationalism whose constituencies are the global poor (Wolf 2004, pp. 14, 308–31). The world needs more cross-border trade and investment, not less, so argue the proponents.

Jagdish Bhagwati in his *In Defence of Globalization* avers that the West must make further concessions in trade to developing countries so that they can reap more benefits from the current phase of globalization. Like Wolf, Bhagwati agrees that trade (merchandise first and then service) has fuelled the growth of the world economy. But the Indian-born economist champions a giveaway of miracle drug formulas and other inventions to developing countries by scrapping TRIPS (trade related aspects of intellectual property rights) in the WTO, which he calls "a collection agency" for the rich. Globalization has been good for the poor (Mexico, Brazil, Korea, and Malaysia) and better for the rich (Japan, the United States, and the European Union). Trade has become an important tool to eradicate poverty, thus contributing to the improvement of human welfare.

1.11 "UNIQUELY SINGAPOREAN"

The World Bank's analysis (and often claim) about the impact of globalization helps us understand why Singapore has succeeded in its development where others in Southeast Asia have often failed. "Globalization" as simply and elegantly defined by World Bank researchers stands for "growing integration of economies and societies around the world" (WB 2002, p. xi). In it, trade is central. So far, globalization has reduced global poverty. China had 250 million people living in poverty in 1978; by 1999, only 34 million were classified as poor. By partaking of globalization, developing countries alone now have three billion people participating in trade and investment activities. China, India, Vietnam, and Bangladesh, all in Asia, have gained from globalization, while two billion people, mostly in less globally integrated and stubbornly resisting countries in Africa, South Asia, and Central Asia, remain left out.

The World Bank claims that these countries participate less in trade and investment today than they did twenty years ago. It also urges the world to accept the fact that trade is the proven solution to global poverty reduction and that the rich must therefore do more for the less privileged by opening up their markets. Ironically, one World Bank study mentions that 70 per cent of all tariff barriers that developing economies confront are not from the developed world, but from sibling developing countries (WB 2002, pp. 9, 56). Panama, which imports half of the food it consumes, charges an import duty of 260 per cent on chicken leg quarters, while Korea charges 226 per cent on corn starch, 176 per cent on dairy products, and 135 per cent on onions (CRS 2009a, pp. 4, 13). To protect domestic interests, the government is called upon to resist globalization and abjure its benefits.

South-South trade has expanded from less than 20 per cent in the 1980s to more than 40 per cent by 1995. In order to increase the volume, developing countries need deeper integration measures such as vigorous enforcement of TRIPS and customs valuation (WB 2002, p. 62). Both measures call for better institutions and qualified civil servants that many developing countries lack. Also, one cannot effectively enforce conditions under TRIPS without the patent registration and protection that a state must provide. Customs valuation can lead to an actual loss of revenues, unless trade facilitation measures are firmly in place (Bhagwati 2004, pp. 82–83, 183–84). Singapore has succeeded because it has invested in institutions and human resources that could frontally meet all the challenges proffered by globalization and its concomitant opportunities. Thus it seems that more globalization is needed and should be embraced by developing countries as well as by developed economies, its promoters in the first place. As for the uneven effects of globalization, the World Bank has demonstrated that since 1980 there has been a "widening gap between the globalizers and those countries left behind" (WB 2002, pp. 3–7).

Singapore's development has been driven by trade and FDI under intelligent political guidance and a cadre of incorruptible state bureaucrats. The World Bank's empirical research demonstrates that "trade goes hand-in-hand with faster growth" and "more trade is *correlated* with higher growth" (WB 2002, p. 5). Those well positioned to take advantage of globalization succeed. Commenting on Latin America's retreat to statism (or what I call the Hugo Chávez syndrome), the report argues that the "extreme inequalities in educational attainment" in that region have contributed to greater wage inequalities (WB 2002, p. 5). Singapore has done admirably well in building up its public education system, and its fair income distribution is a reflection of the quality of its well trained labour force and well educated, large middle classes. Few in Southeast Asia have been able to duplicate Singapore's feat.

In the financial arena, globalization offers a double-edged sword. Without a "sound domestic financial system", integration with the world financial market cannot yield dividends, as seen in Indonesia, Korea, Malaysia, and Thailand in 1997. Well before 1997 and, in particular, since then, Singapore has been modernizing its financial sector. Banks have been required to hold to higher disclosure rules on non-performing loans; the government has imposed lower capital requirements and granted tax incentives for small and medium-sized investment houses; and the government has injected as much as S$35 billion in private portfolios by encouraging government-linked corporations and statutory bodies to invest. Finally, it has given a tax exemption on private fund managers who handle more than S$5 billion to stimulate private investment. By eliminating the cap on foreign currency-dominated shares in pension funds, the government also encourages inflows of foreign money. In addition, the establishment of joint government-private sector committees has produced innovative state-market collaboration in various financial sectors (U.S. Embassy Singapore 1998 and 1999).

1.12 POLITICAL SPILLOVERS OF THE TWO MODELS

East Asia has relied on an activist state for development. But for reasons of different histories and asymmetries in factor endowments, each country has adopted a different strategy, albeit ones that are still state dominated or driven. Northeast Asia (Japan, Korea, Taiwan, and China, in chronological order of industrialization) adopted a "technology licensing" system of industrialization. Unwilling to allow foreign capital to take up dominant positions in the domestic economy, the government preferred to license foreign technology and pass it on to a chosen firm to manufacture products (Emmott 2003, p. 41). Automobiles, electrical products, and electronics from East Asia were produced under licence. It took decades for Korean, Japanese, and Taiwanese workers to master the use of imported technologies, but once they acquired sufficient skills to use them, they moved a notch upward by modifying them and eventually producing their own hybrid technologies, the adaptive phase that Amsden alludes to. Sony and Samsung are prime examples of this transformation. This blending of domestic savings and imported technology granted Northeast Asian countries a measure of autonomy in decision making, while the state and national firms chose a particular project as a national priority.

Lacking well trained labour, a good education system, significant domestic savings, and managerial talent, Southeast Asian countries chose to invite multinational corporations to industrialize their economies. This "turnkey" model offered two distinct advantages that the Northeast Asian model did not. For one, international corporations brought with them their own capital, advanced technology, and managerial personnel. There was no inherent risk for Thailand, Malaysia, and Singapore to assume. If projects failed, MNCs bore the brunt of capital invested, infrastructure built, and technology imported. For another, once products were made, they were exported to ready markets in the home countries of the investors as well as to other markets. This built-in overseas market access, steady flow of modern technology, and presence of experienced production managers and engineering staff shortened the time of industrialization to mere years, not decades.

Japan, Korea, and Taiwan gained market access by exploiting their security relationship with the United States. Malaysia, in which 20 per cent of all FDI comes from America, has emerged as the third largest computer chips maker in the world, after the United States and Japan. Thailand has become the world's largest light truck maker (Dieter 2009, pp. 89–113). For the past two decades, both Singapore and Malaysia have been exporting two to three times the value of their gross domestic products. In 2006, the World Bank showed that the total trade value of Singapore reached US$511 billion, of which exports accounted for US$272 billion (WB 2008, pp. 210–16). These stunning successes were made possible by a combination of the MNCs' massive investment and imaginative state strategies for development.

It is risky to generalize the political outcomes of the two Asian development models, but a simple comparison and contrast of the evolution of political and social democracy in Southeast Asia and Northeast Asia can deepen our understanding of the development phenomenon. On the surface, it can be observed that Northeast Asia's practitioners of the technology-licensing model (Japan, Korea, and Taiwan) have evolved into more open, liberal democracies than those in Southeast Asia (the turnkey model in Malaysia, Indonesia, and Thailand), with Singapore as an exception or hybrid. Such democracy scholars as Seymour Martin Lipset have argued that as a society experiences a rise in income above a certain level, green shoots of democracy will sprout and take root. Social scientists seem to know more about how to build democracy than how to sustain it, however (Lipset and Lakin 2004; Anderson 1999, p. 2). Nevertheless, there must be reasons the technology-licensing countries have produced higher incomes and seemingly stable democracies as opposed to the turn key countries, again with the exception of Singapore. In addition to the head start in social infrastructure (education, healthcare, workers' rights, and the like) that Northeast Asia enjoyed, fair income distribution, growing middle classes, permeating civil society values, and the consolidation of political and economic institutions, have probably played a decisive role as well.

1.13 "THE ROAD TO SINGAPORE"

Bob Hope, Bing Crosby, and Dorothy Lamour made a comedy movie in 1940 that probably created the first popular impression of Singapore in the American psychic. But long before Singapore was romanticized by Hollywood, America's corporate icons, such as the Dollar Shipping Line, operated out of Singapore at the turn of the twentieth century. Later it became the American Presidential Line, founded in 1938 by Joe Kennedy, father of President John F. Kennedy. In 1997 the line was bought by Neptune Orient Lines, former corporate employer of Prime Minister Goh Chok Tong. Dollar linked America to the "mysterious Orient", as the saying of the time went. In 1916, Kodak opened a store in Singapore, its first in Asia; then, Singer Sewing Machine, Ford Motor Company, Citibank, and others followed suit, firmly settling themselves in Singapore as their base of operations for Southeast Asia and India (Baker 2005).

By 1926, Singer had established a network of distributorship throughout Southeast Asia and introduced an innovative sales method using the instalment plan. This was appropriate given the prevailing living standards in the region then. That same year, Ford built its first Asian assembly plant in Singapore. At about the same time, General Motors located its regional headquarters in Singapore, but chose to assemble cars in Batavia (Jakarta), probably for reasons of cheaper labour, an easier supply of inputs, and an earlier version of the integrated sourcing initiative model (Baker 2005, pp. 138–46). Some seventy years later, many American corporations still regard Singapore as their Asian base of operation. In 2003, Singapore hosted some 1,500 U.S. corporations, which in turn were Singapore's most vocal cheerleaders who lobbied Congress, pressured various trade-promoting governmental agencies, and charmed the American media. Singapore has one of the most active American Clubs in Asia, the home-away-from-home for American business people, diplomats, military personnel, and their families, as well as an itinerant scholar such as myself. Singapore is a known quantity to Americans from Hollywood to Washington.

One must add two more critical contributors to this list: governmental institutions and the elite's ideology. Both have been ardent advocates of free trade and an open market economy with appropriate state regulatory measures. Specialists in economic development in the 1990s began to show interest in institutions, the people who manage them, and other intangible norms and practices, which together have contributed to the making of today's prosperous Singapore. Douglass North received a Nobel Prize for highlighting the importance of institutions in development (North 2005, pp. 13–19).

Since then, economists have dutifully followed North. It has been made clear that in Asia, so-called "catch up" development has occurred when a country was able to build a stable political environment comprising good governance, the rule of law, protection for intellectual property rights, fair tax rates, sound macroeconomic policies, and a market-friendly atmosphere. All these took institutions and talents which ran them. The state had to coordinate a set of policies and institutions that would satisfy both public and private sector needs. Singapore's government has spent a fortune in building up the National University of Singapore, to which the most talented faculty staff are recruited from all over the world. All of these have created formal and informal institutions in which policies could be anchored and projects could be carried out by capable civil servants, people of ability, and proper training Asia has come to possess.

1.14 SINGAPORE'S ELITES AND FREE TRADE

But what happens when a country only has human resources, but no natural resources, to develop? Singapore's success in development owes much to the formation of its elite and their pro-business attitudes. In a culture that values the amassing of wealth above anything else, or "moneytheism", to use S. Rajaratnam's felicitous expression (Mauzy and Milne 2002, p. 51), public service has been viewed as a poor second choice for a profession and regarded as the reserve of poorly paid Confucian scholars. In such a culture, it is difficult to recruit state elites. Yet the 150 or so men and women who govern the republic and manage the national economy are extraordinarily talented people by any world standards. Even mid-level civil servants and military officers exude pride and competence in their roles. There is a closely knit and well coordinated working relationship between the government and businesses that has engendered Singapore's impressive economic achievement, matched by few city states in history, with the possible exception of Venice.

An experiment in the 1960s and early 1970s with elite recruitment in Singapore represents a quintessential example of social engineering and has produced mixed results. In particular, intellectuals and academics did not fit into the world of Lee Kuan Yew and his nation builders. Civil technocrats and military officers adapted well to the practices of the ruling party, the People's Action Party (PAP), but key government leaders were not convinced that the military should dominate. By design, Singapore reversed the state-party relationship. In most authoritarian states, the dominant player is the party, such as the Chinese Communist Party, which is an all-powerful entity that can set state policies, as all party states do. Singapore's leaders did not want a party-state system. Instead, they saw PAP as the recruiter of state elites, an incubating and training ground, but one with little direct executive, legislative, or judiciary power.

As a result, the government has become the pacesetter and is still the stronger of the two. Rigorous selection processes were adopted, and the second prime minister, Goh Chok Tong, was put in charge of institutionalizing the recruiting process. Himself the president of a government-linked shipping company, Goh, a quintessential technocrat (a Williams College graduate in economics), is one example. Another is Dr Tony Tan, an academic, a banker, a deputy prime minister, and a minister of defence through the 1990s and early 2000s. Several retired military officers also joined the government. Among them are such "scholar-soldiers" as Brigadier General Lee Hsien Loong (prime minister since August 2004) and Brigadier General George Yeo (the minister of trade and industry who negotiated the U.S.-Singapore FTA and currently foreign minister). But the military presence in the government (as political power brokers) has been non-existent, compared with other Southeast Asian countries.

Routinely, the government has given out overseas scholarships to its future leaders. Lately, the bright ones are sent to American universities, mostly the Ivies and California-based schools. A former Air Force attaché at the United States Embassy in Singapore told me that Singapore is one of the most favoured Southeast Asian countries from which the American military academies also recruit, and that the Singaporean cadets do well at the U.S. Air Force Academy in Colorado Springs (Tietjen 2008, interview). During my fieldwork in the city state, I met a Singaporean lawyer who was selected to go to the U.S. Air Force Academy, but was rejected at the last minute because of poor eyesight. Two years later, his younger brother was selected by the academy and later graduated top of his class (Loh 2008, interview).

Leaders of the government are not a closed group in terms of their education, professional backgrounds, ethnicity, or even nationality. Singapore's elite recruiting is open and global in practice, compared with Japan's or Korea's. The most recent example is the Government of Singapore's recruitment of non-citizens to lead various agencies and corporations. For instance, in early 2009 Temasek selected a former chief executive of Anglo-Australia's BHP-Billiton (an American) to replace its CEO, Ho Ching, wife of the current prime minister (*Financial Times*, "Mild-mannered" 2009). In July 2009, the CEO-select and Temasek chose to end their relationship, however; a few weeks later, a Citibank man was hired to lead the Development Bank of Singapore (DBS) (Stein and Paris 2009). One previous CEO of DBS was an American banker.

Academic achievement, the ability to be a good team player, and innovative and creative thinking are the leadership qualities that PAP recruiters are looking for in its future generation of leaders (Mauzy and Milne 2002, pp. 38–49). The current balanced political culture reflects the positive dimensions of Confucian values (learned men in government; hard working ethics; and austerity), while nurturing the meritocracy of governing elites coming from diverse ethnic and national backgrounds. In less globalized societies, citizenship matters; in the most globalized society, competitiveness, efficiency, and productivity matter. Singapore values the talent, not the individual's citizenship. This has helped Singapore avoid one perennial mistake of governing elites that plague all cultures: inbreeding and its accompanying ills. Instead, this meritocratic approach to governance paid off during the financial crisis of 1997–98 and has shepherded the city state well in weathering the 2008–10 recession.

1.15 WASHINGTON'S TRADE AND SECURITY STRATEGY

In a curious way, Bush chose to continue Clinton's trade strategy: simultaneously pursuing trade liberalization at the multilateral (WTO), regional (NAFTA, the now moribund Free Trade Area of the Americas, and APEC), and bilateral levels. Clinton was Wilsonian in his world view, but Bush was not. Strobe Talbott, a classmate of Clinton's at Oxford (both were Rhodes Scholars) and later deputy secretary of State for the Clinton administration, argued that Clinton firmly believed that good economic relationships can lead to strong security ties (Talbott 2008, pp. 393–96). The U.S. trade deficit in Clinton's first year in office was a mere US$136 billion. When he left in January 2001, it was three times that amount. One reason for this high deficit is that Clinton kept tariffs low to promote good trade relationships, which in turn reduced security frictions. The problem was that not all American trading partners reciprocated. China was one example. Clinton designated China a "strategic partner", worked hard to grant it permanent most-favoured-nation status, and supported its ascension to the World Trade Organization. Many commitments that China made in order to become a WTO member have remained unfulfilled, however (Talbott 2008, pp. 335–36). Also, Clinton worked with multilateral organizations such as the United Nations (U.N.) and NATO when it came to regional and global security issues. The results were poor. These organizations did not always deliver what they promised. Bush disdained them and did not bother to follow Clinton's approach for that reason.

On the multilateral stage, Clinton's approach was what Madeleine Albright termed "assertive multilateralism" (Talbott 2008, p. 335). Paleo-conservative Republican senator Jesse Helms saw the United Nations as a tool of unfriendly countries seeking to undermine "the sanctity of national sovereignty" of America and attempted to modify its behaviour by withholding U.S. dues (US$1.5 billion). The amount represented 15 per cent of the entire U.N. budget, but less than a thousandth of the American budget of US$1.7 trillion (Talbott 2008, pp. 335–36). Crafty Richard Holbrooke, Clinton's ambassador to the United Nations, invited Helms to address the Security Council, allowing the senator to vent his anger and read out a riot act to the Security Council. Soon, the Clinton administration was allowed to pay the overdue debt. One of Clinton's folksy expressions sums up the situation: "We are the biggest dog in the hunt", and the United States must set a good example (Talbott 2008, p. 329). But the Republicans in Congress and President Bush did not regard the U.S. role in the United Nations as critical.

The Clinton administration's contribution to strengthening the security architecture in the Asia Pacific has not been appreciated by either the media or the academic community. To foster a closer relationship and to become more transparent in NATO decision making, the Clinton administration gave Russia a seat at the table, to the dismay of many conservatives in the United States. Former U.S. Secretary of State Henry Kissinger, for instance, thought that Clinton had gone too far in the name of transparency and in an attempt to bolster the sagging political position of Russian president Boris Yeltsen at home; in fact, Kissinger stopped short of accusing Clinton of destroying NATO (Kissinger 2001, pp. 44–45). Security arrangements with Japan, Korea, and Australia were significantly updated. The willingness of the United States to sit down with North Korea abruptly opened the Stalinist state to the outside world. In this context, the Six-Party Talks were a critical vehicle for clearing the path to the multilateral discussions. The engagement of China in military relations through the exchange of visits and greater communication opportunities also eased bilateral tensions. Secretary of Defense William Cohen was the first high-ranking American official to visit China's military installations, which had been closed to foreign dignitaries previously. Clinton also updated and supported the changing relationship between Japan and the United States by agreeing to greater security autonomy for Japan, limiting the more obtrusive presence of the U.S. military there, and allowing continued access to advanced high tech weapons systems in the American arsenal (see Chapter 6 for details).

Where Bush parted from his predecessor was in his security policy. In his last days in office, Clinton invited the president-elect to the Oval Office for a private handover chat. The incumbent painted five short- and long-term foreign policy issues that Bush was inheriting: al-Qaeda threats; the breakdown of the peace process in the Middle East due to "the intransigence of Yasser Arafat"; increasing Indo-Pakistani tensions; North Korea's nuclear threat; and, finally, "the simmering crisis in Iraq" (Talbott 2008, p. 357). None tweaked Bush's interest, or at least did not appear to do so during the conversation. As it turned out, though, making war on Iraq's Saddam Hussein was at the top of Bush's agenda from his first day in office: "We are taking this guy out. After all this is the guy who tried to kill my dad" (Talbott 2008, p. 353). As it turned out, Bush had set his security agenda well before he took the oath of office: attack Iraq.

In his pre-9/11 days in office, Bush changed the fundamentals of United States' foreign security and economic policy by abandoning multilateralism without consulting Congress. What Talbott has called "*a la carte* multilateralism" permitted Bush to pick and choose which institution (the United Nations, NAFTA, the IMF, the World Bank, the World Court, and so forth) to work with, depending on his agenda. The first international move Bush made when he came into office was to suspend the Middle East peace talks. He likewise unilaterally abrogated the Anti-Ballistic Missile Treaty, thus giving the United States the right to deploy a national missile defence system, the core of the neocons' and conservatives' security policy. Not only was he the least travelled American president in history, but he also had no use for international law, institutions, treaties, alliances, or even diplomacy: "Here's what we're *not* going to do: we're not going to abide by old treaties; we don't intend to sign new ones; we're not going to do diplomacy; we're not going to do peacemaking or peacekeeping" (Talbott 2008, pp. 350–51).

Strobe Talbott depicts the Bush doctrine thus: "throwing hard power around to push democracy". Talbott counsels that the best way to build democracy in developing countries is to recognize that "nations build themselves, and democracy emerges slowly and iteratively" (Talbott 2008, pp. 302, 372–73). Neoconservative advisers encircling the Bush wagon were in such a hurry to make their mark that they sought to shorten the "unipolar moment" into Bush's two presidential terms, and hard power was seen as the quickest way to leave a firm footprint of their ideology (Talbott 2008, pp. 330–31; Fukuyama 2006, pp. 60–61).

On the surface, the Bush administration's philosophical disposition was one of bilateralism in interstate relations; a "security first" policy, especially after 9/11, of "preemptive and preventive war" against America's perceived enemies; a pro-business and anti-labour stance in domestic and foreign economic policies; and the ousting of Saddam Hussein at any cost. None of these policies completely turns off Singapore's elites. Nevertheless, the timing of Singapore's instigation of the USSFTA project during a November 2000 midnight golf game between Prime Minister Goh and President Clinton is curious. The U.S. election was over, and a Republican administration would be coming into office in late January 2001. The Clinton administration's second term had only eight more weeks left, and Singaporeans knew that FTA negotiations could drag on for months or even years. The FTA negotiations between the European Union and MERCOSUR, for instance, have been going on for fourteen years and are still not concluded as of 2010.

Why was Singapore in such a hurry? Singapore has been one of the freest trading countries in the world. It levies import taxes only on four items: sugar, samsoo, beer, and medical samsoo. Meanwhile, the United States charges the lowest import tariffs in the world, and it levies no export taxes. The Constitution of the United States specifically bans them. For many Asian countries, as much as 80 per cent of their exports enter the United States duty free or at less than 3 per cent tariff. This meant that in 2000 there was a *de facto* tariff-*free* trade between the two countries. From purely the standpoint of trade, why then was there the need for an FTA? Lee Kuan Yew himself has pointed out in his biography that Singapore has got along *better* with Republican administrations than Democratic ones. Presumably, pro-labour Clinton would be less open to the idea of an FTA.

Also, a year before, Singapore had caned an American teenage prankster who maliciously spray-painted cars in a rich neighbourhood. Clinton's plea for clemency in the case did no good. Singaporeans knew from the Canadian prime minister that Clinton and his people felt that they had lost "face" *vis-à-vis* the American public and could have held grudge against Singapore. After all, when it came to insults, Clinton was known to have a long memory (Felsenthal 2008, pp. 66–67, 182–83, 292–93). In view of this, one might have concluded that Singapore was taking a very high risk in broaching the subject of an FTA with lame duck Clinton, who was soon to leave office. Why would he be interested in granting any favours to Singapore? If the United States was destined to decline in economic power, Singapore had little to gain over time from an FTA deal with a loser. What might Singapore's non-economic motives for an FTA have been? These are some of the questions that the following chapters will try to answer.

2

The Road to the United States-Singapore Free Trade Agreement (USSFTA)

Without security, there can be no economic development. Conversely, stability and security are in serious jeopardy without economic development. This is the basis for the priority that Singapore has placed on ensuring our defence and security since the earliest days of our independence.

Dr Tony Tan, Deputy Prime Minister and Minister of Defence,
February 2002

Singapore was keen to have a Free Trade Agreement with the US, not only for its bilateral economic benefits, but also for the strategic signal it would send to the entire region. The FTA brings not just Singapore, but all of Southeast Asia, closer to the US. It binds us economically and politically, and helps to anchor the US in Asean.

Brigadier General George Yeo, Minister of Trade and Industry,
29 April 2003

2.1 OVERVIEW

Neoclassical economics has long held that trade contributes to the overall economic growth and development of a country (WB 2002; Schott 2004; Wolf 2004; Bhagwati 2004; Dent 2006). This study of the making of the USSFTA contests that assumption through an examination of the empirical evidence surrounding this bilateral agreement and instead posits that political and security considerations may outweigh the economic benefits of free trade agreements for the partners.

An example of a typical neoclassical study of the benefits of free trade was carried out by a group of economic researchers at the University of Michigan using a general equilibrium model of U.S. trade with the rest of the world (D. Brown, Deardorff, and Stern 2002). According to the study, if the entire world unilaterally dropped all tariff and non-tariff barriers, the total gain to the United States in that year would have been about US$497 billion, or 4.5 per cent of a US$13 trillion GDP, not a hefty amount. For Singapore, the study estimated a gain of US$17 billion. If APEC had eliminated all tariffs, it would have added an extra US$244 billion to the American economy, or 1.8 per cent of U.S. GDP (CRS 2007b, p. 15). But these projected gains were based on the assumption that the world or APEC alone would get rid of tariffs unilaterally. In this hypothetical scenario of a world without trade and non-trade barriers, gains could fuel the economic growth of countries that depend heavily on external trade as a source of income, or wealth generator. The Government of Singapore concluded that a free trade agreement (FTA) with the United States could add as much as 2 per cent to its GDP per annum. For the United States, the gain would be minuscule (CRS 2007b, pp. 7–8, 10).

In Southeast Asia, several key countries (Singapore, Malaysia, and Thailand, followed by Indonesia and the Philippines) have been engaged in export-promoting industrialization (EPI) for the past four decades. Singapore housed 6,000 multinational corporations in 2000 (1,500 of them being American) when it began to negotiate with the United States for an FTA (Pang 2007, p. 2; U.S. Embassy Singapore 2005). Soon after the Asian financial crisis of 1997–98, Singapore stepped up its pace of garnering FTAs with its best trading partners. New Zealand became the first country to sign such an agreement with the city state. The negotiations took eighteen months to conclude, and the FTA came into force in 2001 (Hoadley 2002, p. 72).

Both sides considered the closer economic partnership an exercise for future FTA negotiations with trading and investment partners. In other words, it was a political act. At the time, New Zealand ranked eighteenth in terms of Singapore's trading partner hierarchy. But fearing the potential disintegration of the ASEAN Free Trade Area (AFTA, signed in 1993), Malaysia vociferously complained that such bilateral FTAs pursued by Singapore and later by Thailand would give extra-ASEAN trading partners "back door" access to the ASEAN market ("Rafidah" 2001). The Singapore-New Zealand FTA particularly rankled Malaysia, which at the time practised anti-colonialist foreign trade and security policies. In reality, one of Malaysia's largest trading and investment partner is the United States. Singapore's response to Malaysia's concern was that the bilaterals could open up more opportunities in trade and investment for all ASEAN countries (Kesavapany 2001*a* and 2001*b*). Malaysia was not completely convinced.

2.2 AN AMERICAN IN SINGAPORE

An eighteen-year-old Ohio youth, Michael Peter Fay, moved to Singapore with his mother and stepfather in 1992, at the height of the seemingly unstoppable economic boom in East Asia, and when Singapore was attracting a worldwide attention as the second Asian country to become a fully developed nation after Japan. Ultimately, Fay's misbehaviour, and Singapore's response to it, became a metaphor for a larger cultural rift that was growing between Singapore and the West. Unlike the case of Japan, members of Singapore's governing elite were touting their economic achievements and became fond of lecturing the Western political leaders who condemned its undemocratic and illiberal political systems and practices. Concurrently, the Western media were too critical of Singapore's political style, which they called authoritarian or even worse (Safire 1994). In addition, the U.S. Department of State would list Singapore among human rights violators, big and small. With the fastest growing economy in the world, Asian countries (Singapore, Korea, Hong Kong, Taiwan, Malaysia, Thailand, and Indonesia) began to acquire confidence and a new kind of mindset. Those who travelled to the region at that time could sense the palpable changes in attitudes among the public and private elites. Intensely proud of what they had achieved, they began reverse lecturing.

In an interview with *Foreign Affairs* in its March/April 1994 issue, Lee Kuan Yew, who brought about unprecedented economic prosperity to three million people, was in an ebullient mood: the former prime minister observed that while he admired America as an anti-communist country that enjoyed an open attitude of people regardless of ethnicity or religion, but as a society it broke down and Western democracy was not working. The problems of illegal drugs, failing social welfarism, and lawlessness (guns, violent crimes, vagrancy, and a culture of "excessive individualism") contributed to the decay and decline of America, he argued. Commenting on U.S. foreign policy, Lee found it unfathomable that the United States could send an army to a country (Panama), capture its elected president, and put him in jail in Florida to try to solve the drug problem at home. He admitted that Singapore could not send an army to Burma and do the same, although it was not clear if he was referring to the limitations of the republic's military capabilities, or to the official policy of non-intervention among ASEAN siblings. Asia had done better than the West, he believed, because it created "a well ordered society" wherein the government made sure that each individual would enjoy "the maximum of his [her] freedom" (Zakaria 1994, pp. 3–12). Lee stated that it was the culture of Asia that led to an orderly society and responsible incorruptible government that made Asia distinct and therefore different from the United States. He was speaking — unbidden — for Asia as a whole.

Lee's interview was just one of several well orchestrated campaigns that Asian, Middle Eastern, and East African countries had mounted to highlight the rise of Asia and the decline of the West, trumpeting the arrival of the Pacific Century. Elsewhere, one Muslim scholar argued that Victorian English women enjoyed less freedom and rights than today's Muslim women and stressed that Muslim countries have elected women as presidents and prime ministers, conveniently forgetting that these female Muslim prime ministers and presidents came from South and Southeast Asia, not from the Middle East or Muslim Africa, an important cultural point worth remembering.

But it was the late Kim Dae Jung's rebuttal to Lee's interview that dented the Singaporean hubris. The then president of Korea forcefully argued that there is no causal link between "undemocratic" government and economic development. Instead, Kim argued that economic prosperity under undemocratic regimes in nineteenth-century Prussia and Meiji Japan paved the road to twentieth-century fascism, but they did not survive. Contrary to Lee's Asian world view where order, good governance, strong political leadership, and mass obedience served as the foundation for the Asian values, Kim highlighted democratic dimensions that had inherently been rooted in Asia, but had been forgotten long ago, or suppressed and that a new Asia needed to rediscover those roots and rejuvenate them (Kim 1994, pp. 189–94). After this confrontation between Lee and Kim on Asia's past, present, and future, Singaporeans seemed more demure in the Asian values debate. Kim's indirect message was "who appointed Singapore to speak for Asia?" Also, simple logic suggested that if Confucian or Asian values were indeed responsible for the economic miracle, why had Asia not fully developed in the 1820s or the 1890s? Surely there must have been external factors that also contributed to the growth and development of East Asia from the 1970s onward. One undeniable factor was neoliberal globalization, a decidedly Western movement. East Asia was responding very well to it.

Singapore's Professor Tommy Koh called for his country to stop being a "strident spokesman for the East" (Koh 1998, pp. 356–58; Barr 2002). It should be noted that the Asian values debate and the punishment of Michael Fay took place at the time when Southeast Asian countries (in particular, Singapore and Malaysia) were on the verge of redefining their domestic and foreign policy objectives, distancing themselves from the West, and rediscovering their Asian historical roots to rationalize their tremendous accomplishments.

The vandalism committed by Fay and his confederates (offspring of foreign diplomats and businessmen) took place during the three weeks from 18 September to 6 October 1993. The first car they spray-painted belonged to an influential Singaporean Indian judge and his wife, a state-appointed member of parliament. By American cultural standards, such a crime *could* be considered minor. But the Singaporean authorities took it differently. The boys were arrested and questioned. Singapore insisted that Fay and his cohorts confessed willingly, but later the accused stated that they confessed under duress and physical abuse (Nathan 1994; Hinds 1994). William Safire, a former speechwriter in the Nixon White House and a conservative pro-Republican editorialist at *The New York Times*, used the word "torture"(Safire 1994).

The timing could not have been worse. Riding high on the crest of an economic miracle previously unknown to the region, East Asian political leaders, media elites, and academic gurus began to lecture the West for its moral decay, crime, illegitimate births, violence, high rate of other social instability, and its eventual decline in contrast to the rapid advent of the Asian century. America should not be treated as special and should not enjoy extraterritoriality, either *de facto* or *de jure*. It was about time U.S. citizens living overseas be subject to laws of their host countries and be accountable for their actions. This Singaporean position was both sound and reasonable.

In hindsight, the superpower's press, radio, and television media were behaving badly, as if saying that the United States was the world sole superpower and how dare the tiny island treated Americans that way. An imperious arrogance pervaded both the American Government and its media. The Americans were not defending Fay's indiscretion, but considered the Singaporean punishment unusual and even cruel. Public sympathy for Fay and media pressure forced President Bill Clinton to appeal to Singapore for leniency, asking that the caning be waived (Reyes 1994). Singapore stood firm, but helped Clinton save face by reducing the number of lashes by two. Nevertheless, it was basking in triumphalism of teaching the superpower a lesson: you cannot push Singapore around. Both Washington and Singapore made political hay out of the Fay incident.

Then, a scant four years later, the Asian financial crisis let the air out of the vaunted Asian values balloon. It taught Singapore an important lesson: the city state is also vulnerable to spillovers from the economic and financial mismanagement of its Asian neighbours. It was infected by the crisis spreading from Thailand, Indonesia, and Malaysia, which represented as much as half of Singapore's trade ties. Singapore's investment in these countries ran into billions of dollars. All too quickly it became apparent that putting all of one's eggs in the single ASEAN basket could be unwise and even dangerous. Singapore needed to redirect its economic ties not away from its neighbours, but by expanding its extraregional linkages so that another crisis in the region could not affect Singapore adversely. In other words, it needed to balance its losses in the region with its gains outside, or vice versa. The Fay affair, Asian values, the financial crisis, and growing support for China forced the city state's ruling elite to formulate a new foreign economic and security policy within and outside Southeast Asia.

2.3 EXPLOITING CLINTON'S ASIA-PACIFIC ASPIRATIONS

When the Government of Singapore was planning to broach Washington about a free trade agreement, there was a feeling in the city state that Clinton might have a long memory about his being rebuffed in the Fay incident. In the logic of American sports, victory is about winning, not coming in second. Reducing two lashes still meant that Fay received the remaining four lashes. That did not help Clinton save face, in the American view. He had no persuasive power over Singapore. Then again, he was a practical and pragmatic politician. Clinton would ignore his enemies with nothing to offer, but he cultivated foes with present and future value (Felsenthan 2008, pp. 202–07, 292–94). In regards to Singapore, Clinton needed the city state for its geopolitical and strategic value. The past malignity could be forgotten. Also, he must reward Singapore for its unilateral offer of access to its military facilities at a time when the United States had been unceremoniously evicted from the Philippines. Clinton knew that Singapore was also eager to avoid becoming China's beachhead in the region by increasing its military ties with America and expanding its Changi naval facilities for U.S. naval access, at the risk of drawing ire from its neighbours (USDoD/News Briefing 1998).

There were other elements that the Clinton administration was compelled to take into consideration: the Singaporean air force had been using American military bases in Texas, New Mexico, and other states for training; Singapore had been a major purchaser of U.S. weapons; and there was an urgent need to revamp its security relationship with Japan. The United States also needed to assist the Philippines in consolidating democracy under President Corazón Aquino, and Clinton needed to deal with the rapid rise of China in such a way that would not alarm its Asian neighbours. All of these goals were security-*driven* and required a carefully measured response, not one driven by emotion. Singapore's economic and security diplomacy with the United States could hardly be construed as anti-American. Clinton appreciated this fact and must have concluded that the Fay affair could not be allowed to interfere with larger goals.

Thus, in the 1990s, as the United States emerged from the "Japan bashing" of the 1980s and from decades of Cold War uncertainty, President Clinton fully recognized the need to mend bilateral fences throughout East Asia. America felt that it was being left out. Clinton pursued a policy that combined strengthening existing bilateral alliances with Japan, Korea, and Australia with launching a minilateral strategy of engaging ASEAN and its Regional Forum (the ARF, comprising the ten ASEAN countries, plus China, Japan, Korea, India, the United States, Australia, New Zealand, the European Union, and Russia). His strategy for APEC had been flagging. He needed a new vision. In time, that vision was to have the cumulative effect of converging both trade and security policies. With Japan, the Clinton administration updated its defence and security ties in 1996, followed by the Guidelines for U.S.-Japan Defense Cooperation in September 1997.

That same year, Japan was contributing US$5 billion to the cost of the U.S. military stationed in Japan. In the Korean Peninsula, Clinton initiated the Four Powers Talks (later to become the Six Powers Talks and today known as the Six-Party Talks, adding Russia and Japan to the existing four — two Koreas, China, and the United States) to encourage North Korea to disband nuclear weapons development. The four powers met three times: December 1997, and March and October 1998. Clinton's objective remained the establishment of a "non-nuclear democratic, reconciled, and ultimately reunified Peninsula". With Australia, Clinton expanded defence ties in the Sydney Statement of 1996 (USDoD 1998, pp. 5–7). All these efforts needed to be matched by similar initiatives in trade and investment. The United States needed to do more in Southeast Asia.

Meanwhile, by the early 1990s, China's military modernization was in full swing, and an economically vibrant Taiwan was making noises about becoming independent. Clinton recognized that "lasting security in the Asia-Pacific region is not possible without a constructive role played by China", and that "China presents numerous challenges, as well as opportunities in [the United States] regional security strategy". But China saw U.S. bilateral alliances in Asia as "factors of instability", while the United States viewed them as factors that have promoted stability and security for the region" (USDoD 1998). This difference in strategic interpretations between China and the United States is still not reconciled to this day. But in May 1995 Clinton did convince China to establish the highest level of communications link ("hot line") with Washington to consult mutually on a host of issues that would concern the two countries. In January 1998, bilateral relations were so improved that Secretary of Defense William Cohen was shown the Air Defense Control Center in Beijing, making him the first American official to see such military facilities. He was also invited to address the PLA's Military Academy of Science and was assured by the Chinese leaders that Iran would not be getting Chinese anti-ship cruise missiles, although the sales contract was already signed (USDoD/OASD 1998). Even so, the United States Navy did verify that Iran positioned Chinese-made anti-ship missiles on islands in the Persian Gulf. It also acquired long-range missiles from North Korea (Clarke 2004, p. 111). All in all, the Clinton administration endeavoured to manage China as its strategic partner.

Like his predecessors, Clinton realized that Japan was the bulwark for the American security system in the Asia Pacific. The 1997 Guidelines allow Japan to reach out beyond its borders in support of the United States in a variety of military actions. However, a strong caveat was written into the agreement that gives each party the right to decide *independently* if such collaboration would serve the national interest (Clarke 2004, p. 10). This proviso has given Japan a new boost in its military options and can allow Japan to participate in regional and global security activities. In the Philippines, where the United States had maintained two important military bases since the end of World War II (Clark Airfield and the Subic Bay naval facilities), Manila refused to renew the base contracts. In 1991–92 the closing of those bases raised serious doubts about the American commitment to the region. In 1998, as the Philippines was overwhelmed by an Islamist insurgency in Mindanao, Manila needed U.S. assistance. Washington and Manila signed a Visiting Forces Agreement through which the United States has contributed to the military modernization of the Philippines. Once again letting bygones be bygones, Clinton did not hold a grudge against the Philippines for its 1991 eviction of the formal U.S. presence.

In spite of the deepening economic ties between Asia and the United States since 1980, when Asia supplanted Europe as the United States' larger trading partner, mutual security cooperation has not been similarly updated and remains bilateral and even patchy. The rise of China has injected a new variable into the Asian security calculus. The first set of vexatious issues concerns the historic Sino-Japanese rivalry and animosity dating back to their late nineteenth-century war, the subsequent takeover of Manchuria by Japan, and the war against China in the late 1930s that led to World War II. A second set involves the Japanese Occupation of Korea from 1910 to 1945, and the atrocities committed by the Japanese military in Southeast Asia during World War II. In Singapore alone, fifty thousand innocent Chinese residents were massacred by the Occupation army. After the Second World War, the reluctance of Japanese politicians to apologize and come to terms fully with its past incursions in the region caused tensions with its neighbours to worsen; similarly, Japan has never built a war memorial in Singapore as a sign of atonement. Given Japan's advanced economy and technology plus its past misdeeds, the possibility of restoring a military in Japan sends chills down the spine of many Asians. Until this issue is resolved to the satisfaction of Japan and Southeast Asia, there will not be an Asian great power to assure the region of peace and stability. The United States stands out as a reasonable option to be the guarantor of regional stability.

Given this historic enmity and occasional hostility among Asians, it was difficult for any American president to produce a single multilateral security policy that would satisfy the emotionally and psychologically lacerated region. Clinton, like Reagan and Bush (father) before him, chose to continue the hub and spoke approach, but with a twist: he chose to combine a host of existing bilateral alliances with intraregional military exercises and collaborations. One example of this approach is Japan's acceptance to reach out beyond its own territorial waters in regional and international security engagement. Among these were: an attempt to draw North Korea into regional talks to temper its nuclear policy; a recognition of the ARF as a vehicle to mitigate and resolve thorny regional issues, such as those in the South China Sea, which has added much to the agility and stature of the ARF; constant dialoguing and exchange visits of high-ranking military officers; and some sixty port calls to Hong Kong by the U.S. Navy, which shored up bilateral security collaboration between the two giants of the Asia Pacific.

The success of Clinton's low profile Asian policy is manifested in such bilateral and multilateral military exercises as Cobra Gold, Cope Tiger, and Commando Sling (the latest being from December 2009 to July 2010 with Singapore's air force), as well as military access to jungle training facilities in Brunei and Malaysia, in-transit aircraft refuelling in Thailand, and the Changi naval facilities and Paya Lebar Air Force Base in Singapore. Changi has the capacity to berth two aircraft carriers side by side and Paya Lebar boasts an impressive 12,400 feet long by 200 feet wide runway. Also stationed in the base are the personnel of the military support units from Australia, Britain, and New Zealand, three members off a five-party alliance, with Malaysia being the fifth ally. Secretary Cohen revealed with great satisfaction that when the United States signed an accord with Manila to "station" American troops in the Philippines (also called the Visiting Forces Agreement), Singapore announced unilaterally that the United States Navy could access the Changi facilities (USDoD/OASD 1998).

Mark Hong, a distinguished retired diplomat and Singapore's former ambassador to Moscow, made the point that for the time being, history has kept Asia from building a viable security system similar to Europe's. In his 2006 talk at a Beijing conference, Ambassador Hong persuasively argued that it would take another two to three decades to iron out these outstanding differences in Northeast Asia, to say nothing of those plaguing Southeast Asia. Until such time, Ambassador Hong argues, Asian countries will be better off focusing on building economic ties and integration by means of FTAs — bilateral as well as intraregional. Like in the creation of the European Union (EU), Ambassador Hong sees closer economic relations as the first cornerstone for enduring intra-Asian solidarity, peace, and prosperity. In his view, Singapore is leading the charge (Hong 2006). Hong's analysis supports well what the Clinton policy has accomplished. Thus, there has been a synergy between Singapore and U.S. foreign economic and security policy towards the Asia Pacific.

One area in which Clinton did not receive enthusiastic support from China and Southeast Asian countries was how to deal with al-Qaeda threats. Contrary to popular belief, Clinton did have a sound counterterrorism policy, albeit one not publicly announced and unfortunately drowned by his sex scandal. A few months into office, the Clinton administration was briefed by the CIA and FBI about the bin Laden organization, then already in operation from Chicago to Vienna, Milan, London, Canada, Egypt, Germany, Belgium, and elsewhere (Clarke 2004, pp. 135–40). In late 1999 Jordanian authorities disrupted al-Qaeda cells and prevented major attacks in Europe and the United States. The Clinton administration adopted a series of measures to respond to such attacks, including setting up the Counterterrorism Security Group at the White House and giving Richard Clarke the power to manage it with a rank of cabinet secretary. Clarke coordinated Principals Committee meetings, which included both the secretary of state and secretary of defence.

Clinton also increased the budget for terrorism prevention programmes from US$5 billion in 1996 to US$11 billion in 2000 (Soderberg 2005, pp. 162–69). Vaccines were stockpiled in case of attacks; and when a bomb exploded during the Atlanta Olympic Games, the Clinton administration was well prepared. In 1996 the Taliban took Kabul, and al-Qaeda moved its operations there. The *USS Cole* and U.S. Embassy bombings in 1998 were identified as al-Qaeda handiwork. When the United States asked for U.N. sanction against the Taliban regime in Afghanistan, Russia was eager to support it, but China and Malaysia abstained (Soderberg 2005, pp. 172–73). It should be noted that had it not been for the Jordanian breakthrough, the Clinton administration would have fewer reliable intelligence sources, and the Hashemite Kingdom was well rewarded with a U.S. commitment to sign an FTA towards the last days of the Clinton administration. But in East Asia, Clinton had no reliable ally stepping forward to stamp out al-Qaeda activities there.

2.4 EXTRA- AND INTRA-REGIONAL FACTORS DRIVING FTAs

In 1995, half of the world's trade was taking place within regional trade agreement frameworks (Serra et al. 1997, p. x). The opening of the European Union in 1992, the first meeting of the APEC leaders in Seattle in 1993, and the formation of NAFTA in 1994, sent strong messages to U.S. and Singaporean leaders that the multilateral forum of GATT could not be counted on to produce trade liberalization. By 1995 GATT had evolved into the WTO, but continued to be frustrated in its quest to advance trade globally. The collapse of the WTO ministerial meetings in Doha in December 2001, and Cancún in September 2003, convinced the countries *willing* to push for multilateral trade and investment liberalization to move forward with or without the *unwilling* (Schott 2003).

Disillusioned by the mounting paralysis of trade and investment negotiations, the United States shifted its gear to bilateralism as a fallback position, while not entirely abandoning its commitment to multilateralism. This was also Bush's (son) policy. The United States failed to rally support for its multilateral efforts either in the GATT/WTO negotiations, or in its own hemisphere, as Latin Americans ultimately became unconvinced of the wisdom of the proposed Free Trade Area of the Americas. Bilateralism seemed to be the only road left for Washington to trek. One Canadian observer was more blunt: the United States was cornered into the bilateral route because several presidents ignored opportunities to build multilateral and regional alliances through give-and-take with its partners. This alienated America's traditional allies, including Canada, and reduced the options open to the United States (Clarkson 2008, pp. 5–6).

Japan, Australia, New Zealand, Korea, Singapore, and Thailand followed suit. Singapore and Thailand, two of the original five founders of ASEAN in 1967, became the champions of building bilateral agreements with their major trading partners. Investments by Temasek Holdings in Thailand have been growing, and the bilateral economic convergence between the two countries has been moving at a faster pace than AFTA integration (Srisamorn 2006). Singapore has been moderately successful in intra-ASEAN investment, but there have been incidences that have convinced Singapore and Thailand that intra-ASEAN investment liberalization has stalled. Hence, Singapore, as the region's premier service economy, has not been satisfied with the snail's pace of investment liberalization in

ASEAN. In 2000, ASEAN had yet to become Singapore's hinterland, as the founding fathers had hoped.

For Singapore and Thailand, indisputably the two most ardent advocates of free trade within ASEAN, as well as with their external partners, the WTO's failure to produce an integrated single world market played an equally important role in their decision to go *bilateral*. The rise of a prosperous but economically aggressive China added another concern that the Middle Kingdom can divert FDI, as well as trade, away from the region ("Rafidah" 1994). For Singapore, the political instability and economic stagnation of post-Soeharto Indonesia and the on-and-off spats with Malaysia also increased its anxiety about the prospects for a full recovery from the 1997–98 financial crisis. It was also concerned with how to sustain its sterling economic performance, surrounded as it was by failing economies and outmoded authoritarian regimes, which have tarnished the region's reputation and its global image.

For at least a decade or more, Mahathir of Malaysia had been cosying up to Beijing; likewise, Singapore could not afford to ignore the Middle Kingdom. China claimed an annual potential import capacity of US$2 trillion worth of goods during the first decades of the twenty-first century, and Singapore did not want to miss out on the opportunities (Pang 2007). But at the same time the militarily more powerful China was engendering uneasiness, even fear, throughout the region and hence there was a desire among Southeast Asian nations to jump on the Beijing bandwagon (Kissinger 2001; Abramowitz and Boswoth 2006). Yet trade alone cannot build security in an Asia that has shown a greater propensity towards realism than liberalism. Rather, regional security concerns must be addressed concurrently.

So far, neither the ASEAN Regional Forum nor ASEAN Plus 3 (China, Japan, and Korea) has been able to construct a realistic security framework that can reconcile and accommodate the rise of China, the continued presence of the United States in the region, and a yet-to-be-determined role for Japan and India. This conundrum has impelled the Singaporean decision makers to pursue a host of bilaterals, with the dual objectives of deepening economic integration with its trading and investment partners while building a diplomatic, political, and security collaboration network with the world at large. As a matter of fact, ASEAN members have pursued divergent paths in their economic and security interests, at times contradicting and even colliding with one another.

On the economic front, the region has been reformulating its trade and investment relationships with the external great powers. Over half of the region's exports have been going to the United States, the European Union, and Japan: together these three entities account for 70 per cent of all FDI in Singapore. During the Cold War, ASEAN kept the external great powers at arm's length, but at the same time actively cultivated them for closer economic ties (Collins 2003, pp. 161–62). This mix of security realism and economic liberalism paid off handsomely during the Cold War. But with the end of the Cold War and the rise of a prosperous China, this divergence model has been put to test severely. Historically, ASEAN has allowed its members to have a unique way of pursuing group and individual country's interest at the same time, although recently this has not worked well (Severino 2006). At times, this divergence seems to drive a wedge into intraregional relations. In its economic and security relations, ASEAN has been more generous to external partners than to its own members, or so it seems. This split personality has created a series of sibling spats that the group knows it should avoid, but somehow cannot.

This intra-ASEAN situation has led to different and, even conflicting, stances by the various ASEAN members in recent WTO negotiations. The Group of 22, led by India, Brazil, and South Africa (pack leaders of the unwilling), drew from ASEAN adherence by the Philippines, Indonesia, and Thailand, all major rice and sugar growers. In Cancún, Malaysia vigorously objected to Singapore's push for liberalizing trade in services and finance, strengthening intellectual property rights (IPR), effecting competition regimes, and making government procurement open to all foreign and domestic bidders (Sally 2004, pp. 10–14). ASEAN does not have a consensual position on WTO issues other than its support for trade liberalization in a generic sense. Malaysia's proposal to form an "all Asian" economic bloc to rival the United States and the European Union for global prestige, power, and influence has not got off the ground (Sally 2005, pp. 92–115). This division has been highlighted by differences in development, national policy, ethnocentric issues, and external security concerns.

The absolute value of the intra-ASEAN trade *ad valorem* has been steadily increasing since 1970, but its ratio as a percentage of total trade has never surpassed 25 per cent. According to the WTO, 20 per cent of Singapore's trade is with ASEAN partners, the highest among the ten countries. Singapore's trade integration with its neighbours is commendable, but if the city state's share is subtracted from the whole, the regional average falls below 20 per cent (Peebles and Wilson 2002). Indonesia's exports to ASEAN countries stood at 2.7 per cent in 2000 and 5.4 per cent in 2006, while the Philippines' share was a paltry 1.3 per cent in 2000 and 1.1 per cent in 2006 (see Table 2.1). These two countries represent 57 per cent of the ASEAN population, but they have not been the economic locomotives of trade integration. In fact, three-fourths of ASEAN's trade has been with extra-regional partners, and this trend has stubbornly remained unchanged.

TABLE 2.1
Share of ASEAN-5 in Intraregional Trade, 2000 vs. 2006 (%)

Country	2000 Exports	2006 Exports	2000 Import	2006 Exports
Indonesia	2.7	5.4	2.2	4.9
Malaysia	6	5.4	5.2	4.9
The Philippines	1.3	1.1	1.4	1.5
Singapore	9.6	10.9	10.5	9.1
Thailand	3.1	3.5	2.7	3.7
ASEAN-10	24	25.1	23.5	23.1

Source: WTO 2007, tables 1.22 and 1.23.

Another stumbling block to smooth integration has been the result of redundancy, since ASEAN has been the production platform for multinational corporations. Over half of ASEAN-4's (Singapore, Malaysia, Thailand, and Indonesia) exports are in electronics, thus discouraging a closer complementary regionalism from emerging. A single electronics MNC produces similar goods in three or four countries, exploiting the cost differentials, and the final products are often sent to home countries or other ASEAN countries for assemblage. Toyota produces cars in Thailand, but components that go into the car are manufactured in the Philippines (gears, transmissions), Indonesia (diesel engines), Thailand (gasoline engines), Malaysia (electrical systems), and Singapore (designing) (Staples 2006, pp. 99–107). Such a division of labour in production protects Toyota by distributing country political risks across the region. So far, AFTA rules have encouraged the regionalization of production, but have not forged a single integrated, seamless production platform. Furthermore, had it not been for MNC-driven production systems, the pace of AFTA regionalization would have been slower (see Table 2.2).

TABLE 2.2
Share of a Country's Exports to and Imports from ASEAN, 2000 vs. 2008 (%)

	Indonesia		Malaysia		Philippines		Singapore		Thailand	
	2000	2008	2000	2008	2000	2008	2000	2008	2000	2008
Exports										
Agricultural	9.9	17.6	6.4	8.7	2.9	8.1	3.6	2.5	13.2	15.9
Fuels/Minerals	18.6	33	11.8	25.2	4.7	17.5	11.6	26.6	10.1	15.9
Manufactures	68.9	48	80.2	65.4	92.3	74.1	83.2	68.2	73.6	68.7
Imports										
Agricultural	7.7	4.6	6.8	14.7	8.6	17.6	5.2	5.3	6.3	6.1
Fuels/Minerals	26.1	46.6	14.1	27	13.8	25.1	8	26.8	16.5	26.5
Manufactures	66.1	48.8	76.3	56.3	76.8	56.9	86.6	61	74.2	64.6

Source: WTO 2009, table 1.20.

This has contributed to AFTA's expansion, but has shown limits. There is little intraregional division of labour that could encourage and exploit product differentiation. Except for Singapore, no ASEAN country can boast significant research and development (R&D) in technology. MNCs bring technology, assemble final products by exploiting ASEAN endowment factors, and export the value-added products to global markets.

One recent study shows that Malaysia, Thailand, Indonesia, and the Philippines spent far less than Singapore in original R&D. Yet, multinationals continue to invest in the five countries without having to consider their indigenous R&D capabilities, which have made little difference. The reason for this is that MNCs still rely on their home countries for new technology. Southeast Asia is still seen as the place where components and parts are made for final assembly, not the source of original design and innovation. Singapore is an exception since it has launched a strategy of shifting from electronics hardware manufacturing to a knowledge-based economy, in particular, pharmaceuticals and other biomedical and digital fields. According to Ambassador Koh, the tightened rules of intellectual property rights after the FTA with the United States have attracted fresh FDI to these fields, not just from the United States, but also from Japan and Europe. The attraction of the USSFTA has spread beyond the borders of the two parties.

In 2004, Toyota Motor Thailand produced 280,000 units, half of which was exported to Japan, Europe, and Australia. This is the salient aspect of turnkey industrialization. What is produced will be exported; hence, the manufacturer (MNC) determines what should be produced and where it should be marketed. In these circumstances, the EPI model has produced the countervailing effect of confining regional economic activity to a lower rung on the global production chain in technological terms. Additionally, such *production* can shift power from the state to the firm. The loss of power by the state is not confined to the domestic arena since the products are exported. The *market* is shaped by neoliberal globalization and the ASEAN *state* has little elbowroom to manoeuvre. Susan Strange reports that 70 per cent of German-Czech trade in the 1990s was represented by manufactured products, chiefly textiles, which were assembled in the Czech Republic and sold to Germany. This external market dependency has the effect of locking the producer into single-item manufacturing. Japan's nine largest trading companies (*soga shosha*) control 3,000 foreign affiliates, all of which are production platforms. They have enormous power in the countries where they operate. Linda Weiss' thesis that in the age of globalization the state still commands in ASEAN-MNC relations can be easily contested, while Strange's thesis that the state becomes helpless against neoliberal globalization is validated (Weiss 1998; Strange 1996, pp. 44–45).

Another stumbling block to ASEAN economic integration is that new members such as Cambodia heavily depend on import and export duties for government operations. As much as 60 per cent of government revenues comes from trade duties, and duty-free trade can wreck public finances. An IMF report shows that once trade revenue is lost due to liberalization, it is difficult to recover. Other new sources can be developed, but in Senegal's case for example, the country was able to restore only 70 per cent of the lost revenues after years of effort (IMF 2006). Cambodia and Vietnam prefer to trade with the United States, Japan, and the European Union, all of which grant them the most favoured nation status, but do not require them to reciprocate the preferential treatment. Such one-way free trade has contributed to the growth of Cambodia and Vietnam in their industrialization strategies (Chhon and Moniroth 1999, pp. 39–40). The United States alone provides such preferential trade access to 131 countries around the world (USGAO 2008a, p. 7). For these sundry reasons, members of ASEAN began to embrace the growing trend of bilateralism as the region's integration has stumbled, in particular, in the form of what Goh Chok Tong calls "cross-regional" trade pacts. Meanwhile, FDI strategies remain consistently national, not regional. However, when Singapore signed the FTA with the United States, it added a feature that would help Indonesia, thereby making its FDI strategy more *regional* and doing more good for the regionalization of production (a form of economic integration) than all of AFTA's efforts over the previous decade.

2.5 FROM THE ATLANTIC CHARTER TO BIPARTISAN U.S. TRADE POLICY

For nearly eight decades, the United States has been promoting an integrated single world market (Frankel 1997; Pang 2007, p. 9). As discussed in the previous chapter, historians would date the serious onset of global free trade to the Atlantic Charter of 1941. Winston Churchill hand wrote the original draft of the charter. What he did not count on was that the American side was unabashedly Wilsonian. U.S. President Franklin Delano Roosevelt had been Wilson's assistant secretary of the navy. Cordell Hull, working at the State Department, was the author of Point 3 — the convergence of trade and security — of Wilson's fourteen points at Versailles. Georges Clemenceau supposedly complained that Wilson wanted to impose on the world four more "commandments" than God had issued to Abraham.

The Wilsonian vision was certainly global and driven by his concern for how to secure enduring peace for humanity. Also, as a diehard liberal, Wilson was deeply shaken and shaped by the threat of the Bolshevik Revolution and called for free trade to build a peaceful international system in which capitalism opposed communism (Macmillan 2001, pp. 495–96). This vision further holds that international security must be built on institutions that can foster interdependent economic relationship and security arrangements for all. When the Lend-Lease agreement was signed, the Americans built Article IV into it, which specifically required Britain (the borrower) to embrace free trade. The demand was repeated in the Atlantic Charter (also Article IV). British reluctance to give in to the American demand of free trade by abrogating the imperial preferences in the Ottawa Agreement of 1932 almost derailed the conclusion of the Charter. But British acceptance of the general spirit of equal access in international commerce with few or no restrictions for all countries satisfied the Americans for the time being (Skidelsky 2000, pp. 181–89).

Embedding security into economic integration is what post-war Europe pursued. The European Union is the archetypical FTA embedded in security arrangements that ended a century of war by granting Germany the centrality of Europe's economy and by placing the United States as the external counterweight to check future German military ambitions. But in reality, the greater threat was Soviet communism. In Asia, a different kind arrangement was made. Japan, Korea, and Taiwan prospered by selling their products to the United States, also a one-way free trade arrangement in their earlier phase. Japan and Korea granted military base rights to the United States and in exchange enjoyed broader security cooperation with it and arms procurement from it (Fallows 1994; Pang 2007, p. 9). This tit for tat trade-off has been the foundation of American trade and security policy since Wilson's time.

Soon after 11 September 2001 the Bush administration adopted a two-prong foreign trade and defence policy: (1) a pre-emptive strategy that will allow the United States the unilateral right to strike suspected terrorists' enclaves or countries that grant sanctuary to terrorists; and (2) a political economy strategy that links trade policies to "broader economic, political, and *security* aims"[emphasis added] (Powell 2004, pp. 22–24). Towards this objective, Congress granted Bush the Trade Promotion Authority of 2002, or a "fast track", empowering the executive branch to negotiate and sign FTAs. Robert Zoellick, the U.S. trade representative (USTR), was emphatic: the United States should forge FTAs only "with societies of special interest for reasons of history, geography, security, or other ties" ("Unleashing" 2003). Observe that the economic benefits were not even mentioned. The strategy seemed prudent and workable. At the end of 2003, 69 per cent of U.S. trade was conducted with America's FTA *and* security partners, which in turn consumed 73 per cent of U.S. exports (Zoellick 2003). As of 2006, the United States had fourteen FTAs in force that represented 45 per cent of the total US$2.1 trillion value of all U.S. trade. Still, 55 per cent of U.S. trade was with non-FTA partners, such as China, Japan, the European Union, and others (USGAO 2004, pp. 35–36, 64–65).

2.6 A MIDNIGHT GOLF GAME IN BRUNEI

The Clinton Library Archives in Little Rock, Arkansas, does not list the midnight golf game of 14–15 November 2000 with Singapore Prime Minister Goh Chok Tong in the president's daily schedule. Archival staff has suggested that the match was probably arranged after Clinton's arrival in Brunei (Simmons 2008). Clinton was happy to have the diversion of a golf game, a welcome break from the tedious meetings and ceremonial dinners of the 2000 APEC summit. With a handicap of thirteen, golf has been Clinton's favourite exercise. Those who watched the game said the mood was jovial and Clinton won the game, but it was more than likely that a well mannered Goh let him win. One biographer has stated that Clinton's buddies always let him win (Felsenthal 2008, pp. 73–75), something Goh must have known or been told. In the confab on the links, Goh raised the possibility of bilateral free trade. Clinton surprised everyone by readily agreeing to it. On the morning of 16 November 2000, the White House press secretary in Brunei released the news about the proposed FTA.

> The United States of America (USA) and Singapore have agreed to start negotiations on a bilateral Free Trade Agreement (FTA). [The] USA and Singapore are both firm supporters of the Asia-Pacific Economic Cooperation (APEC) and are committed to APEC's Bogor Goals of free and open trade and investment by 2010 for industrialized economies and 2020 for developing economies. The USA and Singapore reaffirm their strong commitment to the multilateral trading system and the launch of a New Round in 2001. *The FTA will be modeled after US-Jordan FTA. We have directed Ambassador Charlene Barshefsky and Minister George Yeo to endeavor to conclude negotiations before the end of the year* [emphasis added] (White House 2000).

The interesting part of the brief press release is that both countries have reaffirmed their willingness to remain with the tripartite strategy of either (a) staying true to the proposed bilateral approach between the two countries, or (b) endorsing a multilateral approach to trade and investment liberalization at the WTO level, or (c) supporting a regional approach at the APEC level, just in case the first two scenarios failed. Goh had his goals of accelerating Singapore's recovery, thus moving forward with restructuring the economy, while Clinton was eager to leave his imprint in the Asia Pacific by signing the first FTA with an Asian country, thereby sending the message that East Asia had been dragging its feet in implementing the much ballyhooed economic integration. Singapore was Clinton's first choice in Asia for a reason.

Two features stand out in the press release. First, it is curious that the United States and Singapore chose to use the U.S.-Jordan FTA as a model. Second, both the president and the prime minister were inexplicably optimistic in expecting the negotiations would take six weeks to conclude. The Jordan FTA was a security-driven cornerstone laid by Clinton for larger Middle Eastern economic integration with the United States. A Wilsonian president, Clinton sought to link material prosperity to security. Trade and investment were those tools. Clinton's term in office was to expire the third week of January 2001, but he might have wished to sign the FTA before he left the White House. Based on the Singapore-New Zealand FTA, which took eighteen months to conclude, Goh might have assumed that the two like-minded and willing partners could shorten the negotiations. In fact, the negotiations took two years to conclude, the longest time taken of all the FTAs that the United States has negotiated to date. It was George W. Bush, Clinton's Republican successor, who signed the FTA.

2.7 FTA NEGOTIATIONS BEGIN

The bilateral trade in 2000 was US$37 billion. When the negotiations were completed in 2003, the total value of the two-way trade was US$31.7 billion. For the first year of the FTA, 2004, the total value reached US$34.8 billion, and between 2000 and 2009, the highest point was 2008, when the total soared to US$44 billion (see Table 2.3). The trade has steadily increased after the FTA went into effect. In 2008, the trade dropped by 1 per cent over the previous year, but in 2009, the bilateral trade was down by 14 per cent, or US$38 billion, almost at the level of 2000. Two things can explain this: the impact of the Bush recession of 2008 and Singapore's geographic diversification of exports. The city state has expanded its exports, but not to the United States.

The eleven rounds of negotiations took over two years and were held in Washington, London, and Singapore. In addition, there were numerous video teleconferences on unresolved issues and on-site visits by U.S. specialists on agriculture and labour to the city state, and by Singaporean lobbying teams to America. The first round took place between 4 and 21 December 2000 in Washington. The Clinton administration held two rounds; then the Bush team took over (Koh 2004, pp. 3–22). The U.S. team was led by Ralph Ives, assistant USTR for Asia and the Pacific. The Singaporean side was led by Professor Tommy Koh, ambassador at large of the Ministry of Foreign Affairs and a veteran diplomat who understands the United States better than anyone else in the republic.

The two chief negotiators agreed to divide the negotiation into twenty-one sections, each of which would be led by subject matter specialists. The final agreement would have twenty-one chapters. Each side was assisted by topical specialists from various ministries, departments, and agencies of the respective governments. The other rounds took place on neutral ground in

TABLE 2.3
U.S.-Singapore Bilateral Trade, 2000–2009
(US$ billion)

Year	U.S. Exports to Singapore	U.S. Imports from Singapore	Total Two-Way Trade	Balance of Trade	Per Cent Change over Previous Year's Total Trade Value
2000	$19.2	$17.8	$37.0	$1.4	
2001	$17.7	$15.0	$32.7	$2.7	−12%
2002	$16.2	$14.8	$31.0	$1.4	−6%
2003	$16.6	$15.1	$31.7	$1.5	+2%
2004	$19.4	$15.4	$34.8	$4.3	+9.2%
2005	$20.5	$15.1	$35.6	$5.4	+125
2006	$23.8	$17.8	$41.4	$6.0	+16%
2007	$25.6	$18.4	$44.0	$7.2	+6%
2008	$27.9	$15.9	$43.8	$12.0	−1%
2009	$22.3	$15.7	$38.0	$6.6	−14%

Source: CRS 2010, p. 3.

London (OAS 2000, 2001*a*, 2001*b*, and 2001*c*; GOS 2001). The eleventh and final round took place from 11 to 17 November 2002 in Singapore, two years and two days after Clinton and Goh announced their intent to negotiate an FTA in Brunei (USTR 2003*d*). The agreement was signed on 15 January 2003, and President Bush notified Congress of his intent to sign the FTA on 30 January 2003. The Trade Promotion Authority of 2002 required the executive branch to notify Congress at least ninety days before the president would sign the bill (CRS 2002*a*, pp. 1–2). He and Prime Minister Goh signed the document on 6 May 2003 at a White House ceremony and agreed that the FTA would go into effect on 1 January 2004 (White House 2003). The negotiations cost the U.S. government US$162,000 (see Table 2.4); the cost to the government of Singapore is unascertainable.

The Singapore FTA involved 139 officials on the U.S. side while Singapore wielded a contingent of 53 specialists. The U.S. negotiating team for the Chile FTA was smaller (112 people), but cost more (US$194,000) and took fourteen rounds (as opposed to eleven for the Singapore agreement). The negotiations with Australia involved 134 staffers from the U.S. Government and cost US$246,000. At the time, the total value of

TABLE 2.4
Cost of FTA Negotiations to the United States, 2003
(US$ thousands)

FTA Partners	USG Official Travel	Translation Costs	Video Conference	Support by State & Embassies	Representation Costs	Total Cost
Chile	$104	$151	$15	$4	$9	$283
Singapore	$162	$0	$4	$5	$1	$172
CAFTA	$258	$80	$0	$3	$0	$341
Morocco	$137	$198	$2	$0	$2	$339
Australia	$246	$0	$10	$9	$1	$266
SACU	$214	$0	$0	$28	$1	$91
Middle East	$63	$1	$3	$23	$1	$91
Total	$1,184	$430	$34	$72	$15	$1,735

Source: USGAO 2004, p. 19.

the two-way trade between the United States and Singapore was slightly larger than that with Australia. If one compares negotiation costs with total bilateral trade value, the Singapore FTA stands tall.

The breakdown of the 139 U.S. officials involved was as follows: 26 staffers from the Office of U.S. Trade Representative; 23 from the Department of Agriculture; one from the Department of Commerce; 22 from the Department of State; 16 from the Department of the Treasury; and another 50 unidentified "others" from thirty-one U.S. governmental entities normally involved in trade negotiations (U.S. GAO 2007, p. 20). Compared with the FTA negotiations with Australia, Chile, and Morocco, and the CAFTA-DR and Southern African Customs Union (SACU), the USSFTA took the largest number of manpower and heavy participation by Treasury officials (sixteen), signalling that the opening of Singapore's financial sector was of the utmost interest to the United States (see Table 2.5). The negotiations with Australia, whose economy (GDP) is several times larger than Singapore's, took 134 U.S. negotiators, or five fewer than Singapore's FTA. The negotiation with Chile took place at the same time as the Singapore FTA and required the participation of 112 people, many of whom were Spanish-English translators. The least number of rounds in the various talks occurred in the CAFTA-DR negotiation, even though the United States had to conduct separate individual meetings with five

TABLE 2.5
Number of U.S. Staff Involved in FTA Negotiations as of October 2003

FTA Countries	Rounds Held	USTR	Commerce	Agriculture	Treasury	State	Other	Total
Australia	5	22 (16%)	20 (15%)	8 (6%)	16 (12%)	23 (17%)	45 (34%)	134 (100%)
CAFTA	7	20 (27%)	10 (13%)	7 (9%)	3 (4%)	12 (16%)	23 (31%)	75 (100%)
Chile	14	25 (22%)	16 (14%)	5 (4%)	8 (7%)	10 (9%)	48 (43%)	112 (100%)
Morocco	5	21 (16%)	19 (15%)	7 (5%)	8 (6%)	19 (15%)	56 (43%)	130 (100%)
SACU	3	22 (47%)	6 (13%)	2 (4%)	2 (4%)	6 (13%)	9 (19%)	47 (100%)
Singapore	11	26 (19%)	23 (17%)	1 (1%)	16 (12%)	22 (16%)	50 (36%)	139 (100%)

Source: USGAO 2004, p. 20.

different countries most of the time. The reason for fewer rounds was that the six parties agreed to use a common template already developed by the United States in other negotiations although each Central American country negotiated a separate timetable for the reduction, elimination, and phasing out of tariffs to suit its own domestic realities.

There were several critical issues for both sides. Singapore presented an issue that American negotiators have never faced. Roughly 266 products (155 product lines in WTO jargon) were manufactured by Singaporean firms in Indonesia, or more precisely, on the islands of Bintan and Batam. Singapore wanted these products to be considered "Made in Singapore". In Batam alone, there are thirteen industrial parks, employing 400,000 Indonesian workers, many of whom are employed by Singaporean firms (CRS 2002a, p. 4; MTI n.d. and 2003). This configuration is similar to the *maquiladoras* in Mexico and Honduras where countless American and other foreign firms have established their manufacturing platforms to exploit relatively cheap labour, even cheaper infrastructure, and looser environment and labour regulations than at home. For the purpose of advancing the negotiations, the United States agreed to insert the integrated sourcing initiative (ISI) clause extending FTA benefits to the Indonesian islands where electronic, medical, and other fine instruments are manufactured and assembled. Neither Singapore nor the United States raised the possibility of extending reciprocal, similar privileges to the maquiladoras of Mexico and Honduras.

Since 266 Singaporean products already entered the United States duty free before the FTA, the real savings to Singapore is estimated to be 0.21 per cent, which represents a merchandise processing fee (CRS 2002a, p. 4). This added gravitas to the concession also sent an important political message to the Megawati government in Jakarta about the U.S. desire to be engaged in Southeast Asia. Also, the Malaysian concern about back door access to the ASEAN market was weakened by granting FTA benefits to Indonesia. It also validated Singapore's claim that the bilaterals it signed with extra-ASEAN partners would be good for the region as well, a point that Singapore's High Commissioner K. Kesavapany made in Kuala Lumpur. This "reverse back door" was expected to contribute to the consolidation of Indonesia's democratization and economic development. The city state was also able to show how its FTA integrated, albeit only partially, Bintan and Batam into the global trade system. Soon after the FTA went into effect, the United Sates and Indonesia resurrected military-to-military relations that had remained frozen from the time East Timor was pursuing independence from Jakarta (USDoS 2005). No one has shown if the USSFTA had a role to play in this military-to-military bilateral cooperation, but it is clear, given the unusual sequence of timing, the FTA could have been of help.

Textiles were another issue that both sides had to grapple with. Singapore has a growing apparel manufacturing industry, which has exported not an inconsequential amount of finished apparel to the American market. Between 1998 and 2001, the United States consistently ran a deficit on "knit apparel" and "woven apparel" with Singapore. The U.S. Department of Commerce reported that in 1998 Singapore sold US$296 million more of the combined apparel items in 1998 to America than the United States did to Singapore, steadily increasing that amount to US$316 million in 1999, US$342 million in 2000, and US$507 million in 2001, when the FTA negotiations were proceeding in earnest (CRS 2003b, p. 6). The value of the textile trade alone was larger than the annual bilateral trade of US$300 million between the United States and Jordan. In 2002 the United States charged an average of 18.6 per cent on imported Singaporean apparel, which added up to a total of US$42.3 million in import duties collected by U.S. Customs (CRS 2003b, p. 24). Because Singapore imported and still imports yarn and other raw materials that go into the finished apparel products, rules of origin became a key issue in the negotiations.

Another U.S. concern was how to control potential abuse of market access by giving Singapore's raw material sources (third countries) the unwarranted temptation of building factories in the city state. Yet another issue was circumvention, specifically, the transshipment of products coming from China, Bangladesh, and other ASEAN countries. As much as 80 per cent of Singapore's trading involved transshipment. The final wording on the rules of origin was built on the concept of "yarn forward", borrowed from the North American Free Trade Agreement, which means that the clothing materials must be made by the signatories, not by outsiders (CRS 2003b; USTR 2003e).

In 2005, during the first annual review of the FTA, the Singaporean side requested a modification of the rules of origin regarding yarn forward (American Chamber of Commerce in Singapore 2007). The U.S. Trade Representative's office invited concerned citizens, corporations, consumer groups, and other interested parties to submit their views in an announcement in the *Federal Register*. In the Chilean FTA, cotton and other raw materials can be imported into the country, but must be converted into yarn and clothing materials *in* Chile. This would meet the conditions of the rules of origin. No such requirement was added to Singapore's case. One requirement qualifying the rules of origin in both FTAs states that fabric cannot be dyed or printed outside the country. Also, in Chile's case, the United States was a substantial exporter of textiles and apparel to the Latin country, but this is not the case with Singapore. Chile and the United States agreed to limit their agreement to one million square metres per year on domestic materials, and two million square metres per year on imported materials for the first ten years (to be scaled down to one million per year thereafter) (USITC 2007). A similar condition was being considered in the Singaporean case.

Yet another issue raised in the review dealt with financial market access, including the safety of investments and investors' disputes with the state. Financial services covered banking, insurance, securities, and other related services. During the sixth round of negotiations in London, both sides began to make breakthroughs on these matters, but it was not until the last minute that issues such as repatriation of capital and investors' right to sue the state were resolved (MAS 2003). The importance attached to these issues had both sides convinced that the FTA was as much or more about services as it was about merchandise exports. Since the conclusion of the FTA, the attraction of Singapore to American investors has been shifting from electronics manufacturing and petrochemicals to financial services and knowledge-based sectors such as pharmaceuticals and digital communication industries.

With Singapore just emerging from the turbulent 1997–98 financial crisis, the city state negotiators were cognizant of the potential impact of unrestricted capital remission, or capital transfers, in times of future economic and financial crises. Lessons learnt from the neighbours' experience in 1997–98 were important. The four countries most severely affected by the crisis experienced significant capital flight: Korea, US$110 billion; Indonesia, US$91.6 billion; Thailand, US$90.3 billion; and Malaysia, US$24.3 billion. Together, these amounts represented 85 per cent of all Asian capital flight between 1987 and 1997. Indonesia in particular did not act fast enough to stem the egress (Moghadam and Ditz 2002, pp. 14, 17, table 1). In all probability, this estimate is probably on the low side.

In the first quarter of 1998, the Economist Intelligence Unit reported that some US$60 billion to US$80 billion were moved out of Indonesia *alone,* presumably to Australia, Singapore, and other destinations that allowed non-resident bank accounts (Economist Intelligence Unit 1999, pp. 15–17). Historically, the Chinese in Southeast Asia have maintained safe havens for their money outside the country in which they live. For instance, the Filipino Chinese have maintained strong ties with Hong Kong banks; Indonesian Chinese have closer relationships with Singaporean banks, as do Malaysian and Thai Chinese businesses. In 1998, the city state had 145 foreign banks, but it is the four Singaporean banks (Development Bank of Singapore, Overseas Union Bank, United Overseas Bank, and Overseas Chinese Banking Corporation) that have dominated the financial sector. Since the 1960s, Singapore has sought to consolidate the Chinese banks in the city state that cater to peoples identifying with some dozen different Chinese dialects. From there, Singapore has used the Development Bank of Singapore as the motor for merging, acquiring, and restructuring the Chinese ethnic banks in the region (Hart 2002; R. Brown, pp. 4–7; Seagrave 1995; Weidenbaum and Hughes 1996).

Given the ethnicity-driven, discrete, and informal nature of these financial transaction practices, it is natural for the United States to seek transparent and tight rules of governance, to which Singapore agreed in the FTA. In Singapore, American banks are small in capitalization and are outsiders to this informal, clan-based system; thus, they play a small role in the Chinese capital market. Penetration into that market could be profitable. Also, credit is due to Singapore for accepting and playing by transparent rules. Although foreign banks can technically compete, culture-driven practices (clan ties, hometown connections, ancestral links, linguistic roots, informality, and secrecy) will take time to be broken or altered, if indeed they ever can be.

Singapore is already Asia's second largest financial centre after Tokyo, the world's third largest foreign exchange hub, and Asia's largest energy trading centre. Outside Tokyo, Singapore has the most sophisticated stock, bond, derivatives, and futures markets in the Asia Pacific. As such, transparent governance, the rule of law, and competitive management can only help Singapore as a rising global financial complex while legitimizing its activities and discouraging shady business and financial practices in which overseas and mainland Chinese have often been known to be engaged. Singapore is eager to shed this image. To this end, greater participation by U.S. financial institutions could help. If this occurs, then we would have an example of an FTA bringing about domestic reforms of consequence.

Capital controls were another issue that concerned the Americans. China, India, and Chile, for instance, have them. But when Malaysia adopted capital control measures in September 1997, effectively blocking the exit of capital invested in the country, it became controversial ("Capital Controls" 1998; "Malaysia's" 1998) and became the target of the wrath of global financial elites as well as the Clinton administration, the World Bank, and the IMF — the Washington Consensus trio. U.S. banks' lending exposure in Southeast Asia was dwarfed compared with that of European and Japanese banks (see Table 2.6) whose combined lending to the region as of January 1997 came to US$242.3 billion while that of the U.S. banks was mere a US$31.8 billion, or 13 per cent (Pang 2000, pp. 570–93, esp. 579). Foremost in the minds of the American FTA negotiators was reducing future risk for the U.S. financial institutions operating in Southeast Asia, first by setting a "high quality" standard, beginning with Singapore. The rest would then follow. This is another example of lateral benefits of the FTA going beyond the signatories. Japanese and European banks, like ISI for Indonesia, have gained from the USSFTA.

Since the implementation of the USSFTA, Singapore has deregulated its banking market further. In 2007, it agreed to grant full banking licences to foreign banks, and as of 2008, five licences were given to American banks. In the first year of the FTA, Citibank was limited to thirty customer service locations, meaning branches or off-premise ATMs, but from the second year onward, it was allowed an unlimited number. Locally incorporated banks could establish an ATM network throughout the city. In 2004, Citibank began to expand and established four branches; by 2006, it had eleven. Citibank also joined forces with other foreign banks (ABN AMBRO, HSBC, Maybank of Malaysia, and Standard Charter Bank) to create proprietary networks of ATMs. By adopting innovative measures such as a biometric payment system (using fingerprints instead of credit cards), a versatile Citicard that can be used in subways and buses, and placing ATMs in subway stations and supermarkets, the American bank controlled 50 per cent of the entire credit card market in Singapore by 2007 ("Citibank" 2007), a feat that it has not achieved in the United States. Citibank re-incorporated itself as a local bank, instead of retaining the status of a U.S. bank affiliate.

TABLE 2.6
International Bank Exposures to Asia, as of January 1997
(US$ billion)

	China	Malaysia	The Philippines	S. Korea	Taiwan	Thailand	Indonesia	Total
United States	2.7	2.3	3.9	9.4	3.2	5	5.3	31.8
Japan	17.8	8.2	1.6	24.3	2.7	2.7	22	114.1
European Union	26	9.2	6.3	33.8	12.7	19.2	21	128.2

Source: Pang 2000, table 3.

With respect to insurance and securities, American firms were fully authorized to offer services under Singapore's regulations. A non-discriminatory commitment was written into the FTA. American insurers could underwrite a variety of policies, including those for maritime and air transport. Almost all restrictions were removed under the FTA, including lucrative reinsurance, brokerage areas, and offshore insurance. The latter measure meant that an American insurer in the United States need not be established in Singapore to access the Singaporean market as long as it meets the regulatory requirements of the city state fully (CRS 2008d, p. 8). In addition, U.S. companies are allowed to sell stocks and bonds, either through their branches in Singapore or through acquired local firms, which allows for unrestricted flows of financial information across borders. American firms are also allowed to sell services such as financial advice.

Pensions represent another area now open to U.S. firms. Although Singapore's pension system is a government controlled and managed sector, the state has begun to allow privatizing of the social security system, and U.S. firms are allowed to participate under the FTA terms. Several U.S. securities firms in Singapore use the city state as the base to branch their activities out to other ASEAN countries, and as the financial integration of the ASEAN market takes firm hold, the FTA will further benefit American companies. This is crucial because some ASEAN countries lack domestic savings to finance their own development and are thus keen on tapping into foreign capital markets. Access to Singapore is one route to this financing and thus represents an example of how a *bilateral* FTA can nevertheless bring *regional* benefits to the poorer ASEAN countries that have no plans to forge an FTA with the United States.

2.8 HIGHLIGHTS OF THE U.S.-SINGAPORE FTA

The FTA's twenty-one chapters, eleven side letters, and nine annexes run to some 1,400 pages. The main chapters alone are 236 pages long and are posted on the website of the Office of the United States Trade Representative. Six chapters are devoted to specific industry sectors: Chapter 5 on textiles and apparel, Chapter 8 on services, Chapter 9 on telecommunications, Chapter 10 on financial services (the longest chapter, comprising twenty-seven articles), Chapter 14 on e-commerce, and Chapter 15 on investment (the second longest chapter, with nine articles).

Other chapters deal with the structure and implementation of the FTA: legal definitions of the FTA (Chapter 1); national treatment (Chapter 2); rules of origin (Chapter 3); customs administration (Chapter 4); technical barriers to trade (Chapter 6); safeguards (Chapter 7); rules on business travellers (Chapter 11); competition or anti-monopoly (Chapter 12); government procurement (Chapter 13); intellectual property rights (Chapter 16); labour (Chapter 17); the environment (Chapter 18); FTA implementation transparency (Chapter 19); dispute settlement (Chapter 20); and "general and final provisions" (Chapter 21). A fuller legal analysis lies outside the scope of this book, but a cursory reading of the chapters and selected documents strongly upholds the view that the agreement is primarily about the trade in services, financial services, e-commerce, and investment. Neither side deemed it necessary to include chapters on agriculture, value-adding sectors, and energy.

The USSFTA is unique in two ways. First, it is not about trade in merchandise, but rather about trade in services by conventional and electronic means. Second, by going beyond WTO standards and practices, or "WTO plus", the USSFTA is groundbreaking: its rules for e-commerce are extensive; intellectual property rights, government procurement, and investor-government dispute resolution rules and enforcement are stronger than in other FTAs; and the rules for investment and financial services are market-friendly, or neoliberal. As Tommy Koh has stated, the USSFTA has set the gold standard for all other FTAs to follow. But it must be pointed out that these gold standards for manufacturing and service sectors will work only between two high-income countries, not between two disparate political economies such as the United States and Cambodia, for instance. Also, when Singapore signed an FTA with Japan, it did not replicate the terms of the USSFTA, going instead for a partial scope agreement.

On the whole, the language of the agreement strongly reflects U.S. jurisprudence, such as due process, right to arbitration, impartial tribunals, and transparency of implementation and enforcement. Furthermore, Singapore and the United States agreed to use international laws and to curb excessive and arbitrary actions by each government. The U.S. and Singapore's common Anglo-Saxon jurisprudence heritage acquired under English colonial rule aided enormously in forging the agreement. Other cultural intersections that facilitated negotiations and common perspectives include similar history and business cultures (both countries have traditionally been traders and champions of freedom on the high seas and in open skies) and the fact that both societies are dominated by elites educated in the English language.

2.9 THE UNITED STATES GOT A BETTER DEAL, *FOR NOW*

The FTA document reveals a lopsided arrangement concerning merchandise trade between the two partners. The United States *immediately* received zero tariff on 100 per cent of the goods that it would sell to Singapore. The city state received the immediate elimination of duties on 93 per cent of goods that it would sell to the United States. Who got the better deal? Over an eight-to-ten year period, the remaining tariff would be completely eliminated. But in reality, these provisions do not represent much of a concession from either side. Singapore has been a duty-free importer for nearly 99.9 per cent of imports, except for four items: beer, sugar, samsoo, and medical samsoo. The United States charges one of the lowest average import duties in the world, and the constitution prohibits export taxes. Both countries are free traders. Hence, one of the cornerstones of the FTA — the elimination and reduction of tariffs — was the least of the concerns for the parties. Instead, Singapore and the United States wanted to forge a cutting edge bilateral economic relationship that focused on trade in services, opening financial markets, government procurement practices, and other innovative areas.

When the WTO held its meeting in Singapore in 1995, it produced an information technology (IT) trade agreement to which forty countries agreed that eliminates all duties on IT and communications products. This pleased Clinton, who fought hard to keep the Internet from being "carved up like radio frequencies" and make sure that it remained a "global free-trade zone" (Felsenthal 2008, p. 86). The WTO reported that by 1997 the total value of IT products in world trade reached US$600 billion, greater than all *agricultural* products sold across borders (WTO 1997). Singapore's major exports to the United States and, in fact, to the world are IT-driven electronics instruments and communication gears. Given this trade structure, Singapore, through the FTA, has the high ground in this type of merchandise trade by setting itself up as a major exporter. Meanwhile, the United States benefited as well because it has been the world's largest producer of high-end IT products and largest consumer of IT components of all grades.

The United States Trade Representative office lists at least ten areas that make the USSFTA innovative and precedent-setting for future high quality FTAs: (1) trade in services; (2) e-commerce; (3) IPR protection and enforcement; (4) competition law; (5) government procurement; (6) simplified customs procedures; (7) easing visa rules for business travellers; (8) immediate elimination of all tariff on all American goods; (9) labour and environmental provisions; and (10) dispute settlement. In several of these areas, the Bush administration went beyond what the WTO would require, such as in e-commerce, government procurement, and licensing U.S. lawyers who graduated in the top 70 per cent of their classes from Harvard, Columbia, New York University, and the University of Michigan to practise law jointly with Singaporean counterparts (USTR 2002). It is interesting to note that there are better law schools than these four in the areas of Asian trade and finance, but during my field research, no one seemed to be able to explain how these four had been chosen.

Singapore also made a political concession to the USTR negotiators on America's sensitive items from the so-called negative list. The National Retail Federation had threatened to oppose the FTA if the textile and apparel section stayed in the agreement (CRS 2002*a*, p. 4). Traditionally the three most vociferous opponents of all FTAs in the United States have been the agricultural lobby, the textile and apparel industry, and steel makers and their unions. But Singapore imports over 90 per cent of its foodstuff, does not produce steel, and produces a small amount of apparel. Indeed, the U.S. agricultural lobby and the Department of Agriculture were enthusiastic supporters of the FTA since the city state imports a huge amount of American produce, from grains and fruits to dairy and meat products and leafy vegetables (USDoA 2000; CRS 2008*e*; Lim 2009). The fact that the top two ranking members of the Senate Finance Committee came from agricultural states (one from Montana and another from Iowa) did not hurt Singapore's case for the FTA since both senators aspired to open up markets for their constituents. The United States may have realized greater gains in these first years of the FTA, but one should not lose sight of the fact that Singapore has acquired the world's largest and richest hinterland, which it has yet to exploit fully. Singapore's economic concessions satisfied Bush's financial and service sector supporters, and its security collaboration was the boon that the U.S. military and arms makers had previously only dreamed about. In short, Singapore pursued a prudent and apt strategy in negotiating with the security-driven Bush administration.

On the whole, the FTA document endorses American business practices and upholds its values and norms. This means that Singapore has agreed to reform its state-driven rules and regulations by introducing such new laws and practices as competition, tighter IPR enforcement, and transparent bank licensing. The United States has succeeded in opening up the Singaporean market as wide as Singapore would ever want to go.

On balance, Singapore did acquire the United States as its newest market for its growing service industries, including such giant corporations as Keppel, the Development Bank of Singapore, Sembawang, Federal International, and Temasek, which variously engage in infrastructure building, energy services, financial services, and shipbuilding and repairing. While the overwhelming majority of U.S. business entities in Singapore are private, the major investors and beneficiaries of the FTA on the Singaporean side are government-linked companies, or GLCs. Given the overwhelming presence and role of GLCs in Singapore's domestic and external economies (as much as 40 per cent of GDP), it seems the privatization-conscious Bush administration obviously chose to overlook the future role of the Singaporean state-owned enterprises in the U.S. economy. The American negotiators were more concerned with competition issues, not ownership issues. Conversely, American corporations will have a curious impact on Singapore, which is now receiving "national treatment" and competing with GLCs on the same footing throughout Southeast Asia and beyond for international market share.

2.10 BYZANTINE AMERICAN TRADE POLITICS

The United States has the most complex and therefore least efficient structure for FTA negotiations of any country in the world. The Singapore FTA was the last one that did not come under more stringent rules. While the Singapore FTA negotiations were going on, the Bush White House adopted thirteen pre-FTA qualifications for selecting FTA partners. The National Security Council, with the participation of the National Economic Council (also at the White House) is in charge of choosing FTA candidates, which strengthens this book's thesis that the United States continues the Wilson-FDR convergence model when it comes to international trade (see Table 2.7). The pre-selection process can be rigorous, but remains essentially political. The president can ignore NSC-NEC vetting and follow his own instincts for whatever political reasons.

TABLE 2.7
White House Guidelines for Selecting FTA Partners and Negotiating Goals

Six Criteria Used by White House National Security Council	USTR, State, Treasury, Commerce, Agricultural, et al.
Country Readiness: security consideration drove the Bush administration to choose an FTA partner; readiness is also determined by partner's will and societal support for trade and economic liberalization	*Legislative Requirement:* objectives stated in 2002 TPA must be followed and met; USTR developed 16 goals to pursue, such as transparency in government procurement, protection for FDI, financial sector liberalization, etc.
Economic & Commercial Benefit: opening up access to partner's domestic market in financial sector, government procurement, e-commerce, trade facilitation, and broader reform	*Foreign and Economic Policy Goals:* FTAs must link to "foreign policy and security policy". FTA must be "comprehensive"; avoid agreements that can undermine WTO rules and regulations
Benefits to the Broader Trade Liberalization Strategy: bilateral FTAs must support U.S. objectives in regional and multilateral FTAs	*Private Sector Inputs:* private sectors (business and labour) must be included in negotiations, so that Congress would support negotiated FTA
Compatibility with U.S. Interests: economic and security interests are highlighted	*Negotiating Strategy:* the baseline for negotiation is to secure "comprehensive" FTAs
Congressional and Private Sector Support: agenda of business, organized labour, human rights, the environment, gender, and other interest groups must be taken into account	
USG Resources Constraints: multiple FTA negotiations can take place if staff and financial resources are available	

Source: USGAO 2007c, pp. 12–13, 18–20.

Historically, there have been three ways to sign trade agreements: by a treaty, by a congressional-executive agreement, or by a joint decision. Article I of the U.S. Constitution gives Congress the power to "regulate commerce with Foreign Nations" (Article I, Section 8, Clause 2). Congress sets duties, tariffs, and restrictions, while Article II grants the president the power and authority to conduct foreign relations, such as "Make Treaties", "appoint Ambassadors, other public Ministers and Consuls", and "receive Ambassadors and other Public Ministers". Article III gives the courts the power to review "Treaties" and assigns the Supreme Court original jurisdiction over "all cases affecting Ambassadors, other Public Ministers and Consuls" wherein the government of the United States is a party (Article III, Section 2). This separation of powers over foreign affairs was the cardinal principle that the framers of the constitution had imposed to reduce the abuse of power by any single branch of the government.

The United States Constitution is arguably the first document ever that devotes more space to curbing the power of government than granting power to it. This has made it nearly impossible for the government to negotiate the reduction of barriers, to grant concessions to partners, and to organize special trade relationships. In fact, to negotiate a free trade agreement on a literal reading of the Constitution would mean that Singapore would have had to negotiate with all 535 members of the U.S. House and the Senate, then persuade the president to sign the bill into law, and enforce or implement it in a timely fashion. Finally, it would have had to hope that along the way there would not have been any irregularities or glaring omissions that the Supreme Court would consider unconstitutional, thus rendering the FTA null and void.

To avoid all these tedious steps and glaring pitfalls, Congress granted the first "fast track" authority to President Benjamin Harrison in 1890 so that he could "bargain tariffs". The court upheld the Trade Act of 1890 as constitutional, thereby opening the way for congressional delegation of a series of fast track authorities to presidents since then. There have been seven other congressional acts that delegated power over commerce to the president, seven of which took place in the twentieth century. Six of those occurred after World War II, or Bretton Woods. In all, the years of fast track authorizations were 1890, 1934, 1962, 1974, 1979, 1984, 1988, and 2002.

The Singapore FTA began without a fast track trade promotion authority (TPA) in place. During the negotiations, Congress granted Bush the fast track authority in the Trade Act of 2002, which contains other trade-related provisions, of which the TPA was one. Although no treaty has been used in the twentieth century to conclude a free trade agreement, a statute was once used to conclude an FTA and that was for the U.S.-Jordan agreement (CRS 2005b, p. 4). Partisan politics and the House's reluctance to give up power over commerce might have contributed to the avoidance of using treaties as FTA tools since only the senate has the constitutional power to approve or reject treaties. Partisan gridlock in Congress as a factor in the making of FTAs in the American political system will be discussed in Chapter 5. In hindsight, the timing of the Singapore FTA was almost fortuitous, given the partisan rancour of American domestic politics, which became sharper and shriller after the conclusion of the agreement. The case of the Korean-U.S. FTA being held up is one example of this partisan imbroglio. And, in all likelihood, without the 9/11 attacks and Singapore's strategic relationship with the United States, the process would not have gone through as smoothly as it did.

It has been said that the USSFTA could serve as the model or template for all other FTAs in Asia. It has worked with Singapore because it is a highly developed economy built on service industries, without a natural resources sector, and with a shrinking manufacturing sector (CRS 2003b, p. 2). Few, if any, other countries in the world fit this profile. Thus, for instance, the USSFTA could not and did not serve as a model for the CAFTA-DR agreement. Similarly, the FTA with Chile was being negotiated concurrently with Singapore's, but the two FTAs are quite different. Chile was a mining country with a growing agricultural sector (winter fruits, grapes, and vegetables), wine, and fishery industries, which, along with copper, constitute the core of the country's exports. The U.S.-Chile FTA's sections on e-commerce, government procurement, and financial services parallel those of the Singapore FTA to an extent, but Chile has no comparable electronics or biotechnology industries. Also, Singapore was not required to remove or phase out its consumption (excise) tax on automobiles, while Chile agreed to remove its "luxury tax" on imported cars over four years (USITC 2007).

The Chile FTA is not about service and has not given an immediate boost to American banks and other financial players in the country. The FTA was more likely a ploy to convince Latin obstructionists of the Free Trade Area for the Americas that the United States had other options and they had better cooperate in approving the FTAA. The ploy did not work, however. When the negotiations failed, the United States simply moved forward with more bilateral FTAs within the Americas. Other Latin countries were eager to follow in the footsteps of Mexico and Chile.

What Table 2.4 does not reveal is that FTA negotiations are time consuming, not between the potential partners, but *within U.S. governmental agencies* and, in particular, with the U.S. Congress. A Government Accountability Office (GAO) study shows that as of November 2007, the United States had negotiated seventeen FTAs with forty-seven countries during the five-year TPA period of 2002–07. Forty-four per cent of U.S. trade is conducted with its FTA partners, and, not surprisingly, the United States does not have FTAs with its major trading partners: the European Union, Japan, and China. To complete negotiations with the forty-seven countries during the five TPA years, the USTR and his staff held 1,605 consultations with Congressional staff. Over half of those meetings took place with staff of four committees: two agricultural committees of both houses; and the Senate Finance Committee and House Ways and Means Committee, the two trade committees in charge of FTAs (USGAO 2007, pp. 4, 8–9). Furthermore, there were twenty-eight U.S. Government-appointed committees with 700 private citizens with whom the USTR was required to consult for their input.

The value of two-way trade between the United States and Singapore in 2008 reached US$44.7 billion: US$28.8 billion for U.S. exports and US$15.9 billion for imports from Singapore. In 2003, when negotiations concluded, the total value of the bilateral trade was US$38 billion. Per negotiator trade value for the United States was US$287 million, given that 139 staffers were involved. For Australia, the number was US$143 million per U.S. staffer; for CAFTA-DR, US$328 million; for Chile, US$59.8 million; and for Morocco, a modest US$18.2 million (CRS 2005*a*, p. 2). Morocco's strategic importance played a major role (as with Jordan under the Clinton administration) in Bush's decision to entice the North African country to sign an FTA. A strong security partner, Australia was rewarded for its hawkish stand in support of Bush's war on global terrorism. The value of Chile-U.S. trade was US$6.7 billion, a fraction of U.S.-Singapore trade, although the South American country is the Saudi Arabia of copper production. The presence of American mining companies in Chile is huge, but until the FTA was signed, American firms had the disadvantage of having to pay higher import and export duties. Many complained that Canada was able to grant mining firms and equipment manufacturers duty-free advantages that U.S. firms did not have, thanks to its FTA with Chile. Also, as mentioned earlier, the Bush administration was eager to conclude the Free Trade Area for the Americas and wanted to woo Latin support with the Chilean example. Undoubtedly, the economic factor figured less importantly than the political in Bush's strategy.

Compared with the CAFTA-DR deal, the Singapore FTA was simpler. The five countries in Central America and the Dominican Republic have been close trading partners as well as home of major U.S. investment. They have been beneficiaries of Reagan's Caribbean Initiative (one-way free trade concessions made to the sub-regional states) of the 1980s in order to garner their security support in isolating the Ortega government in Nicaragua. It was the first time in America's FTA negotiations that both partners agreed to exclude certain products from duty-free trade permanently. Sugar for the United States, onions for Costa Rica, chicken quarters for the Dominican Republic, and rice for Guatemala, Honduras, and El Salvador were protected in perpetuity. This does not prevent CAFTA-DR from selling sugar to the United States. The agreement guarantees that the import tariff rate will not go down; thus there is no phase-in period. Also, when the price of sugar falls below a certain point, the Department of Agriculture can halt its import to protect American producers. Furthermore, the U.S. Government will pay the American sugar growers the difference between the market price and the value of imports. Yet, the sugar lobby of the United States, in spite of the safeguard built into the FTA, opposed the deal (CRS 2008e, pp. 22–24).

The entire CAFTA-DR decision was about political convenience, and Bush's eagerness to collect support from Central America and the Dominican Republic as his security policy in the Middle East outweighed any consideration of trade liberalization. Similar exclusions for beef, dairy products, rice, and other sensitive items were built into the Australian and CAFTA-DR FTAs. It set a bad precedent for long-term trade liberalization efforts. The rhetoric of the president's own Republican Party consistently opposes all forms of state subsidies. Nevertheless, these FTAs include many features whereby the state shields and protects certain agricultural sectors championed by key Republican senators and representatives. To no one's surprise, Bush violated his own policy of pushing competitive trade liberalization for the world.

Finally, the White House signing ceremony for the USSFTA confirmed the view that Bush was using FTAs to build up a network of security partners for the war on global terrorism. In his remarks, Bush could not stay away from the topic of global terrorism; Goh elaborated on the common ground that Singapore and the United States had staked out in their fight against global terrorism in his remarks to humour his host. The White House press release was a reflection of the balancing act: trade is important, but Bush valued Singapore's participation in the security of Southeast Asia, Iraq, and Afghanistan even more (White House 2003).

In a 2008 interview, Professor Koh mentioned to me that he received flack from the Ministry of Trade and Industry (MTI) officials because Singapore "gave in" more to the United States than to the World Trade Organization (Koh 2008, interview). His counterparts in the negotiations certainly brought significant expertise to the table. The U.S. chief negotiator, Ralph I. Ives, had previous experience in international trade matters in APEC meetings. Additionally, the National Security adviser, Sandy Berger, was a trade lawyer. Thus the Clinton White House was not without in-house expertise and was a champion of international free trade. Berger was also a strong advocate of the United States military presence in the Asia Pacific (Soderberg 2005, p. 15). Together they set the initial tone for the Bush appointees in the USTR Office to follow. Contrary to popular notions, it was the Democratic presidents (Wilson, FDR, and Clinton) who gave free trade its greatest push and sought to link it to America's and the world's security.

There was one development that the Singaporeans did not expect from the negotiations. To Professor Koh's surprise, the USTR negotiators offered 5,400 work visas to Singaporeans per year! (Koh 2008, interview; L. Chang [2005?]). The Senate Judiciary Committee expressed displeasure on the visa inclusion because it was an immigration matter, not a trade issue, and obviously, the USTR did not receive prior authorization from the committee to offer Singapore the visa concession (USGAO 2004, p. 51). These are the sweeteners that can be "traded" only between two high-income countries, and even more so between security partners that will not abuse such privileges. Under Bush, Singapore, Australia, and Chile were the three countries to which such visas would be given. Each had a reason to merit the grant, which had nothing to do with bilateral trade. Singapore and Australia supported Bush's policy towards the war in Afghanistan and Iraq. Chile did not. With Singapore and Australia, security collaboration stood tall. But why Chile? The answer lies in Bush's need for its support to conclude the proposed Free Trade Area for the Americas.

2.11 FINE-TUNING THE USSFTA

At the conclusion of the first annual review, Singapore and the United States agreed that the FTA needed to be fine-tuned. In order to accomplish this goal, the FTA has a built-in annual review mechanism (Article 3.18.2). The two parties can also create a Joint Committee to consider and effect amendments to the FTA (Article 20.1.2). The reviews since 2005 have been conducted face-to-face either in the United States or Singapore, as well as via videoconferencing. Between 2004 and 2008, there have been four annual reviews. Both sides are free to propose amendments. By law, the American president is required to seek advice from the International Trade Commission (USITC) on the potential effects of any proposed amendments on the U.S. economy, labour, environment, and other sectors of society. These reviews are classified as confidential and therefore not open to public inspection. However, the requisite announcements of these reviews in the *Federal Register* give big picture concerns. Also, the USTR office and ITC must invite business groups, other interested parties, and the general public to submit their opinions on annual review concerns, and legally they must reveal the annual review topics.

Since U.S. law requires the International Trade Commission to investigate vagaries of trade practices, it posts all the rulings of the cases it had investigated on its website. From these documents, one can glean some aspects of bilateral FTA practices by the United States and its partners. In 2005 (Year 2 review) the USTR specifically requested the USITC's opinion on four issues related to the elimination or faster phase-out of duties on (1) "preparations for infant use, put up for retail sale" (baby formula); (2) "peanuts in snack products"; (3) "polycarbonates"; and (4) changes in the rules of origin for photocopiers made in Singapore (Letter from Schwab to Pearson). The USITC's responses to these issues will be discussed below.

2.11.1 Annual Reviews

One area that U.S. firms filed complaints about and requested improvement in was more effective enforcement of intellectual property rights laws and the imposition of stiffer fines for their violation. For instance, one Singaporean firm was caught illegally using some fifty U.S.-made software programmes, including Adobe, Microsoft, and Autodesk, worth a total of about S$78,200 at retail value. The Singaporean authorities prosecuted the violator and convicted the firm. However, when the fine was imposed, the Singaporean court claimed that the law as it stood in 2006 allowed a maximum fine of S$30,000 for the total of fifty violations.

Although Singapore has the lowest rate of IPR infringement in East Asia, its enforcement has been lax. It has 5 to 10 per cent piracy rates for audio and video materials, but a high 39 per cent for business software. Also, Singapore does not have a "whistle blower" law that protects informers; therefore, those in the know are most reluctant to testify in open court (U.S. Embassy Singapore 2008).

Also, there are cultural prohibitions or taboos that stringent laws cannot address. Squealing or ratting is considered anti-social. Voluntary collaboration with the government is not a popular sport in Asia. Furthermore, it is difficult for affected U.S. firms to ask the Singaporean police to make regular inspection sweeps. According to one informant, when the Singapore police enter the premise of a store or an office upon receiving a tip or a complaint, they look for the specific violation, such as a Microsoft program installed on computers. Once on the premises, though, they cannot act on any other violations they may find. In other words, even if the police discover the illegal usage of an Adobe programme while they are searching for Microsoft programmes, they cannot investigate the case in the absence of a formal complaint about an Adobe programme being filed. This stricture means that the police would confiscate the evidence (pirated software, for instance) pertaining to the Microsoft violation, but not the Adobe case, even though they have a court order to enter the premises and investigate (Overmyer 2008, interview).

During the second annual review Singapore requested that the timetable for the complete elimination of duties on polycarbonate resin (5.8 per cent before the FTA, 4.6 per cent after), originally set for a ten-year phase out. Polycarbonate resin is a raw material used in making optical discs (such as CDs, DVDs, and other products), automobile headlamps, medical devices, and even large water jugs (such as five gallon bottles). Its strength, optical clarity, high temperature endurance, and strong impact resistance are highly valued qualities. The three major makers of the material in the United States are General Electric (GE), Bayer Material Science, and Dow Chemicals. The U.S. imports polycarbonate from Japan, Canada, Singapore, Belgium, and Thailand, with the first three accounting for 75 per cent of all polycarbonate imports. GE has two plants (Mount Vernon, Indiana and Burkesville, Alabama) that produce the material under its trademark, Lexan, employing 2,000 workers. Bayer has one plant in Baytown, Texas. The third and oldest, Dow Chemicals, has its plant in Freeport, Texas (Letter from Gladden to Weisel).

The American manufacturers were opposed to Singapore's request. First, Bayer, Dow, and GE protested that the outright elimination of the duties would give the Singaporean manufacturer a competitive advantage and eat up the American market shares held by the trio. Singapore also enjoyed an 80 per cent cost advantage. Furthermore, American technology and infrastructure were older. These two reasons constituted the crux of the American firms' opposition to any changes in the acceleration of the duty phase out. Contrary to popular economics literature that assumes trade agreements are for their promotion of free trade, FTAs are also used to protect inefficient domestic industries by signatories. Bayer, Dow, and GE are Global 500 companies and can hardly be considered helpless small fries, yet they were asking for the state's protection.

Dow was confronted with a different dilemma that Bayer and GE did not share and that led to its opposition to the Singaporean request. Dow's polycarbonate plant in Freeport has been operating since 1941. Its plant facilities are old and not as competitive as Teijin's in Singapore. Texas produces petroleum — the raw material for making the resin — and has been the chosen home for polycarbonate makers. But, even with higher labour cost and "newer production facilities", Singapore could force Dow out of business simply because it is hard to beat the Singaporean cost advantage (Letter from Walker to Weisel). All three pointed out that the American market for the resin is small and strongly insinuated that Singapore already has 30 per cent of the American market and did not need to expand more. Workers could be laid off; plants could close. Claims of potential unemployment in particular always draw attention from district congressional representatives. The letters certainly did not roll out a welcome mat for the manufacturer of polycarbonate in Singapore, which has increased its production by 54 per cent since the FTA in anticipation of greater access to the United States market. In fact, the GE, Bayer, and Dow letters were an attempt to preserve the American market for those corporations — that is, an effort to push for an oligopoly.

Chapter 5 will discuss in detail the politics of lobbying in Washington, which has been extremely effective in setting national trade policy. Elected officials and career bureaucrats cater to business, labour, and other special interest groups for short-term gains and have few qualms about sacrificing the long-term interests of the American people. This said, there is this peculiar cost to American democracy and capitalism when it comes to free trade. What Dow, GE, and Bayer wanted was regulated trade in order to rein in competition, involve greater government control, and even call for costly protectionism, all at the expense of America's 300 million consumers. American capitalists are not against a big and intrusive government as long as it works in their favour. This mindset constitutes the core logic of lobbying in the American and European political economy.

The sole manufacturer of polycarbonate resin in Singapore is a Japanese company, Teijin Chemicals. One of the three American manufacturers that opposed the tariff reduction or elimination was the German firm, Bayer. Thus, the concerns, interests, and benefits of the USSFTA spill over beyond the borders of the two signatories. Singapore was representing the interest of the Japanese firm; meanwhile, a third of the U.S. opposition came from a German company. In 2005 Teijin Chemicals of Singapore exported 25,300 metric tons of polycarbonate resin, holding 30 per cent of the American market share, thanks to the FTA. In 2002, Teijin produced 13,000 metric tons of polycarbonate resin in Singapore, but in 2005, the second year of the FTA, this figure increased to 200,000 metric tons. North America's market capacity in 2006 was estimated at 108,000 metric tons, and Teijin's production capacity in Singapore alone (not counting the Japanese share of its parent company) in high grade resin was 130,000 metric tons (Letter from Rumer to Weisel). Combining the cost advantage, better technology, and duty free status, the Japanese company in Singapore has the potential to overwhelm its American and German competitors and dominate the North American market in a short order.

2.11.2 Ironies of Globalization and FTAs

Two conclusions can be drawn from the USSFTA case. First, the globalization of production, trade, and investment that MNCs have established around the world places the rationality of the FTA in question since such agreements are typically confined to the signatories' national borders whereas MNCs function globally. Trying to make distinctions between Singaporean and Japanese firms in the city state becomes ludicrous. If Teijin is classified as a Singaporean-incorporated firm, it is entitled to export to the United States. Japan cannot offer this advantage since there is no FTA between Japan and the United States. It also makes good sense that countries that do not have FTAs with the United States and/or Japan should allow their firms to move to Singapore, manufacture products there, then export them to Singapore's FTA partners. The intriguing part of this case is that

Teijin, a company from a decidedly neomercantilist country (Japan), can expand its trade and international market share by taking advantage of the FTA signed between two free market economies. Teijin thus has reason to expand its operation in Singapore. This state of affairs is probably not the back door access that Mahathir and his trade minister were opposing. In fact, with more FTAs, Singapore could attract more FDI from those countries that do not have FTAs with the United States, Japan, and/or the European Union. This is another type of investment diversion that scholars need to investigate. Its positive and negative impacts will be enormous for signatories and non-signatories.

The second conclusion constitutes an interesting commentary on the *trade diversion* versus *trade creation* discourse, a legitimate concern for trade economists. They argue that when an FTA goes into effect, the signatories could divert imports away from their traditional but now non-FTA partner, and create new trading opportunities for the FTA partners. In the polycarbonate case, it is a bit more complex than what economic theory can explain. Teijin also exports polycarbonate to the European Union and China. The former charges an import levy of 6.5 per cent and the latter 12.2 per cent on Teijin's product. The Singapore FTA has already encouraged Teijin to "divert" its exports away from China and the European Union and redirect them to the United States. Workers have already been displaced, and the possibility of GE, Bayer, and Dow plant closings remains. For the European Union and China, Teijin's diversion would be a welcome stimulus for their local producers, which could create more jobs and expand production as a result. Curiously, the USSFTA would have created positive economic effects for the European Union and China, another phenomenon that neoclassical trade theory cannot explain.

It is clear that bilateral FTAs can affect countries that are not involved in FTAs, but that have been investors in the signatories' countries. American firms in Singapore will also benefit from the city state's FTA strategies. This situation raises serious questions. Are Japan, the United States, and Germany getting a free ride? Does the impact of globalization and FTAs on bilateral security arrangements call for restructuring of national economies from the bottom up? The existing preoccupation with national interests must be carefully reviewed as FTAs and globalization can undermine the state's ability to control corporations residing outside its jurisdiction. Certainly both Teijin and Bayer are beneficiaries of the USSFTA. At the same time, the state must find additional reasons to protect those MNCs that it hosts. This aspect of the globalization of trade and security is outpacing the ability of national politics to keep up. It has also not been adequately addressed by international political economy scholarship.

Another interesting case in the second annual review involved a parent-subsidiary dispute. Abbott Pte. Ltd. in Singapore built a powdered milk (infant formula) plant from which it would like to export to ASEAN markets and the United States (Letter from Suro-Bredie to Schlitt). The FTA sets Singapore's total trade quota for infant formula at six metric tons by Year 3 (2006), while for the same year, Chile was allotted 517 metric tons and Australia 1,685 metric tons. The latter two are major dairy producers, while Singapore is not. On behalf of Abbott Nutritionals, Singapore was recommending that the phase-out period for baby formula be shortened from twelve to ten years. For Year 4, the new quota for Singapore should be increased to 554 tons, not the original 6.7 tons. However, Singapore does not have large herds of dairy cows. Instead, it must import raw materials from the United States to qualify for duty free status under the FTA's rules of origin. But neither Abbott nor the Government of Singapore made such an offer (Letter from Suro-Bredie to Schlitt). For Singapore to produce so much baby formula, one must assume that milk and other raw materials would have to be imported from ASEAN countries, thereby taking advantage of the duty-free trade agreement within AFTA, ASEAN's trade group. Or, perhaps Abbott Pte. Ltd. is considering imports from Australia and New Zealand, with which Singapore has FTAs.

At all events, the document failed to explain the origin(s) of the raw materials needed to produce the projected quantity of baby formula. If Abbot pursues one or the other of these scenarios, what kind of back door would that be? One thing is clear: when two high-income countries have an FTA, it is a comprehensive economic integration agreement whose impact invariably goes beyond the bilateral; instead, it becomes regional and inter- or cross-regional. The United States should accommodate Singapore's request for expanding the original FTA concept and revisiting the limits contained in its current rules of origin. Without a revision, the FTA will not work, given that the United States and Singapore already had *de facto* free trade in pre-FTA days.

What is astounding about the baby formula case is that Abbott Pte Ltd's parent firm, Abbott Laboratories (founded in 1888 in Chicago), strongly opposed Singapore Abbott's plan for baby formula exports to the United States. Speaking through its lawyers (Miller & Company, P.C. of

Washington, New York, and Kansas City, Missouri), the Illinois company argued that "Abbott does not support this proposed change", meaning the "accelerated [sic] in the reduction of the U.S. duties on, among other things, preparations for infant use, put up for retail sale" (Letter from Murray to Jensen). It is not clear from the letter why the parent firm was opposing its own subsidiary's plan, but conflicting market strategy could not be ruled out. This is but one example of the irony of the globalization of production. The original intention of Abbott Pte. Ltd. was to target the Asian market, leaving the parent firm and its U.S. plants to supply the domestic market. Also, NAFTA has expanded Abbott's supply chains in Canada and Mexico, thus it does not need additional competition from its offspring in Singapore. But what if Abbott in Singapore has cost and other input advantages over those in the United States, Canada, and Mexico? If so, should Singapore Abbott export baby formula to the NAFTA-3, with which the city state has three separate FTAs? Such conundrums are typical of the vagaries of the globalization of production and FTAs that IPE literature needs to address.

In 2009, Abbott (USA) established a research laboratory in the Biopolis of Singapore for "conduct[ing] stability studies, including studies on active pharmaceutical ingredients and regulatory requirements for new pharmaceutical products". The laboratory will specifically focus on "development of innovative investigational medicines and potentially deliver new treatments to neuroscience and cancer". It is Abbott's first and only R&D laboratory in Asia (Abbott 2009). To a layman, research on cancer and neuroscience is far more sophisticated than infant formula, perhaps akin to comparison between microchips as opposed to potato chips. What is amazing though, is that Singapore can offer comparative advantages in goods and services ranging from baby formula to advanced cancer drug research.

2.11.3 From Baby Formula to Peanut Snacks

Finally, there was a petition by an unspecified number of Singaporean nut snack makers. Under the FTA's terms, Singapore was allowed to export 1.21 metric tons of *peanut* snacks to the United States duty free as of Year 3. Singapore had also requested an earlier phase-out of these duties than what was originally contained in the FTA, even though it has no peanut farms. Above and beyond this quota, Singaporean snack makers were originally supposed to pay 131.1 per cent of import duty. In some ways, these requests made good sense. One container can hold 18 tons of peanut snacks. The quota for Year 3 represented a fraction of one container's capacity. One does not rent a portion of a container in international shipping; the shipping cost of a fully filled container (18 tons) or a partially filled one (1.21 tons) is the same. Either the United States should scrap the duties altogether or it should increase the quota in order to make the economy of scale work in favour of the Singaporean snack manufacturers. The Government of Singapore and the snack makers, both cognizant of the rules of origin under the FTA terms, have readily offered to import peanuts from the United States, value add them in Singapore, and then re-export the finished products to the United States. Singapore has long been doing such intermediary value adding in terms of petroleum refining, and ranks as either the second or third largest petroleum refiner in the world on any given day. The request indicated that the quota would increase from 200 metric tons for Year 4 to 322 metric tons for Year 9. Beginning Year 10, there would be no more quota restrictions (Letter from Morris et al. to Schwab; USTR 2003a).

The response from the American peanut growers changed from guarded support for the FTA in 2003 to outright opposition to any change in 2006. In a 2003 nut-cutting session, the peanut growers' association took the position that as long as the tariff phase-out took place "in the later stages of implementation" of the FTA, it would support the agreement (USTR 2003a). But according to the second annual review in which the Southern Peanut Farmers Federation participated, four states — Alabama, Georgia, Mississippi, and Florida — represent 80 per cent of all American peanut production. In their opposition to the increased quota and an accelerated phase-out of duties, the four-state association pointed out that any concessions would encourage Singapore to build new value-adding facilities. Since Singapore does not produce peanuts, it would be importing (cheaper) raw materials from sources other than the United States, thus precipitating trans-shipments of materials from third countries and even endorsing the "misuse of the trade agreement". This possibility cannot be ruled out. What can be deduced so far is that Singapore would like to amend the FTA restrictions little by little, in a classic guerrilla warfare strategy of first giving in and then taking back, and then some.

The peanut growers' letter also pointed out a technical error in the USTR's announcement in the *Federal Register* that referred to "peanuts in snack products (HS 2008.11)" (Letter from Morris et al. to Schwab). This Harmonized Schedule normally includes peanut butter, which is not "a snack product", suggesting that the loose definition of peanuts in snack products could open a Pandora's Box (Letter from Morris et al. to Schwab). Aside from the missed opportunity to export peanuts to Singapore, the federation of nut growers must have believed the cost of displacing American workers, as well as the competition from Singapore in Asian and ASEAN markets, could lead to the demise of the U.S. peanut and snack making industries. The Singaporean manufacturers would have duty-free advantages within ASEAN over their U.S. counterparts, and within Asian markets, the cost of transportation and lower wages would give Singapore additional advantages. The trade-off would have been the total imports of American peanuts into Singapore as opposed to the future loss of the Asian and ASEAN markets to the U.S. peanut industry. Had the federation accepted Singapore's offer to buy peanuts from the four American states, this would have resulted in Singapore's domination of the American snack market. But over time, transportation costs alone would have resulted in Singapore diverting its buying peanuts from American to Asian sources. Rejection of the Singaporean request in this case did save American farm interests. Coincidentally, peanuts are one of the best protected agricultural products in the United States. Hence, this is yet another example that challenges neoclassical economic theory that holds that FTAs can be win-win deals for all. The FTA certainly protects American peanut farmers, but not the Singaporean snack makers and consumers.

2.12 FUTURE OF THE USSFTA AND ITS IMPACT ON ASEAN

The FTA between the world's largest economy and Southeast Asia's richest country has created and will continue to beget a series of unanticipated consequences for the partners, for NAFTA, and for AFTA. The first four years of the FTA have been *positive* and *profitable* for both sides — what economists call "short term" or "static" gains. Since 1 January 2004 when the FTA went into effect, U.S. exports to Singapore have increased almost by 49 per cent. The value of bilateral trade when the FTA was signed in 2003 was US$38 billion. In 2007, it had increased to US$44.7 billion (US$26.3 billion in U.S. exports, plus US$18.4 billion in U.S. imports), creating US$7.9 billion in trade surplus, up from US$6.9 billion the year before. In 2008, the U.S. surplus grew to US$12.9 billion (for a total of US$44.7 billion in bilateral trade, identical to 2007). That year U.S. exports increased by 9.6 per cent while Singapore's exports to the United States declined by 13.6 per cent. As of this writing, the city state still ranks twelfth in terms of the value of American goods exported abroad (U.S. Embassy Singapore 2010).

In terms of merchandise imports, Singapore bought from the United States the equivalent of 56.5 per cent of the total that China bought, 92.4 per cent of French imports from the United States, and 90 per cent of Taiwan's imports. In terms of the trade surplus generated by U.S. exports, Singapore ranked fifth after the Netherlands, Australia, Hong Kong, and Belgium in that descending order (U.S. Embassy Singapore 2005). Likewise, in the exports of services, Singapore was a good market: the United States sold US$6.7 billion worth of services, and American firms resident in Singapore sold US$7.3 billion. In return, Singapore exported US$3.9 billion in services and the city state firms in the United States provided US$2.1 billion (U.S. Embassy Singapore 2005). A little more than half of all American services exported to ASEAN went to Singapore, and ASEAN bought more services (US$13.1 billion) from the United States than China (US$10.9 billion), Korea (US$11.5 billion), India (US$6.7 billion), or all of Africa (US$8.1 billion) (U.S. Embassy Singapore 2005). Taken together, East Asia represented the major export market for U.S. services.

In 2005, the second year of the FTA, Singapore ranked third in terms of total trade value, behind only Australia and Japan (first and second). At the end of 2005, the U.S. share of FDI in Singapore reached US$54.5 billion; the following year the figure jumped to US$60.4 billion. American FDI in China that year was less than half that amount, at US$22.3 billion. U.S. investment stock in Australia and Japan was US$122.6 billion and US$91.8 billion, respectively (U.S. Embassy Singapore 2005). By the end of 2008, Singapore had become the most popular destination for U.S. investment, moving up from third to first place in just three years. It hosted US$106 billion of American FDI, while the amounts for Australia and Japan fell to US$89 billion and US$79 billion, respectively (U.S. DoC 2009a, Table G2). The United States invested more in Singapore than in the three Chinas (US$76.5 billion): China (US$22.3 billion), Hong Kong (US$38.1 billion), and Taiwan (US$16.1 billion) (U.S. Embassy Singapore 2005). What conclusions can IPE theories draw from this level of economic integration?

Additionally, the impact of the FTA on Singapore has been impressive. Since the agreement went into effect, Singapore has introduced a series of domestic reforms, fine-tuned existing regulations, and upgraded trade procedures by adopting international rules. American business leaders in Singapore welcomed the new competition law (Competition Act of 2004), and praised the considerable improvement in IPR enforcement. They also lauded the steady opening of the financial market, especially banking. At least five U.S. banks hold new licences — one "qualifying full bank" and four full-service licences. The terms of the FTA allow the U.S. banks to open an unlimited number of branches and ATMs, but all the non-U.S. foreign banks as a group are allotted twenty-five locations that they must share. Singapore also lifted ceilings on foreign ownership of Singaporean banks and financial houses. The government has made it clear, however, that the three major private banks (OUB, OCBC, and UOB) are not candidates for takeover, merger, or acquisition (U.S. Embassy Singapore 2005). Whether such a ruling constitutes a violation of the spirit of FTA remains to be seen.

3

American International Trade Practices: History and Theory

A nation can obtain prosperity, civilization, and power by means of agriculture, industry, and commerce.

Quesnay

Perpetual internal peace has stimulated industrial progress at home, whole England's naval supremacy has prevented any decline in trade abroad. Every war that England has fought has brought about a further expansion of her foreign trade.

Friedrich List

3.1 WHAT WE KNOW ABOUT TRADE SO FAR

History has shown that there is an intricate relationship between stability (with security) and material prosperity (through trade). A perfect balance of the two would bring universal and perpetual peace to the world. This is the statecraft that the United States since Woodrow Wilson's time has been seeking to fashion. The inability of nation states to maintain that balance has led to numerous wars. Quesnay saw the link between prosperity of all mankind and free trade. Friedrich List, a most petulant critic of nineteenth-century English free trade policy, recognized that the balance among peace, naval power, and foreign trade has created a rich, prosperous, and middle-class England. Economists have long argued that the benefits accrued from trade outweigh losses from not trading.

This 230-year old theory, first advanced by Adam Smith in 1776 and then a few decades later refined by David Ricardo, still dominates the thinking of American trade economists. Smith and Ricardo were in fact talking about the "absolute advantage" of the cost of production when they argued that the Portuguese would be better off by focusing on producing wine while the English would do better by making textiles. With hindsight, historians could have observed that trading Portuguese wine for English cloth served the interests of Britain, a manufacturing and therefore high-income country, but not those of Portugal, which to this day remains less developed and less wealthy than its English trading partner. Some have even argued that wine specialization might have contributed to Portugal's relative underdevelopment (Sideri 1970). First Alexander Hamilton, then Friedrich List (a German exile, refugee, and a long-time resident of Reading, Pennsylvania, where he edited a local newspaper) forcefully argued that America must not embrace "the cosmopolitan [similar to today's globalized] system of free trade advocated by Adam Smith". This argument launched a rival school of thought on economic development that vigorously defended protectionist policies for infant industries and managed trade practices that condemned the British policy of unfettered trade as unfair, labelling it "selfish and greedy" (List 1983, pp. 48–51).

List wrote twelve letters to J. Ingersoll of the Pennsylvanian Association for the Promotion of Manufacturing Industry, arguing that there could not be free and fair trade between the United States, a still-developing country, and England, a fully developed economy, or between low- and high-income countries. National wealth, the thinking continued, comes from a political economy (synonymous with a public policy-driven economy) that generates its own powers of production. Laws and public institutions are not direct agents of production, but List recognized their value and role as having corollary "productive powers" (List 1991, pp. 144–45). Hence, the state and its agent, government, have an important role to play in the formative phase of development and economic growth. Japan, under the Meiji elites, and Korea, under Park Chung Hee, are historical endorsements of List's trade and development theories. James Fallows, author of the best seller, *Looking at the Sun*, observed that no one in American universities knows much about List, but in Japan and Korea his works are required reading. Korean university students read List, while American students at Berkeley, Harvard, and MIT read Smith (Fallows 1994, p. 191). Japanese and Korean trade policy, development strategy, and income distribution now reflect the cumulative effect of decades-worth of implementing List's theories.

3.2 TRADE IN HISTORY AND THEORY

By the time of World War I, two Swedish economists (Heckscher and Ohlin) argued that trade emerged from exploiting advantageous "factor endowments"; thus, China and India with labour advantages, would choose to make and export labour-intensive products, while Switzerland and England, with huge financial resources, would likely export capital-intensive goods (Gill and Law 1988, pp. 235–37). When Smith, Ricardo, List, Heckscher, and Ohlin were theorizing trade policies, the world did not allow restrictionless, free cross-border flows of factors of production: in other words, capital did not move from country to country without restrictions. Instead, these theories assumed that capital was *stationary*, not mobile. Furthermore, national debt in those eras was incurred by the government of a country and was owed to its citizens, thereby making it possible to control with domestic monetary and fiscal policies. After the Second World War, the world opened up, barriers came down, countries' borders became porous, and capital migrated from place to place for higher returns. To maximize value, technology transfers also began to take place, along with the migration of skilled workers as factors of production as well. These supply chains have been the basis for the globalization of production, or, to be more precise, the globalization of finance, production, and trade.

Restrictions still exist, though. However for the past five decades (1950–2000), the mobility of today's factors of production (capital, skilled and unskilled labour, non-renewable and renewable raw materials, and technology) has become a fact of life. Countries with labour shortages, such as Singapore, Japan, the United States, and many in the European Union, import workers to build infrastructure, provide low-end social services, work in manufacturing industries, and toil away as agricultural labourers. Corporations from rich countries that have expensive input costs often migrate to other locations where the cost of production, infrastructure, and other inputs are lower. Relocation, outsourcing, and divestiture have become fundamental parts of development and growth for an increasing number of countries, but have also become policy cornerstones for trade practices. Such social policy issues as the environment, health care, wage control, the right to organize unions, and universal access to education, have become vital components of development and also define the scope of all free trade agreements.

No longer is it desirable to formulate trade policy without taking into consideration the input costs of factors of production, the quality of education and public health, and the state of infrastructure, all of which can determine the competitiveness of a country's economy and its agents, whether they be private corporations, government-linked companies, or multinationals. As a whole, the ideas developed by Smith, Ricardo, List, Heckscher, Ohlin, and their followers have limitations in explaining the emerging integrated political economy of the twenty-first century. But their originality still remains vibrant and their applicability, germane, with timely modifications.

In America, it is not contradictory to find that a strong hawk (or realist, in IR terms) in foreign policy advocates free trade and forsakes industrial protectionism (or liberalism, in IPE terms). Frequently, it has been commonplace to argue that the other side of IR's realism or economic nationalism is IPE's (neo)liberalism. James Fallows recounts a televised public debate in the mid-1990s in which Henry Kissinger, William F. Buckley, and Congressman Jack Kemp — all foreign policy *realists* — forcefully argued that America must forgo all forms of protectionism and must not respond in kind against those countries practising protectionism such as Japan, Korea, China, India, and continental Europe. On the other hand, foreign policy liberals — or seekers of interstate cooperation through multilateral institutions on a regional or a global scale such as Congressman Richard Gephart, MIT economist Lester Thurow, Governor Jerry Brown of California, and journalist James Fallows — favoured protectionism and trade retaliation against the violators (Fallows 1994, p. 472n10). American conservatives believe that the unilateral opening of the market could persuade mercantilist and statist countries to do the same for their markets, while liberals reckon that a tit-for-tat response could pressure trading partners to open up. This seeming riposte in policy thinking is uniquely American and has resurfaced during the making of the USSFTA.

3.3 AN AMERICAN TWIST ON STRATEGIC TRADE THEORY

Historians have argued that the state has always played a role in economic activities, whether in commerce, moneylending, or building toll roads. Paul Krugman pioneered a strategic trade theory and was given a Nobel Prize in 2009 for his lifetime contribution. Jagdish Bhagwati, Krugman's mentor, has pointed out the flaws of free trade, especially regional and bilateral arrangements that can harm universal welfare. He has condemned bilateral FTAs as too preferential, arguing that it could block all roads leading to a single global barrier-free trading system in our lifetime. Krugman's contribution to trade theories is complemented by the five principal political economy approaches to development and trade: (1) the Smith/Ricardo's free trade argument; (2) List's call for infant industry and trade protectionism; (3) Heckscher-Ohlin's *best factor* advantage-driven trade strategy; (4) the developmental school of East Asia and Latin America, wherein the role of the state is paramount and even critical for the success of development policy; and (5) some of all of the above, and their variations as advocated by others (Krugman 1993).

In 1984, Krugman sponsored a conference in Washington D.C. on how to devise a strategic trade theory and implement it (Krugman 1993). Since then, no new ground has been broken on strategic trade thinking, however. What Krugman said in 1984 still holds true today. Because the world has changed so much, the future Nobel laureate convincingly argued that the old assumptions (Adam Smith and his followers whose ideas Krugman called advocates of "supply and demand" rules) cannot explain the new emerging international trade patterns. He submitted three factors that not only redefined international trade, but also reshaped globally corporate strategies for becoming more competitive and profitable: (1) large-scale production (an economy of scale); (2) a learning curve (accumulation of knowledge); and (3) the dynamics of innovation (the ability to generate and incorporate new technology in production) (Krugman 1993, pp. 5–19, esp. 15). These aspects redrew the old boundaries of trade. The old assumptions and principles that hold that markets function perfectly, and hence that the distribution or allocation of resources (capital, labour, and raw materials) is brought about by the ebb and flows of supply and demand, no longer hold true.

Krugman argues that the time has come to identify those industries and firms that can generate greater returns on labour and capital by maximizing the three new factors: scale, knowledge, and innovation. Firms with these factors must be identified and their expansion supported. Spillover effects can boost other allied firms and sectors (Krugman 1993, pp. 8–13). But Krugman leaves unanswered the vital question of *who identifies and chooses the strategic winners*. In East Asia, the state did and, to an extent, still does. This is fully understandable. When Krugman was advancing his theory, the United States was just coming out of the recession that had begun under the Carter administration (1977–81), and the new Reaganites were playing with neoliberal market theories. The Laffer curve, the Third World debt crisis and solutions to it, the Republican euphoria for a smaller state, and Reagan's opposition to using interventionism to deal with the yawning trade deficit with Japan, constituted the core of the conservative economic debate. The U.S. trade deficit with Japan was US$28 billion when he came to office in 1981. The deficit rose to US$60 billion by the first year of Reagan's second term in 1985. When he left the office eight years later it had ballooned to US$127 billion, all indicating that a "strategic trade" policy through state intervention would not have been popular. The political mood in the 1980s was not conducive to Krugman's ideas.

The predominant neoliberal thinking of Reagan's advisers on the trade deficit, in particular with Japan, was that the culprit was not the Japanese predatory, mercantilistic trade practice, but rather "the savings and investment imbalance at home" (Armacost 1996, p. 32). As such views gained currency, the Reagan administration forged a new economic doctrine: the Washington Consensus, which it pushed the world over as a panacea for achieving a favourable trade balance. Today the outcomes of applying the tenets of the Washington Consensus have been stiffly contested and questioned, especially in Latin America. The strategic trade policy, as defined by Krugman and his colleagues at the 1984 conference, would have required government intervention in the form of choosing the winners and discarding losers by selecting the proper scale of production, funding basic R&D policies to create new innovative technology, and adopting new institutional regimes to maximize the bank of knowledge and institutional memory. Such a role could not be left to the market, however. How to create the proper balance between the role of the state and that of the market in international trade without subjecting the American economy to excessive government intervention still remains unresolved.

Until the mid-1980s, the Asian model of "the state leads, the market follows" was one strand of the strategic trade policy. The state has decided how the merger of an industrial policy for economic development with mercantilist guidance is to play out: who produces, how to finance production, who can invest in strategic sectors, and where to export the goods produced by this model. This model has worked wonders in the Asian context. It goes without saying that Singapore has practised its own version of this strategic trade policy. The city state is small and compact enough to create a consensus around which the state and the market can rally. But this has not been the case for the United States.

Herein lies the rub: when trading with a mercantilist and interventionist state, what would be the best strategy for the United States to pursue? So far, there has been no clearly defined trade policy coming from the various administrations or the U.S. Congress. Too many theories and not enough consensus have undermined America's search for a good trade policy. This shortcoming was the case when the United States dealt with Japan in the 1970s and is now the case with China. So far, the United States does not use two separate templates — one for neoliberal and another for neomercantist-statist trading partners — when it signs an FTA. On the surface, the systemic differences between say, Chile and Korea, would call for a different framing of FTA terms, but in reality, they have not. On par, the lack of formalizing this distinction has been motivated by the American desire to employ a neoliberal FTA framework in order to instigate reforms in neomercantilist political economies.

It is absurd to claim that Adam Smith and David Ricardo were the first to pioneer trade theories. Their intellectual debt to history was enormous. Merchant rulers of the Hansa (a cluster of port cities on the Baltic and North Sea coasts of today's Poland, Germany, Denmark, Sweden, Norway, and western Russia, whose commercial peak occurred between the twelfth and fourteenth centuries) built their prosperity on trade. In the Mediterranean, Venice and Genoa became rich by seaborne trade. Jean Baptiste Say, Quesnay, and Immanuel Kant all argued that free trade begot material prosperity and could bring about peace among nations. (Now we know where Woodrow Wilson got his ideas.) To sustain material well-being for all humankind, the world must have a Kantian "perpetual peace", the expression that Adam Smith borrowed from his contemporary. Similarly, Quesnay, who was rebelling against the *dirigiste* mercantilist state of the eighteenth century and the most inequitable society in European history (France), is credited with having coined the concept of "universal free trade" as a way of promoting human dignity, prosperity for all humankind, and continental commonweal, which he called "cosmopolitan political economy". Kant saw the value of "perpetual peace" as the incubator of stable prosperity (List 1991, pp. 114–23; Talbott 2008, pp. 87–103). One must point out, however, that the Kantian "perpetual peace" can be built *only* when there is no external intervention, in other words, trade partners must eschew all forms of interference in their partners' domestic affairs. This was the original core concept the political economy at the time.

The proponents of the ASEAN way have failed to credit Kant for the approach they have adopted towards trade among the member nations. Kant obviously believed that trading partners should respect each other's autonomy and sovereignty and that doing so would lead to material prosperity for both sides. But as demonstrated in the Michael Fay episode, Singapore perceived the pressure exerted by the United States as an undue exercise of suzerainty over a small state, or outright intervention. This asymmetry could have disrupted the process of wealth and power allocation between Singapore and the United States. Wealth and power could reduce, if not deter, such an interference. Small rich countries such as Switzerland and Luxembourg invite less external interference than poor ones such as Haiti and Zimbabwe.

The first three schools of trade-related thought (Smith-Ricardo, Hamilton-List, and Heckscher-Ohlin) *assumed* that nations would not allow unencumbered flows of capital, labour, raw materials, and technology from outside their borders into their domestic economies. The practice of globalization as we understand it today, as embodied in such phenomena as multinational corporations, offshore production platforms, tapping into external savings for domestic development, externalizing national economies, and revolutionary informatics and communication technologies, did not exist in those times. This means that what we consider today to be free trade and its ramifications have derived from social science thinking developed since the end of World War II. A brief review of the dominant ideas and ideals that have shaped our thinking about free trade can help us understand how and why the United States and Singapore have chosen to expand bilateral free trade as a form of economic integration.

Regardless of earlier schools' nuances, all have relied on how to maximize nature-created comparative *cost* advantages and policy-inspired competitive *systemic* advantages in international economic competition. But in reality, whichever trade theory a country adopts, there are other non-economic issues that either block fuller implementation of the theory or that dilute it so much that the theory fails to explain actual practice. Milton Friedman commented that the best theories "will be found to have assumptions that are wildly inaccurate descriptive representations of reality, and … the more significant the theory, the more unrealistic the assumptions" (Mearsheimer 2001, p. 30). This is no place to delve into a litany of failed trade theories, but it is sufficient to argue that the thinking of Smith, Ricardo, and his nineteenth- and twentieth-century heirs cannot explain the *peculiar cost* of the political economy of today's bilateral, regional, and global trade policymaking, implications, and practices, or their long-term consequences. Thus for a proper understanding of the consequences of FTAs, we must delve into the domestic, bilateral, and interstate politics that have led to such economic integration.

3.4 OPPORTUNITIES FOR TRADE AND INVESTMENT EXPANSION

The Uruguay Round of the General Agreement on Tariffs and Trade (GATT) was concluded in April 1994 and produced its Final Act, on which the World Trade Organization (WTO) was built and from which its governing principles were drawn. The United States participated in GATT under its trade promotion authority granted in the Omnibus Trade and Competitiveness Act of 1988. One of the most salutary outcomes of the round was to expand GATT coverage to areas not covered until then, such as trade in services, intellectual property rights, and agriculture. This also made world trade more complicated.

Proper protection for intellectual property rights was and still is the chief concern of pharmaceuticals, informatics, entertainment, and similar knowledge-producing industries. In 1987, 167 American firms claimed that they had lost US$23.8 billion from foreign infringement of those rights (USGAO 1994, p. 8). The Final Act did cover such losses by adopting stringent rules for TRIPS (trade-related aspects of intellectual property rights), a victory for developed high-income economies such as the United States, Japan, and Europe, but a tremendous loss for developing countries. Jagdish Bhagwati lamented that TRIPS turned the WTO into "a collection agency" for rich countries; that the poor of the world could not make generic drugs any longer (which in reality is not true); and that two U.S. trade representatives (Carla Hill and Mickey Cantor) misled poor countries into believing that strong patent protection is good for them as well (Bhagwati 2004, pp. 82–83, 183–85).

What Bhagwati didn't say explicitly is that TRIPS has pitted the economic rights of inventors (knowledge producers) *against* the human rights of the poor (consumers) who could not benefit from the innovation at market prices. How to balance the rights of an inventor and the rights of users remains an unresolved issue in international trade and in all FTAs between developed and developing countries. Bhagwati urges the rich to give miracle drugs to the poor free of charge. Thus, free trade has been politicized not just in academic circles, but also in the public policy arena as well.

3.5 AN AMERICAN VIEW ON TRADE BENEFITS

The Council of Economic Advisers for the U.S. president concluded that when the terms of the Final Act were fully implemented by the tenth year, the United States would add between US$100 billion and US$200 billion to its GDP, or an increase of 1.5 to 3 per cent (Bhagwati 2004, pp. 1–3) Also, the Government Accountability Office (GAO) report on GATT stated that world trade would increase by US$755 billion by 2005 and that the United States would be a top beneficiary, including its agriculture sector, which would add 105,000 new jobs and an additional US$4.7 billion to US$9.7 billion in exports. A joint study by the World Bank and the Organization for Economic Cooperation and Development (OECD) also indicated that by 2002, US$213 billion would be added to world income, if all the terms of the Final Act were met. The GAO report also predicted that the U.S. trade deficit would *decrease* by US$13.5 billion to US$24.6 billion per year, which would add as much as US$48.9 billion to the GDP (Bhagwati 2004, pp. 8–11).

This rosy picture was contested by the political losers, especially the textile and apparel industries and their workers. The study predicted a loss of 72,000 to 255,000 workers over ten years. An Institute for International Economics study showed that the nation's subsidy to the two sectors amounted to US$24 billion in 1990, or US$139,000 per job in the textile and apparel industries. Seventy-five per cent of all subsidies to protect twenty-one of the least efficient and uncompetitive jobs in the economy went to textiles and apparel (Bhagwati 2004, pp. 3, 11). Free trade benefits, but only for those that are competitive and efficient.

3.6 THE END OF BIPARTISANISM AND THE RISE OF UNIPOLARISM

One popular American assumption is that if you are poor, you have nothing to trade. Thus, a poor post-World War II Europe had to be rebuilt. The Marshall Plan contributed to the economic recovery of war-torn Europe in the mid-twentieth century and set it on the road to the integrated European Union of today. That plan is a superb case of bipartisanism. Democrat

Truman was an unpopular president in Republican-controlled Congress at the time and knew that the European recovery plan would be derailed if his involvement was too strong. For this reason, he preferred the plan to be named after his secretary of state, George C. Marshall. Ironically, a group of the most ardent isolationists — led by the Republican Party's Arthur Vandenberg of Michigan (chairman of the Senate Foreign Relations Committee), Everett Dirksen of Illinois, and Karl Mundt of South Dakota — rallied the troops to push the bipartisan bill through the U.S. Senate. They understood that without economic reconstruction, Europe would be an easy target for communism and a burden to America in the coming war against the Soviet Union. Such business tycoons as Will Clayton (founder of Anderson Clayton), Paul Hoffman (president of American Motors), Averell Harriman (heir to the Union Pacific Railroad fortune), the wife of a Republican presidential candidate, and many others from both parties constituted a citizens' committee to support the Marshall Plan. Even Governor Thomas Dewey of New York, the Republican presidential candidate in 1948, came out endorsing the plan.

On the House side, Republican Congressman Christian Herter led a committee of sixteen bipartisan members on a fact finding trip to Europe. Among the members were Congressmen Richard Nixon (Republican), John F. Kennedy (Democrat), and Henry Cabot Lodge (Republican) (Behrman 2007, pp. 114–23). Herter became secretary of state in the last years of the Eisenhower administration and Lodge served as U.S. ambassador to Saigon in the Kennedy administration. It was a time during which American political leaders had a sense of *noblesse oblige* and were eager to help those who could not help themselves. U.S. politics and American society were permeated with the sentiment that the noblest of all noble causes must rise above the partisanship and sectarian interests. Furthermore, as a trading partner, a rich Europe would serve America's interests better. Pre-war Germany represented as much as half of the continent's industrial output, and Americans understood that a new Europe had to be moored in a collective security system, while economically it had to be integrated with the German economy.

3.7 POLITICIZING THE TRADE AGENDA IN CONGRESS

For the past four decades, though, American politics have become a playpen for those with special political agendas to promote ideological axes to grind. Numerous "think tanks" in and around Washington D.C. are in fact factories for generating trade, security, and social policies. Some are intellectually honest and appear to be non-partisan (in order to qualify for a tax exempt status), while others are downright partisan. The Project for the New American Century is one of the latter. Such organizations produce a political agenda and sell it to plausible presidential candidates. The neoconservatives ("neocons") rallied around Ronald Reagan, who was a devout anticommunist and strongly in favour of regime change in the Soviet Union and its satellite states in Eastern Europe. The elder Bush was less enthusiastic about being surrounded by advisers from the right wing fringe, but tolerated them by having some of them in his cabinet. Bill Bennet became secretary of education; Dick Cheney ("the phlegmatic" as Bacevich calls him) became secretary of defence; and the son of neocon guru Irving Kristol became chief of staff to Vice-President Dan Quayle.

But after Bush (father), a new power base was put together — the coalition of conservative southern voters (the sun belt), big businesses, Wall Street bankers, conservative religious organizations, defence contractors, energy companies, and what Kevin Phillips calls the triple alliance of "petropolitics (the petro belt), fundamentalist or radical religion (the Bible belt), and debt financing (Wall Street) (Phillips 2005, pts. I and II). This set of interests also constitutes the new right wing political coalition, "the base" that sets the agenda for the Republican Party (Phillips 2005, p. xi). They choose a candidate who will implement their political agenda. Since Bush the father, no candidate has been able to receive the party's nomination without the support of "the base".

Kevin Phillips, a one-time Republican Party operator and now a prominent political commentator, argues that the end of bipartisanism began under Richard Nixon in the late 1960s and that its momentum gathered slowly under Ronald Reagan. During the first Bush administration, the Republican Party completed its swing to the far right. The election of George W. Bush in 2000 was also the work of the Republican Party "base". The re-election of George W. Bush in 2004 was the finest hour for the coalition of religious radicals and ultra-conservative fringe groups. The horrific attacks by al-Qaeda (ironically also translated as "the base") on 11 September 2001 galvanized right wing groups and many moderates alike. Nixon's middle-of-the-road "silent majority" made a sharp turn to the right after 9/11. Their ideological cheerleaders were neoconservative media celebrities, cable TV moderators, and extreme right wing radio ranters. Members of the Project for the New American Century provided fodder for a new foreign security policy. Their ideological imams are Irving Kristol, Charles Krauthammer, Francis Fukuyama, Richard Armitage, Bill Bennett, Paul Wolfowitz, Elliott Abrams, Robert Kagan, Donald Rumsfeld, Robert Zoellick, and other well known Republican luminaries (Bacevich 2002, pp. 205–06). Trade is not their main agenda; security is. In practice, they do not object to FTAs and have often tied trade to security.

In January 1998, eighteen neocon luminaries wrote a letter to President Bill Clinton calling for the removal of Saddam Hussein from power, arguing that the dictator must be unhorsed before he could deploy chemical weapons and other weapons of mass destruction. Eight of the eighteen signers of the letter came to hold high visibility posts in the George W. Bush administration. The letter reveals that five years before the U.S. invasion of Iraq, war against Saddam had already been foremost on the neocon signers' minds (Abrams et al. 1998). One signer was Francis Fukuyama, who came to Washington as an intern to Paul Wolfowitz and worked at the Department of State under his tutelage. Another was Robert Zoellick. After the Iraqi invasion, Fukuyama began to move away from the neocon crowd, convinced that the war had been mismanaged and would lead to greater negative consequences. Several founders of the neocon movement were former Marxists and anti-Stalinist intellectuals who were predominantly Jewish and mostly educated at the City College of New York. As émigrés and exiles they harboured a strong patriotism for their newly adopted country, having often been victims of Old World political and social convulsions such as communism, fascism, Nazism and, in particular, anti-Semitism.

What brought them together was their common cause, the global struggle against Stalinist communism. After the collapse of the Soviet Union in 1991, the neocon agenda changed: they harboured the strong conviction that America's foreign policy must contain three elements: (1) the espousal of the liberal values of democracy, which are deemed to be good for humanity and which must be promoted around the world, even by force; (2) the use of American power for higher moral purposes and to reach neocon standards; (3) the rejection, or, at least, the questioning of the legitimacy, effectiveness, and morality of international institutions and systems that oppose neoconservative aspirations; and (4) opposition to all forms of "social engineering", the practice of which was deeply ingrained in the excesses in Stalin's Russia and during the New Deal era of the Democratic Party's programmes, especially under Lyndon Johnson. Over the years, the neoconservative agenda crept into a succession of Republican administrations and key Congressional leadership posts. The two philosophical fathers of the group, Irving Kristol and Robert Kagan, advocated *regime change* as the centrepiece of Reagan's foreign policy. Dick Cheney and Bill Bennett were powerful advocates for removing Saddam from power in the Bush (father) administration. This same theme would reappear in the 1998 letter to Clinton, and by the time George W. Bush came into office, the neocon agenda became the cornerstone of his foreign security policy.

Many neocon luminaries (Cheney, Rumsfeld, Armitage, Wolfowitz, Zoellick, Feith, and Perle) became key foreign security and economic policymakers in the Bush administration (Fukuyama 2006, pp. 37–42, 45–49). Neocons have been preoccupied with ideology, security, military force, and the domestic social agenda. Fukuyama stresses that some of the agenda items appealed to realist foreign policymakers such as Kissinger, to some journalists, and to many in the military. They are less concerned with issues concerning globalization, such as trade, investment, labour, and the environment (Fukuyama 2006, pp. 43–46). The neoconservative forces set the principal agenda for the Bush administration and were obsessively preoccupied with the Middle Eastern security. The security of Israel was one calculus in their thinking, which included the belief that a regime change in Iraq could instigate a cascade of democratic changes throughout the region. Such a change would presumably produce an environment conducive to Israel's survival and security. In fact, it was the pro-Israeli neocons, not American oil companies, that lobbied for the war in Iraq (Mearsheimer and Walt 2008, pp. 232; 254–55). Unfortunately, this obsession resulted in the complete neglect of U.S. geoeconomic interests in the Asia Pacific.

To show its disdain for East Asia and Southeast Asia, Secretary of State Condoleezza Rice failed to show up for the annual ASEAN meeting twice, in 2005 and 2007 (CRS 2008j, p. 3). One senior diplomat told me in the summer of 2008 that she was considering not attending the ASEAN meeting for a third time and consulted Singaporean Foreign Minister Yeo (the host of the event) about it. Yeo used an American baseball analogy to explain what Rice's absence would mean: three strikes and you're out. Rice attended, albeit briefly. Although it is too early for former Bush advisers to start finger pointing, Fukuyama has attributed this Iraqi policy failure to the excessive influence of neocons behind closed doors. Both the *Washington Post* and the *New York Times* initially supported Bush's foreign policy, in particular the invasions of Iraq and Afghanistan, but by 2005 these publications began to turn away as well (Rickes 2006). The two foundations of Bush's foreign policy have been regime change and preventive war or pre-emption, the very goals of the neoconservatives. Neither of these two worked out the way Bush's neocon advisers wanted. The overall unpopularity of the Iraqi and Afghan invasions has since discredited Bush's neocon agenda altogether (Rickes 2009, pp. 74–105).

The timing for the Singapore FTA could not have been more perfect. In recent years, the Indian Ocean has emerged as the focal point of a naval power contest among India, China, Japan, and the United States. This situation is the logical outcome of the rapid economic growth of India and China over the past few decades (Mohan 2009). Also, as Robert Kaplan has persuasively argued, the Indian Ocean belonged to the Muslims prior to the arrival of the Europeans. Arab, Indian, Chinese, and Persian merchants intermingled in the lands along that ocean for centuries before the arrival of Europeans. It took the Portuguese, the Dutch, the English, and the French two centuries to gain hegemony in the region. Once Muslim dominance receded, it was never fully restored, although a significant Islamic presence has remained (Abu-Lughod 1989; Margariti 2007; Bernstein 2008, pp. 77–109). The twenty-first century may witness the revival of Indian Ocean trade, once again dominated by Muslims and their Chinese and Indian partners. Thus, the future "centre stage" of all potential conflicts in the twenty-first century is likely to be in the Indian Ocean, the third largest body of water in the world (Mohan 2009; Kaplan 2009). It carries 85 per cent of China's hydrocarbon imports, 40 per cent of world trade, 45 per cent of Middle Eastern oil, and 50 per cent of the world's container ships.

The U.S. Pacific Command in Honolulu estimated that in 2007, some 70,000 ships carrying 20 million containers (more than a third of the entire world trade) passed through the Indian Ocean, the Malacca and Singapore Straits, and the South China Sea. This set of statistics has drawn significant attention from American military and naval strategists (USDoD/AFPS 2007). Without securing safe passage through the Indian Ocean and through the straits, the allies of the United States in East Asia cannot sustain their economic prosperity. One Indian strategist argues that without security in the Indian Ocean, these Pacific powers will be putting their economic futures at risk (Mohan 2009). Placed in this context, Singapore's geostrategic importance to the United States, Japan, Korea, and even to China, becomes starkly evident. The city state will continue to grow economically, making it *the prize* over which the great external powers will vie, now and in the future. Both China and India are the two great power aspirants and are busily building dual purpose ports in Burma, Pakistan, and Iran to protect their flanks and long-term Mahan-*esque* maritime interests. Policymakers are keenly aware of the implications of the convergence of trade and security in this region, a reality that is not intrinsic to the Central and South American FTAs that the United States has negotiated. As in the days of Mahan, international commerce cannot thrive without safe ports, naval bases, and like-minded maritime allies.

3.8 AMERICAN TRADE POLICY AND POLITICS

I.M. Destler in his seminal work argues that American trade policy began to fail in the late 1980s and has never since been restored to its former effectiveness (Destler 1995). Through the years, Congress found it convenient to shift the public pressures from protectionists to the president by delegating control of trade negotiations. After the Trade Act of 1930 (also known as the Smoot-Hawley Act) and its disastrous provocation of foreign retaliation against U.S. products, the Roosevelt administration began to veer away from excessive protection. Smoot-Hawley imposed as high as a 60-per cent rate in import duties on over 11,000 items. In 1929, the United States exported US$5.6 billion and imported US$4.4 billion. In 1933, three years into Smoot-Hawley, trade dropped precipitously: US$1.65 billion for exports and US$1.45 billion for imports (Destler 1995, p. 11). Trade expansion was one option for the Roosevelt administration to pull the country out of the Depression. Also, FDR and Secretary of State Cordell Hull firmly believed that trade expansion through lower tariffs or elimination of them would lead to peace among nations. The mood for trade began to shift from draconian protectionism to limited liberalization (mutual tariff reductions). Disenchantment with Smoot-Hawley was sinking in. In 1910, 50 per cent of federal revenues came from import tariffs, but in the 1930s, this dependence was considerably reduced. While isolationism on security issues still persisted and remained strong in Congress, FDR successfully pushed Hull's free trade agenda. The result was the Trade Act of 1934.

Hull believed that "unhampered trade [is] dovetailed with peace; high tariffs, trade barriers, and unfair economic competition [can lead to] war"

(Destler 1995, p. 14). Security considerations also played a role, albeit a hidden one, because officially the United States remained neutral. Hull wanted an indefinite time frame for the law, but a guarded Congress granted the authority for three years. It was subsequently renewed four more times, in 1937, 1940, 1943, and 1945. By the mid-1930s, the major change in trade policy was a mere shift from the "statutory tariff" to a "bargaining tariff". The former represented a unilateral setting of protectionist rates to protect American manufacturers and farmers, while the latter sought a "give and get" deal in which the president would negotiate for mutual reductions of tariffs, up to 50 per cent of the existing rates. Interestingly, the law did not require Congressional approval once the agreement was reached. The global trend in the mid-1930s did not represent a "free trade" movement (Destler 1995, pp. 5, 8, 12, 15–16). The world was not ready for free trade. It was ready for war.

The real push for free trade did not take place until the early 1960s under the Kennedy administration. GATT was one reason. Free trade gained real momentum only after the ascent of Ronald Reagan to the presidency in 1981. As the largest industrial economy in the world, the country had two primary concerns. The first was how to rebuild war-ravaged Europe and contribute to the economic recovery of Japan. Towards this end, the Marshall Plan and similar aid programmes were devised. Second, by 1947, it was clear that the world was heading towards another military confrontation, this time between the Soviet Union and the United States, each seeking "the destinies of half the world" to cite Tocqueville (Gaddis 1997, p. 26). The Cold War began and trade became a vital soft power vehicle to bolster American allies.

By 1949, the United States led the establishment of the NATO while the Soviet Union had already seized several eastern and central European countries and propped them up as its satellites. The line was drawn, for Stalin seemed to know where and when to stop. Truman and Secretary of State Dean Acheson, though not sympathetic to communist expansion, were willing to cut their wartime ally some slack. By then the strong link between economic prosperity and military security was firmly established in the minds of the American and Western European leaders. This convergence model (economic growth and security stability) would serve as the bedrock of American and NATO policy for the next five decades.

In Asia, the United States had the civil war in China with which to deal. In 1946, Truman dispatched George Marshall to China to bring about a reconciliation between the Maoist and Kuomintang forces. The mission failed and led to the American policy of first isolating and then containing Communist China (Gaddis 1997, pp. 62–70). The economic isolation and military containment of Marxist-Communist states then became the twin foundations of American foreign policy. The conventional wisdom that a rich and well-to-do democracy would make a better security partner in the anti-communist crusade has been the ideological linchpin of the United States ever since. Japan, Korea, Taiwan, the Philippines, and others were allowed to export to America with little or no barriers, to build up their military capabilities. But no reciprocity was demanded.

The United States' trade profile began to change after 1971. Between 1960 and 1970, the United States consistently produced a small trade surplus each year. Since 1971, the United States has yielded a trade deficit, *nonstop*, except in 1973 and 1975. In 1984 and throughout the Reagan years, and for the first time in history, the trade deficit went over the US$100-billion mark, or to be precise, US$112.5 billion. Another milestone was reached in 1999 when U.S. imports surpassed US$1 trillion (US$1,025 billion) and its trade deficit came to a whopping US$346 billion. It would take another eight years to reach the next milestone, that of exporting over a trillion dollars, US$1,037 billion in 2006 (CRS 2008*f*, p. 9). In 2003, yet another record was broken for the merchandise trade deficit, which went over the US$500-billion mark (US$547.6 billion) for the first time. And in 2005, the deficit soared to an unprecedented US$828 billion, or roughly six times Singapore's gross domestic product that year (Destler 1995, p. 46, table 31; WB 2007, pp. 202–05, 206–09). By 2006, the trade deficit reached US$838.3 billion and the year after that, down to US$819.4 billion, thanks to the cheap U.S. dollar that increased overseas demand for American goods and services (see Table 3.1) (CRS 2008*h*, p. 9).

By the time Reagan came to office, trade had become a national issue. Destler points out that during his first term (1981–85), the Reagan administration heeded a lot of protectionist pressures, especially from three of the least competitive sectors in the American economy: textiles and apparel, steel, and automobiles. But once he was re-elected, Reagan swiftly abandoned his earlier policy of protecting these endangered industries. This position was more consistent with his own conservative ideology. He pushed for an all out free trade policy, which put him completely at loggerheads with a more liberal Congress.

What prompted Reagan to change his mind? First, the trade deficit went over the US$100 billion mark for the first time in history. In fact, economists estimated that the dollar was so overvalued that America's competitors

TABLE 3.1
U. S. Merchandise and Service Trade, FDI Income, and
Current Account Balances, 1985–2007, Select Years
(US$ billion)

Year	Merchandise Trade Balance	Service Trade Balance	Investment Income Balance	Current Account Balance
1985	–$122.2	$0.3	$25.7	–$118.2
1990	–$111.0	$30.2	$28.6	–$79.0
1995	–$174.2	$77.9	$20.9	–$109.5
1997	–$198.1	$89.8	$12.6	–$140.9
1999	–$346.0	$82.6	$13.9	–$300.1
2000	–$452.4	$74.1	$21.0	–$416.4
2001	–$427.2	$64.5	$25.2	–$389.4
2002	–$485.0	$61.2	$27.4	–$461.3
2003	–$550.9	$54.0	$45.3	–$523.4
2004	–$669.6	$61.8	$67.2	–$625.0
2005	–$787.1	$75.6	$72.4	–$729.0
2006	–$838.3	$85.0	$57.2	–$788.1
2007	–$819.4	$119.1	$81.7	–$731.2

Source: CRS 2008h, p. 14.

had a 30 to 40 per cent cost advantage. Second, the U.S. trade deficit with Japan, America's second largest trading partner and the world's second largest economy in 1984, reached US$33.6 billion. Congress was besieged by protection-seeking industries, unions, and grass roots groups that worried about the soaring deficits and job losses. It was under Reagan that trade lobbying politics took on a life of its own. Reagan believed that a change in monetary policy would correct the trade woes.

But international trade *per se* had no champion in the Reagan *laissez-faire* government. The post of special trade representative (STR) to the president was created in the late 1950s as U.S. involvement in GATT negotiations intensified. Two top Congressional committee chairmen responsible for international trade issues (Wilbur Mills of the House Ways and Means Committee and Russell Long of the Senate Finance Committee) had a strong dislike of State and Commerce. Mills and Long ignored the departments' trade agenda. When Kennedy came into office, he picked Christian Herter as his STR. Thus the Kennedy Round was launched.

Jimmy Carter had a Texas businessman, Robert Strauss, as his STR, one of the best until that time in terms of mobilizing Congressional support for Carter's trade policy. Preoccupied with his re-election though, Carter chose a former governor of Florida to replace Strauss, who was packed off to Moscow as U.S. ambassador. But the replacement lacked Strauss' political savvy and connections in Congress. The office languished. With an unpopular president sitting in the Oval Office, Congress could ignore the STR without fear. At the end of Carter's term in office, Congress persuaded the White House to accept a plan to establish the Office of the U.S. Trade Representative, which would pull together the trade-related efforts of dozens of agencies and work as the head of trade policymaking. The USTR office went into action in January 1980 and has since been an integral part of the White House (Destler 1995, pp. 18–21).

3.9 THE U.S. TRADE REPRESENTATIVE AS A POLITICIAN

Reagan chose a former senator from Tennessee, William Brock, a candy tycoon in Knoxville, as his trade representative. To pay off a political debt stemming from his election, the president chose Malcolm Baldrige, a businessman from Connecticut, as secretary of commerce. These two strong-willed individuals in charge of Reagan's trade policy started off badly. Reagan's chief counselor, Edwin Meese III, liked Baldrige and preferred to fold USTR duties into Commerce. As the result, Reagan proposed the creation of a Department of International Trade by merging the two contending agencies. Senate leaders were split over the new cabinet level department, and the House leadership was outright hostile to the plan and refused to support the bill. The chairman of the House Subcommittee on Trade tartly observed, "Every President that comes in wants to throw the USTR Office out of the White House" (Destler 1995, pp. 18–21). With this divided Congress and the president consenting to the creation of the new department, the USTR office lost much of its power and the disenchanted Brock left soon afterwards. His successors had even less power.

3.10 HOW THE PLAZA ACCORD GAVE AWAY SOUTHEAST ASIA

By 1985, the approach among Reagan's advisers to correcting the trade imbalance was leaning towards a monetary solution, not a trade bargaining bill. The weakened USTR could not be counted on to contain the mounting trade deficit. The overvalued dollar must be realigned, and the G-5 (the United States, Japan, Germany, Britain, and France) met. Meeting at the Plaza Hotel in New York, the leaders agreed to increase the value of the yen precipitously over the next few years. The official rate was ¥360 to the U.S. dollar before the Plaza meeting in September 1985. The Government of Japan was willing to accept an appreciation of the yen by 20 per cent. The first week after the accord, the yen was revalued by nearly 12 per cent (Volcker and Gyohten 1992, pp. 228–58). Soon, the value of the yen continued to soar. In theory, Japan would buy more from the United States and Europe. That would have relieved the trade deficit overhang. But this did not happen. In 1995, the dollar was at ¥80, and in late November 2010, it was trading as low as ¥81.

As it turned out, the Reagan monetary policy projection has never been realized. It had lopsided but unforeseen benefits for Japan. The appreciated yen bought more dollars, and Japanese multinationals financed the relocation and expansion of their production platforms throughout Asia — first to Korea and Taiwan, and then to Southeast Asia — by using the cheaper dollar. By the end of the 1980s they were firmly established in Southeast Asia as the largest investor, and Japanese firms exported in ever larger quantities to the United States and Europe, this time from their Asian production platforms at less cost than at home. The outcome of the Plaza Accord from the standpoint of the United States and Western Europe was, at best, mixed, but it amounted to handing over Asia's entire market and production base to Japan. It was a misguided economic policy that lost the primacy of the United States and Europe in Southeast Asia, not the scaling down of their military commitment to the region. In the second half of 2010, the United States, the European Union, and Japan demanded China to revalue its *yuan*. China has been resisting. One wonders if we will witness a similar outcome — China's expansion into raw material-rich Africa, Central Asia, and Latin America.

3.11 CONTENTIOUS TRADE CONSTITUENCIES

There have been four major groups which have had a say in trade issues in the United States: organized labour, business, environmental groups, and special interest groups, including human rights and issue-specific think tanks. Many are ideological groups with lofty goals in the tradition of the nineteenth-century American Protestant missionaries who went to

China to save millions of souls. The two most vocal groups of the four are organized labour and the U.S. Chamber of Commerce, a business lobby. In any discussion of trade policy, these two constitute the proverbial list of the "usual suspects": labour is blindly against FTAs, while business is blindly for them. The decline of organized labour over time had considerably eaten into its political clout by the 1990s where trade issues were concerned. Total membership of unionized workers shrank to 15.4 million in 2009 from a peak of close to 30 million in the 1950s. In 2002, the entire workforce of the United States was about 145 million. The American Federation of Labor and Congress of Industrial Organizations merged in 1955 to form today's AFL-CIO. It is composed of fifty-six unions, boasts eleven million members, and is an important player in Washington politics, especially in the Democratic Party. In principle, the union is dedicated to the protection and enhancement of the working people's interests. When free trade undercuts inefficient American manufacturers and threatens job security, the AFL-CIO and its sibling unions actively lobby Congress and the White House to oppose free trade.

In the case of the Singapore and Chile FTAs, the AFL-CIO's major concern was the standards for enforcing domestic labour law and protection of workers' rights, which it considered to be below world standards in the case of both countries. It also claimed that the standards in the Singapore and Chile FTAs were lower than those found in the US-Jordan FTA. Jordan accepted the practices of both the International Labor Organization and those adopted for countries qualifying for the Generalized System of Preferences (GSP). In the Singapore and Chile cases, emphasis was placed on enforcing existing domestic labour laws, not expanding them to provide greater protection and rights to the workers. Also lacking in both agreements was the worker's right to correct violations or non-enforcement of the labour laws and standards. The Labor Advisory Committee (LAC) and AFL-CIO reports called this "a step backward". In Chile's case, the labour standards it met under the GSP terms were far superior to those negotiated by the USTR (USTR 2003c; USC/H/SCTCPTSE 2003).

The LAC was one of the twenty-eight committees (one presidential committee and twenty-seven sectoral and world regions committees) and went beyond labour issues, often probing into human rights, external debt, financial autonomy, and intellectual property issues. In the Singapore and Chile joint review (conducted concurrently because the two FTAs were completed almost at the same time), the committee pointed out that the

external debt situation for the two countries could get worse once the
FTA went into effect (USTR 2003c). *The faux pas here is that Singapore has
no external debt.* Also, LAC loudly complained that the trade deficit for
the United States would go up as soon as the FTAs went into effect. In
the case of Singapore, the United States has been running a trade surplus
every year since 2004. According to the U.S. Embassy in Singapore, the
United States yielded its largest trade surplus in 2005 with the Netherlands
(US$11.7 billion), followed by Australia (US$6.7 billion), Hong Kong
(US$6.5 billion), Belgium (US$4.4 billion), and Singapore (US$4.3 billion).
In that year, the United States exported US$47.9 billion to the ASEAN-10,
US$19.6 billion to Singapore, and US$34.7 billion to China (U.S. Embassy
Singapore 2005). The tiny city state (three-and-a-half times the size of
Washington D.C.) bought 41 per cent of the U.S. exports to ASEAN, equal
to 38 per cent of what China bought from it.

Because labour unions use a common template for reviewing all FTAs,
such egregious errors are found in several places in their position papers.
Also, LAC objected to the inclusion in the FTA of two Indonesian islands
(Bintan and Batam) where Singaporean firms produce electronic equipment
and medical instruments which, under the terms of the FTA, would be
treated as "Made in Singapore". Two concerns were raised: (1) Singapore
could be misused as a trans-shipment point by other Asian producers,
thereby undercutting American jobs; and (2) American multinationals
could relocate their production facilities to those islands to take advantage
of cheap labour. Furthermore, both the LAC and AFL-CIO pointed out
that the USSFTA labour rules do not apply to the workers on the two
Indonesian islands (U.S. Embassy Singapore 2005). The last point was a
legitimate concern because Indonesian labour rules were not subject to
scrutiny during the FTA negotiations; therefore the higher standards would
not apply to the workers on the two islands. In fact, neither Singapore nor
the United States has control over Indonesian labour practices.

The Center for International Environmental Law (CIEL), a Washington
lobbying group, reviewed the Chile and Singapore FTAs and found several
flaws in them (CIEL 2003). The single foremost objection was that the FTAs
failed to include "robust provisions to promote environmental improvement
in all three countries". CIEL further claimed that the environmental
standards required of Singapore and Chile were inferior to those of earlier
standards in the US-Jordan FTA. CIEL contended that WTO rules assure
"a general environmental exception" that environmental laws cannot be

challenged by investors. In the Singapore and Chile FTAs, investors can bring suit against the government, challenging its decisions concerning natural resources, for instance. In the Trade Promotion Act of 2002 (TPA), Congress made it explicit that the environment is a "negotiating objective" in FTAs, but the CIEL report complained that the language in the FTAs was "ambiguous", leaving little or no assurances that the contracting parties would enforce environmental laws. Also, unlike the NAFTA side agreements, citizens in Chile and Singapore are not given the right to initiate litigation by bringing allegations of non-compliance. For example, the CIEL reports pointed out that citizens in New York, Connecticut, and Rhode Island sued Canada for its failure to enforce clean air standards for power plants (CIEL 2003).

Such blanket criticism and generic observations seemed out of context and even egregious when one considers the differences between Chile and Singapore. Chile is a mining and agricultural economy, much of whose exports are copper and winter fruits and vegetables; hence, the environment is a legitimate concern for extractive industries and agricultural activities. But Singapore, predominantly a service and non-smoke stack manufacturing economy, has one of the highest environmental standards and safeguards in the world, if not on par with or surpassing Japan's. In fact, those who visit Chile, Singapore, and the United States can attest to the fact that Singapore has the highest air and water quality among the three FTA partners. Along with the AFL-CIO's out-of-place observation on the external debt of Singapore, CIEL's judgement on the poor environmental quality of the city state seemed to be based on patently wrong facts. It is appalling that such ill informed positions on the part of lobbyists could have a legitimate place in shaping American public policy.

3.12 LOBBYING POLITICS GONE OVERBOARD

Kenneth Dam identifies three structural cornerstones for how lobbying the White House and Congress functions. The first is what he calls "logrolling", in which each senator or representative finds political bedfellows in Congress to push through his or her bill. This back scratching has become the core of lobbying politics in and outside Congress. The AFL-CIO opposition to FTAs includes some strange bedfellows indeed: supporters from human rights, religious, anti-abortionist, and environmental groups. When the time is right, labour will reciprocate its support by backing various non-labour causes promoted by these other interests. There are several such "lobbying blocs" whose interests on the surface have no sectoral ties and no philosophical kinship, but they will pull together when it comes to lobbying for an interest of their allied member.

The second foundation is a centrist position on all issues, thus allowing frequent but temporary alliances by the two parties. In fact, Dam concludes that there is no major difference between the Republican and Democratic members of Congress on critical issues, such as protectionism for trade. Clinton was only able to push the NAFTA project through Congress with Republican support because an overwhelming majority of Democratic members in Congress voted against NAFTA.

Dam's third cornerstone is "political contribution". The cost of an election is so exorbitant that no single senator or representative could mount an effective (winning) campaign without deep pockets. Thus, many are forced to trade political support for financial contributions. Study after study has shown that there is a direct, positive relationship between the amount of money organized labour contributes to elected officials and the level of their support for projects presented by the contributors: "the larger the contributions from labour PACs [political action committees, fund raising units of an elected official], the more likely House members to vote against NAFTA, the GATT Uruguay Round legislation, and the 1998 fast-track bill" (Baldwin and Magee 2000, p. 41). In fact, a cogent argument can be made that private campaign financing is the root cause of congressional corruption.

In 2000, Congress was voting on the permanent trade status of China, known as Permanent Normal Trading Relations. Before then, Congress had to renew the special trading privileges annually upon certification by the president on a host of issues, including human rights practices, religious tolerance, and even political prisoners. Lobbyists from labour and business had the means to influence Congress on how to vote. The U.S. Chamber of Commerce did not hesitate to threaten those who voted *against* the China bill. Senators and representatives were sternly warned that they could not expect financial contributions (to PACs) from the Chamber's numerous political funds. The Teamsters' Union, which was against granting China permanent normal trading status without annual Congressional review, warned Congress that those voting *for* the China bill could not expect to be recipients of a portion of the union's US$9 million political fund. Such money withholding threats have become a routine national lobbying tactic. Although no public record exists, one can assume that China spent a small fortune in this lobbying war. The bill passed, granting China the permanent and normal status it sought, the penultimate step to receiving the support of the Clinton administration to ascend to the WTO. The vote turned out to be 237–197 in the House, and 83–15 in the Senate (Dam 2001, pp. 70–71). Money well spent.

3.13 SINGAPORE'S LOBBYING EFFORTS

Singapore knew exactly how the lobbying system worked. For the USSFTA, the Embassy of Singapore, the U.S. Chamber of Commerce, the USSFTA Business Coalition, the US-ASEAN Business Council, and several governors (of Indiana, California, Washington, Nebraska, North Carolina, Utah, and Hawaii) mounted the most effective (and probably expensive) lobbying campaign ever for an FTA. A bipartisan Congressional caucus was set up to disseminate information, and lobbyists individually met 352 Congressmen and 78 senators. At the House, Representative Solomon Ortiz, a Democrat from the 27th District of Texas, was recruited to organize the caucus. Keppel-FELS and Singapore Technologies have been major investors in his district in the city of Corpus Christi. Republican Representative Curt Weldon (Pennsylvania) came aboard as co-chair for the bipartisan caucus. Also, Ortiz recruited a fellow Texan, albeit a Republican, Representative Pete Sessions, to speak at a Ways and Means Committee hearing in support the FTA bill (Chan 2004, pp. 163–76). Sessions highlighted the Singaporean role in the war on terror as much as the mutual economic benefits that the FTA would bring to the United States and Singapore (USC/H/CWM 2003g), the core philosophical foundations for Republicans — that is, advocacy of a strong security-defence stance along with a free market and free trade.

Interestingly enough, Sessions had nothing to say about the concerns for labour and environmental issues raised by the AFL-CIO, the Labor Advisory Committee, and CIEL. The final vote was 272–155 in the House, and 66–31 in the Senate, in support of the FTA. The lesson is clear: money politics holds sway in Washington decision making, and Singapore mastered the intricacies of American lobbying politics in which peculiar alliances are formed and disbanded as economic interests evolve. It worked.

In the fall of 2008, I contacted forty-seven local American chambers of commerce (often known as AmCham) that the ASEAN coalition for USSFTA had listed as endorsers of the agreement in a quest to determine the reasons behind their support of the measure. Often local chambers enjoy unrestricted access to congressmen and senators of the state. Many were in Midwestern states such as Michigan, Indiana, and Ohio. I received twenty-eight responses. The astounding fact is that none of the chambers contacted indicated that they knew anything about the FTA project or having endorsed it. One chamber in Indiana stated that its support for the USSFTA could have been prompted by the fact that a former governor of that state became Bill Clinton's ambassador to Singapore. A chamber in northern California referred me to the Oakland city government for more information. And finally, one Michigan chamber official stated that her organization was merged with another one (both were on the ASEAN coalition lobbying list) and hence the executive director did not know anything about the USSFTA. The astounding feature about these e-mail communications is that none of the chambers connected their local interest to the FTA. This is not to say that the ASEAN Business Council made up the list. But Congress has been warned repeatedly that lobbyists do exaggerate and at times concoct non-existing cases of support by various entities for a given cause.

3.14 GEORGE W. BUSH AND THE TRADE PROMOTION ACT OF 2002

From the beginning, George W. Bush needed to tread carefully where trade matters were concerned. Brazil, the largest exporter of orange juice to the United States, paid US$418 in import duties per ton the year that Bush came into office. Bush only barely won Florida, a major orange and orange juice producing state, with an official difference of 537 votes over Al Gore. With a historic intervention by the Supreme Court, Bush came to office. He was faced with a difficult choice between upholding his support of free trade and adding to the unemployment rate in Florida, where his younger brother was the governor. Bush's advisers were already planning his re-election for the White House in 2004.

The political calculus mattered. The duty represented 40 per cent of the value of orange concentrate, and free trade would make orange juice cheaper to American consumers. As a free trader, Bush was in favour of the reduction or elimination of the duty on Brazilian orange juice. But as a politician, he understood that the removal of duty would put 90,000 workers out of a job in Florida alone. California is the other major orange producer, and in the 2000 election, Bush did not carry the state. In fact, no Republican presidential candidate has carried California since Reagan. In the end, the electoral calculus did not allow Bush to grant duty-free status to Brazilian orange juice. Similarly, in steel producing states such as Pennsylvania, Indiana, Ohio, and California, the free trade president was quick to impose a surcharge on imported steel (also a major Brazilian export item), again for political reasons in order to get blue collar votes, which normally go to Democrats.

Six presidents had the TPA before him, and history showed that without TPA, Bush's foreign economic policy could not be effectively implemented. The United States would be left out of the FTA race from which the European Union and other countries could write new rules and standards on intellectual property rights, information technology, agricultural products, government procurement, and customs procedures, leaving the United States with no role to play. Robert Zoellick, Bush's USTR, argued that the European Union had twenty-nine FTAs and Mexico (a NAFTA partner) had nine with twenty-nine countries, but the United States had only three: the U.S.-Israel FTA, the Canada-U.S. FTA (CUSFTA), and NAFTA. One third of American farm land was devoted to the international market and generated US$53 billion in revenue in 2001. Accounting for one quarter of the U.S. GDP growth, the agricultural export sector sustained 12 million jobs and represented far more than 12 million votes, a powerful argument that Zoellick made to the president (Zoellick 2002). Meanwhile, a typical American family of four would benefit from between US$1,300 and US$2,000 per year in additional income and lower costs of consumables, thanks to free trade.

Eight trade promotion authority acts were created by Congress between 1890 and 2002. The Trade Act of 2002 (the name that Congress put on the final bill), originally known as the Bipartisan Trade Promotion Authority Act, or, more commonly, the Trade Promotion Authority, is the most recent one. But it expired at midnight on 30 June 2007 and has not been renewed since. The Trade Promotion Authority (TPA) of 2002 was in fact Title XXI of the Trade Act of 2002. A House-Senate conference committee produced the final bill, which passed in the House by a vote of 215–212 on 27 July, and the Senate by a 64–34 vote on 1 August, right before the summer recess. On 6 August, President Bush signed the bill into law, known as Public Law (PL) 107–210 (CRS 2003a). The TPA is one of the four cornerstones of PL 107–210 which are: (1) Trade Adjustment Assistance (TAA); (2) Trade Promotion

Authority (TPA); (3) Andean Trade Preferences; and (4) Generalized System of Preferences. It is interesting to observe that Singapore was willing to negotiate *without* the TPA. When the trade act came into force, both sides were meeting in London for the seventh round of negotiations.

Between April 2002 and July 2007, the Bush administration negotiated fourteen FTAs. The Trade Act of 2002 produced six successful FTAs which were with: Singapore, Chile, Australia, Central American Free Trade Agreement-Dominican Republic, Peru, and Morocco. It also completed three agreements that are still pending Congressional approval or disapproval (Korea, Panama, and Colombia), plus one suspended negotiation with the Southern African Customs Union. The Free Trade Area of the Americas proposal, initiated by Clinton but also pursued by the Bush administration, is essentially moribund, derailed by formidable opposition from MERCOSUR and Hugo Chávez and his followers — Bolivia, Ecuador, and Nicaragua. Negotiations with Malaysia are suspended; and with those Thailand are still alive, but have stalled. Malaysians are in no hurry to conclude the FTA, given the fact that it has been generating its largest trade surplus ever with the United States. Furthermore, the issue of Prime Minister Abdullah's successor was consuming much of the political leaders' energy recently, but now that a new prime minister is in place, negotiations may resume. Prime Minister Najib Tun Razak has been wanting to reignite relations with the United States, but the FTA is not a burning issue. In Thailand, the military coup that ousted Prime Minister Thaksin in 2006 compelled Bush to suspend the negotiations; to date, no major breakthroughs have been made with the civilian governments that have succeeded the military. However, not all FTAs have been negotiated under fast track authority or the TPA. The Singapore and Chile FTAs began without TPA, and as negotiations were concluded, Congress granted the authority to the president. Jordan also began its negotiations for an FTA with the United States when there was no TPA. When that agreement was completed, a separate statute was written to approve it (CRS 2005*b*, p. 4) and was the only one secured with statutory approval, instead of by way of the conventional TPA.

The eighteenth-century framers of the American Constitution sought to avoid a concentration of power in the hands of any single branch of government. Montesquieu's principle of separation of powers was duly incorporated into the U.S. Constitution, thus dividing the power to conduct foreign relations and the power to regulate commerce between the president and Congress. This arrangement worked well during the nineteenth century, when international trade was simple and direct, often between just two countries. The predominant exports were agricultural products represented by a single interest group. But in the twentieth century, trade became more complex, often pitting agricultural and industrialized products against services, thus spawning multiple but conflicting constituencies. Issues governing tariffs, both formal and informal, as well as direct and indirect non-tariff barriers, customs procedures, transportation rules such as trans-shipment, warehousing, rules of origin, intellectual property rights, and other trade-affected domestic concerns (unemployment insurance, training for new skills, and health care), have all crept into the mix and have different impacts on various sectors, thus overwhelming bilateral, regional, and multilateral negotiations (USGAO 2007*a*).

In the process, international trade has created domestic multiplier effects, both positive and negative, on certain sectors of the domestic economy, often to the detriment of overall trade objectives and outcomes. A Congressman or Congresswoman represents a district within a single state; as such, each representative is a guardian and promoter of *local interests*. This means that a representative from a steel producing or textile making district would take a radically different position on trade from his/her colleague who represents a banking district, even though they belong to the same political party. The former, regardless of party affiliation, would oppose free trade *in principle*, while the latter would favour it. With these district-specific economic interests driving Congressional voting patterns, it is no longer possible to expect a single consensus from a state delegation, let alone from the party. Exceptions to this pattern are found in the predominantly agricultural states of the Midwest and the South, which is often thrown into a single voting bloc when it comes to trade issues. In this regard, the Republican Party, with its predominantly white Southern and Midwestern supporters, has a clearer position on trade (generally in favour of FTAs) than the Democratic Party with its multiple constituencies, including labour and environmental groups (generally against FTAs).

Job displacement and collapses of inefficient companies have created a major political problem for Congress. To deal with potential unemployment arising from FTAs, Trade Adjustment Assistance programmes were built into all trade legislation since 1962 to help those American workers and small businesses displaced by imports. In 1988, the "Buy American" provision was written into law to safeguard against predatory practices of other countries, such as dumping or using prison labour. In 2002, the Democrats were determined to use the trade bill to enlarge workmen's entitlement from job training or retraining for new skills to health care subsidies. The Democrat-controlled Senate favoured a plan that would allow a 73 per cent tax credit for displaced workers' health insurance costs and a special health care benefit for retired steel workers (CRS 2003a, p. 4). In the 2002 TPA bill, Democrats added a series of generous benefits for those displaced by FTAs and by the relocation of companies to sites abroad. Republicans blocked those provisions. The compromise was a modest increase in the job training programme, the portability of health insurance from old jobs, and the payment of salary differentials between old and new jobs. But the management of the programme was left to individual states, with the Department of Labor exercising oversight. The implementation of the programme has been uneven, and benefits vary from state to state. Workers and companies participating in the programme also have to plough through dense bureaucratic procedures (USGAO 2007a). All told, the Bush administration did little to meliorate the programme.

Regarding unemployment caused by free trade, Congress spends as much as US$1.2 billion a year for TAA programmes that cover 65 per cent of health care premium subsidies for workers who lose their jobs due to trade, or to their employers moving abroad. It also grants other entitlement provisions for the displaced. Republican senators opposing the entitlement provision of the TAA produced a trade remedy amendment that would have tied the hands of the president in anti-dumping and countervailing duty issues. The compromise was that the TAA contributions were scaled down to satisfy the Republicans, and less stringent provisions were formatted for labour and the environment to satisfy the Democratic constituents. In some ways, this was a remarkable achievement, given the fact that the Democrats controlled the Senate and the Republicans the House at the time. The bill was passed in July 2002 in the House and in early August in the Senate, and Bush signed it into law on 6 August. Then, twenty minutes later, he left for a month-long "working vacation" in Texas (Bumiller 2002). It was a *peculiar* victory, not fully satisfying for free traders and profoundly dissatisfying for anti-free traders. Both got only a little of what they wanted.

3.15 FAST-TRACK AUTHORITY OR TRADE PROMOTION AUTHORITY

There have been other reasons for the fast-track authority to be created. Its origin is found in GATT negotiations. Multilateral negotiations during

GATT rounds in 1948 necessitated the creation of fast-track authority. To be taken seriously, American negotiators needed to back up what was negotiated at GATT rounds and assure other countries that what was negotiated would be honoured. Otherwise, foreign negotiators would not take America's commitment seriously. In order to launch tariff reduction negotiations at GATT rounds, the Kennedy administration asked and received the authority, called the Trade Expansion Act of 1962, which launched the Kennedy Round (1964–68). All six rounds of GATT meetings (devoted to tariff reductions) were attended exclusively by developed countries. Developing countries would participate in later rounds (Das 2004, pp. 4–6). Also for the first time in history, the Kennedy administration incorporated a provision which has come to be known as the Trade Adjustment Assistance. The objective of that provision was to help those workers and businesses displaced by trade diversion as the result of tariff reductions or free trade agreements. This TAA has come to play a critical role in the making of the Trade Promotion Authority of 2002, which in turn directly affected the US-Singapore FTA as well as those with Chile, Australia, and others that have followed.

Richard Nixon sought a different kind of authority in 1969. The more critical issue in international trade then were non-tariff barriers (NTBs), while the negotiating parties volunteered to reduce formal barriers at GATT rounds. Nixon proposed that he be given "proclamation authority" which would allow him to negotiate the removal of NTBs and submit the results to Congress. If Congress did not object, the negotiated agreement would become a law by presidential proclamation. The House approved the Nixon request, but the Senate rejected it. A compromise was reached: as long as the president met the conditions laid down by Congress, the legislative branch agreed not to amend the terms of the negotiated agreement.

In other words, Congress could vote the agreement up or down, but it could not make any changes to the terms that the president negotiated. This arrangement allowed the United States to participate in the Tokyo Round (1973–79) in which ninety-nine countries participated (CRS 2003a, pp. 2–3). That round was the first in which many developing countries got to participate. Its key achievements include the establishment of a series of codes of conducts, such as the Subsidies Code, the Anti-dumping Code, and the Technical Barriers to Trade Code. Congress was convinced that the Tokyo Round should continue and renewed the presidential authority in the form of the Trade Agreement Act of 1970 (PL 96–39) (CRS 2003a, p. 3).

The fast-track arrangement has proven its worth. In terms of the sheer number of bilateral FTAs, George W. Bush used it more than any president in history for a total of fourteen FTAs negotiated, the highest among all presidents. However, there was a twist: his principal motivation was to use the FTAs to open the door for security collaboration after 9/11.

Other Republican presidents mindful of the importance of interstate security cooperation have used trade as a wedge. The Trade and Tariff Act of 1984 allowed President Ronald Reagan to negotiate an FTA with Israel (CRS 2003a, p. 4). The Iran-Iraq war of the 1980s seemed to be dragging on, while the terrorist attack on the U.S. Marine barrack in Beirut, plus the Nicaraguan Contra war, were the key security issues for the Reagan administration and Congress. Forging an FTA with the Jewish state would renew America's commitment to the region. Complicating the global economic scene further at the time was the Third World debt crisis, whose opening salvo was fired in September 1982 by Mexico and then spread to the rest of Latin America, crippling that region for the entire decade.

The economic collapse of Latin America in the 1980s, and especially its import-substitution strategy for development, ushered in an era of the now infamous Washington Consensus measures. Despite the merits of the Washington Consensus, free trade emerged as an important adjunct to the Reagan administration's security agenda in the Middle East and the Americas. The next important step that Washington took was the negotiation of the Canada-United States FTA that came to fruition in 1988. The next milestone fast track was adopted in 1988 to allow the United States to participate in the Uruguay Round (1986–94) that eventually involved 117 countries and resulted in the creation of the World Trade Organization by 1 January 1995 (Ostry 1997, pp. 175–76). The Tokyo Round produced a "shallow integration" of the world trading system, but that in and of itself was encouraging. All in all, it can be argued that the fast tracks have worked: the Kennedy Round, the Tokyo Round, the US-Israel FTA, the Caribbean Initiative, CUSFTA, the Uruguay Round, and NAFTA were the proud achievements of the fast-track approach.

As Bill Clinton took office in late January 1993, the outgoing Bush (father) administration had nearly completed the negotiations for NAFTA, leaving Clinton's people to conclude it by putting the final touches and shepherding it through Congressional approval. Three issues came to the fore as either incentives or disincentives for the making of NAFTA. The oldest of the three dealt with labour standards that trading partners are encouraged to adopt and practise. The second issue was how to fund the trade-affected adjustment programmes. The third concern was to ensure environmental protection measures.

In many ways, special interest groups were able to exploit these issues to block FTAs. At times, American negotiators would use domestic lobbying pressure and politics to extract commitments from trading partners to implement their own domestic reforms. This was the case with Jordan, Central America, Peru, the Dominican Republic, and the Southern African Customs Union (SACU) negotiations. Either way, trade legislation had broadened its scope and gone beyond trade. Now it is a tool for introducing domestic reforms for the United States and its partners. Some partners such as Mexico and Singapore have effectively used FTAs to launch key domestic reforms that they would not and could not have done on their own.

3.16 REPUBLICAN RADICALS AND CLINTON

As it turned out, Clinton became the only president in recent memory without any trade promotion authority, although Congress was in the hands of a free trader Republican majority during his administration. Trade had been a major national and Republican Party issue since the Reagan years, so it seemed only logical that presidential negotiation authority for trade should be extended to Clinton as well. In 1995, the Clinton administration requested trade promotion authority from Congress so that it could induct Chile into NAFTA. However, both parties were disenchanted by Clinton's labour and environment provisions in the final version of NAFTA and thus were not willing to grant him fast-track authority. Chile refused to negotiate with the president without fast track, and Clinton chose to wait for the next Congress (the 105th, of 1997–99) to reintroduce his TPA bill. Waiting out one Congress for the next has become a political ploy that all presidents have used when unable to overcome congressional resistance or a partisan snag in a current Congress. Congressional elections take place every two years, and if a president campaigns successfully for enough congressional and senatorial candidates, he could move a new Congress to approve his agenda. However, presidents are known to often lose their party's majority control of Congress in midterm elections. Clinton certainly did.

His second try for fast-track authority came in 1997. The preceding November, Democrats gained control of the Senate, but not the House.

The Senate Finance Committee approved the Clinton TPA bill by adding labour and environmental measures as a separate section under the title of "political objectives" (Ostry 1997, pp. 175–76). This was prudent, considering public opinion. Clinton's vice-president, Al Gore, was a strong environmental supporter, but the political reality was that Congress was divided on the issue along partisan lines: the Senate had had a Democratic majority while the House was in the hands of the Republicans. The Democrats favoured strong labour and environmental provisions in all trade bills. The Republicans did not. Predictably, it was in the Republican-dominated House Ways and Means Committee that Clinton failed to line up his own Democrats to support the bill. Only four of the sixteen Democratic members on the committee were satisfied with the Senate version and voted for the bill. Others voted against Clinton. With a vote of 24 to 14, the bill did make it out of the committee. But when the White House was unable to get more support from the House, Clinton and Speaker Newt Gingrich agreed to withdraw the bill before a floor vote (Ostry 1997, pp. 175–76).

In July 1998, the Senate Finance Committee passed the 1997 version of the bill with partisan altercations, but it never reached the Senate floor for a vote. When the bill did go to the House for a vote, it was rejected along partisan lines, 180 for and 243 against. The Republican side wanted to protect the interests of agriculture and big business, while the Democrats sought to safeguard and even enlarge the rights of labour. Neither side could agree on a compromise. Further aggravating the situation was the presidential sexual indiscretion incident (the Monica Lewinsky affair). It was not the TPA, but Clinton's resignation which the Republican Congress was after. The House later indicted the president. The Senate failed to convict him, however (Mitchell 1998; Clines 1998; Mitchell 1999). No one seemed to care about fast track.

When George W. Bush took office in late January 2001, Congress contained three broadly defined pro- and anti- free trade blocs. One group called for strong enforcement of labour and environmental provisions in FTAs, with the possibility of sanctions if the FTA partner failed to honour the terms of the agreement. The second bloc supported the inclusion of stringent labour and environmental protection measures, but left enforcement to the president. Yet a third group of senators, congressmen, and congresswomen favoured the complete exclusion of labour and environmental provisions in all free trade agreements (CRS 2003a, p. 5). This was the congressional line-up that Singapore faced in its pursuit of an FTA with Bush's America. It explains why Bush-appointed the twenty-eight committees (presidential; USTR; the Commerce, Labor, and Agriculture departments; and the Environmental Protection Agency) that reviewed the Singapore and Chile FTAs were not overly preoccupied with loose environmental and labour standards in the agreements. The Labor Advisory Committee was the only one which opposed both FTAs.

4

The USSFTA Bridging Economic Regionalism and Security Regionalism

Without stability and security, there can be no economic growth, no investments, no trade.

Lee Kuan Yew in *Parliamentary Debates*, 1 June 1988

4.1 REGIONALIZATION AND REGIONALISM

There are certain fundamental and similar characteristics in all *regionalisms*, regardless of their construct. When social scientists invoke the term *regionalism*, it can mean any multistate free trade or security agreements such as ASEAN, AFTA, APEC, NAFTA, the European Union, MERCOSUR, SACU, CAFTA, NATO, or AZNUS, to name a few. When economists talk about NAFTA, they refer to *economic regionalism*. When political scientists discuss critical security issues in NATO, they are referring to *security regionalism*. Other scholars employ the term to suit the needs of their own disciplines as well. For instance, in literature, regionalism can be a genre. In languages, it represents going beyond distinct accents or intonations and into the more elaborate realm of what constitutes a separate cultural identity. For physical geographers, it can have ecological meanings as well. Moreover, the non-state or corporate-driven realities of economic regionalism and security regionalism can have political, social, and cultural nuances embedded in these systems that their creators did not intend or envision. Hence, in order to be a little more precise in the use of the concept for our purposes, this chapter will develop a typology of regionalisms that different academic disciplines use.

In the past, physical barriers such as mountains, rivers, deserts, seas, and oceans often defined what constitutes a region. Once societies formed state systems, political barriers served a similar purpose in insulating and self-containing an area. Regionalism has often been defined by a single set of cultural values, norms, customs, and history that bind the inhabitants of the locale. Brittany, Scotland, Quebec, Texas, the Nordeste, and Mindanao are different from the rest of France, the United Kingdom, Canada, the United States, Brazil, and the Philippines respectively, in terms of cultural uniqueness (religions, languages, folkways), the way of life, social values and mores, and even a history of common sufferings and blessings, all forging and reinforcing the psychic unity of the inhabitants — what Asians might call spirit, or Europeans and Americans call national identity. What has brought them into the larger system of the nation state is common political belief in or vision of a single nationhood or statehood.

Separate *cultural* identity from the rest, *political* autonomy from the overbearing central state, security from geographic isolation, perceived threats from outsiders, and self-sustaining *economic* life, have all become the basis for the making of these provinces, departments, or states into "regions" distinct from the rest. But the strong desire to build a single nation state and, for less developed regions, to catch up with the most advanced areas of the country reinforced the regionalism. The instruments for change have often been economic development projects, internal market linkages, and a common sharing of factors of production across physical and political barriers (Kollmorgen 1945, pp. 377–89). In the United States, a superb example of internal regionalism within a single country is the Tennessee Valley Authority (TVA) hydroelectric dam project of the 1930s. Begun as a flood control and hydroelectric power generation project, the TVA's electrical grids integrated half a dozen American southern states economically. The availability of power brought in new industries, which in turn fuelled the rapid growth of regional agriculture and spurred industrialization. Textile plants dotted the South, and the Franklin D. Roosevelt administration was able to coalesce new political forces that worked as a southern voting bloc, one of several regional power groups within the Democratic Party until the late 1960s. No Democratic president won an election without the support of the southern voters, except Harry Truman in 1948. The bloc also brought enormous political power to the federal government. One can analyse similar economic and political changes as ASEAN deepens its integration through trade, investment, and common infrastructure over time.

This type of regionalism is a natural type. The focus of this book, by contrast, is a regionalism that is deliberately constructed, and artificially held together by interstate integration engines and systems such as ASEAN, APEC, the European Union, and MERCOSUR (Mercado Común del Sur). They are *political* and *economic* constructs. The political objectives of the member states of these entities are the motor of regionalism and are often complementary to the economic activities of state and non-state players. In both cases, economic integration has enhanced the political objectives. While the etiology and process may be different, the two regionalisms were politically driven or political constructs.

There are some similarities between the role of the natural region of the 1930s and 1940s in the United States and the political construct of the interstate region of Southeast Asia today. The cultural cohesion and common identity that International Relations' constructivists relish still remain the glue of both natural regionalism and its politically constructed cousins. The notion that globalization must be resisted by the formation of regionalism is also found in both as a familiar retrogressive political response to rapid change. Such retrogressive regionalism as a planning unit can interfere with the economic and political objectives of municipalities or could undercut the sovereignty of nation states, which in turn can provoke resistance to the further deepening of regionalism. This is a politically sensitive issue in bottom-up regionalism such as that which brought the European Union and APEC into existence, and less of an issue in such top-down regionalism as MERCOSUR, ASEAN, or SACU.

Complicating ASEAN regionalism is the resurgent and resentful nationalism of smaller states, such as Cambodia and Myanmar, against their larger, more prosperous, and politically more expansive neighbours. Not all members gravitate to tariff-free trade and investment, or are prepared to welcome political interference from other members. Laos is not even a member of the World Trade Organization and hence is not considered an FTA candidate by developed countries. Myanmar has battled with ASEAN peer pressure to loosen its dictatorial rule. In view of these contradictions, the foremost value of ASEAN regionalism has been political for the poorer states, and economic for the wealthier states. One can imagine that further economic and political changes can occur over time, as ASEAN deepens its integration through trade and investment, as well as shared infrastructure. It will have become a single region, more complete, more compact, and even politically manageable. The political and economic power derived from this structure will be quite different from what ASEAN can grant today.

4.2 GLOBALIZATION REDEFINING REGIONALISM

The traditional meanings of "natural" and "constructed" regionalism have lost their viability as globalization gets in full swing. In cases where globalization provokes regionalism, political barriers are removed through trade liberalization, structural reforms, and overcoming physical barriers through new technology and infrastructure improvement. But they reinforce or even distort the power of a globalizer such as the United States, and magnify the feebleness of the smaller countries such as Malaysia and Chile impacted by globalization. Each responds to its own circumstances and its own capabilities. ASEAN has not adopted Mahathir's foreboding — only Asians are welcome — as its core principle of regionalism, however. For a small state, regionalism can help strengthen its capabilities in international relations and international political economy.

The case of Portugal in the European Union during the East Timor independence movement is a good example. In late 1975, Portugal was alone and helpless when Indonesia invaded Timor with a nod from the Ford administration and the blessings from Canberra. But by 1998, Portugal, which has been a member of the European Union since 1986, was able to mobilize the European Union behind its demand that Indonesia quit East Timor and grant independence to the former Portuguese colony. For a smaller state, the appeals of regionalism can quickly become magnified. Stanley Hoffman argues that for a large country such as the United States, too many international and regional institutions and rules can restrict its power (Gelb 2009, p. 23). For a larger state, regionalism constricts its mobility and reduces its autonomy of action, but grants it the larger cover of speaking for the region. Brazil's resistance to the Washington-led Free Trade Area of the Americas (FTAA) is another example. Peeved by the orange juice tariff issue with the United States, Brazil led MERCOSUR and anti-American states such as Venezuela, Bolivia, Ecuador, Nicaragua, Paraguay, among others, to join forces in opposing the Washington-sponsored FTAA.

Unwittingly caught in the battle between the two behemoths (Brazil and the United States), several Latin states preferred bilateral FTAs with the United States, which the Bush administration put together as a second best option. None has turned to Brazil for economic integration initiatives.

To some in ASEAN, regionalism is a defence mechanism against out-of-control globalization forces and its key drivers, while to others, regionalism is a most appropriate tool to maximize whatever benefits and opportunities globalization has to offer. These divergent views have also tempered ASEAN regionalism. Those in the former camp have been championed by anti-globalization proponents and *less* developed political economies such as AFTA, MERCOSUR, SACU, India, and a legion of developing countries, while the latter set has been cheered on by pro-globalization promoters, or *more* developed economies, such as the European Union, Japan, Singapore, and NAFTA. This philosophical divide has made ASEAN regionalism less productive and has placed the group's integration at risk. Walden Bello has flatly stated that "We had 30 years to build an ASEAN house, and we blew it" (Bello 2004). He is not alone in this belief.

4.3 THE WEALTH OF NATIONS AND FTA-DRIVEN REGIONALISM

Wealth has played a role in a nation's ability to project power and stir up fear. Smaller and poorer countries bordering on larger and more prosperous neighbours may be eager to form a collectivist entity to expand and exaggerate their power on international relations. Hence, regionalism appeals to them. Economic differences illustrate and reinforce this perspective. In 2006, Mexico's per capita income at a market exchange rate of US$8,000 was one-seventeenth of America's US$45,000. The gross national income (GNI) of the United States (US$13.5 trillion) was a little over 100 times that of Singapore's GDP (US$130 billion). The city state is the richest country in ASEAN in per capita terms and the fourth largest in economic output among the ASEAN-10, trailing after Indonesia (US$316 billion), Thailand (US$194 billion), and Malaysia (US$147 billion). One might add that Singapore has achieved development with only a fraction of the larger neighbours' populations. The quality of human capital also matters, and that has made all the difference for the city state. Laos, the smallest economy in GNI terms among the ASEAN-10, posted a per capita income of US$500 in 2006 and, like the Mexico-U.S. ratio, its per capita GNI is one-seventeenth of Singapore's (WB 2008, pp. 14–17).

Cambodia's expectations of how it can benefit from ASEAN regionalism are quite different from Singapore's, and each pursues different state (political and disparate) objectives within and outside the region. This situation has hindered ASEAN integration.

The USSFTA was decidedly the product of pro-globalization and high-income countries. Globalization can benefit them because the FTA is between fully developed service and manufacturing economies with advanced infrastructures, including informatics and path-breaking communications technologies, systemic competitiveness, well trained human capital, and abundant managerial capital. Long-term dynamic gains will be shared by the partners.

FTAs work best between political economies of similar levels of development, not between developed and developing, or between developing and developing, countries. In the latter two cases, asymmetries can overwhelm smaller partners with trade deficits and high external debt, as shown in the case of MERCOSUR. Uruguay and Paraguay have been running chronic trade deficits against their physically and fiscally larger neighbours and MERCOSUR partners, Brazil and Argentina. In MERCOSUR, Brazil has emerged as the regional banker, holding much of the external debts incurred by smaller members. In some sectors, even Argentina has been struggling to compete against Brazil. As a result of the extreme lopsidedness in size of these economies relative to one another, Uruguay has been threatening to forge bilateral FTAs outside the region (Pang and Jarnagin 2009, pp. 87–127). In this context, the USSFTA is a unique form of regionalism, bridging the two regions of Southeast Asia and North America, and cannot easily be replicated elsewhere without open financial market access, protection of intellectual property rights, e-commerce, and open access to government procurement contracts, cross-licensing of professionals, and even shared political economy values and global strategic visions. Conventional wisdom has held that the U.S.-Singapore FTA could be the model for other bilaterals in the region (Daquila and Le 2003, pp. 908–28), but this has not happened and will not work.

4.4 WEALTH AND POWER PROJECTIONS WITHIN REGIONS

Nation states since Westphalia have sought to acquire power on the world stage, first within a single region of geographic confines, then in an international system of multiple regions, finally becoming an unchallenged global economic and military power. Empire builders such as the Romans and the Mongols went through a similar three-stage expansion. Andalusia, the Byzantium Empire, Genoa, Venice, the Ottoman Empire, and China wielded considerable regional influence, while conjuring up fear among smaller neighbours. But they lacked an economic strategy of integration with other regions: their economic wealth was well confined to one or two regions, but it never spanned the globe. Immanuel Wallerstein makes a distinction between "empire" and "world-system". The former is a politico-military organization lacking economic linkages outside the realm, while the latter is a more comprehensive political economy with hierarchical links among a trilevel division of labour: the core (the most advanced and developed in terms of capital and technology as well as political and social systems); the semi-periphery; and the periphery (the least advanced and either un- or underdeveloped).

These three have constituted the co-denizens of a single capitalist world system since the early sixteenth century. By contrast, historical empires did not establish networks of cross-border productive systems to generate rent, while the world system set up elaborate systems of colonization and mercantile exploitation (Wallerstein 1974, pp. 15–16). It should be noted that the neo-Marxist notion of "empire" emerging in the post-modern era lacks the historical grounding found in Wallerstein's analysis, but includes both institutional and non-institutional players from the environment to "biopolitics" (Hardt and Negri 2000; Passavant and Dean 2004). In recent years, the indiscriminate *ahistorical* use — or, more appropriately, abuse — of the concept of empire has proliferated. Regardless, all empires and nation states have resorted to a set of foreign economic and military-security policies to achieve their imperial and national aspirations. The bases for projecting the national power in the international system are wealth, fear, and force (Bobbitt 2002, pp. 215–16).

Is modern-day regionalism the moral equivalent of Wallerstein's world system or empire? Not all nation states have the same capabilities of projecting power both at home and abroad. Without military or sea power, a country cannot attain greatness. The military power of a country is not always a reflection of the actual size of its GDP. John Mearsheimer calls a country's ability to mobilize natural, industrial, and financial resources, "latent power" (Mearsheimer 2001, pp. 61–68). A country with larger economic resources, but with lesser mobilization capabilities (due to peculiarities of its political system), will remain a smaller military power.

During the Second World War, Germany had a far larger economy than the Soviet Union, but the Russians outproduced Germany in armaments and eventually won the war, albeit with Allied support. This raises a fascinating question about the future mobilization capabilities of China, India, and the United States as the rival superpowers in the Asia-Pacific region and the Indian Ocean basin, and how they will reorder the security landscape of Southeast Asia. At the end of the day, it is a country's political economy that defines its military capabilities. But how to project those capabilities as a military force may depend on the political system, its leaders' will, societal support, and other organizational capacities (Gelb 2009).

Myanmar and Cambodia have the domestic power to quell rebellions, enforce law, collect taxes, and even suppress ethnic minorities and opponents of the government, but they lack a latent capability to project power in the ASEAN region. Singapore may be small, but it is globally influential in wielding *soft power* because it is a regional economic power and boasts the region's best armed forces. How a nation-state can mobilize comprehensive sets of resources, domestic as well as foreign, to project power depends on how a regional system of economic and military relationships is fashioned. In Southeast Asia, ASEAN has not been able to restrain the exercise of power by member states and its non-binding rules; hence, its IR system is structurally *anarchical*. This characterization reinforces the view that there is no higher authority or power above the state that could coerce a Southeast Asian country to abide by it. The "ASEAN Way" has institutionalized this absence of supranational enforcement, voluntary or otherwise (Haacke 1999, pp. 581–611). The most recent ASEAN heads of government meeting in Bangkok in 2009 demonstrated this point. ASEAN's frustrated inability to deal with the junta in Yangon is one such example of the limits of regionalism.

In the European Union system, the exercise of power is hierarchical, but symmetrical. Member states have willingly given up parts of their sovereignty on key policy domains and have willingly accepted the decisions and rules reached in Brussels as well as the general laws of the European Union as agreed upon in the parliament at Strasbourg. Germany is restrained by European Union rules, but also by its own volition. To lead the European Union, Germany must behave in a manner that gains the trust of others.

The future success of the European Union will depend on the continued practice of restrained *primus inter pares*. This cohesive political regionalism is unique in history and cannot be replicated in Asia because Japan, China, India, and Indonesia have so far exhibited neither the will nor the spirit to behave like Germany, or an altruistic and self-sacrificing regional power. Singapore's case illustrates that economic power has gained importance in international relations, but without military power, on its own it can have limits. In the absence of any cohesive regionalism forged by internal great powers, Asia may have to rely on the existing system of ASEAN-chaired economic and security regionalism for decades to come. The downside of this arrangement is that in the age of brutally competitive globalization and proliferating regionalism a country's economic power can rapidly wax and wane. This can affect ASEAN members more severely than the Asian great powers.

4.5 KNOWING THE LIMITS OF REGIONALISM

Peter Katzenstein argues that there have been two supranational movements which have contributed to the political rise of a region, namely, *internationalization*, in which states are the sole actors, and *globalization*, in which both state and non-state actors commingle and share the space (Katzenstein 2005, pp. 14–23). One might add that the determination of the relative prominence of state or non-state actors is a function of a given region's culture, history, and choice of political strategies. In the Anglo-Saxon world of liberal political economy, non-state actors can wield as much influence as the state and can often challenge the state; but in the more nation-centric and mercantilistic Asia, non-state actors can rarely override state decisions. Dynamic social and economic activities across borders, encouraged by globalization as well as by interstate political action, reaction, and transaction have created "a world of regions". Some are politically conceived while others are geographically constructed. Still others are put together by political and economic designs, or human imagination. But all tend to respond to external economic stimuli in one way or another. Each region (or "society of states" in the lexicon of the English school of IR) possesses a distinct personality with its own strategy to act, react, and transact in a given situation. A successful region must sensibly prioritize goals to be achieved (whether security or economic), manage its resources prudently by knowing its own limits as well as its adversary's capabilities, and sequence its growth in realistic steps (Gelb 2009, p. 93). Both internationalization earlier and globalization now bring states together into a region for economic, political, security, socio-cultural, and environmental reasons. When a region is made of disparate states, such as ASEAN, this is hard to do and is a very slow process.

In sum, regionalism is a political structure with an economic purpose that reflects and shapes the strategies of the state and non-state actors within it (Katzenstein 2005, pp. 14–23). Successful regionalism must harmonize the activities of both. In a tightly regulated market system such as Singapore, the state and non-state actors would meet in the market and should mutually reinforce one another; in a classic liberal market, the state and non-state economic actors compete for the dominant position. Foremost, such a cooperative strategy must reflect and shape the region's core aspirations. Goh Chok Tong has commented that ASEAN will never become another European Union, where bureaucrats in Brussels call codfish *"gadus morhua"* and determine the size, weight, and colour of cucumbers and how to wrap or unwrap cheese (NAS/Goh 2003*b*). The former Singaporean prime minister swore that such regulatory excesses will never intrude into ASEAN/AFTA.

One cannot imagine that culturally rich and diverse Southeast Asia will allow the AFTA bureaucracy to give a new generic name to durian and set rules regulating the size, weight, and scent of the fruit. Asian regionalism will function better if it is defined more loosely and less restrictively. Harmonization and standardization are good measures for all regionalisms to adopt in order to establish a level playing field for big and small players, but regions must know the cultural and political limits of how and when to set such common denominators. Each region has to design its own architecture, which in turn defines the shape and content of the community. A community of states abiding by regional rules and regimes can set limits for how far regionalization can proceed and what it can bear or tolerate without interfering with the pursuit of collective progress and its individual members' interests.

4.6 DENATIONALIZING A REGION

There are several definitions or concepts of regionalism that can often be confusing. But there have been at least five types that social scientists have recognized: *natural, political construct, economic, outcome of process, and historical.* Allen Scott, a geographer, identifies a region as a cohesive *economic* hub, or a production cluster. He identifies forty cities in the United

States that accounted for 63.5 per cent of the all American merchandise exports in 1994. The ten largest cities claimed 33.8 per cent. Each of these economic "clusters" includes geographically surrounding areas replete with supply and production chains, constituting a single, coherent region (Scott 2000, pp. 57–59). This is what Singaporeans are fond of calling "hinterland". Peter Dicken, another geographer and one with Singaporean living experience, uses the term to mean a subunit of the global economy such as the European Union and NAFTA, which are only two of several regions that globalization has begot (Dicken 2007, p. 8). For the purpose of fostering economic-financial primacy, political integration, and security for the whole, a region with Sassen's "global city", Braudel's "*superville*", and/or Castells' "informational city" can deftly manage both "geographic dispersal of economic [and financial] activities" (the bedrock of today's globalization) and at the same time integrate these "geographical[ly] dispersed activities" (Sassen 2001, pp. xix–xx).

Therefore, as regions are political creatures, differences exist. These differences can be exploited by the strategy organized by a rival region of state *cum* non-state players who choose to mobilize their resources and capabilities for exploitation. To develop, a region requires social interaction and transaction among constituent members, as well as integration with extra regional players. Trade and cross-border investment have been the two vehicles for achieving this development. Once fully developed, each region becomes an economic cluster and can serve as a subunit of a larger global system, such as Wallerstein's world-system. The emphasis placed on economics in defining regionalism (Scott, Dicken, and Sassen) strongly reflects the influence of globalization, especially the perception that globalization can be reined in to promote the economic integration of countries and firms.

Kenichi Ohmae, MIT-trained nuclear scientist-turned business strategy guru was the first to identify such economic clusters as "regional states" that share a single financial hub, a cohesive infrastructure, a transportation network, a competitive production network, and an integrated consumer market (Ohmae 1995, pp. 79–100). A subunit of the larger globalized world economy, Ohmae's regional state — or better yet, region-state — can be located within a single country, or can straddle two or more countries. One type of region-state is an economically rational cluster of cities, a hinterland supply source, urban production centres, and a manufacturing hub within a single country, such as Osaka-Kobe-Kyoto (the Kansai region).

Hong Kong-Shenzen-Southern China is another example, as is the Silicon Valley and the greater Bay Area of northern California. Some region-states incorporate more than two or three countries, such as Los Angeles-San Diego-Tijuana, Lyon-the Rhône-the Alps of France and Northern Italy, and the Singapore-Johor-Riau growth triangle (Ohmae 1995, pp. 80–81). Since Ohmae's region is typically intra or interstate by structure and has its own governance rules and distinct system of operation — typically reserved to a state — it seems justified to label such a unit of globalization as a "region-state".

The first example of a natural region-state within a single country is driven by economic integration and interdependency — a network of suppliers and buyers with the overt political encouragement of the nation-state. The second type of a cross-border region-state is a decidedly political project, driven by economic motives such as harmonization and integration as the first step towards eventual political union, de jure or de facto. The most prominent aspect of this region-state is the cross-border production platform and marketing found in Europe, North America, and Southeast and Northeast Asia. This regionalization of production can draw countries with diverse factor endowments, as well as co-join developed and developing economies into a single integrated economic hub, all to contribute to the total welfare of the region. Also, products are exported outside the region-state, thus globalizing marketing and tapping into extra regional capital, technology, and natural resources. In ASEAN, extra regional workers are also an important factor for prosperity. Extra regional linkages are important for ASEAN's growth and expansion. The combined force of the regionalization of production and the globalization of financing and marketing makes the region-state a unique political and social creature.

At the moment, ASEAN, the European Union, NAFTA, MERCOSUR, and SACU, to cite a few, are examples of regionalisms at varying stages of maturation. Leaders of these entities reaffirm from time to time that economic integration, not political union, is their ultimate goal. But when economic integration deepens and interstate socialization accelerates, new political challenges and conflicts emerge. To make the system work better and respond more effectively to external competition posed by other region-states, the larger states must lend helping hands and make concessions to smaller partners so that the group as a whole can become competitive. Now it is the collective, not individual, survival that is at stake. Success of one state can have a cascading multiplier effect for the group, but cannot sustain collective welfare alone. Such political collaboration fosters regionalism and can pave the way for eventual political integration. This bottom-up process can endure, as opposed to the top-down version of the Roman, Chinese, or even Mongol systems.

To grow and prosper, the region-state will eventually have to adopt a single currency, or a unit of account, coordinate members' macroeconomic policies, promote common social goals, and ultimately forge ahead to a political union. Such regionalization will require sustained political commitment and will take time — decades or perhaps even centuries. It took more than a decade for the American Confederation of the eighteenth century to become a loosely federated "united states". It took another hundred years and a devastating civil war for America to produce a truly unified state. And it took another century-and-a-third to elect the country's first biracial African-American president, thereby granting full political voice to minorities. In Europe, it was Charlemagne's time in the tenth century that launched the Holy Roman Empire project — one god, one nation, and one Europe — and it has taken a thousand years and numerous wars since to arrive at the current state of the European Union.

4.7 AN ECONOMIST'S REGIONALISM

Economists seem to have an unspoken consensus when they talk about regionalism. In their lexicon, regionalism refers to regional economic entities such as trading blocs, investment zones, and common manufacturing areas in which two or more states and their non-state actors participate (Frankel 1997; Schott 2004). They are politically created interstate systems for economic purposes. When Edward Lincoln talks about "economic regionalism" for East Asia, he offers no definition. He assumes that economic regionalism automatically promotes economic integration of the region (East Asia) through interstate and cross-border trade and investment activities, drawing state and non-state actors in a single region (Lincoln 2004).

According to this inferred definition, a culturally cohesive Europe contains several economic regionalisms: the European Union, the European Free Trade Area (Norway, Iceland, Liechtenstein, and Switzerland), the European Economic Area (Norway, Iceland, and Liechtenstein), and other sundry economic agreements. Furthermore, this type of regionalism

— or better yet, subregionalism — has woven a series of overlapping supraregionalisms, to use Lincoln's concept, among themselves, as well as with extra-regional states and regionalism in Latin America, Africa, Asia, and North America. Admittedly, this definition is a bit loose, but it conveys the sense that there is a hierarchy of regionalism.

Specialists in international political economy and international relations seem to agree that regionalism is a cluster of institutions, regimes, and norms. Since the collection of institutions, regimes, and practices affect the overall well-being of the denizens in a region, architecture matters. When it is put together by two or more states in order to promote and enhance the commonweal, regionalism is political, cultural, economic, or security-driven while being either *de jure* or *de facto*, formal or informal, or even binding and non-binding. It is a creature of choice, or a creature of necessity. Some political scientists adopt the economist concept of regionalism, namely an economic bloc (Pempel 2005, pp. 1–28), while others have included both economic and security dimensions in their definitions (Katzenstein 2003). As such regionalism has both international political economy (state and market) and international relations (war and diplomacy) implications. Whichever definition one embraces, regionalism has two faces: economic and political.

For this book, region, regionalism, and regionalization are defined more narrowly to accommodate the diverse needs of the situation whereby high, middle, and low-income countries can co-mingle and pursue different objectives while using similar regional mechanisms. *Region* is foremost a geographical unit which, over time, has evolved into a *social* organization moved by peoples of diverse cultures, but with shared historical bonds. As the society evolves into a more sophisticated political organization, the region acquires the *political* means to pursue its objectives. The necessity to survive creates a collective strategy for economic prosperity as well as security against external threats and natural disasters. Thus, the region has acquired an *economic* and a *security* role. In this sense, the European Union *region* is a tightly knit social, political, economic, and security organization, whose common aspirations at the moment are to achieve primacy in the globalized world system. Its laws, history, and strategy have the power and capabilities of reaching beyond its geographically defined confines. If its projection of power were to become global, it would be considered a global superpower. If the limits of its power end within the borders of Europe, it is a regional power.

All politically constructed regions aspire to become the core of a global region as the borders of their economic, political, and social power and capabilities expand. This kind of expansion is currently driven by globalization. It requires military resources and capabilities to thwart undue disruption in order to achieve ongoing global expansion. In the past, it took wars to accomplish the same goals. Some regions have successfully taken advantage of the opportunities and challenges offered by the last four decades of globalization, while others have not ("the left behind"). To bastardize Toynbee's historical building blocks, the current phase of globalization as a civilization is built on the *economic province*. Economics predominates and shapes all other *provinces* of the world civilization. In it, regions constitute a strategic foundation for survival, defence, prosperity, and security.

Regionalism should then be understood as a political expression of the total sum of the region's history and culture, and a current and future economic strategy for state and non-state actors to survive, manage, and prosper. Even in the era of neoliberal globalization, *de jure* regionalism has always been *state-led*, but corporations (actors in the market) have built a *de facto* regionalism of *market-driven* interlinked systems of resources extraction, value adding, and manufacturing in several countries within a region, then exported these products and services to the world. Elsewhere, we referred to Toyota's production platforms scattered throughout Southeast Asia. Such corporate regionalism has created its own governance rules. While this brand of regionalism has contributed to the growth and integration of ASEAN in several sectors of the regional economy, it has also encouraged states to act. To create more jobs and grow economically, ASEAN members are increasingly taking into account and catering to corporate wishes when cross-regional economic and social decisions are made.

Once this system is in place, non-state actors may become the principal drivers for the making of culture, history, and strategy. For NAFTA, corporations, individuals, and NGOs play a significantly more important role than the state. In ASEAN/AFTA, the state still reigns and rules. For the European Union, reflecting its core regional history and culture, co-governance of the state and non-state players has been fine-tuned in practice. This different architecture can make regionalism perform in a superior manner at a given moment of globalization and internationalization. The waxing and waning is a fact of life for the "world of regions". If gains for the state and non-state constituents diminish, it can be assumed that regionalism is failing and in need of restructuring. Regionalism is a construct, and, as such, it can be *re*constructed or *de*constructed, depending on external and internal circumstances.

ASEAN regionalism is a political and economic expression of a group of ten countries that are democratic and liberal, authoritarian and illiberal, or mercantilist and semi-democratic. If regionalism is inhabited by democracies, liberalism, and open and transparent rules, all structural and functional changes will come from below, that is, an instance of bottom-up regionalism. In top-down regionalism, the demands and calls for reforms and change will come from state members, or even from outside. Today, there are neoliberal regionalisms such as NAFTA, soft mercantilist regionalisms such as the European Union, and developmental regionalisms such as ASEAN/AFTA. Which of the three systems can perform best in the age of globalization constitutes a topic in and of itself for investigation, but this book will address this matter in part through the prism of the bilateral free trade system of the USSFTA.

4.8 A POLITICAL SCIENTIST'S REGIONALISM

Christopher Dent, one of the rising stars in studying the international political economy of the Asia Pacific, defines regionalism in a more comprehensive, albeit a bit dense, way: "structures, processes and arrangements that are working toward greater coherence within a specific international region in terms of economic, political, security, socio-cultural and other kinds of linkages" (Dent 2008, p. 7). In this context, the USSFTA can be considered regionalism. Dent's regionalism will work best when members of the region establish overall cohesion of political, economic, social, and security objectives that they pursue collectively and individually. It is based on institutions and regimes; hence, the level of the partners' development of political economy matters.

Other students of regionalism have introduced a host of lexicons that have made the appreciation and understanding of the concept more difficult. Hettne, for instance, discusses "open, extraverted regionalism" where the state may lack the means, resources, and know-how required to manage challenges of globalization *alone*, and hence choose to join forces with NGOs. His list also includes the "hegemonic regionalism" of Europe; the "peripheral regionalism" of the Balkans, South Asia, Africa, and even the former USSR; "developmental regionalism" in which weak and ineffectual states and markets must depend on external resources to survive and prosper; and "security regionalism" which is a follow-up tool for economic regionalism to sustain itself (Hettne 2000, pp. xx–xxi). His regionalism is topical, geographical, or ideological, but never all three concurrently. Hettne focuses more on the state concerns of development in the swiftly moving times of globalization and its proper response to defend itself. The like-minded must organize. This may not reflect reality, however.

The distinguishing feature of the "old regionalism" is the paramount role that the state assumed and continued to exert in the process of regionalization, which Hettne defines as a region's attempt to "increase their [sic] level of region-ness" (Hettne 2000, p. xxi). There are more sophisticated definitions, however. But Hettne captures the core notion of regionalization, which is a process to deepen the political, economic, and social cohesiveness among many disparate countries. Another feature of the old regionalism is its excessive emphasis on *trade* related issues (thus ignoring the role of investment, security and even homogenizing cultural and political values, as well as roles of extra regional players), and the drive for political cohesion and social integration. This has led to the gross underestimation of the role of non-state actors in the building of regionalism, or the process of regionalization. The old regionalism, as defined by Joseph Nye, Jr., for instance, stands for a congregation of states: "a limited number of states linked together by a geographical relationship and by a degree of mutual interdependence" (Schultz, Soderbaum, and Ojendal 2001, p. 15). Observe that the key word in the old regionalism is *interdependence*, not integration. Nye's regionalism is both political and economic. Interdependence can enhance state sovereignty; integration requires voluntary reduction, or even abandonment, of sovereignty in favour of regionalism. Regionalization is the process by which a group of states and non-state actors creates a common set of rules to promote their political, economic, social, and security-driven objectives, which, in turn, when embraced by all, becomes regionalism.

The old regionalism theories were built on the "cost-benefit analysis" of the reduction or elimination of tariff barriers within given geographical confines. So long as opportunities for trade creation were greater than trade diversion, regional economic interdependence worked. Trade promotes interdependence, but trade *and* investment lead to integration. It should be pointed out that today the world has globalized financing and marketing, but also has regionalized trade and production. One regionalism can checkmate another regionalism. But in single regionalism, one corporation can scatter its production system through several member countries, thus maximizing FTA benefits. Resources are produced locally (within a single state), but value adding and trading take place *across* a region with FTAs. Today's "world of regions" is still working towards building a global FTA. But financing production systems can be globally outsourced. In fact, corporations want to do this to reduce the political risks of host countries, as well as encourage project diversification. Another example of single regionalism is the environment. The impact of its degradation is global, with its contagion effect ignoring political borders or regional barriers, but environmental mitigation is typically regional, often paid for by individual states or a region-state.

There are limits to applying the theories of old regionalism to new situations, however. For the past two decades, and to be sure, since the stalemate in Doha (2000) and the collapse of Cancún (2003), globalization, with its pervasive economic integration of the world, has rendered the old regionalism (focusing on trade alone) less effective. Razeen Sally makes an important point: of the 151 WTO members (153 in 2011), some twenty to thirty countries account for slightly more than 80 per cent of global trade. Some 120 countries account for less than 10 per cent. The United States alone provides 131 countries with preferential treatment in trade (which I call one-way free trade). But it is this group of countries, often led by China, India, Brazil, and South Africa, which blocks the trade liberalization agenda by turning the WTO into a world "tirade" organization.

These states already enjoy one-way free trade privileges with the United States, the European Union, and Japan. But they fear being taken over by the developed countries and are unwilling to reciprocate by joining a single global market system, within which they would not have clear control. The developed are willing to forge ahead with trade liberalization without the participation of the unwilling. The Doha blockage has involved the refusal to compromise on the both sides — refusal by developed countries to open their markets to agricultural products from developing countries, and refusal by developing countries to open their markets for manufactured and service products from the former. This political friction has been impeding the creation of a single, seamless world market. This state of affairs has driven the willing countries to go alone in their quest for expanded cross-border trade and investment. Bilateralism has become the preferred route.

Because of this stalemate at the WTO, the European Union and NAFTA have gone beyond the respective regions in search of new trading and investment partners, *with or without the WTO* — collectively in the case of the closed regionalism of the European Union, and individually in the case of NAFTA's open regionalism. The outcome has been varied: new regionalism, extra regionalism, cross-regionalism, and minilateralism. Whatever nomenclature one chooses, all are designed to accommodate the new requirements of a country's (and by extension, a region's) expanding needs for the regionalization of production and globalization of financing.

Cross-regionalism, in the definition of Goh Chok Tong, is, therefore, one form of new regionalism that can satisfy the needs of members that cannot be satisfied within the current ASEAN format. This may also come about when the region cannot offer economies of scale, product sophistication, or market access. The inability to produce a consensual security community can also result in the search of like-minded partners outside the region. Hence, crossing over or going outside ASEAN has been a viable option for such developed economies as Singapore, Thailand, and Malaysia. In the absence of the security mechanism in the region, the economic interests of ASEAN's advanced economies must be protected and defended at home and abroad with the help of extra regional partners. Thus, the primary motivations for forging cross-regionalism are economic and security.

Goh Chok Tong was clear on this: without defeating anti-globalist Muslim terrorism, the future of free trade and, therefore, the material prosperity of Singapore, Southeast Asia, the Asia Pacific, and the world, will be in peril. For Singapore, which depends on outside world market (open, not closed) for its living and prosperity, anti-globalization movement can be disastrous. This prospect was one reason Singapore championed Bush's strategy of linking trade and security in ASEAN and APEC (NAS/Goh 2001), although the prime minister was not totally comfortable with the Bush's unilateralism and America's unrestrained use of force, which Goh termed "discomfort to Asia" (NAS/Goh 2003a).

The major difference between the old and new is not just a matter of semantics: *interdependence* for the old regionalism and *integration* for the new. The two terms are not interchangeable. These differences notwithstanding, the new regionalism makes room for non-state actors (foreign and domestic) and the state's willingness to accept a subordinate role as a regulator, not the developer, of the region. Often, new regionalism is not defined by geography, but by common aspirations to gain from globalization. New regionalism can also be imagined. The theories about new regionalism, however, must not only incorporate trade creation opportunities for state and non-state actors, but must also highlight the interaction between trade and flows of FDI and foreign portfolio investment (FPI).

In short, the services sector has come to garner an equal, if not greater, voice in FTAs driven by new regionalism. This sector is usually the base of an FTA signed by two high-income countries. Transnational production systems (dispersed or otherwise), cross-border financing, and access to world markets are new factors that have come into play. The new regionalism must build a safety net for a country's external economy, assets, and investments outside the political jurisdiction of the state. For the past two decades, if not longer, worldwide FDI and FPI flows have been on the rise, and countries need to design region-state regimes and even global institutions that can protect these extraterritorial investments. For this purpose, a new security format is needed.

The dorsal fin of the old regionalism was state-sponsored "neo-mercantilism" while the new is decidedly market-driven "neo-liberalism". In the latter, the state's role is confined to institution building and regulation. In the old form, the *state* was the prime recipient of gains, while in the new regionalism, *market* agents such as multinational firms and their regional and host country allies (suppliers, component manufacturers, and infrastructure service providers, to name a few) remain the primary beneficiaries of gains. In the old regionalism, gains remained at the top; in the new regionalism, gains are filtered down to local firms and individual levels. The state also seeks to maximize the benefits it realizes for its national and multinational firms by instituting timely reforms and modernization. The USSFTA grants all Singaporean and Singapore-based firms investing and manufacturing in the two Indonesian islands the privilege of accessing the U.S. market. Cross-regionalism and cross-regionalization, then, can best be understood in the context of the roles that the state and non-state players *share* in diplomacy, war, and security, as well as in trade, investment, and the environment. A country's multinational corporation can pave the way for new security relationships or alter existing ones.

Singaporean leaders have taken pains to point out that the city state has the capability to provide security to the 6,000 multinational firms in residence, the majority of which are Western, and the declared targets of al-Qaeda and its Asian subsidiaries. A weak state will adopt restrictive and nationalistic policies to drive foreign firms out, thus pre-empting potential threats. In Singapore's case, the state is responding quite differently: it is keeping pace with change by constantly fine-tuning its policy. Herein lies the societal need to link economics and security. It is a proven fact that a country with weak security (such as chronic social instability, failed state syndrome, and poor physical and human infrastructure) cannot attract FDI, the lifeblood for economic growth and societal development at large. Even if a country has good domestic savings, it will still need FDI for new technology, new managerial know-how, overseas market access, and security links. Strong government (such as the junta in Yangon), cheap labour (such as in Bangladesh), and abundant natural resources (such as in Indonesia) will not automatically attract foreign investment at a sufficient level to ensure wider and deeper development.

4.9 PROFILING ECONOMIC REGIONALISM

When a region or a group of like-minded countries agrees to combine and share their resources and experiences, and to establish a common trade and investment strategy for the region's development and collective prosperity, they will build institutions, write up rules of engagement for FDI, and even create a pool of capital to share. This is "economic regionalism". In open regionalism such as ASEAN and NAFTA, members are free to pursue extra regional economic ties. In closed regionalism such as the European Union and MERCOSUR, member states do not have the individual freedom of developing economic ties with extra regional countries. Both types of regionalism can develop external economic ties, but in closed regionalism, all members must sign on as a group, while in open regionalism, group action is not required. Instead, members can do what their economic needs dictate. Some regions such as the European Union, MERCOSUR, and SACU began as customs unions and then gradually evolved into free trade areas. Others began as free trade areas but acquired some of the characteristics of economic integration areas (EIAs) that go beyond trade. This is the case with NAFTA, the EU, and AFTA (a work still in progress). Still others chose to incorporate aspects of an FTA while pursuing EIAs bilaterally, but comprehensively, as in the case of the United States-Singapore Free Trade Agreement. Or, partners can agree to limit their agreement to merchandise trade or partial scope trade, as in the case of the China-India agreement.

As of May 2009, the World Trade Organization classifies all trade agreements into five categories: (1) regional trade agreement (RTA); (2) FTA; (3) customs union; (4) EIA, and (5) partial scope (PS) agreement (see Table 4.1) (WTO n.d.). Furthermore, the WTO distinguishes all agreements as pertaining to either goods or services or both. China and ASEAN have two separate FTAs, one for goods and another for services. In other agreements, such as that between the United States and Singapore, goods and services are combined and comprehensive in scope. Japan prefers EIAs, which it calls "economic partnership agreement" (EPA). It can cover more than goods, or trade in partial scope with investment or non-trade related measures. The Japan-Indonesia EPA, for instance, includes a measure that the Southeast Asian country must export health care workers to Japan (Stott 2008). Also, the EPAs seldom cover over 80 per cent of traded goods ("substantial" in Article 24), the threshold set by the WTO to be an acceptable bilateral or regional FTA. Politically sensitive items such as rice and sugar are left out. The Japan-Thailand and Japan-Indonesia EPAs, can be considered partial in scope (Dieter 2009). One must question the merit of developed high-income countries such as Japan signing agreements that are anything but comprehensive and that can enhance global trade liberalization. But the reality is that neither Japan nor the United States has taken this step willingly due to political sensitivities at home and in partners' countries. Such FTAs and EIAs are inherently more political than economic (see Table 4.2).

To follow Japan's strategy, China and India signed an FTA in February 2009. The agreement is restricted to "goods" and is a "partial scope"

TABLE 4.1
FTAs and EIAs for ASEAN Plus Three and NAFTA, 2009

Region-Markets	EIA	FTA and EIA	Total
ASEAN-10	17	30	47
Plus Three	6	15	21
NAFTA	7	22	29
Total	30	67	97

Source: WTO n.d., A-Z Table and individual country profiles.

TABLE 4.2
FTAs in Force and WTO Legal Cover as of April 2009

Type of Regionalism	Enabling Clause	GATS Art. 5	GATT Art. 24	Total
Customs Union	6	—	13	21
FTA	9	—	137	146
EIA	—	65	—	65
Partial Scope	13	—	—	13
Total	28	65	140	243

Source: WTO n.d., A-Z Table.

agreement. Neither side was interested in deeper economic integration, nor has either proposed plans to convert the agreement into a comprehensive FTA or EIA. This PS could be a building block for a better bilateral security relationship, not the principal tool for economic growth and development for the signatories. It can hardly be considered a way forward for Asian economic integration since the large economies of the region could do so much more for smaller states.

The popularity of FTAs and EIAs is obvious. For high-income countries, they can cover a range of issues that the WTO regimes cannot and have not. They can be flexible — structured to confine the agreement to trade in merchandise and/or services. Or they can go beyond WTO regimes by covering investment, intellectual property rights, government procurement, e-commerce, bilateral professional certification, and even the immigration of professionals and skilled workers, as in the case of the USSFTA. Furthermore, both models allow flexible time frames for further integration, encouraging lower-income members to move at a pace that suits their needs. APEC has two liberalization dates, both being voluntary and non-binding: 2010 for developed countries and 2020 for developing, but members' commitments to implementation have not been forthcoming. CAFTA-DR adopted a liberalization time frame suitable to each member's capabilities. This variable speed of integration can lead to potential conflicts if the generosity of high-income countries is abused. But such concessions are called for by the reality of income disparity, differentials in state and economic development, and even diverse history and culture. Both NAFTA and AFTA allowed such variable market openings in which the speed of liberalization and deregulation reflect the different capacities of the signatories.

In order to have a viable, working, economic regionalism, however, the region must have several internal and external endowments to exploit. In addition, contracting parties, or the states, must have certain institutional infrastructure, as well as similar levels of development in: macroeconomic policy; regulatory regimes for open trade and investment practices; working trade facilitation systems; the political will to implement necessary reforms when needed; and a modernization strategy that can incorporate capacity building along with its intra or extra regional partners. The United States has spent millions of dollars in capacity building for SACU (US$2 million), Central American (US$47 million), and Moroccan (US$40 million plus) negotiators and civil society participants (USGAO 2004, pp. 48, 53, 56). If a region comprises uniformly low-income countries with little or no internal capital, technology, or knowledge, such economic regionalism has little or no chance to survive. The earlier experiences of the Central American Common Market of the 1960s and the Andean Pact of the 1970s fit this description. They failed.

An IMF study demonstrates that openness and liberalization in trade policies can contribute to the overall economic expansion of any country. For the past twenty years, all countries that have grown economically had also adopted open, liberal trade regimes and practices (IMF, 2006, pp. 3–4). In addition, the study emphasizes the impact of open, liberalized trade practices that can also lead to poverty reduction. Trade liberalization, while being competitive, can generate greater effects, if it is reinforced by other domestic reforms: sound macroeconomic policy; domestic market deregulation; more realistic exchange rates; opening of capital accounts; social safety net reform; and more investment in human capital formation, among others (IMF 2006, pp. 5–6). By no means is it an easy task for countries to adopt these IMF recommendations. But once such a free and open trading system is put in place, the poor can reduce poverty by 2 per cent per annum when it is fully integrated into the free trade system (IMF, 2006, pp. 5–6). These political and social reforms can also work as additional stimuli for faster growth. The IMF also claims that trade liberalization can lead to the reduction of "monopoly rents" and moral hazards by reducing the value of political connections (IMF, 2006, p. 2). Of course, this is how trade liberalization works *in theory*.

In fact, low-income countries rely on trade revenues as the principal source of government income. In the case of Cambodia, the government derives as much as 65 per cent of its operational budget from import and export taxes (Chhon and Moniroth 1999). The poorer a country is, the greater its dependence on revenues from trade taxes. This was also the case for the United States in the nineteenth century. The IMF study goes on to show that for the past twenty years, low-income countries that have reduced or eliminated tariffs also lost their trade revenue income. By shifting to other revenue sources, half of the countries that liberalized trade and cut tariffs were able to recover only 70 per cent of their pre-liberalization income. The other half could not. This has discouraged poor (low income) countries from adopting trade liberalization. Introducing such new taxes as consumption taxes — valued added and excise — can be politically unpopular and even impractical, if evasion is widespread.

In poor and middle-income countries, trade constraints and barriers are also numerous. Many have been accumulating barriers over time due to domestic pressures. Eventually, this makes a country's exports uncompetitive and imports more expensive, which in turn can cause economic stagnation and perpetuate underdevelopment. Some constraints are obvious, overt, and political: exchange controls; higher trade taxes, and surcharges; import and export quotas; repatriation requirements; exemption and dispersion of tariffs; excessively high tariffs on intermediate and capital goods; corruption in trade facilitation practices; and poor governance (IMF 2006, p. 14). All countries suffer from this malaise, but low- and middle-income countries seem to be more severely affected by it. In Senegal, a new tax system had to be adopted by merging the multiple VAT rates into a simplified single flat rate in order to recover lost revenue from trade liberalization. Senegal had the political will to launch the reforms that many countries lack (IMF 2006, p. 10). This means that the new regionalism of low-income countries cannot produce as positive dividends as those of high-income countries. This may be why some economists argue that South-South regionalism does not work. Not all regionalisms are the same.

4.10 FTAs AMONG LOW-INCOME COUNTRIES

Indeed, one World Bank study advises against South-South (or low income to low income) economic integration (WB 2003, pp. 124–35). The theoretical implications are clear. First, there is strong product redundancy among low-income countries, which intensively focus on raw material production and the export of natural resources, often not value added. In the 1960s, all Central American Common Market members grew bananas, other fruits that are the same, coffee, and sugarcane. Guatemala could have no trade gains by selling its bananas to Honduras and buying Honduran bananas in return.

Second, an FTA has to be comprehensive to accrue benefits. Most South-South FTAs are politically motivated, tend to be "partial scope", and fail to include items that are politically sensitive, thus not covering WTO's minimum requirement (Sally 2006, p. 6). Trade integration must be followed by an influx of capital in order to go beyond the static gains of the early years of trade creation. There was little cross-border investment in the Central American Common Market. South-South FDI cannot offer either advantages on the scale needed or advanced technology that competitive production platforms require. If anything, South-South FDI tends to be speculative in nature. Without new technology, productivity will stagnate.

Third, another theoretical implication for the South-South FTA is that the consumption power of low-income countries is limited; rather, their market growth depends on the expansion of personal income. The autarkic South has a history of low growth. It has traditionally *un*welcomed foreign investment. But for the past forty years, the fastest way to expand an economy has been through international trade and investment. This means that after initial gains, the South-South FTA has little room for trade to expand. Hence, the temptation is high to turn economic integration into a political mechanism to protect the domestic market against foreign competition.

The Andean Pact of the 1970s and 1980s fulfilled the role of protecting import-substituting industrialization and the home market, and of resisting FDI inflows by establishing region-wide discrimination and restrictions against non-members. An average African state belongs to four such FTAs, while an average Latin American country, seven (Sally 2006, p. 7). None has worked as well as the planners intended. Thus, this type of regionalism (between South-South, or low income countries) acquires an undue political significance, but undermines all possibilities of economic gain. For a while, the Andean Pact and the Central American Common Market functioned as bulwarks of anti-Americanism, a political reaction from the informal "colonial" hinterlands of the United States.

In theory, one can also expect that an economic regionalism of middle-income countries will do little better than one of low-income economies. But this may not be the case. As manufacturing economies, middle-

income countries have something to export, but if all members are good
at producing iron, steel, textiles, electronics, and auto parts, and if they
practise a state-led development strategy, it is not likely that trade barriers
will come down fast enough for each country to benefit. Furthermore,
because the core of the state-led model is to protect domestic markets
and to prolong comparative and competitive advantages, each country
has a tendency to mobilize more state-owned and -managed resources,
and to practise an autarkic strategy, occasionally tapping into external
savings overseas. This is what happened to the Latin American Free
Trade Association. Mexico, Brazil, Argentina, Chile, and Peru (the more
advanced industrialized economies of the region) failed to open up their
markets to one another.

By contrast, advanced ASEAN countries are producers of electronics
and auto parts. Intraregional trade on these items has been responsible
for the region's economic growth. But the key difference between ASEAN
and LAFTA is that the former hosts a large number of MNCs, which use
the parts and components to assemble finished goods and export them
worldwide. As a coalition of import-substituting countries, LAFTA never
had such MNC connections on a regional or global scale. In both cases, the
convergence of growth, development, and income could not occur without
the participation of external capital, technology, and market access. Without
a locomotive pulling the rest of the region's economic wagons, no convoy
of trains could reach the destination of common prosperity. In Japan, the
Flying Geese model worked because the country was willing to invest
and produce throughout Southeast Asia, and then buy the finished goods
and export them to Europe, the United States, and even Japan itself. In
the new regionalism, external linkages are more vital to economic success
than ever before.

4.11 FTAs AMONG HIGH-, MIDDLE-, AND LOW-INCOME COUNTRIES

Economic regionalism between disparate or asymmetrical income
countries (low and middle; middle and high; and high and low) — as in
the European Union, the NAFTA, and potentially APEC — can generate
different gains for the members. The objective here is convergence of
income, that is, poor countries catching up with the rich. But in reality,
not all member countries will benefit, nor will they do so equitably, due to

national differences in growth, development, and distribution strategies. Equal gains cannot happen even between two high-income countries, as seen in the USSFTA. One partner can benefit more from trade while the other benefits from non-trade arenas such as investment and security. But trade theories hold that gaps in development, growth, and income between partners can be closed by borderless, barrier-*less* preferential trade and investment. This outcome cannot be achieved overnight, however. There is, nevertheless, room to exploit differentials in factor endowment, as in the case of the European Union and to a lesser extent, in NAFTA. When regionalism allows greater latitude in development for its members, as in an open format, opportunities for external trade and investment ties can attenuate the income differentials over time. Open regionalism offers more opportunities for growth and development than closed regionalism, however.

When trade and investment asymmetry occurs in closed regionalism, the aggrieved member has little recourse to redress the asymmetry by remaining within the region market. This has been the case for Uruguay and Paraguay in MERCOSUR. It takes time and external stimuli to increase competitiveness, invest more money in infrastructure, inject new technology into production systems, and upgrade human capital. The European Union experienced this problem in its earlier days, and to solve it, cash transfers were made from the richer to the poorer members as a way of bringing up the income levels of Portugal, Spain, Greece, and Ireland closer to those of the older and more advanced members. Also, it welcomed investment from the United States, Japan, Canada, and other developed countries. Symmetry in development and personal income was seen as being conducive for EU integration and expansion. Decades later, Ireland has achieved income parity with developed siblings in the union and others are catching up. But this has not happened in MERCOSUR, where Paraguay and Uruguay, which together represent less than 10 per cent of the group's GDP, have been forced into indebtedness and run trade deficits with the larger members (Pang and Jarnagin 2009). This means that free trade *cum* customs union alone will not do the job. Other development policy coordination and stimulus measures for the members are also needed. The European Union has done so, while MERCOSUR has not. External links and inputs are vital in both cases.

In NAFTA, Canada and Mexico have run deficits against the United States in some sectors, but on the whole, the overall trade deficit has been borne by the largest member; hence, in reality, there has been a steady income (wealth) transfer from the richest to the less well-to-do. This situation cannot last forever without the reciprocity of lesser members making concessions. Mexico will have to open up its financial market and service sectors; Canada will have to allow more U.S. FDI into its natural resource sector. Both will need to carry out domestic reforms for further liberalization and deregulation. But in reality, this has been politically unpopular in Canada and Mexico. They both loath American domination in all forms. Open regionalism has allowed each member to redress asymmetries by going outside the region. Mexico, Canada, and the United States have actively pursued extra regional FTAs in Latin America, Asia, the Middle East, and Africa. The European Union has locked out the United States in trade, but has welcomed U.S. investment, which has increased from US$1.2 trillion in 2005 to US$1.8 trillion in 2008 (USDoC 2009, table G2). In addition, the United States could make up its losses in NAFTA by expanding its trade and FDI relations with countries in Asia, Latin America, and Africa. But this option of entering into FTA accords for EU and MERCOSUR countries with others outside their regions *on an individual basis* does not exist. Neither Portugal nor Britain can sign an FTA with Canada or Singapore. EU and MERCOSUR rules require a single collective decision for all members, denying an individual member the freedom of choice; instead these entities operate on a "one for all and all for one" principle.

The theoretical implication here is clear: open economic regionalism with its *sovereignty enhancing* mechanisms grants greater latitude in devising economic strategies to its members than closed regionalism, with its restrictive but *sovereignty pooling* gains. These choices are trade-offs. It can be argued that closed regionalism is ideal for advanced, high-income countries while open regionalism can accommodate countries with disparate income and development levels.

Trade is often enhanced by investment. This explains why USTR negotiators insist on including investment liberalization and deregulation in all FTAs. It is not surprising then that U.S. multinationals prefer to invest in America's major trading partners. The income from American overseas investment is critical for offsetting trade deficits with those countries. Expatriation of corporate profit abroad can create jobs at home and further finance research and development of advanced technology. When major trading partners welcome an unrestricted entry of U.S. investment, it has generally led to positive effects. Of the top ten destinations for American investment, six are in Western Europe and three are in East Asia. In terms of the total amount of hosting American FDI, Singapore ranked sixth in the world (excepting NAFTA) in 2008 (see Table 4.3). Within Asia, Singapore is the number one destination for American investment (US$106.5 billion), followed by Australia (US$88.6 billion), Japan (US$79 billion), Hong Kong (US$51.5 billion), and China (US$45.9 billion) (Table 4.4). The American gains in the FTA with Singapore are unusual in that the larger partner has benefited from both trade surplus and return on investment.

4.12 IMPLICATIONS OF REGIONALISM FOR ASIA-PACIFIC BILATERALS

When two high-income countries integrate their economies to form bilateralism or regionalism, they bring to the table a greater variety of factors of endowments than low- or middle- income countries do. It also causes a high level of political friction because the stakes are so high. When the U.S. automobile industry becomes a victim of Japanese competition, or when the Korean financial market is taken over by European investors, the losing side will resist, and its resistance has more firepower than what middle- or low-income countries can muster. But when matched correctly, the direct benefits from the economic integration of high-income countries

TABLE 4.3
Total U.S. Investment in Top European and Asian Countries, 2005–08
(US$ billion)

Country	2005	2006	2007	2008
Australia	76.7	67.6	83.5	88.6
Hong Kong	36.4	39.7	50.2	51.5
Japan	81.2	84.4	81.9	79.2
Singapore	76.4	81.9	94.8	106.5
France	60.5	63.0	70.0	75.0
Germany	100.5	139.8	166.0	181.0
Ireland	55.0	86.4	114.9	145.2
Netherlands	240.0	279.0	389.0	443.0
Switzerland	100.7	102.4	98.0	123.4
United Kingdom	380.0	418.0	509.0	563.8

Source: USDoC 2009a, table G.2.

TABLE 4.4
Total U.S. FDI Stock in Select Asia-Pacific Countries, 2004–08
(in US$ million)

Countries	2004	2005	2006	2007	2008
Australia	—	75,669	67,632	83,340	88,549
China	17,616	19,015	26,459	28,579	45,895
India	7,658	7,162	9,746	14,540	16,104
Indonesia	—	8,603	9,484	17,679	17,909
Japan	71,005	81,175	84,428	81,923	79,235
S. Korea	17,747	19,760	27,299	26,854	27,673
Malaysia	8,909	11,097	11,185	13,037	13,291
New Zealand	4,620	5,191	5,933	5,395	5,266
The Philippines	6,176	6,522	6,948	7,066	5,914
Singapore	61,076	76,390	81,879	94,810	106,529
Taiwan	—	14,356	16,999	15,711	16,604
Thailand	7,499	10,252	10,642	8,850	9,128
Others	—	4,082	5,367	6,010	8,510
Total	374,754	375,689	403,637	453,997	491,910

Source: USDoC 2009b.

could be immense and even create positive spillovers for the region. When merging superior capital, technology, and managerial know-how in a single sector such as banking, the financial regionalism of two or more partners can dwarf the next largest competitors. In this case, each partner contributes to the weaker part of the other partner, whereas in the bilateralism or regionalism between middle- or low-income countries, such synergy cannot be had. The free flow of skilled labour through preferential visa quotas (as in the case of the U.S. FTAs with Singapore, Australia, and Chile), in addition to the cross-licensing of engineers, accountants, lawyers, and other technical professionals, can lead to the creation of a common pool of human capital.

Furthermore, no industry can improve its efficiency and increase productivity without innovative technology, which generally comes from expensive investment in original research and development. Without transparent and rigorous enforcement of intellectual property laws, though, there will be no investment in original R&D in advanced technologies. The integrated sourcing initiative that Singapore persuaded the United States to accept in their FTA is an important "support" infrastructure for high-income countries. A high-income country brings capital and technology to Bintan and Batam to produce goods that Indonesia cannot manufacture with its own factor endowments. By providing physical space, infrastructure, and cheap labour that Singapore does not have in the city state, Indonesia has provided the support structure for Singapore's economy, and, in the process, acquired market access to the United States. Because of well developed social and physical infrastructure, such an FTA can offer two immediate benefits: first, static gains can be quicker but larger than those from the low- and middle-income FTAs, and second, the time to reach the onset of dynamic (ongoing and sustainable) gains can be shortened. When a small advanced economy such as Singapore forges economic integration with the world's largest economy, the profits and impact will be greater still for the smaller partner. But the real benefits and gains are not confined exclusively to the economic realm but to the political, social, and security arenas as well.

The Asia Pacific hosts several economic regionalisms. Razeen Sally has observed that FTAs are relatively new to Asia (Sally 2006, pp. 1–3). Until 2001, neither China, nor Japan or Korea had signed FTAs within and beyond the Asia Pacific. Then, the number of FTAs mushroomed. In 2001, China joined the World Trade Organization, thus making itself a prime candidate for free trade partnership with other WTO members. All success of regional integration must begin with trade expansion among the constituent countries in a region. Without a high degree of integration (economic, political, and social), the security of a region can only be tentative and tenuous. There must be a common interest to defend and rally around. Collective well-being in material prosperity and military security must be firmly rooted in economic integration. Europe, for instance, displays the highest intraregional trade ratio, thanks to the European Union and other subregionalisms (72.8 per cent of their exports and imports in 2008 were conducted among themselves), while Asia and North America attained 50.1 per cent and 49.8 per cent, respectively.

Here, one can argue that there is cohesion and a thread for closer collaboration in economy, politics, culture, and security. Other regions of the world have not achieved the threshold of the 50-per cent mark for intraregional trade. In 2008, Latin America reached an intraregional trade ratio of 26.5 per cent while Africa attained 9.6 per cent. The Middle East, the lowest among world regions, reached only 2.5 per cent (see Table 4.5). A lower ratio, as in Africa and the Middle East, indicates that the regions are hampered by a lack of political collaboration and by little desire to

TABLE 4.5
Intra- and Inter-regional Trade as a Percentage of Total, 2008

Region	Asia	N. America	Europe	Mid East	Latin America	Africa
Asia	**50.1**	17.8	18.4	4.5	2.9	2.8
North America	18.4	**49.8**	18.1	3.0	8.1	1.7
Europe	7.5	7.4	**72.8**	2.9	1.5	2.9
Middle East	20.4	11.4	12.3	**2.5**	0.7	9.6
Latin America	16.8	28.2	20.2	2.0	**26.5**	2.8
Africa	20.4	21.8	39.1	2.5	3.3	**9.6**

Source: WTO 2009, table 1.4.

fashion a common strategy in international political economy and security. Without the convergence of these two universes, there is little basis for collective social harmony and a grand political vision for the future.

WTO statistics show that in the spring of 2009 the world had 243 working FTAs of four types: customs unions, free trade agreements or areas, economic integration agreements, and partial scope agreements. Of these, 211 are combined agreements for merchandise and services trade. Customs union seems to be popular among geographically closely knit regions, such as Western Europe, the Southern Cone of Latin America, and the Southern African region, but not North America. Even so, the goods trade agreements, or FTAs, represented 60 per cent of all agreements of the four types — RTA, FTA, CU, and EIA. Partial scope agreements tend to take place between low-income countries (South-South), as in the India-China FTA, as well as a North-South set of asymmetrical income countries, such as the Japan-Indonesia EPA. The combination of a comprehensive FTA and a deeper EIA is favoured by such high-income countries as Singapore and the United States. Regional trade agreements can include any two or more of the four types. Partial scope FTAs often fall below the 80-per cent mark of the WTO recommendation for tariff-free trade and also exclude sensitive areas from the agreement. Rice, for instance, has been one item that Japan has excluded from its EPAs with various countries.

Also, a closer examination of the FTAs already in force and in negotiations by Singapore and the United States reveals another interesting picture. Singapore has thirteen FTAs in force with twenty-three countries, while the United States has seventeen FTAs in force, with three agreements signed but pending congressional approval. A total of forty-seven countries have negotiated FTAs with the United States. Both Singapore and the United States have several ongoing negotiations, some at a very early stage of just launching discussions. Both are also involved in negotiations for a Trans-Pacific Partnership agreement with Australia, Brunei, Chile, New Zealand, Peru, Malaysia, and Vietnam. Several bilateral agreements already exist among subsets of this group of nations. The ASEAN Free Trade Agreement binds Singapore, Brunei, and Vietnam. The United States has bilaterals with Singapore, Peru, Chile, and Australia. Singapore has bilateral FTAs with Australia, Peru, and New Zealand. Brunei, New Zealand, Singapore, and Chile have been jointly members of the Trans-Pacific Strategic Economic Partnership Agreement since June 2005. Finally, Vietnam and the United States have been discussing a bilateral FTA. And Malaysia decided to join the TPP negotiations in August 2010 ("Malaysian Cabinet" 2010). The Philippines has also expressed its interest (Cahiles-Magkilat 2010). As of November 2010, Japan was keenly interested in joining the TPP, but could not make a firm commitment to join the negotiations, with divided public support — not surprisingly, with business *for*, and agriculture *against*, the region-wide FTA (Ohata 2010; Editorial 2010; "US praises" 2010; Fukue 2010; "Japan, Peru" 2010). The group's economic integration strategy confirms the belief that a fallback position of bilateralism or minilateralism is not only possible, but also the most viable alternative, given the fact that the Doha and Cancún meetings failed to advance an integrated single world market agenda. A U.S trade official stated that the TPP negotiating parties plan to unveil the new region-market in November 2011, when APEC holds its summit in Honolulu (Barkley 2010). Assuming the Trans-Pacific Partnership is set up, we will find that it will have both political and economic significance for the Asia Pacific.

But the geographic foci of the FTAs pursued by the United States and Singapore also confirm their desire to remain linked to major resource producing regions as well as regional security hubs: the Middle East (for energy access and security concerns), Latin America (raw materials and potential markets for manufactures and services), East Asia (expansion of current economic stakes and updating the security role for the United States, plus Singapore's need to balance the emerging regional great powers with the United States). The United States has pursued comprehensive and inclusive trade and investment agreements (not partial scope or customs union), while Singapore has been more flexible. It has signed both comprehensive and partial scope agreements. The USSFTA for instance, is a more comprehensive agreement than the Singapore-Japan EPA. Finally, both have signed and are negotiating an FTA plus an EIA, often exceeding WTO standards and adding an innovative mechanism to expand and integrate partners into e-commerce, comprehensive labour and environment rules, government procurement access, amplified protection for intellectual property rights, mutually reinforcing professional licensing governance, and migration of highly skilled workers. Publicly unsaid but implicitly accepted in these FTAs is a strong commitment to enhancing mutual cooperation in security interests in the respective region and around the world.

4.13 SECURITY REGIONALISM

One argument posed in this book is that economic regionalism alone cannot thrive without a matching complementary security regionalism. The sole exception is NAFTA, because neither Canada nor Mexico has pretentions of challenging U.S. military superiority. Economic wealth has historically led to military power. Nations with military power projection capabilities do not shy away from a show of force, or even resort to it, when diplomacy fails to resolve conflict. Economic regionalism is not without the potential pitfall of creating trade disputes, and escalating claims can tempt the militarily more powerful to use force. Ostensibly to avoid such an eventuality, ASEAN has developed the ASEAN Regional Forum. The ARF has worked to promote constant dialoguing and confidence building among its participants. But it has not sought to become an institution of arbitration or a resolution vehicle to deal with present and future conflicts. Its role in the Northeast Asia's Six-Party Talks is marginal, but it has provided opportunities for the United States, the two Koreas, and Japan, to meet and ventilate their grievances away from the glare of the public eye. All six countries are part of the ARF.

In May 2010, when the South Korean naval vessel, *Cheonan*, was sunk by a torpedo, Seoul quickly blamed Pyongyang for the aggression. Japan was concerned. The United States and South Korea chose to move forward with their planned military exercise in the Yellow Sea. By the middle of the summer, the crisis reached a boiling point, and a North Korean representative at the Shangri-La conference in Singapore was threatening to respond with force (presumably missiles and possibly nuclear weapons) if the naval exercise went ahead. The ARF called for moderation on both sides, but the dialoguing degenerated into a propaganda forum. China could have taken a stronger position of defending North Korea, but in view of its huge economic stakes in South Korean and Japanese trade and investment, it demurred and chose a wait-and-see attitude. For a similar logic, economic stakes guided the decision by Seoul to restrain. Powerful business groups opposed a military retaliation because they feared the loss of their investment in North Korea. Some 700 South Korean companies are doing business *in* and *with* North Korea. In the Kaesong Industrial Park alone, just across the border from South Korea, there are 121 companies that have established production platforms for *chaebol* exports. In the end, economic interests overrode the security response of the South Korean Government (Fackler 2010).

Over a century ago, Captain Alfred Thayer Mahan, a U.S. Naval Academy professor, presciently observed that the role of a "cruising" navy is to protect national commerce around the world while disrupting an enemy's commerce, which "strikes down the money power of a nation" (Mahan 1987, pp. 135–38). In the Seven Years War (1756–63), the combined British and Dutch fleet closed off France and seized profitable overseas colonies in the Americas, thus strangulating French trade with the colonies. In the War of 1812, it was American privateers who did more damage to British commerce than the U.S. Navy, thus laying the first cornerstone for a link between trade and maritime security for the United States. Mahan was also explicit about the responsibility of the navy: to protect the commercial sea lanes that a country's merchants exploit, first in the home coastal waters and then the world over. A powerful state must establish overseas naval bases and commercial staging grounds that can preserve the link between sea power (a security concern) and the country's economic opportunity to generate wealth (trade).

Mahan argued that the United States could not become a world trading power without safe harbours for commerce and naval bases around the world. President McKinley's decision to retain the Philippines after the Spanish American War of 1898 was in accord with Mahan's strategy that as an aspiring Asia-Pacific power, the United States needed a naval base to protect America's expanding commercial presence in the Western Pacific. Global trade interests require a global navy. To a certain extent, Mahan is still relevant, especially when 85 to 90 per cent of world trade still moves over the seas. This means that trading partners must bear in mind maritime security, which in turn requires the participation of non-FTA partners whose commercial stakes in the regional maritime zone are just as high as those of the FTA partners. But in security relations, the question of free riding becomes a thorny issue.

Much like the role of foreign great powers in the Vietnamese withdrawal from Cambodia, it was Napoleon's fleet that tied down the British navy in European waters, thus providing breathing space for the small American navy. It was the naval alliance and coordination of the United States and revolutionary France that brought Britain to its knees in 1812. The end of the Cold War and the evacuation of the Soviet air force and naval fleet from Da Nang and Cam Ranh Bay, as well as the withdrawal of matériel support to Hanoi, did more to end the Vietnamese occupation of Cambodia than the ASEAN initiative did (Yahuda 2003). This observation is not meant to minimize ASEAN's part in the episode, but rather to serve as a reminder that external events also played a role along with ASEAN's initiative. Yet the eviction of Vietnam contributed mightily to the forging of ASEAN regionalism, just as 1812 shaped the American belief that the British navy would remain a threat to the consolidation of U.S. sea power in the Atlantic. This thinking remained dominant in U.S. Naval War College teachings, right up to the beginning of World War II — Britain posed a greater threat than Germany.

There are two requisite questions touching on security regionalism that must be posed. The first is: can a country or a region "buy" security from external sources such as FTA partners? A Dartmouth College political scientist argues that security can be "produced" at home and abroad (Brooks 2005), the implication being that it can be purchased. Singapore and the Netherlands lack the resources to deploy their naval presence on a global scale. But trade is a lifeline for them. Thus, they must rely on someone else's navy or instigate security regionalism in their respective geographic spheres in order to build sufficient naval strength to keep the world's oceans and sea lanes safe. The Dutch can rely on NATO. Asia does not have a regional security organization or even a security community that could project its naval power to protect its regional and global trade lanes. Singapore has to rely on its own power, coupled with a willing external power, for good reasons.

The second question is: how does a regional "system", whether it be political or economic, work *for* or *against* security? Joseph Nye has defined a "system" in international relations as being "a set of interacting units [meaning states] having behavioural regularities and identity over time. Its structure defines the ordering of its parts. Structure involves an ordering principle, specification of the functions of different parts, and the distribution of capabilities. In international politics, the ordering principle is anarchy" (Nye 2004, p. 25). When Nye's definition is applied to Asian regionalism, the interacting units (states) would need to establish rules, regimes, and institutions that can "regularize" their behaviour to deal with anarchy. This construct would require a more mature security mechanism, either indigenously built or externally imposed. ASEAN leaders have agreed to build an ASEAN Community by 2015. That is the first step towards several of formal regional forums, including a security concert.

Until a decade ago, the region lacked an indigenous hegemon, or a superpower, which could impose order and set up rules or regimes that could shape state behaviour in the region. After World War II, that role fell to the United States by default. Now that the region has produced at least three leading contenders (Japan, China, and India) and possibly a fourth candidate in the offing (Indonesia), there is reason to believe that Asia should build its own security system. This process is just now unfolding and could move faster, if there is a clear and present threat to regional security. At the moment, the United States is not seen as a threat to Asia. But over time, these regional great powers will seek to replace the United States, thanks to the past three decades of non-stop economic growth that has given impetus to military and naval modernization in the region. Asian countries are building FTAs within the region, as well as outside it.

For the time being, however, rivalries among the regional contenders have impeded the construction of a viable security system, while the intraregional economic and security contest has been heating up. China, India, Japan, and Australia have each been gearing up to fill the vacuum left by the wilfully negligent Bush administration. Their separate initiatives will not clash with one another for another two or possibly three decades. For now, the individual pursuit of national economic and security interests in Asia has not degenerated into uncontrollable conflicts that could lead to war. In his November 2009 visit to Asia, Obama made it clear that he will strengthen and expand American engagement in the region and at the same time strongly support the ASEAN attempt to construct a community (White House 2009b). The *National Security Strategy* of May 2010 also reaffirms Obama's position of keeping the United States visible and deeply engaged in the Western Pacific (The White House 2010).

The dynamics of security regionalism have currently experienced both growing pangs as well as severe pressure to restructure. There is little doubt that the United States, the historical and current hegemon, needs to shift from its historical bilateralism in security and trade relations to a more amenable multilateralism. Shifting from bilateralism to multilateralism over decades in the economic arena, while downgrading hegemony to indispensability in security, would constitute a process that can be termed "gradualism", or a long goodbye to the old order. The United States must accommodate the dominant and rising economic powers of the region and woo them as security partners. The erosion of American hegemony as the region's sole stabilizer has accelerated since the end of the Vietnam War and became a fact of life under the Bush administration. The Obama administration must scale down America's current not-too-subtle profile as hegemon to one of being an indispensable security ally and partner.

The best way to achieve this shift from U.S. "hegemony" to U.S. "indispensability" is through merging the multiple sets of trade and FDI bilateralism with individual Asian and Oceanic (Asia-Pacific) countries gradually. But until the region produces a functioning institutional framework, bilateralism in trade and security must remain. Once economic multilateralism is put in place, security regionalism will evolve from it. The United States, Japan, China, India, Korea, Australia, and Singapore must lead others to build Asia-Pacific security multilateralism. This can be done through strengthening the current role of ASEAN and its subsidiaries such as the ARF and AFTA, while modifying the Six-Party Talks into a permanent forum. The Asian great and middle powers, the United States, and Russia are the logical leaders with high stakes in the region. It will take at least three decades (by 2040) for such an arrangement to come to fruition. Until then, the United States will have a dual role to play: continuing as the current security stabilizer of the region and as the *primus inter pares* in the Asia-Pacific economic system. However, the United States must not hold unchallenged primacy in both Asian international relations and political economy, even if it can. The strategy of voluntary reshaping from hegemony to indispensability must be carefully crafted. The condominium of economic power and security exigencies will be the pathway to Asia-Pacific prosperity and stability that the Obama administration must promote and its successors must embrace. The core of Wilsonian multilateralism for global security and prosperity is *inclusiveness*. Security and prosperity must benefit all, not just some, of the Asia-Pacific region. For this strategy to work, the United States must lend support to ASEAN from the outside, while Singapore and other American partners in the region do their part from the inside.

Given the current trajectory of economic integration, intra-Asian trade will continue to expand for another three decades. This will initially reduce its dependence on the United States and the outside world. Conversely, intra-Asian trade expansion still requires more overseas market access, innovative technology, and fresh capital. By then, the majority of Asian countries will have attained high-income status. This will create greater opportunities for extra regional trading partners and will not necessarily eliminate the U.S. role in regional trade and security, just alter it. But without the convergent strategy of melding the two — sharing the economic benefits of trade and investment along with sharing the burden of security needs — the United States will continue to be challenged by the regional great powers and will even be seen as an intruder and a threat.

In that event, the Asia Pacific will remain a source of instability and insecurity that could eventually undo five decades of building regional economic prosperity. Therefore, the Asia-Pacific condominium is a better alternative for all, despite the view that nothing short of America's complete withdrawal from the Asia Pacific can bring stability to the region (Kang 2003, p. 164). How the United States can modify its role to fit the changing dynamics of Asian security requirements has to be the basis for all American policy responses.

4.14 AMERICAN SECURITY POLICY SINCE NIXON

To reinforce the argument for the gradualism, a bit of recent historical perspective is in order. The major shift in U.S. foreign security policy towards Asia occurred in the summer of 1969. Apollo 11 successfully landed Neil Armstrong and Buzz Aldrin on the moon; they returned home to Planet Earth by splashing down in the Pacific near Guam. Richard Nixon was besieged by the intractable peace negotiations in Paris with the North Vietnamese, who were bent on forcing the United States into unconditional withdrawal. Nixon wanted a simultaneous withdrawal by both sides. The peace negotiations threatened to end the very existence of South Vietnam's Thieu government, but Nixon was willing to gamble on that account. In order to gain the upper hand in the media, Nixon chose to go to Guam to welcome the astronauts home.

There, unbeknown to his staff, including Henry Kissinger, the president announced that there would be a major shift in U.S. foreign security policy towards Asia. Three principles, Nixon said, would reshape his *post-Vietnam* Asian policy. First, mindful of Asian nationalism, the United States would not push a policy that would collide with the aspirations of nationalism. Second, the United States would "shift primary responsibility for Asian security to Asians". Third, the United States would avoid any policy that would drag the country into another war in Asia, which he summarized as "no more Vietnams" (Dallek 2007, pp. 144–45). The press immediately dubbed the pronouncement the "Guam Doctrine". Nowhere in Nixon's statement or in the subsequent consultations with Asian heads of state was there any indication that the United States would reduce its military presence in Southeast Asia, but it was understood as such. It was obvious that the end of the Vietnam War was coming near, and it was assumed that the Americans would pull up stakes and go home afterwards. A Harris Poll conducted in the summer of 1969 showed that 71 per cent of Americans favoured pulling out of Vietnam (Dallek 2007, p. 150). In some quarters of Asian governments, alarm bells went off. A total withdrawal from Vietnam could lead to greater instability in Southeast Asia than the war itself.

By May 1973, Nixon pulled out all U.S. ground, air, and naval forces from South Vietnam, got prisoners of war back from Hanoi, and began to increase security cooperation with Beijing, to the dismay of many countries in Southeast Asia. The importance of the Guam Doctrine for Asia was then and is now that the United States cannot be counted on to play the stabilizer role. Instead, Asia must prepare for and get used to a future with a reduced U.S. role. Who will pick up the slack? This question must be settled by Asians, but the stakes for China, Japan, and India are so high that Southeast Asia, at the crossroads of the Western Pacific and the Indian Ocean, will play a greater role than it has bargained for.

Robert Dallek, a priceless biographer of Nixon and Kissinger, insists that the Guam Doctrine was Nixon's idea, not Kissinger's. In fact, Nixon never discussed it with Kissinger (Dallek 2007, p. 143). The national security adviser elaborated on the three-part doctrine. First, "[T]he United States will keep all its treaty commitments" (meaning it would come to the defence of South Korea, Japan, the Philippines, Thailand, South Vietnam). Curiously, Kissinger left out Australia and New Zealand, with which the United States has had one of its oldest security alliances in the Asia Pacific, namely, ANZUS. Taiwan was not mentioned either. Second,

"We shall provide a shield [of defence] if a nuclear power threatens the freedom of a nation allied with us, or a nation whose survival we consider vital to our security and the security of the region as a whole." Third, "in cases involving other types of aggression we shall furnish military and economic assistance when requested and as appropriate" (Kissinger 1979, pp. 224–25). It was clear that Kissinger doctored or rephrased much of Nixon's original pronouncement as the summer trip around the world wound down. Neither Nixon nor Kissinger even hinted that there would be a unilateral disengagement of the United States by its pulling its military stakes out of Asia. But this has happened. At the height of the Vietnam War, the United States had 500,000 troops in the region. Today, it has fewer than 100,000. The war (a decade of the one in Afghanistan and still going, and six bloody years in Iraq) has taken its toll.

The final version that Kissinger (ever mindful of his proper place in history) crafted states that "of all the achievements of Nixon's first term, I consider the preservation of the sinews of our military strength among the most significant" (Kissinger 1979, p. 225). This statement hardly reflects what happened in 1975, as "the fifth-rate agricultural power" (read North Vietnam) humiliated the United States by forcing it to quit Indochina altogether (Dallek 2007, p. 152). After 1975, Kissinger's worst fear was realized: the credibility of the United States as the guarantor of security for the region plummeted throughout Asia, especially in Southeast Asia.

In Northeast Asia, it was a different story. With Japan, the United States increased security collaboration, joint research and development of weapon systems, and co-production of combat aircraft (USGAO 1989 and 1995). The U.S. collaboration in advanced military technology with Japan has offset the Northeast Asian fear of outright U.S. withdrawal. Successive administrations from Jerry Ford to Bill Clinton have been unsuccessful in shaking off the shame of the Vietnamese withdrawal. But when Jimmy Carter made the decision to pull American forces out of Korea, it inflamed more fear. In the end, the adverse Asian reaction, the U.S. Congress, American public opinion, and the media forced Carter to reverse his earlier decision. Reagan abandoned the draw down plan altogether. Yet the image of America as an unreliable ally in the region has lingered like a bad odour in some countries. Others such as Singapore, Korea, and Japan have sought to keep America militarily engaged in the region. This division still exists today.

In referring to U.S.-Japan relationship, U.S. Ambassador Mike Mansfield, former Democratic majority leader in the Senate and a vocal opponent of the war in Southeast Asia, observed that this is "the most important bilateral relationship in the world, bar none" (Fallows 1994, p. 136). In the late 1970s and through the 1980s, Japan's security strategy was to play second fiddle to the United States by building its military capabilities for "self-defence" against possible small-scale invasions, while leaving large conventional war and nuclear confrontation to the United States. Such dependency has meant that the United States had an obligation to modernize and bolster Japan's self-defence capabilities, and both sides have struggled with updating and modernizing the alliance.

By the time Bill Clinton came to office, U.S. Asian policy had not changed since the Guam Doctrine, but no administration since Nixon's had made any serious effort either to implement the doctrine or lay new security institutional foundations. U.S. economic and security policy towards Asia has lacked cohesion and is still plagued by partisan views. Singapore and Malaysia have taken two extreme positions. China and Japan, lukewarm about the prospect of the U.S.-Australia-Canada hegemony, have thrown many road blocks along the path to trilateral security regionalism, supporting non-binding rules for APEC decisions. Mahathir spent a decade obstructing APEC, especially all initiatives from the "white" countries (Ravenhill 2001, pp. 105, 108–12). Most recently, post-9/11, George W. Bush's incessant push to turn APEC into a security organization (which would have amounted to regionalizing his agenda for a global war on terrorism) during his eight years in office almost wrecked any chances to nurture economic regionalism.

U.S. foreign policy tends to have a split personality, no focus, and no resilience. Obama has addressed the imbroglio forcefully, however. He visited India, Indonesia, South Korea, and Japan in November 2010, following two cancellations. In November 2011, Obama will be hosting an APEC meeting in Honolulu, where he was born and grew up. All in all, the Obama administration has sent a strong message that the United States will remain in the Western Pacific as a player, a tradition that President Andrew Jackson began when the United States signed its first commercial treaty in Asia with Siam in 1832 (Herring 2008, p. 168).

4.15 REGIONALISM FOR OR AGAINST GLOBALIZATION

If the concerns of nation states such as Singapore and the United States include a sound strategy for economic prosperity and continued internal and external stability, the tools for economic prosperity must be accompanied and reinforced by the tools for promoting and defending those interests at home and abroad. The globalization of financing and the regionalization of production have rendered NATO-style security regionalization less effective, if not completely out of date. So far, irregular threats in the region have not de-railed either globalized financing or regionalized production systems, which are fundamental to the growth and prosperity of the Asia Pacific.

At this time, there are two impending concerns. The first is the perception of regional power shifts: China is on a roll, while the United States is haltering. This dynamic has created uncertainty in the security outlook. The traditional role that the United States has assumed since the end of the Second World War as the linchpin of the region's security and stability is stiffly challenged by a rising China. India has responded to this shift by upgrading and modernizing its own military. Japan has been stepping up its rearmament by reconciling itself to the reality that it cannot count on the United States for military support forever. North-South relations in the Korean Peninsula are far from being settled. The recent claim by China for its historic ownership of the South China Sea has not sent an assuring message to its small neighbours ("Don't internationalise", 2010). Tensions in the East China Sea between Japan and China have increased. All in all, the countries in Southeast Asia will need to move quickly to establish a security system that can thwart or, at least, mitigate coming threats and conflicts. It is a daunting task.

The Philippine academic Renato Cruz de Castro argued that his country chose to reduce military dependence on the United States by refusing to renew U.S. base rights at the Subic naval station and Clark airfield in 1991. Part of the naval base was buried under volcanic ashes and lava. By 1992, the United States handed over Clark airfield and left the Philippines. By then, like many ASEAN countries, the Philippines was ready to "address the country's vulnerability to external security threats by veering away from its traditional bilateralism and moving toward multilateralism". Riding on the crest of Asian values and exuding confidence in their future, the ASEAN nations were convinced that the ARF could be counted on to be a substitute for the U.S. role in the region (De Castro, 2004, pp. 154–71). But it did not turn out that way.

Soon after that, China issued an irredentist map of the South China Sea, laying claim to all islands and islets in the Spratly and Paracel groups. The Mischief Reef in the Spratlys has been claimed by Manila, Beijing, and Taiwan. Between 1995 and 1998, China was probing the South China Sea and occupied "a reef deep inside the Philippines" (De Castro, p. 155). Manila hoped the ARF would "assume a more substantial role in fostering regional security cooperation...." It would make American bilateralism "anachronistic" and Manila could count on "a new and an untested ASEAN Regional Forum as an alternative to its bilateral alliance with the United States". Manila considered ASEAN "the most effective, resilient, and universally accepted regional organization providing new initiatives to preserve the environment of peace, prosperity, and cooperation in Southeast Asia and the entire Asia-Pacific" (De Castro, p. 155). The Mischief occupation would demolish Manila's optimism for the ARF.

When China sent in a military force to occupy the reef, that rattled the Philippines, now unprotected by the U.S. military bases. It could have been a test by Beijing to determine the level of response from Manila as well as the United States' reaction. The Philippine Government anticipated strong ASEAN support to counter the Chinese move. None came. The result of this confrontation was the decision for the Philippines to return to the United States for help. After 9/11, the Philippines became the first Asian country to support Bush's campaigns against Afghanistan and then Iraq by reopening Subic and Clark as transit points for the U.S. military. A Visiting Forces Agreement allowed the deployment of a small number of American military advisers to assist in the fight against Muslim insurgency in Mindanao and other islands. The United States also provide military funding to modernize the Philippine armed forces. The moral of this episode is that the ARF was the wrong institution for the expectations of Manila then. How this misunderstanding could have occurred constitutes a topic of investigation in its own right.

Rodolfo C. Severino, a distinguished Filipino diplomat and secretary general of ASEAN (1998–2002), participated in the creation of the ASEAN Regional Forum in 1994. He mentioned that the second meeting of the ARF in Bandar Seri Begawan in August 1995 definitively laid down the architectural foundation and objectives of the entity: (1) confidence building, (2) mechanisms for preventive diplomacy, and (3) conflict resolution. The membership must be approved by ASEAN as well as participants. A country could apply for it through the president of the ARF at the time. The three objectives would evolve in a sequence. De Castro asserted that

China, then a Dialogue partner, blocked any adoption of ARF's role in the South China Sea dispute (De Castro, pp. 154–56). Severino has pointed out that the ASEAN Way culture drove the founding principles of the ARF; hence, such issues as the Taiwan Straits, as well as Aceh, East Timor, Sabah, southern Thailand, and other points of conflict (but not Korea), were considered domestic, culturally internecine, and separatist; thus they were off limits to the ARF (Severino 2009, pp. 16–17).

China did not want any conflict resolution mechanisms built into the ARF but indicated it would support an "elaboration of approaches to conflict" [resolution] and that with the presence of the United States and China, any designing of preventive diplomacy rules would be extremely difficult. The United States encouraged the ARF to become "more operational" and make it a "stronger institution", but Severino rejects flatly the characterization of calling the ARF "a talk shop". Malaysians have a more benign view of the ARF: it has not been hijacked by either China or the United States, a success in itself. Daljit Singh, a fellow at the Institute of Southeast Asian Studies in Singapore, is more cynical: "Do not dismiss the ARF, but do not be seduced by it" (Severino 2009, pp. 128, 130, 133, 135). Some may see this bestriding as opportunistic, but must acknowledge it is a good survival strategy. The Thais have done it for centuries.

The reasonable conclusion on the state of the ARF is that it is a work in progress. Its future shape will depend on how well the great power partners will behave and how well ASEAN can defend its "centrality", or more popularly, the rights of the "driver's seat" in the organization. Perhaps this is a blessing in disguise because ASEAN is not forced to take stand on the region's critical security issues and does not need to take sides, especially between the United States and China. But all can see that the future economic prosperity of Southeast Asia will depend on stability in Northeast Asia, especially the tripartite relationship among the United States, China, and Japan. The spillover effects of a mismanaged security situation in the north could be devastating. At the same time, the ARF cannot miss out on the larger security affairs of the Asia Pacific. It must take both a pro-active and reactive role. For ASEAN, its challenge is, and continues to be, how to remain neutral and fully integrated with the outside world, but not be dominated by either China or the United States. America's interest is to assist ASEAN in retaining its strategic and economic centrality, while China's interest will be to continue to be the dominant force in Southeast Asia.

5

The American Politics of FTAs, Lobbying, and Trade Reforms

Sept 11 does not merely mark the conflict between civilized behaviour and terrorism. It also marks the conflict between globalization and isolationism, between free trade and protectionism.

Goh Chok Tong, Singapore, 13 October 2001

5.1 IPE OF TRADE *AND* SECURITY

The Singaporean mantra that FTAs are not about trade, but about everything else can be rephrased as: FTAs are about domestic reform in the economy and the modernization of security so that a country can be positioned more competitively in the globalized economy and can buy more security from the great powers to defend its own interests at home and abroad. The convergence of economic and security interests have become more imperative than ever in an era of globalized finance and markets, of regionalized investment and production, and of a reconfiguration of security issues after 9/11. The USSFTA is a political expression of the two partners' common desire to meet the new economic and security challenges emanating from rapidly changing global and regional developments in trade and security patterns.

For the past half century, American foreign policy elites have believed that diplomacy and security (the use of force) have been two sides of the same coin. Henry Luce's American Century began with the big bang of the total defeat of fascism and Nazism in Europe and Japan's militarism in East Asia. Core American values such as a free market, open and liberal democracy, the rule of law, social justice, human rights, shared prosperity, security at home and abroad, and world peace, have been promoted through economic diplomacy and security tie-ups. When and where these Wilsonian core values are threatened, the United States has responded with a show of force. This approach has been honoured by every American president since the end of the Second World War and has been supported by bipartisan leaders in Congress. Political leaders educate the American public, which normally comes aboard in support of a policy that promotes American values or the American Creed wherever an opportunity arises. The tradition of bipartisanism that originally forged the convergence of economic and security interests into the bedrock of American foreign policy began to erode in the 1980s and experienced a serious breakdown by the early 1990s.

In that decade, Luce's American Century was replaced by extreme right wing views such as those advocated by the Contract with America in 1994, and the Project for the New American Century in 1998, whose goals were inherited and embraced by George W. Bush. The unfortunate outcome of this shift in policy from bipartisan collaboration to an ideologically extremist and unilateralist approach has been to place economic diplomacy under the giant shadow of excessive security considerations. In part, the events of 9/11 played a larger defining role in this process. But this shift was also the result of the political dominance of right wing interests in American politics, as well as of fringe groups driving the Republican Party's main agenda.

The Clinton administration conceived of the USSFTA in a Wilsonian framework in which the bourgeoning trade relationship between Singapore and the United States would lead to closer security collaboration in Southeast Asia. Such institutional ties could also advance common and shared objectives in the larger international system (Soderberg 2005, p. 98). As in the Europe of the Marshall Plan and then NATO, the sequencing of the U.S. strategy — first identifying common bilateral security interests and then formalizing them in the FTA — was consistent with Washington's foreign policy towards Asia. Also, the choice of bilateralism is consistent with Washington's Asian security policy. The USSFTA remains one of several principal linchpins of America's twenty-first century foreign policy towards

East Asia and has been put forth, incorrectly, as the model to emulate. But the post-9/11 ideological lurch to unilateralism — or the *a la carte* multilateralism of the Bush administration — subordinated the nurturing of economic integration to security interests. Doing so is a mistake. Bush's New American Century, unlike Truman's original American Century (built on the twin pillars of the Marshall Plan and NATO), has tainted the FTA as a political instrument designed to buy security cooperation from Singapore and, in exchange, allow the city state preferential access to the world's largest economy.

The relationship between international political economy *and* security has not been sufficiently explored to formulate a coherent theory in the literature in this area. However, it is the contention of this book that the economic universe and the security universe are intricately joined through a variety of IPE actors (trade, finance, the environment, and development) as well as security goals (transfer of matériel, access to bases, joint naval and air exercises, and weapons interoperability) in three important ways: the *globalization of finance*; and the *regionalization of production* through cross-border foreign direct investment by MNCs for overseas production platforms (which have created a network of corporate regionalism); and *trade liberalization* (importing inputs, assembling them locally, and exporting final products to the world's major markets). These three factors promote a growing number of *bilateral free (preferential) trade agreements* among producers and consumers. As seen in the previous chapters, when Toyota, Sony, Microsoft, IBM, and other advanced technology firms establish a set of production platforms in geographically dispersed locations to produce the cheapest components and parts, then assemble them into finished products in ASEAN or NAFTA, this is corporate regionalism. Together, these multinational corporations have created an additional layer of economic regionalism on the top of the existing political regionalism. This superimposed economic integration must be fostered and protected, and thus creates a need for security regionalism.

On another level, co-production and collaboration in weapons manufacturing (as occurs between Japan and the United States), plus cooperative research (between Singapore and the United States) bring U.S. firms as partners to a variety of economic endeavours in both Japan and Singapore. These are two cases of linking IPE *and* security. They reinforce each other's structure and eventually harmonize their objectives. This convergence often crosses and goes beyond the bilateral confines of the market, shaping and reshaping the regional market and security ties in the process. Conversely, a good bilateral security relationship can lay the groundwork for a bilateral FTA as in the cases of the U.S.-Israel, U.S.-Jordan, U.S.-Oman, U.S.-Morocco, and U.S.-Singapore, and U.S-Korea (the last still pending) agreements. When security relations drive FTAs, or vice versa, embedding the former into the latter is the usual outcome. Existing international relations theories and paradigms do not clearly explain this trend towards convergence.

Theories of the old mercantilism have asserted that the primacy of the state is to generate a trade surplus, which creates the foundation for national wealth, which in turn finances military power. This interlinking of wealth generation and national security has been justified by the need to defend national interests at home and abroad. The theory of the new mercantilism subscribes to many of the old tenets, but it eschews military conquest options and colonialism. Instead, it supports building interstate, regional, and global institutions and regimes that can safeguard trade activities and investment flows.

This approach has been the proven path to national wealth and power. Where a collective security mechanism within a region is not an option, nations opt for bilateral security arrangements with extra regional great powers. Japan is the *prima facie* example of practising this brand of combining IPE and extra-regional security alliances. To the old and new mercantilists, wealth generation is a zero sum game. Country A's gain in trade is Country B's loss, which is absolute. As a trade surplus accumulates over time, Country A will have greater wealth at its disposal to build superior military and naval capabilities, not only for home defence, but also for the promotion and protection of its interests overseas, as well as those of their like-minded partners, wherever they may be. This extra territorial shift in the enlarged national interest embedded in the international political economy has necessitated state participation in the globalization of finance, the regionalization of production, or the bilateralization of trade. This creates the need for a better security strategy for the protection of burgeoning national economic interests within the region and around the globe. The crux of all mercantilist thinking is based on the assumption that wealth and security are closely knitted together. One without the other has no *raison d'être*.

As Wallerstein and others have pointed out, the lifespan of the world-system's core (or hegemon) can be short (Wallerstein 1974; Abernethy

2000; Bernstein 2008). Spanish hegemony lasted for fifty years; the Dutch for eighty years; the British for 150 years, and the United States for sixty years thus far, though now stiffly contested, especially in the Asia Pacific. Each of the historical hegemons set the agenda for the international system for its time. Each also imposed its own national interests as being also the regional or global agenda, and its dominant political economy, values, and systems set the limits of other state and market behaviours. The critical difference between the international system that the Americans have put together in the post-war era and the Spanish, Dutch, and British versions of the earlier centuries, is that the world under American hegemony has experienced both economic growth and the advancement of political democracy. European colonialism did not accomplish either.

In theory, the liberal economic system should have created greater inequalities among countries, but since 1945, this has not been the case under the aegis of American liberal hegemony. Both developed and developing countries have experienced growth. Income distribution in developed countries has become more equitable. Such income equality further legitimizes the political regime of a country, which in turn buttresses open, liberal society values (Nau 1990, pp. 20–25). Developing countries on the whole have been less successful in devising ways to bring about fair income distribution, which in turn has hindered political democratization. The problem of global inequity between post-industrialized and industrializing societies remains, and is a source of global friction and insecurity. Henry Nau argues that inequity emanates from each country's choice to become rich or poor by a mix of sound policies for development, foreign exchange, trade, and investment, which in turn determines the country's trajectory in terms of dependency, interdependency, or integration with the international system (Nau 1990, pp. 18–19). This proposition is similar to the view that each country chooses how and when to develop; in other words, development is what a country wants to make of it (Harrison 1985), or policy is as good as the people who make and implement it (Barro 1996; Petras 2003; H. Chang and Grabel 2004; Fforde 2009). Singapore, Korea, and Taiwan are certainly cases in support of Nau's argument.

A Western model of IPE assumes that there is an inherent *tension* between the state and the market (Balaam and Veseth 1996, pp. 7–8). An Asian model assumes that there is an inherent *harmony* between the state and the market, hence the practice of "the state leads, the market follows". This difference has impacted interstate and regional relations in a starkly contrasting manner. Country A's actions can affect the outcome of Country B's market. Or, the performance of Country A's market can cause Country B to respond with policy measures to take advantage of, or thwart, Country A's initiative. Over time there will be actions, reactions, interactions, and transactions between the states and the markets of Countries A and B. How to take advantage of the IPE of trade, finance, and, therefore, development has become the foundation of a country's economic diplomacy, which in turn will shape and reshape its security objectives. In the ideal Western world, *the market leads, the state follows*. In the ideal Asian world, *the state leads, the market follows*. In theory, the interplay between the state (politics) of Country A and the market (economics) of Country B results in a neat convergence, since both want to be economic winners and both seek interstate and regional peace. This *convergence of economic interests and security goals* is the lubricant of the modern international system for both Western and Asian political economies.

Divergence typically occurs when the economic interests of Country A clash with the political interests of Country B. For instance, B might refuse to welcome A's foreign direct investment into its market. Or, B might engage in unfair trade practices such as subsidizing, dumping, or manipulating exchange rates. When such conflict takes place between two similar income countries, the use of *force* — or more precisely, military power — is not an option. When the divergence occurs between a high-income and a low-income country (that is, there's an asymmetry in development levels), the economic conflict bedevils bilateral security relations, and war cannot be ruled out. This may especially be the case when one partner grows in economic capabilities and military strength faster than the other. As economic asymmetry (whether in terms of trade deficits, external debt, foreign exchange rates, or even energy and environmental policies) widens, differences in security objectives loom larger.

If regionalism or bilateralism is too rigid and ideologically restrictive, opportunities for reconciliation decrease, and conflict will ensue. Mistrust, a lack of transparency in policymaking, and the chauvinistic pursuit of national interests, can add to a miscalculation of each other's intentions. War can also ensue from this situation. A well calibrated nexus between IPE and security can produce material prosperity, regional stability, and the fulfilment of national interests for the partners. To produce good synchronization between the two, a country must possess a political system that can generate consensus, harmonize sectoral differences, and focus on its national aspirations in international relations.

5.2 A PROFILE OF THE U.S. CONGRESS AND U.S. FOREIGN POLICY

Samuel Huntington has a legitimate concern: he fears that the flood of illegal immigrants into the United States has debilitated American power by diluting the country's traditional Anglo-Protestant national identity (Huntington 2004, pp. 29–30, 37). Hispanic groups have condemned Huntington as a racist. Those who have studied historical circumstances that can lead to civilizational clashes may consider Huntington's views a bit excessively driven culturally, but he does have a point. Similarly, Zbigniew Brzezinski has noted that the domination of the WASP (white Anglo-Saxon Protestant) elite in American foreign policy ended with the Vietnam War. That also coincided with the decline of Anglo-American hegemony of world politics. The world of Washington's policymakers when he became the national security adviser to the Carter administration in 1977 was no longer in the hands of the Eastern Establishment (Brzezinski 1983, pp. 43–44).

Whatever the merit of Huntington's argument and the Hispanic community's rebuttal, it is also an undeniable fact that traditional American civic values and commitment are hard to find nowadays: the kind of citizenship that prevailed during World War II no longer exists. In spite of many visible examples of successful Hispanics in America, the group as a whole has not performed as well in schools and professions as other ethnic minorities. An overwhelming majority of Americans are still divided over whether the country should be "race-blind" or "race-conscious" when it comes to social and political policies (Huntington 2004, pp. 157, 232–34). This social and cultural diversity has undoubtedly reshaped American democracy today, and no other institution seems to be more out of step with this reality than the U.S. Congress. The trouble is that Congress makes critical decisions for the well-being of some 300 million Americans by writing race-blind and equality granting laws, but its action is not always an accurate reflection of the social, cultural, and economic realities of American society.

The contrast between the profile of the general public and the political universe tells an interesting story about American reality. The

111ᵗʰ Congress (meeting from 3 January 2009 to 3 January 2011) does not reflect the increasing socio-cultural gulf of ethnic minorities in America, which indirectly underscores the complexity of making coherent foreign policy. People may not accept what Congress adopts. Since, no representative or senator is elected with a majority but a plurality vote, a close election outcome sends a divided message, which often puts the elected officials in a quandary. A nation of 300 million people from every corner of the world is a difficult political stage to direct. One problem is the nature of Congress itself, where 535 members promote their individual constituencies' interests which may clash with a president's agenda, even if they are from the same political party. The first priority of a member of the House of Representatives is to represent his/her district's local interests. Two senators represent the interests of a state, regardless of the size of its population. California's thirty-eight million people are represented by two senators, just like Montana's one million. The president, however, represents the national interest, but cannot afford to ignore local interests. If he does, he will put his agenda at risk. Congress has the power of the purse and can refuse to fund a president's project. The Constitution has made the president and Senate share the power to appoint and confirm the highest administration officials, both civilian and military. Together, the House and the Senate wield enormous power over the president's foreign economic and security policy by virtue of their control of the budget and power to confirm (advise and consent to) nominated officials. In fact, since the end of the Vietnam War, Congress has claimed even more oversight power over the executive branch. This has come about at the expense of the national interest and in defence of sectarian or special interest groups.

When a president is popular in the polls, his power to persuade senators and representatives increases, and he may even ride roughshod over Congress to get his way. When the president's popularity is plummeting, Congress often ignores his requests for funding and appointments. At present, the U.S. Congress is no less pro-free trade than any other in the past ten years, but the economic crisis has sapped much presidential and congressional energy and attention. Obama understands that any undue interruption of trade flows, especially when the American dollar is low, can disrupt his recovery plan. For the first half of his presidency, Obama has been more concerned with the domestic agenda, not because he did not care about foreign economic and security policy, but because he inherited an intractable economic crisis from his predecessor. Thus, a problem that he did not create overtook much of his agenda, time, and efforts.

The age distribution of the members of Congress has also been changing, which has implications for foreign policy. Congress has become more conservative, cautious, and risk averse, as an ageing institution. In the 111th Congress, the average age of senators and representatives was 58.2 years, some twenty-five years older than America's mean age. The average age of senators was 63.1 years, while that of House members was 57 years. The youngest member in the House was twenty-seven years old (Aaron Schock, Republican-Illinois) and the oldest was eight-five (Ralph Hall, Republican-Texas). In the Senate, the oldest member was ninety-one (Robert Byrd, Democrat-West Virginia) and the youngest was forty-seven (Mark Pryor, Democrat-Arkansas) (CRS 2008j, pp. 1–2). In the fall of 2009, Senator Byrd completed his fifty-sixth year in Congress, the longest serving federal legislator in U.S. history.

Ethnically, the members of Congress are overwhelmingly white, but are not always WASPs. Forty-two (roughly 8 per cent of Congress) were African-American (all Democrats); forty-one of these were in the House and one was the senator from Illinois who was appointed to replace Obama after he assumed the presidency. Ninety-five of the 535 in Congress were women, seventy-eight of whom were in the House and seventeen in the Senate, the largest number of female representatives in history. There were twenty-eight Hispanics in the House and three in the Senate. Three sets of Latino brothers and sisters were represented in Congress: the first set, two brothers from Florida (both in the House); the next set, brothers from Colorado (the younger one in the Senate and the older one in the House), and a third set, sisters from California (both in the House). Eleven in the 111th Congress claimed Asian/Pacific Islander/Hawaiian ancestry. There was one Native American member in the House. Twelve members of the House and one senator are foreign born, hailing variously from Canada, Cuba, Japan, Mexico, the Netherlands, Peru, Taiwan, and Vietnam. One member in the House was of Filipino and African-American ancestry. Furthermore, women and ethnic minorities have been represented in the both houses in greater numbers than ever before. Two states, Maine and California, are represented exclusively by women senators. One was the first lady of Maine while another was the mayor of San Francisco. Obama's secretary of state, Hillary Clinton, is a former first lady of Arkansas, a former first lady of the nation, and a former senator. A Hispanic senator from Colorado became Obama's secretary of the interior.

Occupations of the members of Congress are not as diverse as those of the country. Those from the single largest bloc come from the "political class" and were former legislators at the state level: 229 in the House and forty in the Senate. Former staffers of federal and state governments also loom large in Congress: 112 congressional staffers, thirteen White House staffers and fellows, and one pilot of Marine One (the president's helicopter), three state supreme court justices, one federal judge, one ambassador, and one admiral. In addition, the 111th Congress had thirty-eight former mayors, thirteen state governors, ten lieutenant governors, three cabinet secretaries, three carpenters, one waitress, one textile worker, one taxicab driver, one hotel clerk, one toll booth collector, one border patrol officer, one mortician, and one auctioneer, among other mundane occupations (CRS 2008j, p. 2). All of these "formers" add diverse class as well as cultural perspectives to foreign policymaking, the debates on which often become a cacophony.

Educational backgrounds are more cohesive, but elitist as well. Ninety-five per cent of the 111th Congress members had university degrees, while twenty-seven representatives and one senator never went to college. Lawyers predominate in the 111th: 168 House members (38.6 per cent) and fifty-seven senators (57 per cent) were lawyers. Twenty-three House members held doctoral degrees (Ph.D.), but none did in the Senate. No single president can match the experiences and perspectives of the 535 legislators in policymaking. If mobilized and used constructively, the collective wisdom of the members of Congress could add value to U.S. foreign policymaking and implementation. Unfortunately though, this has not been the case. The late Senator Everett Dirkson of Illinois said it well: politicians are only as good as the people who elect them. The quality of citizenship is especially critical in a liberal, open democracy where success depends on well informed voters. Without this input, the democratic system will not work.

Over the last three decades, this diversity of representation has lacerated Congress, however. It has injected harsh partisanism, upheld extreme religious values, and idealized political cannibalism, all of which have contributed to the politicization and collapse of the bipartisan tradition of compromise and respect for different opinions in American politics. This clash of political values has made it difficult for the president to work closely with Congress. At the same time, it has also created greater space for political exploitation by corporations, unions, special interest groups, and lobbyists. Foreign countries now need to hire professional lobbying firms in order to be heard in Washington. The days when ambassadors alone could sway Congress and influence the White House are long gone.

5.3 MONEY POLITICS DEBASING DEMOCRACY

The midterm elections of 2010 were the most expensive in U.S. history, costing taxpayers US$3.98 billion. The total media advertising campaigns ran to another US$4.2 billion. In many cases, these ads were paid for by partisan political groups that had no connections with the candidates they either supported or opposed. The U.S. Chamber of Commerce alone spent US$75 million for such ads. Congressional representatives and senators who ran for re-election collectively raised US$1.2 billion for their campaigns. The three Republican gubernatorial candidates in California, Connecticut, and Florida together spent US$243 million out of their own pockets ("Democrats question" 2010; "Election Spending" 2010; "Media Spending" 2010; "Three GOP candidates" 2010). Only one of the three won (Florida's Rick Scott). On balance, these outlays seem ill advised in light of the fact that over the past seventy-five years, the incumbent president's party has been able to win a majority in the midterm elections only twice. Getting elected to office in the United States costs an enormous amount of money and is having a debasing effect on American citizen democracy.

In the 111th Congress, the average term of service for the House was eleven years, or 5.5 terms, while for the Senate, it was thirteen years, or 2.2 terms. John Dingell (Democrat-Michigan) has served in the House for fifty-three years, having first been elected in 1955; and by the fall of 2009 Robert C. Byrd (Democrat-West Virginia) had served fifty-six years in Congress, the longest continuous tenure in history (CRS 2008j, p. 4). The Federal Election Commission estimated that the 2008 elections cost US$5.3 billion. As of October 2008, the presidential election cost US$1.5 billion and was projected to go up to US$2.4 billion by the time it was over in November. An individual contribution to a candidate (not to a PAC or political action committee) is legally set at US$200. In the 2008 election, at least one million people donated $200 each to Obama's campaign. (Center for Responsive Politics 2008). A single House district can cost a given candidate US$1 million to get re-elected. At this rate, Congressman Dingell would have spent US$25 million for his re-elections, although he would have spent less than a million dollars at the beginning of his career, but more than a million for his recent re-elections.

In 2008, the most expensive congressional campaign ever was conducted in New York's District 20, in which the candidates spent US$11.5 million (having raised US$11.7 million). The ten most expensive elections for the House ranged from US$6.5 million (Georgia's District 13) to US$11.5 million (the said New York district). The most expensive Senate race in history took place in Minnesota and cost US$43 million (the two candidates raised US$46.4 million); the outcome was not resolved until July 2009, some eight months after the election in November 2008. The ten most expensive Senate elections ranged from US$16.1 million (Louisiana) to US$43 million (Minnesota). For the presidential race, Obama raised US$745 million and spent US$730 million. John McCain raised US$368 million, of which he spent US$333 million, not counting the federal election allowance. Obama declined to accept federal funding so that his campaign could exceed the federally set advertising spending limit. For the first time in history, the two major presidential candidates raised over US$1 billion for their campaigns (Center for Responsive Politics 2008). With so much money spent, the re-election rate for incumbents for the past three congressional elections (2004, 2006, and 2008) has been very high: for the House, it was 98, 94, and 94 per cent, respectively; for the Senate, it was 96, 78, and 86 per cent, respectively (Center for Responsive Politics n.d.[c]).

America's foreign policy has struggled to be a faithful reflection of the American Creed (characterized by such features as liberal democracy, open markets, individual freedom, human rights, and the rule of law), as well as a true mirror of the constantly changing nature of American society. As the country emerged as the global economic and military power after 1945, it had the power to cultivate peace and prosperity in the world. The export of the American Creed *at that point in history* became and remained the core principle of U.S. foreign economic and security policy. The events following 11 September 2001 have weakened the Creed's foundations, forcing a president and his team to become more capricious in designing foreign policy in the name of fighting a war on global terrorism. In the process, presidents and cabinets have also come to ignore the grand tradition of bipartisan collaboration that Obama promised during his campaign to restore. This voluntary abandonment of American principles, the embracing of unilateralism in foreign security policy, and the unrestrained use of American military power have turned the world against America (Talbott 2008; Gelb 2009).

Once core values and principles are abandoned as foundations of foreign policy, it becomes problematic to analyse and judge decisions and actions. There is no yardstick against which to measure one's choices anymore. Instead, convenience and prudence at a given moment take over as long-term objectives fall by the wayside. By the 1980s, the core values of Huntington's WASP America had dissipated precipitously. Indeed, over the past three decades, Washington has become politically paralyzed, a prisoner of special interest groups, and a depository of failed and undelivered campaign promises. Unless the president and Congress can show a willingness to give and take, the American political paralysis will persist.

The first lesson in today's American democracy is that money matters. The election of Richard Nixon in 1968 ushered in the era of big money politics and weakened bipartisanism by virtue of the sheer personality of the man. His entire political career was built on the political extremism of virulent anti-communism (Pearlstein 2008, pp. 27–34). In this same partisan atmosphere, Ronald Reagan was elected, and during his eight years, the power of special interest groups grew exponentially, ranging from religious fundamentalists to abortionists and anti-abortionists, major corporations and their trade associations, labour unions, universities and colleges, banks, insurance, and other financial groups, transportation and communications industries, including airlines, truckers, and telephone companies, and health and pharmaceutical sectors. For business and labour groups, a Washington "presence" is a must because the federal government regulates how they operate. For single-issue groups, federal funding can spell the success or failure of their agendas. They want to influence Congress and the president to make regulations favourable to their particular interests. Three groups (the American Medical Association, the Pharmaceutical Manufacturers, and the Hospital Association) spent US$526 million lobbying on health care issues between 1998 and 2009. In America, money makes public policy and carries weight, especially among elected officials. It is not that a president wants to ignore East Asia; rather, it is the nature of American politics that makes it necessary for the president to marshal his resources in order to balance the domestic agenda and foreign policy needs. Often, the president can do neither.

5.4 THE MAKING OF AMERICAN LOBBYISTS

Major corporations hire former senators, congressmen, cabinet and subcabinet officers, and top staffers in Congress and at the White House to be their Washington representatives. John Castellani, president of the Business Roundtable (which "represents 150 chief executives from top U.S. companies"), identifies three qualities for the making of good lobbyists: first, they must be honest brokers for the clients they represent and for the lawmakers they lobby; second, they must know the issues they advocate or oppose; and third, they must know how law-making works and must have access to key members of the committee who hold the power over passing or defeating a given bill (Kisluik 2009). The best lobbyist is a senior staffer who has easy access to, and enjoys a good reputation among, those colleagues who actually write and route bills through Congress. With twenty years of experience on Capitol Hill, a senior staffer can make a better living as a lobbyist. For many, it is a second career. It is not uncommon that former staffers from the Hill will write a draft of legislation for senators and representatives whom they seek to influence. A good lobbyist should have the ability to identify which Republican or Democrat power holders he or she must approach.

The cost of lobbying can run into millions of dollars per year. Between 1999 and 2009, the United States Chamber of Commerce (known outside of the country as the American Chamber of Commerce or "AmCham" for short) and General Motors spent US$477 million and US$103 million respectively in lobbying. Of the twenty top spenders, sixteen shelled out more than US$100 million *each* for a political universe that has about 750 policymakers. The least amount spent from the twenty was US$84.2 million — by the Altria Group. It should be noted that eight of the top twenty have a large presence in Singapore and were active members of the U.S.-Singapore FTA Business Coalition. Their names are highlighted in Table 5.1. Two from this group, ExxonMobil and Boeing, served as co-chairs of the Coalition. The third co-chair was UPS.

Often a firm or a trade association hires a law firm or public relations agency to lobby Congress and the executive departments. Covington & Burling, LLP, a law firm with international offices, had a clientele of 989 in 2008 just for trade issues. That year, the firm grossed US$9.9 million in lobbying revenue (Center for Responsive Politics n.d.[a]). The Center for Responsive Politics, a watchdog organization on political abuses, lists the Government of Singapore, the Ordnance Development & Engineering Co., Singapore Technologies Engineering (plus its two subsidiaries, Singapore Technologies Automotive and Singapore Technologies Telemedia PTE), and the Textile and Fashion Federation of Singapore among Covington &

TABLE 5.1
Top 20 Lobbying Spenders in American Politics, 1998–2009
(US$)

	Lobbying group	Total $ spent		Lobbying group	Total $ spent
1	**US Chamber of Commerce**	$477,005,680	11	**ExxonMobil**	$120,356,942
2	American Medical Association	$204,357,500	12	**Lockheed Martin**	$115,974,103
3	General Electric	$187,239,000	13	Blue Cross/Blue Shield	$115,278,490
4	American Hospital Association	$167,858,661	14	**Boeing**	$106,158,310
5	AARP	$158,772,064	15	Verizon	$104,293,908
6	**Pharmaceutical Manufacturers**	$154,163,400	16	General Motors	$102,771,483
7	*Northrop Grumman*	$129,955,253	17	Southern Company	$98,390,694
8	Edison Electric Institute	$126,045,999	18	Freddie Mac	$96,164,048
9	National Association of Retailers	$124,117,380	19	Ford Motor Co.	$84,319,808
10	*Business Roundtable*	$121,840,000	20	Altria Group	$84,195,000

Source: Center for Responsive Politics 2009.
Highlighted: Companies with operations in Singapore.

Burling's clients (Center for Responsive Politics n.d.[b]). But Covington & Burling's own website lists only Temasek, Neptune, and the Government of Singapore, in its disclosure form as Singapore clients.

In 2008, Temasek Holdings (Private) Limited paid the law firm US$280,000 for trade and foreign investment facilitation (Covington and Burling 2008). Two of the five lawyer-lobbyists working for Temasek were Stuart Eizenstat, a former deputy secretary of the Treasury Department as well as a former undersecretary for Economics, Business and Agricultural Affairs of the State Department, along with Alan Larson, who had also served in the same position as Eizenstat at the State Department. Eizenstat, a Harvard law graduate who worked for the Carter and Clinton administrations, has impeccable credentials as a Washington insider. He has had an even longer association with Singapore: at one time, he represented the Neptune Orient Lines, the government-linked company where Goh Chok Tong's civil service career matured. The report filed by the Covington & Burling lobbyists with the secretary of the Senate showed that the general area of lobbying for the Singaporean clients covered "trade" and "foreign investment issues". The report also referred to having lobbied unnamed members of the House of Representatives, the Senate, and officials at the departments of State, Treasury, and Homeland Security (Covington and Burling 2008).

In addition to the paid lobbying, the Singapore International Foundation sponsored briefing and study tours for congressional members and staff to the city state. For the FTA, Singapore focused on Congress. The Embassy of Singapore hired a "boutique" lobbying firm, Fontheim & Associates, for the purpose. A small firm could pay more attention to a given client than a large one. The Government of Turkey hired a retired assistant secretary of defence in the Republican administration to represent its interest in Washington. In fact, the firm was established by a group of powerful Republican politicians for the sole purpose of promoting Turkish interests and was created with Turkish financing (Weisman 2007, pp. 116–20). Interestingly, two of the lobbyists were closely associated with Israeli interests as well. One became a top deputy to Secretary Donald Rumsfeld at the Department of Defense and was considered the architect of the Iraqi war. Another was a former assistant secretary of defence.

American multinationals in Singapore — led by Boeing, ExxonMobil, and UPS — actively lobbied Congress. Governors of key states came aboard. With bipartisan support for the FTA, the Singapore Caucus came to have support from fifty-six members of the House of Representatives from both sides of the aisle. The Singaporean lobbying arm touched 353 of the 435 House representatives (81 per cent) and 78 of the 100 senators (H. Chang and Grabel 2004, pp. 163–76). This was indeed an impressive achievement for lobbying and has set an unmatched record for influencing Congress.

No specific figure is available for the total number of lobbyists who work in Washington, but a figure somewhere between 10,000 and 12,000 cannot be too far off. They exult in power, lavish gifts, making financial contributions to elections, and moving Congress in the direction they want. In the first three quarters of 2008, 1,460 (Q1, or first quarter), 1,592 (Q2), and 1,082 (Q3) *new* lobbyists registered with the secretary of the Senate and the clerk of the House (USGAO 2009*b*, p. 13).

The first lobbying law was put into force in 1946. The many abuses and perfidy committed by some lobbyists drive Congress to clean its own house from time to time. The Lobbying Disclosure Act of 1995 was found to be loose and unsatisfactory and was amended in 2007 as the Honest Leadership and Open Government (HLOG) Act. The new law requires a quarterly report to be filed with both houses, identifying more clearly the lobbying targets and issues discussed. The report must also disclose lobbying expenses, including any political contribution above US$200. When a lobbyist fails to comply with HLOG rules, the secretary of the Senate and the clerk of the House are required to report this to the U.S. Attorney for the District of Columbia who then brings a criminal or civil charge against the violator. The Government Accountability Office examined 40,169 reports in the first three quarters of 2008, of which 6,048 included "contributions" (typically, money to campaign chests). The report found the majority complying with the lobbying act (USGAO 2009b, p. 18). The report does not include information on who received how much from whom and when, however, that information can be obtained from the Federal Election Commission.

There are at least three reasons for legislators to be willingly lobbied. First, they need to be informed on issues in order to get re-elected. Second, the cost of re-election is so exorbitant that campaign funds must be raised. Lobbyists are an important source of that revenue. Third, well chosen lobbying can directly enhance the interests of the home district of a House representative, or those of a senator's state. Representative Solomon Ortiz of Texas (27th District) is one such example. Singapore Technologies Engineering and Keppel-FELS have been the major investors in his district, which includes the Port of Corpus Christi. Ortiz became co-chair of the Singapore Caucus, which played a major role in getting the FTA approved (Chan 2004, p. 168).

Also, key congressmen and senators as well as chairs and ranking members of committees (the highest ranking member of the minority party) are perennial targets of lobbyists and fellow elected officials. Trade issues are handled by the Finance Committee in the Senate and the Ways and Means Committee in the House. Each has a subcommittee on trade. When the FTA was approved in 2003, the chair and the ranking member on the Senate side came from Iowa and Montana, respectively. In the House, the chair of the Ways and Means Committee came from California and its ranking member from New York. The two senators (Grassley of Iowa and Baucus of Montana) came from agricultural and cattle raising parts of the country, and welcomed an opportunity to open Singapore's food market for their constituents. The House leaders (Thomas and Rangel) represented two of the most international trade-driven states (California and New York, respectively) in the country.

Hence, the FTA received 66 votes in the Senate (31 against) and 237 in the House (197 against). A breakdown of the favourable votes indicates a reflection of the economic ties that each state has with Asia. California, Texas, Washington, New York, Illinois, Oregon, and Louisiana are the top seven traders with Asia in terms of export values, each exceeding US$10 billion or more per annum (see Table 5.2). Given these trade connections, Singapore's enormous lobbying resources, and its skilful negotiators, the FTA was really won long before Congress was asked to approve or reject it. Just to be sure though, the Government of Singapore still invested time and resources in the project and cultivated congressional delegations, caucuses, and staffers.

TABLE 5.2
Top 15 American State Exporters to East Asia, 2008

State	Export $ Value (US$ billion)	Asian Share as % of Total Exports	Per Capita Value of Exports	Exports to Asia as % of State GDP
California	$60.73	41.9%	$1,661	3.4%
Texas	$37.30	19.41%	$1,560	3.5%
Washington	$35.11	52.5%	$5,428	12.5%
New York	$18.07	22.7%	$937	1.6%
Illinois	$13.77	25.77%	$1,072	2%
Oregon	$11.4	58.9%	$3,045	5.9%
Louisiana	$10.93	26.08%	$2,547	4.4%
Massachusetts	$8.24	29.11%	$1,277	2.5%
Florida	$7.48	13.78%	$410	0.7%
Ohio	$7.4	16.26%	$645	1.4%
Pennsylvania	$7.35	21.23%	$591	1.25%
Georgia	$7.16	26.04%	$750	1.6%
North Carolina	$6.73	26.83%	$743	1.7%
New Jersey	$6.68	18.82%	$769	1.5%
Arizona	$5.7	28.88%	$899	2.6%
Total	$244.06			

Source: East-West Center 2008.

5.5 LOBBYING FOR AN FTA

Between March 2001 and June 2003, the House Ways and Means Committee and its Subcommittee on Trade held open hearings on trade issues from business, labour, academic think tanks, and professional trade groups. The salient impression emerging from these testimonies and hearings was that sectoral interests overshadowed larger national interests. This was expected. Often, business and labour take opposite sides on free trade, the former supporting and the latter opposing. This sector-specific view went well with the partisan rhetoric in American politics and in Congress at the time. Lobbyists often cast their support or opposition to a bill in terms of the particular views held by key members of the committee. Business groups in particular are adamant about excluding stringent labour and environmental standards on American trading partners that would only result in higher costs of doing business. This stance will also garner support from anti-labour and anti-environment members. Labour goes out of its way to impose U.S. labour standards on workers in trading partner countries, hoping to improve their lot by linking free trade to better environmental and human rights practices. Adopting these practices would increase the cost of business to foreign competitors, thus levelling the playing field. Environmental NGOs tend to support labour's position (anti-free trade), seek greater benefits for workers displaced by trade, and impose more restrictions on immigration that free trade tends to promote.

Remarks and observations by congressional leaders confirm that they tend to champion the one-sided views of a particular business or labour sector that has supported or will likely push for their re-election. If sectoral interests can be linked to national interests, so much the better. If not, then the tactic is to tie the trade issue to district interests. Job loss and job creation are critical issues. Environmental degradation is another. Ideally, if both local and national interests can benefit from free trade, a representative will support an FTA. Democrats tend to oppose FTAs whereas Republicans wholeheartedly endorse them. This generalization is a bit simplistic, but it is the starting point for lobbyists when they approach committee members.

5.6 FTAs HELPING SMALL BUSINESS

Congressional representatives have always been interested in expanding international market share for small business firms in their districts. To facilitate the process, Congress established a federal interagency, the Trade Promotion Coordinating Committee. It has directed the Export-Import Bank (Ex-Im) to devote a minimum of 20 per cent of its programmes and funding to assist small businesses (USGAO 2009a, p. 4). In his opening statement at the House Subcommittee on Trade, Chairman Phil Crane (Republican from Chicago and author of the chewing gum section in the USSFTA document) made it clear that there were 130 FTAs around the world, of which Europe had twenty-seven and the United States only two.

As a result, American exporters were being discriminated against around the world. Congressman Crane argued that small business firms with fewer than thirty people in particular were hurting. One specific example Crane cited was Automated Food Systems of Duncanville, Texas (even though he was from Chicago), a manufacturer and exporter of food processing equipment with eleven workers. Because the United States had (and still has) no FTA with Brazil, Automated was charged an import duty of 14 per cent on its products. A similar story occurred with Purafil, Inc., a water purification system manufacturer in Atlanta, Georgia. It exported 60 per cent of what its seventy workers produced, but the lack of FTAs with its major international markets (Egypt, Brazil, and Chile) robbed it of its trade advantage. The owner of the company pointed out that the profit or loss of the company (and its ability to keep its workers employed) came down to tariffs. He was forced to pay 14 per cent in Brazil, 13 per cent in Egypt, and 9 per cent in Chile, whereas Canadian and European competitors established a strong duty-free presence in those markets, thanks to their FTAs (USC/H/CWM – Weiler 2003i, pp. 6–7).

Following the tone and pace set by Crane, the president and CEO of the U.S. Chamber of Commerce reinforced the Chicago congressman's position by adding that the United States cannot afford to be left out in the rule-making for global trade and investment. He pointed out that the European Union had 909 bilateral investment treaties, while the United States had only forty-three. The United States was handicapped in trade negotiations because every president since Gerald Ford had track authority, except Clinton. Then he touted the official line of big and small businesses alike: the trade promotion authority (fast track), which George W. Bush was then seeking, should not be "encumbered by extraneous labour and environmental positions" (USC/H/CWM – Donohue 2003a, p. 4). He was not recommending that the committee grant TPA to Bush; rather, he was just making the case that the new TPA should not include pro-labour and/or pro-environment provisions.

Violation of intellectual property rights was another hot button issue. Harold McGraw III, chairman and CEO of McGraw-Hill Companies, pointed out that American companies lost a staggering US$8.7 billion per year worldwide due to piracy. Brazil charged 35 per cent on information technology products and furthermore was a champion of IP infringement, causing the loss of US$920 million in 1999 (USC/H/CWM – McGraw 2003e, pp. 5–6). Samuel L. Maury, president of the Business Roundtable, was far more critical of the lack of U.S. government action and alleged that it has hurt the competitiveness of American companies globally. The EU-Mexico FTA remains virtually silent on agricultural issues as the partners did not wait until proper conditions were in place to sign a comprehensive FTA. They just moved forward with whatever immediate interests dictated, thus going for a partial scope FTA. By contrast, the United States insisted on a comprehensive FTA. The worst part was, according to Maury, that "standing still means falling behind" and that was exactly what the United States had been doing (USC/H/CWM – Maury 2003d, p. 6). The core message of the business community was that the United States could not afford to be left out of the FTA race and must take immediate remedial actions. The first step was to grant trade promotion authority to the president.

When the House committee asked the witnesses about the Jordan FTA, business and labour stated that it was a security-driven agreement with more strategic than commercial value. Annual bilateral trade between Jordan and the United States came to "less than US$300 million"; one witness even said "there is no trade going on" (USC/H/CWM – Tarullo 2003h, pp. 7–9). The U.S. Chamber of Commerce witness and others warned against the potential use of the Jordan FTA as a model for other FTAs. Labour and environmental groups had injected the highest standards into the Jordan FTA with the blessing of the Clinton administration.

Because of the small trade volume, American business was less inclined to object to the stringent labour and environmental rules it contained. Even if Jordan were to enforce them, the economic impact would be minor. Clinton persuaded Goh to replicate the Jordan FTA model for the USSFTA in their November 2000 agreement in Brunei. This secured the support of labour and environmental groups, Clinton and Gore's core constituencies. As in the Jordan FTA, Clinton would have Asian security constituencies and interest groups rallying around the proposed FTA. The Clinton people might have thought that it was easier for the United States to dictate its own terms to a small country in a bilateral rather than multilateral setting. This assumption goes a long way towards explaining why the United States has persisted in bilateral trade and security relationships in the Asia Pacific. In the case of the USSFTA, Singapore was not short-changed.

During the House hearings on the U.S.-Jordan FTA, the Purafil executive warned of the unwise use of trade opportunities with a small country for security reasons, instead of focusing on a larger country, such as Egypt (USC/H/CWM – Tarullo 2003*h*, pp. 8–9). No doubt that Purafil's market in Jordan was probably non-existent compared with its larger Arab neighbours. This firm-driven view was at loggerheads with the Clinton administration's wider perspective of how the Middle East could be secured for peace and stability. Later Bush (son) sought to use the Jordan FTA as a building block for a larger Middle Eastern economic integration scheme.

One of the three co-chairs for the USSFTA Business Coalition, the UPS representative, reinforced the AmCham Singapore presentation. UPS, an American express delivery services (EDS) company, employs some 320,000 workers in the United States alone and handles some 13.3 million pieces of documents and packages daily in 200 countries. In 2003, the EDS industry transported US$11 billion worth of goods between the United States and Singapore. By 2008 this figure grew to US$17 billion. Twenty per cent of the total trade conducted between ASEAN and the United States in 1999 (US$68 billion) was transported by air and handled by an EDS. The UPS representative's projection was optimistic: she believed that the market could grow 20 per cent per year with the USSFTA in place. One UPS demand was that the Singapore Post should not be allowed to receive a "cross-subsidization warrant" in EDS, thereby gaining an unfair competitive advantage (USC/H/CWM – Jackson 2003*b*, pp. 1–3). The UPS official was worried about *unwarranted* competition from a company supported by the Singapore Government and was asking U.S. Congress to remove such an unfair business advantage. Both the Singapore Post and UPS sought to use government intervention to improve their respective playing fields.

The AmCham representative in Singapore, testifying before the Crane committee hearing, also pointed out that the U.S. military had full access to Singapore's military facilities and relied on Singapore's enthusiastic participation in the war on terrorism. It is interesting to observe that a business person cited military ties as a compelling condition for the making of the FTA. Singapore offered both military-strategic and economic value to America and its companies, which needed to be safeguarded by the

FTA (USC/H/CWM – Paulson 2003*f*, pp. 1–4). Linking economics and security in this manner was not unusual in the minds of American and Singaporean business leaders and government officials. It seemed that there was a popular belief that the convergence of IPE and security would benefit business. Both activities were reinforced and have remained deeply embedded in each other's embrace.

The strong support from American businesses for the FTA with Singapore was also mitigated by other factors such as taxes. The average corporate tax rate on a U.S. business at home is 25 per cent, while taxes on overseas income can be as low as 4 per cent. American MNCs do not pay taxes on foreign income until it is repatriated home. A U.S. Government study identifies Singapore as one of six countries with the lowest taxes in the world, while Italy, Japan, Germany, Brazil, and Mexico are considered high rate countries. As much as 40 per cent of all American business activity takes place outside of the country. Finance and insurance have the lowest international presence (19 per cent), followed by manufacturing (36.2 per cent), and wholesale (42.9 per cent) as of 2004 (USGAO 2008*b*, pp. 1–4). When an MNC has five production platforms in five different countries, it can shift income among the affiliates by taking advantage of the higher or lower transaction costs among them. This is one way to lower the tax burden. U.S.-based MNCs located in Singapore and operating throughout ASEAN/AFTA can have advantages that Latin America or Africa (where there is no region-wide free trade entity) cannot offer, thanks to the city state's low tax rates and the tax deferral and credit that the U.S. statute allows. The combination of its low taxes, pro-business government, and geostrategic values, allowed Singapore to reinforce the elements of the convergence model, which was an easy sell to Congress.

The most innovative thinking about the convergence model came from the testimony of the representative of the American Chamber of Commerce in Japan (ACCJ). In addition to being an enthusiastic supporter of the president's trade promotion authority, he considered FTAs to have strategic economic and security values in the wider context of the Asia Pacific. The existing bilateral security relationship between the United States and Japan is a starting point. The ACCJ representative made the point that these two countries can continue to play a leading role by coordinating their foreign *economic and security* interests. One must look at mutually interlocking relationships between international economic interests (or international political economy) and security (the ability to protect one's own military interests *abroad*).

This comprehensive security concept hinges on two complementary parts: (1) the embedded nature of security into trade to bring about the two countries' economic integration; and (2) practices of this new security concept against the backdrop of this wider IPE strategy. I define the concept of security in three broad contexts: *(1) the absence of external and internal threats to a country; (2) a nation's capability to produce and ability to buy security in a globalized and regionalized context; and (3) the effective mobilization of resources under the control of the state and a firm to advance realist and institutionalist goals in a comprehensive way and in a timely fashion.* Charles D. Lake II of the ACCJ seems to support the above definition. When mingled with the latent power and capabilities of Japan and the United States, the above definition resonates greater meaning because it links economic capabilities and security enhancement.

Lake drew the congressional committee's attention to the fact that in 2005 bilateral trade between the United States and East Asia came to US$817 billion and was growing faster than that between the United States and Europe, which stood at US$492 billion. However, he cautioned Congress that the bilateral economic relationship between the United States and Japan was declining as Japan shifted its economic weight towards Asia and, in particular, towards China. Between 2001 and 2005, total Japanese trade with Asian countries went from US$312 billion to US$473 billion, while its trade with America was down from US$193 billion to US$189 billion. The direction of its FDI was also shifting from the United States to East Asia. Japan invested US$14.1 billion in the United States in 2000, but only US$12.1 billion in 2006. A sharp rise in FDI outflows from Japan to elsewhere in Asia was also noticed: from US$2.1 billion in 2000 to US$16.2 billion in 2006, or US$4.1 billion more invested in the region than in the United States (USC/H/CWM [2008?], pp. 1–2).

In light of these statistics, one can raise the concern that the two different economic integration policies that Japan and the United States have been pursuing contain potential pitfalls for both. Japan has proposed an Asia-only East Asian Free Trade Agreement for ASEAN Plus Three, plus Australia, New Zealand, and India. This would amplify Japan's arc of economic influence, thus redefining foundations for future security ties. Tokyo has already signed FTAs with the two Oceanic partners and is in hot pursuit of India for an economic and security partnership. Lake also stated that he suspected that Japanese senior officials favoured the Asia-only approach over the more inclusive proposal by the United States for a Free Trade Area of the Asia Pacific (USC/H/CWM [2008?], p. 2).

In economic terms, Japan's current approach (an Asia-only trading area, plus its bilaterally aggressive pursuit of economic partnership agreements with individual Asian countries) can pay off and would constitute a complementary liberalization, Japanese style. What cannot be done at the ASEAN level is being done bilaterally. But over time, an unarmed Japan cannot defend its vast economic holdings and interests in the Asian landmass and archipelagic locations. Its old historical suspicion of, and power rivalry with China can wreak havoc for Japan's long-term strategic vision. Furthermore, to balance China, Japan will need the United States. Adding India to the mix could strengthen Japan's position. To expand its trade and other economic ties with Asian countries, Japan will have to minimize its military build-up to assure them of its peaceful intentions. These are not easy waters to navigate, even for such a seasoned maritime and mercantilist power as Japan.

Lake's testimony contained an ominous warning for American firms operating in Japan. In spite of historical bad blood and political dissension between Japan and the rest of Asia, economic integration of the region has been moving forward at a faster pace than Washington officials have been willing to admit. With a slow but continuing decline in trade and investment relations between Japan and the United States, a significant change in their security relationship is bound to occur, sooner or later. If the current trend of economic closeness among the Asian countries accelerates, it will be sooner rather than later. In light of these developments, AmCham Japan proposed a new vision for a comprehensive bilateral relationship, built on the common values Japan and the United States share: representative democracy; freedom of speech; an independent media and political parties; the rule of law; a commitment to international institutions; and participation in global and regional peace building and peace keeping.

In business the convergence between Japanese and American practices has been forging ahead: transparency; stakeholders' rights and participation in corporate decision making; accountability; independent regulatory regimes; positive aspects of globalization; opening Japan's financial market and its rule making; and more transparent competition practices, among others. Japan still needs to implement its reform obligations to international organizations. One example is the postal banking system, which remains outside the supervision of the Financial Services Agency and receives special treatment. This is inconsistent with Japan's World Trade Organization (WTO) obligations under the General Agreement on Trade in Services (GATS) (USC/H/CWM [2008?], p. 4). The bilateral differences in business practices still remain, but they are minimized and could be better calibrated now than some three decades ago. Japan and the United States have also built mutual security ties that have endured for half a century and have played an important role in guaranteeing the entire region's stability and, therefore, prosperity. President Obama and Prime Minister Hatoyama were well aware that any substantive change in the U.S.-Japan bilateral relationship could alter the two countries' strategic interests, as well as endanger those of the Asia Pacific.

Meanwhile, Japan's dependency on the Unites States in some areas is growing. The production of Japan's multinationals in the United States often "exceeds 50 per cent of [their] total output" (USC/H/CWM [2008?], p. 2). Such a deepening of ties must be taken advantage of so as to consolidate bilateral economic integration. ACCJ has pointed out that both countries would stand to gain from the further globalization of trade and investment practices. Had the WTO's Doha Round been successfully concluded and implemented, Japan would have added US$401.8 billion to its economy, according to a study by the Government of Japan. For the United States, the gains would have been equally impressive: each American household would increase its income by US$4,500, or a total of an additional US$500 billion for the U.S. economy. ACCJ urged Congress to strengthen U.S.-Japan bilateral economic ties to match the close security relationship they already have.

The real outstanding issue for Japan and the United States is not opening the Japanese domestic market wider, but rather an overall improvement in the current Japanese business environment. Lake proposed "an ambitious 'FTA-plus'" agreement for Japan and the United States to set new heights for a future economic integration agreement in the Asia Pacific. This notion of going beyond a bilateral FTA is intriguing, given the fact that the bilateral economic foundation for Japan and the United States is already there. Japan and the United States need a bold joint initiative to balance the China-led integration with Southeast Asia. Without the fuller participation of Northeast Asia (Japan, Korea, Hong Kong, and Taiwan) the China enterprise will yield limited results.

Furthermore, no one in the Asia Pacific *at the moment*, with a possible exception of Burma, seeks a security umbrella from China, which *at the moment* is not capable of providing the kind of region-wide protection, stability, and peace that the United States has done for the past six decades. Given these drawbacks, the ACCJ proposal for a United States-Japan Economic Integration Agreement makes good sense as an additional cornerstone for the region's material prosperity and security framework. Additionally, if one adds Japan's burden sharing contribution to the U.S. military stationed in the country to this economic project, it leaves little doubt that the United States needs to upgrade and rethink its current foreign economic and security policy towards East Asia (American Chamber of Commerce in Japan 2006). The gateway to twenty-first century economic prosperity and military security in the Asia Pacific is still Japan. The continuing well-being of the USSFTA may just as well impinge upon the evolving but more innovative, deeper, and more comprehensive bilateral relationship between Japan and the United States. The reader should remember that Singapore and Japan have an FTA, or more precisely, an EPA. All three (the United States, Japan, and Singapore) seem to embrace the concept of comprehensive security presented above. This triangular linkage can produce benefits for the region and for signatories down the road.

5.7 THE AFL-CIO AND OXFAM VIEWS ON FTAs

The premier labour group in the world and its most influential NGO often cast their opposition to FTAs. The AFL-CIO's position on FTAs is well known and was discussed earlier. Once the leading power in American politics, organized labour has lost much of its luster and influence as the American economy has ceased to be driven by manufacturing and heavy smoke stack industries. Its membership has declined precipitously in recent decades. It still considers itself a role model for the workers of the world, and the AFL-CIO has a strong ongoing relationship with its counterparts around the world. As such, it reserves for itself the primary role of watchdog over the present and future welfare of working classes. When it comes to the domestic impact of FTAs, AFL-CIO leaders pay particular attention to their potential to cause unemployment in the United States.

Because American lobbying politics make for strange bedfellows, the NGO Oxfam has played a major role in influencing Congress and other political elites on trade issues. When their interests converge (such as on labour and environmental sections of an FTA), organized labour and Oxfam are thrown into a marriage of convenience. In the case of the USSFTA, it must be noted that Oxfam's complaints were broadly conceived and philosophically addressed, and wide ranging: labour and the environment; investment protection and investors' rights to challenge state rules and actions; and intellectual property rights and protection.

Aware of the existing stringent environmental laws and enforcement standards in Singapore, Oxfam had little to say on this matter, except that the USSFTA wording was weak and does not encourage future adoption of more rigorous practices. With respect to labour, Oxfam's chief criticism evolved around the FTA's failure to provide protection for internationally recognized workers' rights and the omission by both parties to "harmonize upwards" or push for higher labour standards (USC/H/CWM – Kripke 2003c). But what Oxfam did not acknowledge was that both parties agreed to keep their labour standards on par with ILO requirements. The difference between the American business community's position and Oxfam's was found in the potential use of the labour provision for human development (Oxfam's concern) and for domestic protectionism (the business community's concern). The Oxfam representative wrote this to President Bush: "Both [the U.S. and Singapore] will not fail to enforce their labour laws in a way that could affect trade. Both also agree to strive to ensure they will not weaken their labour laws in a manner that would affect trade" (Letter from Janisnowski to Bush). At best, this statement constituted lukewarm support for the FTA.

Labour's dissenting views of the Advisory Committee for Trade Policy and Negotiations (ACTPN) were aired by James P. Hoffa, general president of the International Brotherhood of Teamsters. Hoffa's observations were in line with those of the AFL-CIO, as expected. He pointed out that the USSFTA adopted lower labour standards than those found in the Jordan FTA. For instance, the dispute settlement provision exempts the Government of Singapore from being contested when it fails to enforce international (ILO) or U.S. standards. Dispute settlement applies only to the violation of domestic laws. The minimum age for child labourer is twelve years in Singapore, where a public assembly of five people or more requires a police permit, thus inhibiting labour organizing activities. Additional flaws include Singapore's weak guarantee of freedom of association and the right to collective bargaining, as well as a prohibition on public employees' rights to organize.

The Teamsters' leader was aware of the fact that the value of U.S.-Jordan trade was a fraction (US$300 million) of the U.S.-Singapore trade (US$41 billion); hence a weaker labour provision in the USSFTA could have potentially greater stakes and consequences in dispute settlement. Also, Hoffa had a problem with the manner in which disputes are settled. The Singapore FTA, unlike the Jordan FTA, grants a sixty-day period for consultations; if they fail, the provision grants a second chance. Once a violation is proven, there will be a monetary fine, not a trade sanction. The limit of the monetary compensation is capped at US$150 million, and the compensation will go to the general fund of the state to improve the labour standards and practices of the violator country, not to the victims (USTR 2003b, pp. 2–3). This is a reasonable criticism from the labour chieftain whose father had fought and secured greater rights for the working class in the United States. As the result, the American worker is among the most protected species of its kind in the world.

Hoffa's comment on the environment is flat wrong, however. The ACTPN report must have assumed that Singapore has a large natural resources extraction and exploitation industry. "The Teamsters Union is concerned that the definition of 'environment' in the Environment chapter excludes laws or regulations whose primary purpose is managing the commercial harvest or exploitation of natural resources" (USTR 2003b, p. 4). Neither has anyone in the Teamsters Union bothered to tell Hoffa that Singapore has no ongoing commercially harvestable forestry industry or exploitable mineral or hydrocarbon resources. Nor has anyone bothered to tell him that Singapore may be the only country on earth that tags every tree in the country for environmental monitoring. Perhaps Hoffa's comments were coming from the template of phrases that his union and the AFL-CIO chronically pronounce.

On the question of immigration (granting 5,400 visas to Singapore annually) and excessive investors' rights to challenge the state, Hoffa was very much in line with the prevailing views of the AFL-CIO. This was done unilaterally by USTR negotiators without seeking prior approval from the appropriate congressional judiciary committees (USGAO 2004, p. 51). On the visa issues, the Teamsters Union argued that in times of high unemployment, importing more workers would exacerbate the problem at home and that the USTR went beyond its 2002 TPA mandate. Furthermore, the union believed that the investors' rights to challenge state actions could weaken the power of government to direct its own economic development policy and made the case once again that the USTR negotiators overstepped their boundaries (USTR 2003b, pp. 3–6).

It is safe to assume that USTR negotiators were aware of the not-too-subtle hostility of Bush and the Republican Congress towards organized labour, thus reflecting the prevailing pro-business climate in the final draft of the FTA. Under Bush, close USTR and business ties were well known. One deputy trade representative went to work for General Electric (a major investor in Asia) after he left the USTR office (Peterson 2008). Major corporations and Washington lobbyists often choose former congressional or executive branch staffers to work for them after these leave government service. There is no doubt that had the FTA been negotiated under the Clinton administration (especially its first term when the president was eager to get re-elected), the views of labour and environment groups would have received greater attention. The Singaporean negotiators must have been fully aware of these philosophical nuances and know that they could get lenient terms on labour and environment from the Republican administration — a point worth emphasizing. As Lee Kuan Yew pointed out in his memoirs, Singapore has worked better with Republican administrations than Democratic.

Oxfam's overall conclusion about the USSFTA was pessimistic. During the joint USSFTA and U.S.-Chile FTA review, the NGO found it "hard to identify how these agreements will promote the goals of sustainable development and poverty reduction" (USC/H/CWM 2003c). Oxfam must have decided that both Chile and Singapore were typical Third World basket cases, thus misstating that they "suffer extremes of poverty and vulnerability"; hence, its pessimistic prospects for FTA benefits. Like labour unions and other anti-free trade NGOs, Oxfam's understanding of the political economies of the United States' FTA partners is appalling and downright wrong. To advise Congress and the USTR based on incorrect information and assumptions has done more damage than good. More often than not, opposition to FTAs from such NGOs is nothing more than a reflection of their philosophical predisposition; thus they have created a one-size-fits-all position. Their main message to Congress was that the FDI and IP protections written into the Chile and Singapore FTAs are too excessively pro-market. As such, they called for the Singapore FTA not to serve as the template for all future FTAs with developing countries. It is a fair warning. Like any other enterprise, it would be wise for the United States to keep in mind the unique circumstances and peculiar realities of its FTA partners, as well as their relative positions within a given region, instead of blindly copycatting the WTO-plus FTA regimes for all.

5.8 FTA-DRIVEN COMPETITION LAW

In 2004, the Singaporean Parliament debated the proposal for a Competition Act that was first conceived in a subcommittee soon after the USSFTA was signed. The law went into effect in 2005 (CRS 2010). The Ministry of Trade and Industry dispatched a senior minister to the Parliament's Q&A session (MTI 2004). The Competition Act is the first such law for the republic and is broadly conceived. In places, it is a bit too general. The USSFTA spurred the reform of various Singaporean laws in order to comply with the FTA terms, but in reality, such changes were long overdue for the economy in which the state's role has been evolving, retreating from direct ownership of manufacturing and services to one of regulation and asserting greater control in financial services. Also, Singapore was transforming its core economy from electronic manufacturing to a more knowledge-based one in pharmaceuticals, biotechnology, and advanced digital sectors. It also sought to strengthen existing IPR laws by more efficient and systematic enforcement. New regulatory regimes have had to be put in place in order to facilitate this transition and growth. In general, American observers in Singapore reported that the economy has been opening up more space for private sectors and international investors through the years.

The Competition Act (Chapter 50B, enacted in 2004) lays down three areas that specifically address USSFTA concerns: (1) anti-competitive agreements, practices, and business decisions; (2) the creation and abuse of dominant position; and (3) mergers and acquisitions that can reduce competition (CCS n.d.). The draft bill of the Competition Act drew heavily from the Canadian Competition Act, U.K. Competition Law (1998), and U.K. Enterprise Law (2002). The Act covers all commercial and economic activities carried out by foreign, domestic, and "Government or statutory" entities.

This comprehensive act overrides and supersedes exiting rules and regulations by creating the Competition Commission of Singapore. Its single statutory body has brought under its jurisdiction all existing regulatory regimes (sector-specific regulatory bodies still continue) and functions as the administrative court ("powers to investigate, adjudicate, and sanction", Clauses 63 through 69). The commission can recommend policies for the

Trade and Industry minister to carry out, and the minister's decision on matters of competition is *final* (CCS n.d.). To respect the rules and practices of an open market, the law allows a modicum of individual autonomy. For instance, in mergers and acquisitions, firms are required to report to and obtain permission from, the commission, but they are free to consult staff and seek guidance (Clauses 57 and 58). The law will prohibit mergers and acquisitions that will "substantially lessen competition and have no offsetting efficiencies" (Clause 54). It is the commission that will evaluate the case and render its decision.

In reviewing the bill, members of Parliament expressed several concerns. First, parliamentarians questioned whether the very creation of the commission (additional layers of bureaucracy and compliance) would add costs to doing business. Singapore has separate regulatory (statutory) bodies for each sector: telecommunications, utilities (electricity, gas, and water), the media (print, radio, and television), banking, the environment, labour, and so forth. Conflicts of jurisdiction as well as duplication were also concerns. Appeals procedures were not clearly spelled out. Appeals for a sectoral decision normally go to the minister of the relevant agency, whereas those from the commission go to a separate appellate council.

In the event of a telecommunications firm found guilty of violating the Act, for instance, the bill caps the penalty at 10 per cent of the annual revenue. But the current Telecommunications Code limits a penalty to a maximum of S$5 million per case. Clause 83 empowers the District Court to hear a violation case. Under the rules of the District Court, it could impose a fine of S$10,000 or imprisonment for one year. The "quantum" allowing the District Court is capped at S$250,000. Still another controversial section (Clauses 34 and 35) proposed that the Commission would review violations even before the law was enacted. Frivolous and unjustified complaints brought up by uncompetitive rivals for the sake of stalling legitimate mergers and acquisitions (whether among domestic firms, or between Singaporean and foreign firms) could wreak more havoc (CCS n.d.). All these could run up the cost of doing business. These remained legitimate concerns as the Act went into effect.

The most controversial part of the bill dealt with exemption and exclusion clauses for certain industries and sectors. One parliamentarian wilily observed that Singapore started as a socialist economy before it embraced a market friendly approach. The result was that the Government of Singapore is now the largest landowner and has been the richest sector in the economy through its numerous government-linked corporations (GLCs) and statutory bodies. The bill never named names, but it could be deduced that those areas that GLCs and their partners dominated were excluded from competition. The senior minister responded that the ministry's justification was that those entities are already covered by statutes and thus require no additional supervision and coverage.

A member of the subcommittee that produced the bill stated that monopolies themselves should not be condemned because of their dominant market share and market power. But the Competition Act must prohibit wilful predatory use of that power and must safeguard the country from pervasive abuses of the dominant position. Here the unsaid concern was multinational behemoths, GLCs, and statutory bodies, which could stifle competition. Predatory pricing by a private firm or a GLC to keep new entrants out of market, undercutting existing competitors and forcing them into bankruptcy, or favouring pro-government firms must all be strictly banned by the act. Parliamentarians with business backgrounds were keenly concerned with additional red tape, collusion, and the high cost of doing business. Those with legal backgrounds came to question if the act would grant too pervasive and sweeping power to the minister (of Trade and Industry), and if the act contained too many areas that are grey and not specific enough.

Curiously missing in the debates was any discussion of the potential abuse of the Act by the government bureaucracy. It has been commonplace in Europe, the United States, Japan, Korea, and Singapore, as well that regulatory bodies tend to promote and protect their sectoral interests. In the United States, business leaders have taken up positions in the regulatory commissions and agencies with which they had previous dealings. Conversely, former commissioners and senior staffers have accepted prominent positions with industry that they used to regulate.

Such cosy relationships have weakened regulatory integrity and, in some cases, have destroyed the legitimacy of the regulating body. In the summer of 2009, a U.S. House of Representatives committee accused the Securities and Exchange Commission of failing to regulate and supervise the American financial sector. In essence, it blamed the current recession on their negligence. Hours after acrimonious congressional testimony, one senior lawyer on the commission resigned. In Singapore's case, top civil servants are seconded to GLCs and, after the passage of several years, are often brought back into government. Herein lies the problem. This is not to say that Singapore practises bureaucratic nepotism, but the potential abuse of "influence" exists nonetheless. The USTR negotiators, well aware of this subtle nuance, pressed the need for containing the potential abuse of the monopolistic influence that GLCs enjoy, against which U.S. companies could not compete. A compromise was struck by including a special chapter in the USSFTA. That provision is Chapter 12.

Regardless of the merits and deficiencies of the law, it has accomplished two things. First, the traditional business practices of using Chinese clan and linguistic connections, which have created monopolies and monopsonies, are now under pressure. Second, the core of all capitalism and its success depends on building a network of partners and collaborators. The Act prohibits culture- or clan-driven mergers and acquisitions, which are often predatory. In this sense, Singapore has created a law that will promote a secular business environment network (in the sense of non-Chinese clan culture and practices) and that can secure its competitive position in the global economy. Such modernization has yet to occur in any of the other ASEAN countries, and Singapore is blazing a new trail for others to follow.

The U.S. Congressional Research Service reported that between mid-2004 and 2005, the Government of Singapore updated and modernized a slew of laws governing the environment, trademarks, copyrights, and other matters that cover the protection of intellectual property rights. Specifically, the government updated and unveiled vastly improved legislation in the following areas: Trademarks Act, Patents Act, Layout Designs of Integrated Circuits Act, Registered Designs Act, Plant Varieties Protection Act, and Manufacture of Optical Discs Act, the last two being new pieces of law. In 2005, the government also unveiled a Copyright Act (amended) and Broadcasting Act. Additionally, Singapore has signed and ratified a host of new IPR-related agreements and treaties. Singapore also became the home for the World Intellectual Property Organization that seeks to deal with IPR issues emerging from the fast growing economies of the Asia Pacific (CRS 2010, p. 10). Altogether, updating these exiting laws and adopting new higher standards for IPR protection have brought fresh FDI into high-tech and biomedical industries.

5.9 LEGALIZING MONOPOLIES IN THE USSFTA

Chapter 12 of the USSFTA has a long-winded title: "Anticompetitive Business Conduct, Designated Monopolies, and Government Enterprises". In spite of the title, it has not led to the abolition of government monopolies.

The chief concern of the chapter is to prevent or pre-empt potential abuses of monopoly power. In deference to the Singaporean economic system and its long history of state-led and -managed development, Article 12.3.1(a) reads: "Nothing in the Chapter shall be construed to prevent a Party from designating a monopoly", and Article 12.3.2 (a) states: "Nothing in this Chapter shall be construed to prevent a Party from establishing or maintaining a government enterprise" (USTR 2003e).

This stance is hardly consistent with American antimonopoly jurisprudence, going back to the times of Theodore Roosevelt, America's era of trust busting. In these two articles, Singapore has shielded itself from future pressures from the United States to dismantle its GLCs, thus pre-empting all efforts by its trading partner to privatize and acquire them. If the divestment or privatization of GLCs were to occur, it would have to be at Singapore's initiative, at the time of its own choosing, and on its own terms. Thus, in the case of the USSFTA, the U.S. strategy of using FTAs to impose domestic reforms on partners was effectively thwarted. Unlike the case of the U.S. Congress prohibiting China's CNOOC from acquiring Unocal (a California oil company), the United States cannot prevent a Singaporean GLC from merging with or acquiring an American firm. Were a Singaporean GLC to acquire a U.S. company and the American court upholds the deal, this would set an important precedent for the future of American business.

Also of interest in the USSFTA are two different definitions of the term "government enterprise". Article 12.8.6 (a) states: "for the United States, an enterprise owned, or controlled through ownership interests, by that Party'; and (b) states: "for Singapore, an enterprise in which that Party has effective influence". The dichotomy of ownership versus influence goes beyond legal distinctions in a society where clan ties, common ancestral hometowns, and even simple linguistic ties lubricate business deals. One comforting thought is that GLCs are known quantities, but many high officials of the Singapore Government have pointed out that GLCs are operated and run like private firms and often hire talented non-Singaporean managers. This is true. Several high-profile GLC managers are non-Singaporean businessmen and businesswomen, who, therefore, do not have vested local interests or links. Hence, the ownership or financial stake is less of a concern; rather, the concern is that if GLCs function like governmental agencies, will the owner-government influence the operation of GLCs? The Singaporean response is negative. But there is no denying that a ministry or a government board has the power to appoint and remove top officials of GLCs, regardless of nationality or citizenship, and hence can have pervasive, albeit indirect and hidden, influence.

There were several follow-up commitments from the Singaporean side to the USTR, assuring it that GLCs will not impede American firms from penetrating into new markets and expanding existing ones. The same day Prime Minister Goh and President Bush signed the USSFTA (6 May 2003), Minister George Yeo of Trade and Industry wrote to USTR Robert Zoellick reaffirming Singapore's commitment to "reducing its existing stakes in these companies [SingTel and ST Telemedia] to zero". As of 2010, this has not occurred. Zoellick has moved on to the World Bank, and it is not all clear if Obama's USTR Ambassador Ron Kirk (former mayor of Dallas) is interested in pursuing the case. Probably not. Neither has the United States raised the issue during the last four annual reviews. The *Federal Register* makes no mention of it.

This pressuring of Singapore to implement Yeo's promise should have been an issue of philosophical urgency for the pro-business Bush crowd, but in this case, security concerns overrode it. Furthermore, Yeo assured the USTR that "the Singapore Government exercises no control over the commercial policy of SingTel and ST Telemedia" and the government holds no "golden share" to veto their business decisions. The privatization of SingTel began in 1993, and ten years later, the government's holdings in that GLC were reduced to 67.56 per cent. Furthermore, Yeo added that an independent regulatory agency Infocomm Development Authority of Singapore (IDA) has the power to prevent any "anti-competitive behavior" by the two GLCs (Letter from Yeo to Zoellick 2003).

It is not clear if the American side was firmly convinced by the argument and if the Singaporean commitment will yield positive results. My interviews with American business leaders and Singaporean executives in the summer of 2008 demonstrated that the telecommunications market has not yet been opened and that there are still restrictions on access to the underground cable owned by SingTel. American cable television firms report experiencing difficulty in direct marketing of their product. Each year, Singapore has been cited as resisting "reasonable access to leased lines" to American telecom firms (USTR 2005 and 2008). Again, Bush did not take any retaliatory action. Rather, he was more eager to nurture the existing security ties. Also, an American firm cannot sell services to several channels. HBO is seen in Singapore on a single channel owned by a GLC. If one accepts the thesis that Bush's need to get Singapore onboard and keep it committed to the Afghan and Iraqi war efforts was really compelling, it is easy to understand why pro-market Bush wilfully neglected to pursue the issue of GLCs and monopolies. When viewed in this security-couched context, future historians will have little trouble in explaining the security-driven motivations behind the USSFTA.

6

A New Strategic Relationship in the Western Pacific: Asia's Preferences and America's Choices

This is where we engage in much of our commerce. This is a place where the risk of a nuclear arms race threatens the security of the wider world. In the twenty-first century, the national security and economic growth of one country need not come at the expense of another.

Barack Obama, Tokyo, 13 November 2009

6.1 THE EVOLUTION OF AMERICA'S FOREIGN POLICY

Trade and security have been the bedrock of America's foreign policy towards Asia for over two centuries. The grand strategy since the times of George Washington has been the conviction that good commercial relations will lead to good political and security relations with partners. In this sense, America has been a liberal nation-state from the beginning, believing in the value of building commercial relations and institutions, which would in turn foster a good security environment among them. President Washington's sage advice of not getting entangled in the old continent's politics was a quintessential divergence strategy to keep the young republic focused on economic, not military, alliances. Today's young and developing countries would be wise to heed this advice until they become economically and militarily strong enough to withstand sudden changes in international relations. ASEAN's strategy has been exactly that: vigorously pursuing trade relationships with external great powers while gingerly navigating the treacherous waters of their power politics.

Thus the linking of trade and security becomes the nineteenth- and twentieth-century cornerstone for America's foreign policy. A newly industrialized and booming economy gave Theodore Roosevelt and his successors the need and resources to pursue an imperial strategy in the Asia Pacific. Woodrow Wilson expanded the concept in a different mould (liberalism as opposed to Teddy Roosevelt's hard realism), but was unable to implement it due to strong imperialist opposition in Congress. Franklin Delano Roosevelt seized the mantle and secured British support to internationalize it, but did not live to see the United Nations and Bretton Woods institutions come alive. It took nearly a century for the United States to make its presence felt in East Asia, but the outcome of the Second World War defined the way forward for the foreign economic and security policy of each of the greater powers: the victorious (America and Russia), the defeated (Japan), and the resurgent (China and India). The United States ended up deciding the future of Japan and half of Korea while ceding half of Sakhalin Island and all of Kurile to the Soviets, as agreed upon at Yalta.

The sweeping tide of communism in the Asia Pacific was a new variable in American foreign policy. John Lewis Gaddis states that Stalin was less optimistic about the victory of the communists in China's epochal civil war, continuing to deal with the corrupt Nationalists, but Truman had already accepted the prospect of the communist state in Asia (Gaddis 1997, pp. 54–55). The Maoist victory and the deteriorating relationship with Moscow over the future of Europe preconditioned the Truman administration on how to respond to the rapidly changing dynamics of power in Northeast Asia. By 1949, the Americans and Russians were entering the Cold War in Asia. The fall of China that year, the Korean War (1950–53), and the defeat in Vietnam (1975) hardened America's resolve to contain Soviet and Chinese communism in the region, while at the same time Washington was eager to develop a strategic anti-Soviet alliance with Beijing. This has denied the United States opportunities to look *anew* at the region and reshape its foreign policy towards it into a Marshall Plan-like strategy. Overwhelmed by the insecurity created by the recent advances of communism, the United States was too preoccupied with putting out brush fires in the region. In the end, without a grand strategy, the United States failed to prevail in Asia. Secretary of State Dean Acheson ruefully observed that Truman's task after the end of World War II in Asia was "just a bit less formidable than that described in the first chapter of Genesis" (Herring 2008, p. 595).

America has had three broad objectives in Asia, and later the Asia Pacific, over the past six decades. Does FTA, especially the USSFTA fit into these objectives? The short answer is yes, but too little, with some luck, not too late. The first and foremost has been to prevent the rise of a regional great power, or a coalition of states, to rival and oppose America's post-war interests. The second objective has been the establishment and maintenance of peace and stability in the region that could guarantee the freedom of sea lanes for U.S. commercial engagement of Asia. In Europe, the United States was able to fashion a collective military alliance and infuse a massive amount of funds to stiffen Europe's economic and security position. In this venture, a vision of the common values, shared kinship, open liberal democracy, and joint economic prosperity in the North Atlantic world, is the glue that has held Europe and the United States together for six decades. They have something in common to defend and nurture.

No such historical vision has been observable in Asia. Its history could not allow it to collaborate with America's efforts to lay down the first cornerstone for regional economic prosperity and collective security. Not finding a Europe-like environment in Asia, the United States chose to do this on a bilateral basis, creating the U.S.-*centric* "hub and spoke" system of several bilateral security alliances and tie-ups, typical of all interstate political economy relationships forged by disparate partners. The history of the region and, the post-war development of China, Korea, and Indochina in particular, have prevented all attempts at implementing collective approaches to security and trade relationships.

The third U.S. objective has been to contain the expansion of an alternative ideology or philosophy, first international communism, and now radical political Islam. The Truman administration and its successors believed that rich and prosperous countries would share democratic and free market values and would make better allies in the fight against global communism. To this end, the United States has contributed to the economic reconstruction of Japan and to the development of Korea, Taiwan, the Philippines, Thailand, and other states willing to be America's allies and partners. The Korean War hastened Japanese economic reconstruction as did the Vietnamese War for Korea's development. While both wars had salutary effects on the economic growth of Korea and Japan, neither produced a region-*wide* system of trade and security cooperation.

A revision of these traditional U.S. foreign economic and security objectives is more urgent than ever now because there is a growing sentiment among Asians to exclude the United States from the region. These objectives reflect a mix of traditional American interests and Cold War vintage preoccupation. They need to be updated and revised. Of the three existing and proposed economic foundations of the region — the East Asian Economic Community (the ten ASEAN countries Plus Three, identical to Mahathir's original East Asian Economic Group); the East Asian Free Trade Area (an economic side of the sixteen-country East Asia Summit [EAS] consisting of ASEAN Plus Three, Australia, New Zealand, and India, proposed by Japan), and the Asia Pacific Free Trade Area (twenty-one countries from APEC, favoured by Washington) — the United States was excluded from the first two. During August 2010, however, the United States and Russia were invited to join the EAS, the result of quiet behind-the-scenes diplomacy by Singapore.

In the security leg of the architecture, the plan for an ASEAN Security Community excludes the United States while the ASEAN Regional Forum includes it. The Six-party group in Northeast Asia includes the United States but excludes ASEAN members, and at the moment solely focuses on North Korea's nuclear issue. The Bush administration proposed a North East Asia Forum of the five in the Six-Party (less North Korea), while Kissinger called for a more inclusive approach that would include all six parties forming a regional forum. If the trouble spot is North Korea, the exclusion of it hardly makes good sense, unless Bush's intention was to build an anti-Pyongyang group. Obama seems to have no such ideological predisposition to exclude North Korea, Myanmar, and other anti-American states from his inclusive diplomacy (The White House 2010, p. 42).

Asia prefers multilateral approaches to both economic and security integration in the public utterances of political leaders, but many have not resisted bilateral ties with external powers. It is accurate to state that Southeast Asia in particular has preferred a dual track: bilateralism and multilateralism. In September 2010, ASEAN leaders as a group were eager to meet in New York with Obama to test America's resolve, and in late October they met with China's premier in Hanoi to reaffirm the Middle Kingdom's benign diplomacy. At the same time, leaders of several ASEAN countries met one-on-one with their counterparts from Russia, China, Japan, and the United States at the margins of the Hanoi meeting. Bush certainly preferred bilateralism. As late as 2006, the National Security Strategy Statement of the United States called for "a foundation of sound *bilateral* relations with key states in the region" (CRS 2007*a*, p. 7). This Bush policy was construed as, and was, a belated response to China's strategic gains. Meanwhile, the Shanghai Cooperation Organization (SCO), founded in 2001, is an effort to counter and even isolate the United States. China and Russia have led it, and four Central Asian countries (Kazakhstan, Tajikistan, Kyrgyzstan, and Uzbekistan) have joined, with Mongolia, India, Iran, and Pakistan as observers. The outward objective of the SCO is to contain Islamist separatism and terrorism, both being the primary preoccupation of China and Russia, and to evict the United States from Central Asia.

In 2005, the SCO called for the closing of the U.S. Air Force base in Uzbekistan. The Central Asian state signed a status of forces agreement with Washington on 7 October 2001 and allowed the United States to launch "the air campaign against Afghanistan...an hour later". The U.S. criticism of the Uzbeks for human rights violations and the subsequent cutting off of aid in 2004 strained the bilateral relations further. Uzbekistan was the only Central Asian state that supported the U.S. invasion of Iraq a year earlier. There were also disputes over insufficient payments for the use of the air base, and the Uzbeks thought that the United States was slow in coming up with funds to modernize the air strips. The shooting of anti-government protesters in the Uzbek city of Andijon resulted in many deaths, and the U.S. Department of State quickly endorsed an international condemnation and investigation. Uzbek leaders were stunned and may have felt betrayed. In 2005, the Uzbek Government asked Washington to vacate the Karshi-Khanabad (K-2) air base (CRS 2005*c*, pp. 1–5).

The old system of security alone to cement bilateral relationship is not working. To respond to the rise of multiple threats and challenges in the Asia Pacific, the Indian Ocean, and Central Asia, some American policymakers and academics believe that Washington should adopt a new bilateral *cum* multilateral approach to security relations. U.S. security *alone* bilateralism in Central Asia has certainly lost much of its dynamism. The SCO has also displayed its first major objection on a global stage: China and Russia opposed the proposal to enlarge the United Nations (UN) Security Council, which could have allowed Brazil, Germany, India, and/or Japan to have a seat (CRS 2008*b*, pp. 24–25). Russia and China may consider Brazil and India as their partners in building a multilateral bloc known as BRIC (Brazil, Russia, India, and China) to rival and checkmate the United States in international political economy and world politics, but their action on the issue of UN Security Council enlargement told a different story. China and Russia did not hesitate to block the aspirations of Brazil and India to sit at the Security Council table as permanent members.

Frustrated by the lack of firmer grounding of American foreign policy in the Asia Pacific under George W. Bush, the master realist Kissinger made eight recommendations on how to moor America's interests in the region (Kissinger 2001, pp. 160–63). First, the United States must "prevent domination of the continent by any single power". Second, the United States must retain "a superior military" presence in the region against any hegemonic threat. Third, Japan must continue to remain the linchpin of the U.S. alliance in the region. Fourth, the United States must engage India to create a safe and stable order between Singapore and Aden. Fifth, the United States must recognize China as "an indispensable component of a constructive Asian policy". Sixth, the United States must nurture the six-party engagement in North Korea and turn it into a new foundation for regional security. Seventh, the United States must lead others to "prevent or at least limit the further spread of nuclear weapons" in the region. Eighth, the United States must fashion a strategy of equilibrium in a new Asian order "without appearing to dominate", but "with subtlety, persistence, and a firm long-range perspective".

On close examination, none of these Kissinger recommendations is new. Aside from the time that has lapsed between Truman and Obama, during which the conditions of the region obviously and vastly changed, America's overall interests in the Asia Pacific have fundamentally remained the same: remaining militarily engaged; guaranteeing stability; expanding trade and investment interests; promoting liberal democracy throughout the region; and, finally, retaining overall economic and military superiority, or indispensable centrality, in the Asia Pacific. Why are the United States and its key strategic thinkers such as Kissinger treating Asia as if nothing has changed over more than half a century in the Western Pacific? An intriguing question suggests itself: is the world (including East Asia) challenging the United States, as Washington challenged Moscow during the Cold War? Kissinger wisely warns: "A deliberate quest for hegemony is the surest way to destroy the values that made the United States great" (Kissinger 2001, p. 288). The Obama administration should heed this tenet.

Since the opening of China by Nixon-Kissinger initiatives in the early 1970s, and, in particular, since the Deng Xiao Ping's unilateral liberalization in 1978, China should have occupied centre stage in the formulation of America's foreign economic and security policy towards East Asia, as Germany did in the post-WWII years in Europe. America's chief focus on its security and economic policy has been Europe, in spite of the fact that East Asia's economic ties (measured by trade alone) with the United States have eclipsed Europe's since 1980. Yet the United States has remained focused on sustaining the security structure of Western Europe. When the Balkans blew up, the Bush (father) administration's first policy choice was to let Europeans handle the crisis. Secretary of State James Baker used a folksy Texan aphorism to explain why: "We don't have a dog in this fight" (Soderberg 2005, pp. 21–24). Europe, however, proved both unwilling and unable to address the situation in the Balkans.

Thus, by the mid-1990s, the Clinton administration was drawn into the ethnic cleansing war. No amount of the American bombing of military installations and infrastructure in Yugoslavia did the trick, however, until Clinton ordered the bombing of private assets, factories, and other properties held by Milosevic and his claque who then agreed to negotiate (Rothkopf 2008, pp. 87–88). For the Bush (son) administration, the real test of the resilience of the existing European system came when NATO agreed to contribute to the Afghanistan effort to fight global Islamist terrorism. Nevertheless, Germany, France, and others balked at joining the Bush administration in its overthrow of Saddam Hussein.

As the largest economy and most lethal military power in the world, the United States has been appallingly clumsy in mobilizing its imagination and resources to cope with the development of East Asia and the rise of China as the world's aspiring superpower. The Clinton administration considered it a strategic *partner*, while the Bush administration viewed it as a strategic *rival*. This sent, at best, a mixed message to the region: America was abandoning its traditional commitment to Asia. In the past, East Asian countries and the United States have gone through tribulations in their various trade and security bilateral relations since the Truman administration. The difference under George W. Bush was that the United States was slow in acknowledging that the old policy of treating East Asia like a group of Cold War-era client states would not work. The dazzling economic prosperity of the Asian tigers (Korea, Taiwan, Hong Kong, and Singapore) in the 1970s and 1980s, and the equally impressive economic achievements of the second-generation tigers (Malaysia, Thailand,

Indonesia, and China) have injected a huge reservoir of self-confidence and even nationalistic hubris in their international relations, spurred a spirit of competitiveness, and even mounted challenges to America's paternalism. Japan and Korea are cases in point.

The Europeans have reconciled with Germany, taken it into their fold of security and economic architectures, and assigned Berlin a leadership role. For the last four decades, a repentant Germany and a forgiving France have been willing to bury the past and have provided new continental leadership in condominium which effectively replaced America as the anchor of a peaceful and prosperous Europe before the end of the Cold War. Europe's most advanced and largest economy has curbed its desire to be a new military power, thus successfully reducing the fear of German militarism among Europeans. Instead, it has focused on an economic growth and expansion strategy by investing throughout Europe. German firms, like their Japanese counterparts in Southeast Asia, reign in Eastern and Central Europe, the Iberian Peninsula, and now energy-rich Russia. Even so, Germany with strong support from France, has not been able to replace the United States in the North Atlantic security system.

In East Asia, Japan, China, and Korea are still endeavouring to reconcile their past and present differences, and, in particular, Japan's stubborn refusal to recant has kept East Asia from forging a more enduring home-grown cohesion and stability in the region. Although China has the bulk — money, market, and military might — it is no Germany. Neither China nor Korea has been willing to grant Japan remission. In the absence of clear and uncontested indigenous leadership and vision, America has filled the vacuum. But some six decades later, with the booming Asian economy, self-confidence, and its renewed historical awareness, the Asians should take more responsibility for their own security. The time has come for the United States to rethink and reorder its grand strategy.

6.2 CHINA AS REGIONAL SUPERPOWER

What Kissinger and his successors at the Department of State have loathed most is that they have had to deal with regional changes around the world over which the United States has not presided or has little control. China sees itself as an unfulfilled superpower and commensurate with its size, human resources, growing economy, and history — the rightful heir to the mantle of regional leadership that Japan has usurped by default for almost a century. Right or wrongly, China's neighbours have accepted the huge market as the future El Dorado, capable of replacing those of Japan and the United States combined. This realignment of trade relationships calls for different security landscaping.

The decline of the United States, whether real or perceived, will create a vacuum in the Asia Pacific that cannot be filled by Japan or Korea or India. Russia is a potential candidate, but unlike the United States, it is still a Euro-centric state and, more importantly, it has no history of imparting visionary ideas and ideals that are attractive to Asians. Like China, the foremost preoccupation of Russia is to protect its own interests in the Asia Pacific. India has a limited historical presence in Northeast Asia. Indonesia could become a hegemon, but only in Southeast Asia. The cultural divide between insular and continental Southeast Asia is vast and will persist. This leaves China as the sole heir of regional leadership. The United States would be making a monumental error if it were to block what the Chinese view as their rightful path. Instead, the United States should help reconfigure the region — beginning with Japan and Korea, then with ASEAN — so that the rise of China will be both peaceful and measured. This soft landing is what the United States must target.

Another possible scenario is that China is the sole candidate to inherit the Japanese mantle in regional economic leadership, as well as America's seat in the regional security arena. Malaysia, Thailand, Korea, the Philippines, and Indonesia have begun to hedge or balance China against Japan, China against the United States, and China against India. In all these balancing scenarios, China remains central. But no Southeast Asian nation has proposed or volunteered to dismantle the U.S.-Japan, U.S.-Korea, or U.S.-Australian alliances, or any of the numerous bilateral security partnerships to hasten the rise of China. The countries which have not had a good relationship with China in the past are suspicious and even unwilling to accept it as America's replacement. China's support of post-war communist insurgency throughout Southeast Asia to balance the U.S. presence has been completely withdrawn and abandoned.

In its place though, China has mounted a highly effective charm offensive in resolving old disputes peacefully and opening its market to recalcitrant neighbours. Its foremost concern is to make Southeast Asian small neighbours feel secure and comfortable in dealing with Beijing. Territorial conflicts have been negotiated, not resolved, in the South China Sea. Laos, Cambodia, Myanmar, and North Korea could not do without

China's trade and aid. Vietnam has had a thousand years of a turbulent relationship with China and is for the time being treated by Beijing with generosity and amity little known in their tormented history. Washington's inattention to its East Asian policy and the Bush-Cheney obsession with Iraq and Afghanistan over the past decade have given China an unprecedented free hand to expand and consolidate its position throughout the region, while exposing America's allies and leaving its partners unattended and to their own devices. The unfortunate outcome was that the United States, under George W. Bush, was unable to offer a vision and soft power diplomacy that could match China's.

The Obama administration should learn from America's own role in the history of the Atlantic. When Europe and America sought to prevent the rise of Prussia/Germany as the continent's dominant power, it resulted in war. When England and France sought to contain German Nazism, it provoked another war. After 1945, when the United States and Western Europe accommodated the rising West Germany, giving it the mantle of Europe's leadership and turning it into a bulwark of continental security, the outcome was more felicitous. Perhaps there is a lesson to be learnt from this *managed* rise of Germany. A peaceful future, therefore, is not the sole issue in the bilateral behaviours and responses between China and the United States. If the European lesson is valid, much of the burden of accommodating China has come from *within*, that is, from other key players of the region — Indonesia, Vietnam, Japan, India, and Australia — as much as from the United States. A second pivotal question is: can China respond as West Germany and then a resurgent united Germany did by (a) abandoning its own military ambitions; (b) being willing to use its economic wealth to build up poor and less fortunate parts of the Asia Pacific; and (c) concurrently allowing an external great power to serve as the stabilizer of regional power?

China's eventual rise as the Indian and Pacific Ocean zone's premier power notwithstanding, many have questioned if the rise of China as the world's leader is as inevitable as its advocates would have us believe. From a Goldman Sachs forecast to such best-sellers as *The New Asian Hemisphere* (Mahbubani 2008) and *The Second World* (Khanna 2008), many opinion makers are unabashedly pro-China, predicting that within the foreseeable future (twenty-five to thirty-five years), China will overtake the United States in both economic and military power. A Goldman Sachs study predicts that China's economy will be larger than everyone else's in the world by 2016, and will surpass the United States' by 2041. India's GDP will be larger than Japan's by 2032, and the combined economic weight of BRIC will be greater than the G-6 (the United States, Japan, Germany, France, the United Kingdom, and Italy) (Goldman Sachs 2003, p. 3).

A future forecast exercise by the United States National Intelligence Council supports the Goldman Sachs study: by 2025, it states, China will be the second largest economy after the United States. It concludes: "By 2025, the United States will find itself in the position of being one of a number of important actors on the world stage, albeit the most powerful one" (USNIC 2008, pp. 7, 29). The report omits any mention of how this economic multipolarism will affect security relationships around the world. And nothing was mentioned in the report about China's moral authority and its grand vision for the world.

Pro-China arguments for superpowerdom, based on excessive *economism*, have been persuasively countered by others who hold that the current world order is dominated by the United States, the European Union, and Japan (that is, the G-7) and cannot be easily replaced by BRIC or any given Asian country. While China's GDP of US$3.3 trillion (2007) will double to US$6.6 trillion by 2015 and then double again to US$13.2 trillion by 2025, the United States will remain the world's economic behemoth with a US$28 trillion GDP (Joffe 2009, pp. 21–35). These doubting Thomases, who are not sanguine about China's rise, cite social, cultural, environmental, and even demographic constraints (all-consuming domestic issues) that can hold China back from claiming a hegemonic mantle, a sort of revenge of Confucian values. For instance, Bill Emmott of *The Economist* argues that the weight of China's domestic problems and ecological degradation could wreak serious havoc before the consolidation of its superpowerdom. He does not see the tense bilateral relations between China and Japan abating any time soon. When China and India reach the level of Japan's development, pollution alone will destroy the planet (Emmott 2008, pp. 106, 175).

And Minxi Pei is even less optimistic: according to his calculations, it will take China forty-seven years to reach the income level of today's average American (US$48,000), seventy-seven years for the average Asian to do so, and 123 years for Indians to reach this level. He even doubts that China can dominate Asia, although Pei readily admits that China would overtake Japan in 2009 as Asia's largest economy and the strongest regional military power. Domestic constraints such as a secession-minded insurrection in the west (30 per cent of China's territory), the persistence of one-party rule, and the question of Taiwan's status, all of which absorb much of China's military attention and resources, can effectively stall its efforts to consolidate its pre-eminence in East Asia, not to mention potential resistance from its neighbours — Russia in the north, India in the west, and Japan in the east (Pei 2009).

Between these two extreme forecasts, much of whose assessments are based on hypothetical scenarios, econometric calculations, and human assumptions, some degree of truth can be found: China is an unstoppable juggernaut with gigantic domestic problems both man-made and nature-endowed that no outside power can solve. How Asia will respond to it will depend on how future relations between the United States and ASEAN, the United States and Japan, and the United States and India will unfold. ASEAN, Japan, and India each offer different endowments that the United States can explore and that China can fear.

6.3 KOREA'S ASPIRATIONS AS AMERICA'S EQUAL SECURITY PARTNER

Even Korea and Japan, the two staunchest Asian allies of the United States, have been seeking to restructure their security relationships, in part to meet the changing political environment at home and commensurate with their growing economic weight in the regional and global arena. Since the mid-1980s, Korea and the United States see differences in many issues. First, Korea would like to pull out its armed forces under U.S. command in future wars. In peace time, Korea retains full command. The United States has agreed to end the control over the Korean armed forces by 2012 and further reduce its forces by drawing down from 30,000 to 25,000.

Also, President Roh Moo-hyun (2003–08) objected to aspects of the U.S. Strategic Flexibility Policy that would allow Washington to redeploy small but globally mobile forces stationed in Korea, to crisis points wherever in the world. Roh's position was that if Korea has no dog in the fight, it should have the right to "veto such deployments" of the American forces stationed in, and partially paid for by, Korea. In 2006, Korea refused to join the U.S. proposed Proliferation Security Initiative (CRS 2007a, pp. 21–22). This is a serious divergence of global strategy between the two allies. It goes beyond a show of nationalism and flaunting sovereignty. Roh and his supporters did not see the bilateral alliance as unalterable. In early 2010, as the North-South relations became tense and especially after the sinking of the *Cheonan* in May, Seoul requested and Washington agree to postpone the handover of the command until 2015 ("U.S. Presence" 2010).

Korea's perception of China and Japan is quite different as well. The refortified defence ties between the United States and Japan make Seoul uncomfortable for historical and geopolitical reasons. In one recent poll, 53 per cent of the Koreans surveyed believed China is taking up a constructive role in guaranteeing regional peace (CRS 2007a, p. 21). Then there is the Korean free trade agreement issue. Already contentious as it is, the Korea-U.S. (KORUS) FTA proposal has been held up in Congress for three years and still lacks approval as of March 2011. At times, South Korea has behaved like a mediator, not a stakeholder, in the Six-Party talks and hence has pursued on its own account the engagement of North Korea (the Sun Shine policy of Kim Dae Jung and his successor Roh Moo-hyun's Peace and Prosperity Policy). This irked Americans and Korea's unilateral action did not go down well with Washington (CRS 2007b, p. 21; CRS 2008g, p. 13).

The Koreans took offence to the KORUS-FTA being delayed, not just because of Bush's inattention, but also as a slight to an important security ally in the U.S.'s efforts in Afghanistan and Iraq. Korea is one of the three remaining Asian allies and partners with a military presence in both theatres. Singapore and Japan are the other two. All three are high-income countries, two of which have signed FTAs with the United States, and one of which is virtually integrated economically with many sectors in the U.S. economy. Korea's attitudes are similar to key European allies who seek equal treatment, but see the hubris of United States as *passé* and even repugnant to their regional and global interests.

6.4 JAPAN'S NEW ASIAN SECURITY POLICY

The sweeping electoral victory of the Democratic Party of Japan (DPJ) and the ascension of Yukio Hatoyama (a Stanford graduate) to premiership in August 2009 gave Washington a pause. The DPJ government stated that, come January 2010, it would not renew the U.S. Navy's right to refuel its vessels in Japan, possibly a prelude to fundamental changes in the security relationship between the two nations (White House 2009a). The bilateral relationship has been under significant pressure because of the rise of China. Japan is uncertain about future responses of a more economically prosperous and militarily assertive China, given Japan's wartime indiscretions. In spite of all the predictions by wise pundits that China will surpass Japan in GDP and trade at anytime, it is doubtful that China could offer the kinds of superior technology that often go with foreign direct investments from Japan to other Asian countries, or could match Japan's vision for shared commonweal. Singapore and Korea definitely would not expect massive technology transfers from China to boost their economies. Indonesia and the Philippines cannot expect China to implement the kinds of community development projects that Japan has financed.

The two countries have followed a different vision of development. China has been Japan's competing bidder for raw materials in Southeast Asia (as well as elsewhere) and thus will hardly co-opt Japan to fashion a common strategic partnership in regional development. Countries in the region have encouraged this competition, or bidding war, to maximize their bargaining power and balancing position. There are eighty-nine U.S. military facilities and 53,000 troops stationed in Japan, with Okinawa carrying the heaviest burden, hosting as it does 18,000 marines, sailors, and airmen, and thirty-nine bases in an area about the size of Los Angeles County. One estimate shows that 20 per cent of Okinawa's prime agricultural land is occupied by the bases; in the 1960s, there were as many as 117 bases. The United States military controlled twenty-nine zones in the sea and fifteen air spaces above Okinawa's Ryukyu island chains (Johnson 2000, pp. 36–37). Okinawa is basically a colony and an occupied country.

Aside from the physical burden that Okinawa has been asked to carry, Japan has been paying more than Germany in terms of a burden-sharing contribution to the U.S. military stationed in the country. Since the mid-1990s, Japan has been contributing US$5 billion annually (Table 6.1). The end of the Cold War and the collapse of the Soviet Union, which removed an important source of threat to Japan in the north and east, increased popular demand for a reduction, or even the outright closing of the U.S. bases and removal of their personnel. Those who have lived near the American military bases in the Philippines, Korea, Japan, Vietnam, and Thailand could testify that the social and sociological consequences of the presence of a base are not always positive to either the occupiers or the occupied. The subculture tends to be sleazy and even creates a peculiar form of poverty, culturally, economically, and psychologically.

Combat Capabilities and Burden Sharing by 10 of America's 27 NATO and non-NATO Allies and Partners, 2003 (US$)

Country	Defence Spending in US$ as % of 27 Allies	Ground Forces Combat Capability[a] (of 27 allies and partners)	Naval Combat Capability[b] (of 27 allies and partners)	Aircraft Combat Capability[c] (of 27 allies and partners)	US$ of Burden Share and as % of Total Cost of US Forces Stationed[4]
1 United States	$383.72bn (54.36%)	37.84% (1/27)	56.72% (1/27)	51.05% (1/27)	n.a.
2 France	$45.08bn (6.43%)	4.56% (4/27)	4.56% (4/27)	5.03% (3/27)	n.a.
3 United Kingdom	$42.43bn (6.06%)	6.46% (3/27)	6.46% (3/27)	4.40% (4/27)	$228m (27%)
4 Japan	$41.67bn (5.96%)	3.60% (7/27)	7.80% (2/27)	4.20% (5/27)	$4.411bn (75%)
5 Germany	$34.67bn (4.95%)	8.0% (3/27)	2.07% (11/27)	5.41% (2/27)	$1.564bn (33%)
6 Italy	$27.38bn (3.91%)	1.70% (14/27)	2.67% (6/27)	2.51% (10/27)	$367m (41%)
7 Saudi Arabia	$22.22bn (3.17%)	2.57% (10/27)	0.88% (14/27)	3.61% (8/27)	$53m (65%)
8 South Korea	$14.64bn (2.09%)	10.28% (2/27)	2.32% (7/27)	3.86% (7/27)	$843m (40%)
9 Turkey	$11.56bn (1.65%)	6.49% (4/27)	2.81% (5/27)	4.11% (6/27)	$117m (54%)
10 Canada	$10.02bn (1.43%)	0.44% (23/27)	2.20% (9/27)	1.26% (15/27)	n.a.

Source: USDoD, 2004.

[a] Ground combat capability includes major combat systems, tanks, artillery, attack helicopters.

[b] Naval combat capability includes aircraft carriers, submarines, principal surface combatants (cruisers, destroyers, frigates), mine layers, patrol combatant ships, strike and defence category.

[c] Aircraft combat capability includes fixed wing combat aircraft (of the air force, navy, and the Marines), fighter-interceptors, fighter-bombers, conventional bombers, tactical fighters, reconnaissance aircraft, combat-capable trainers, electronic warfare aircraft, transports, air-to-air refuelling aircraft, support or special mission aircraft.

[d] Contributions are "direct" and "indirect". Direct contributions include rents on privately owned properties and facilities, utilities, and vicinity improvements; the indirect contributions include forgone rents and revenues, rents on government owned properties and facilities, tax concessions, and customs duties waived.

For instance, one September evening in 1995, two U.S. marines and one sailor decided to rape a Japanese girl "just for fun". The Commander of the U.S. Pacific forces, Admiral Richard C. Macke, commented: "I think that [the rape] was absolutely stupid. For the price they paid to rent the car, they could have had a girl" (Johnson 2000, p. 35). This insensitive remark cost him the PACOM job. Clinton swiftly relieved and retired the admiral unceremoniously, but neither an official enquiry nor a congressional uproar took place thereafter. This callus handling of the case led one prominent American political scientist and Japan expert to observe that Okinawa is America's last colony in Asia (Johnson 2000, p. 35). At the time, it seemed that the United States could do whatever it wanted there and get away with it. Those days are now gone though, not because of Japan's insistence, but because of the rise of China and the economic prosperity in the region that makes it less and less dependent on American help. The aggrieved Okinawans and outraged Japanese have taken notice of the changing dynamics of the East Asian security landscape. Hatoyama's 2009 campaign pledge to remove the Marine airbase of Futenma from Okinawa had to be abandoned a year later, and the prime minister had to resign. His successor compromised by reverting to the original base relocation plan ("Japan's PM announces" 2010).

The United States has agreed to remove 8,000 military personnel from the island to Guam by 2014. The total cost of the relocation to Guam is US$10.27 billion, of which Japan has agreed to contribute US$6.09 billion, or 59 per cent (CRS 2008f, p. 3). This is a *prima facie* example of buying security and a case of security being embedded in an economic relationship. The new thinking is that the cost to the United States of anti-Americanism cancels out whatever value a well thought-out U.S. policy could generate, a point worth remembering in the implementation of U.S. soft power diplomacy. In this case, keeping Japan on the side of the United States at all cost outweighs holding on to the military bases. All in all, the United States has drawn down from a height of 108,774 troops in Asia in 2000, to 82,741 in 2005 (CRS 2007a, p. 13). At one time, the United States stationed 100,000 troops each in Europe and Asia, respectively. To implement the surge in Iraq in 2007 and 2008, both regions saw a reduction of U.S. forces to a little over 80,000 each.

Japan's chief security concerns can be divided into two parts: economic and military. Some policy analysts are convinced that Japan would like the United States to continue to provide an overarching nuclear umbrella for Japan and America's Asian allies while Japan is allowed to exercise its leadership in the regional economy, an arrangement that creates a neat division of labour in the Asian regional architecture in which each country has a distinct role. Japan needs to bury its ugly past with its neighbours first though, before any policy change can be made and accepted in the security arena. Moreover, arming itself too fast could set off alarm bells and aggravate painful memories.

China has skilfully taken advantage of this Japanese guilt complex by extracting huge sums of aid (formally not called war reparations) and has done so on more than one occasion. In addition, the Flying Geese model of the regional economic architecture cannot be easily converted into a security arrangement without the head goose being the major military linchpin. Kissinger argues that Japan should stick to its economic store and leave security concerns to the United States (Kissinger 2001, pp. 118–25). Moreover, some of the geese that used to follow Japan have waffled and begun to divert their flight path towards China. Japan seeks to accommodate China and could even consider conceding a leadership role to the Middle Kingdom without completely kow-towing to the centre of gravity. If this becomes the case, Japan needs to decide how far it is willing to go. Its decision will then have an impact on America's security policy for the region.

Japan has been feeling militarily naked, thanks to Article 9 of its Constitution and its waning but still popular pacifism. The prevailing view has been that it was Japanese leaders who sought to include the war renunciation clause, not the Americans who oversaw the creation of the Constitution. MacArthur gave credit to Japan's post-war prime minister, Kijuro Shidehara, for Article 9. But this view has recently been challenged. Revisionist scholarship indicates that the original Japanese Constitution writing committee was blamed for supporting an unaltered role of the emperor, and an international uproar persuaded MacArthur to disband the committee. He then created another committee under his command to write the Constitution, but this time in full consultation with Japanese leaders. His original instructions, known as the MacArthur Notes, included the complete abolition of "war as a sovereign right of the nation...as an instrumentality for settling its disputes and even for preserving its security". In the final draft, the part addressing the abandonment of the use of force for self-defence was left out, against the American Shogun's draconian instructions (Tsuchiyama 2007, pp. 50–53).

This revisionism might explain why Koizumi and Abe attempted to revise Article 9 in order to modernize Japan's military capabilities and even expand them, with or without the help of the United States. The first step was the creation of the Ministry of Defence in 2006. But the premature retirement of Koizumi and the unexpected fall of Abe have disrupted the process. The prime minister who succeeded Abe was said to be lukewarm about the constitutional revision, although poll after poll in the 1990s demonstrated that the majority of the Japanese public favoured the move (Tsuchiyama 2007, p. 67). For sure, Japan has not abandoned the plan to become militarily more "normal". The events of 9/11 and its aftermath gave Japan an opportunity to beef up its security role in line with new global security challenges. In 2006, the United States and Japan fortified their mutual security agreement, going beyond its previous limits, creating new military-to-military cooperation, and heightening Japan's role in the Indian Ocean (Tsuchiyama 2007, pp. 70–71). That worries Korea in particular as well as China and some countries in Southeast Asia.

In 1996, when China threatened Taiwan with testing missiles in the Taiwan Straits, Japan supported the United States and committed to providing the United States with logistical support. Until 1972, the United States administered the nearby Senkaku islands (Daioyu in Chinese) as part of the Ryukyu islands, but then turned its jurisdiction over to Japan when Okinawa reverted to Japanese sovereignty. Ever since then, Japan and China have had conflicting claims over the islands in the East China Sea. The discovery of hydrocarbon resources (natural gas, and possibly some oil) has intensified their respective claims. Both the Clinton and Bush administrations supported Japan's position. In September 2005, China dispatched its ships to strengthen its claim. Japan countered with its coastguard ships. It is the stated position of Washington that the protection of Senkakus falls under the U.S.-Japan Security Treaty (CRS 2008f, p. 5).

In the summer of 2010, the Japanese Coast Guard detained a Chinese fishing vessel that had rammed into two Japanese cutters. The crew was released, but the Japanese authorities held the captain and ship for months. They were finally released in October, in what seemed to be an exchange for Japanese citizens who had been arrested for entering and photographing Chinese military facilities ("Chinese premier" 2010). The core of U.S. security concerns is how to avoid future confrontations that could set off unwarranted military responses from both sides and draw the United States into the conflict. Neither China nor Japan can benefit from each other's strengthened security posture in the East China Sea and the strained economic relationship between them. In the October 2010 ASEAN and EAS meetings in Hanoi, China and Japan's delegates were hardly in a talking mood ("China dismisses" 2010; "Japanese comments" 2010). In the event of war between the two, the United States is obligated to defend Japan by virtue of the terms of its alliance treaty with the Land of the Rising Sun.

Meanwhile, Japan's concern for North Korea's growing nuclear arsenal and missile delivery capabilities is shared by the United States and South Korea. China has assumed an interlocutor role, but like the case of the United States to Japan, Beijing has military and economic treaty relationships with Pyongyang, and, as a result, it has not always been sympathetic to Japan's security perceptions. In October 2006, Japan and the United States agreed to develop a joint missile defence shield against North Korea, on both land and sea. Australia has shown some interest in joining the venture. The United States and Japan each use the Aegis combat systems for the shield and Australia has ordered such systems from the United States (CRS 2008c, p. 13). Such interoperability will enhance the shield capabilities of all three, but China sees such cooperation as part Japan's larger militarization push.

Japan has also taken the initiative of building security ties with Australia and India through its expanding economic links. In March 2007, Japan and Australia signed the first ever security collaboration agreement in Asia; a month later, the two began negotiations for an FTA. Bilateral trade between the two stood at US$60 billion. The security agreement fosters broadly gauged collaboration (also called a "strategic partnership") in counter-terrorism, international law enforcement, disaster response, and international peacekeeping operations. In Iraq, the Australians have provided escort and protection service for the Japanese Self-Defence Forces. Tokyo and Canberra also share a common concern for China's expanding military power throughout the region, its diplomatic success, and its growing influence in Southeast Asia, whose instability (especially Indonesia's) can directly impact Australia (CRS 2008c, pp. 9–10).

The Japan-India relationship is relatively new and still unfolding. The first convergence between the two is over a common interest in an enlarged UN Security Council. Both have been aspiring candidates for a seat. Although bilateral trade between them remained small (US$7 billion in 2006), India has displaced China as largest recipient of aid from Japan.

Foreign direct investment from Japan to India has soared, serving as a hedge against China. Recently, contentious bilateral relations provoked the Chinese public to carry out violent demonstrations against the Japanese embassy and corporations. Some intimidated Japanese firms pulled out of China and diverted their FDI to India instead. Japan has extended loans and made private investments amounting to billions of dollars towards the Delhi-Mumbai industrial axis, as well as in the New Delhi subway system. Reciprocal visits by each other's military chiefs have been frequent for the past few years, and in 2007, the Indian fleet visited the Yokosuka Naval Base.

In late July 2009, India launched the first of its nuclear submarine fleet. Japan and India signed a civilian nuclear power programme, much to the displeasure of Beijing ("Japan faces" 2010). This is a significant reversal of Japan's imposition of sanctions against India in trade and investment when New Delhi tested nuclear devices in 1998. Also, India and Japan joined the United States in the "Malabar 07" naval exercises off Okinawa, and in a second exercise in the Indian Ocean, which was broadened to include Australia and Singapore. The exercise reportedly included an impressive army of 20,000 men, twenty-eight combat ships, 150 aircraft, and three aircraft carriers. Less than a month earlier, China and Russia had led the Shanghai Cooperation Organization's first military exercise, featuring 4,000 ground troops, 500 combat vehicles, and 1,000 pieces of special equipment from the five-member countries in "Peace Mission 2007". Nevertheless, China "bristled" at the U.S.-Japan-Australia-Singapore-India naval and air exercises (CRS 2008c, pp. 14–15).

6.5 CHANGES IN SECURITY POLICY DOWN UNDER

Australia and New Zealand, security allies of the United States since World War I, have been hedging their security arrangements in the Asia Pacific as well for economic reasons. The Australia-New Zealand-U.S. (ANZUS) alliance is practically dead and is only registered on paper. The original intent of the alliance was to keep the two Oceanic countries safe from the potential impact of renewed Japanese militarism. In the 1980s, New Zealand abandoned its commitment to the alliance unilaterally over the issue of visiting nuclear vessels of the United States Navy. The United States and Australia have had to find alternate ways to recement their bilateral relationship and have done so through the USAFTA, followed by the

U.S.-Australian Treaty on Defense Trade, and a series of bilateral military projects (CRS 2007d). The treaty will speed up the process of arms sales and technology transfers to Australia, whose requests will go through fast track, and can increase the interoperability of the countries' armed forces. No other country in the Asia Pacific has similar privileges. Also, it will open access for Australian firms to bid on U.S. defence procurement projects, which the USAFTA also guarantees. The only other country to have such a treaty with the U.S. is the United Kingdom (CRS 2008c, p. 5).

The careful observer will note that Australia is not a major purchaser of arms from the United States, relative to other nations in the region. Between 1995 and 2008, Australia's largest arms purchase (delivered) worth US$391 million occurred in 2005. In 2006, Australia spent US$2.44 billion to modernize massively its aircraft fleet, missiles, Aegis Weapons Systems, MK 41 Vertical Launch Systems, aircraft engines, and other materiel (CRS 2008c, p. 6). With a few exceptions, Asia as a whole increased its defence spending, for whatever reasons, from US$179.6 billion in 2003 to US$195.7 billion in 2004. India has decided to increase its defence spending by 44 per cent during the five-year period of 2007 and 2012. Australia spent US$17.84 billion in 2006, ranking it twelfth in the world (see Table 6.2).

In spite of China's assurances and reassurances of its peaceful rise and development, the neighbourhood feels uneasy about the present and future security picture, as shown in defence spending. In spite of this development, Australia loathes to alienate China. Kevin Rudd's defence minister, Brendon Nelson, stated " we do not wish to have formal

TABLE 6.2
Asia-Pacific Countries' Defence Spending and Their World Ranking, 2005

Country	Defence Spending (US$ billion)	World Ranking
United States	$518.10	1
China	$81.47	2
Japan	$44.47	4
South Korea	$21.05	8
India	$19.04	10
Australia	$17.84	12
Taiwan	$7.92	19
North Korea	$5.00	23
Singapore	$4.47	24

Source: CRS 2007a, p. 6.

quadrilateral (U.S.-Australia-Japan-India) strategic dialogue in defence and security matters…We do not want to do anything which…may otherwise cause concern in some countries, particularly China". Nevertheless, China formally filed diplomatic protests against such an arrangement, which it perceived as being inimical to its interests. Despite Nelson's remarks, Australia's defence budget has gone up by 47 per cent since 1996 (CRS 2008c, pp. 4, 16).

Michael Yahuda observed that in 1956 China refused to buckle under a Soviet demand that it could not compromise their worldwide strategic interests, as the ideological gulf between the two widened. China was not willing to accept that there was the only one correct path to communism, the Marxist-Leninist variety. In 1959, the Soviets refused to give China nuclear technology, and the following year, Soviet economic and technical advisers left China, or were forced to leave. At the time, both the United States and the Soviet Union shared the common goal of keeping China from becoming a rival nuclear power. In the 1962 short war between China and India, the Soviet Union, Britain, and the United States backed India (Yahuda 2003, pp. 54–59).

Whether communist or capitalist, China's relations with European countries and America have never been pleasant and rewarding; hence, Beijing's perception of America today is a guarded one, in spite of the good times during the Nixon-Kissinger era. Is China treating the United States like it did to Soviet Union in 1960? China's economic and security interests in Northeast Asia and Southeast Asia have been made clear: lock the United States out of the region. China's stance, however, may not represent the dominant view of all East Asia. The big question is if, and when, the rest of greater Asia shares China's view and agrees to pursue China's strategy in banishing America from the region.

6.6 CURRENT CHALLENGES AND FUTURE OPTIONS FOR THE UNITED STATES

The exigencies of the Cold War defined U.S.-Asian security relations for the past six decades. Now, a Congressional report observes: "the strategic and defence context in Asia is largely defined by regional trade and economic ties" (CRS 2007a, p. 28). This means that U.S. foreign economic and security policy, whether bilateral (with individual countries) or multilateral (with ASEAN, APEC, EAS, ASEAN Plus Three, the ARF, and the coming

Trans-Pacific Partnership-TPP of potentially ten to thirteen countries, with Japan, Canada, and South Korea still considering), will hinge on the convergence or divergence of these two spheres of interests. In some cases, economic interests should shape the security relationship; in others, the security relationship should pave the way to future expansion of trade and investment ties. Either way, the convergence model will benefit both America and the Asia Pacific. This fits well with the liberalism found in International Political Economy: "economic and security arrangements increase opportunities for communication, establishing personal ties between people, and cooperating in diplomatic endeavors" (CRS 2008b, pp. 8–9). So far, the United States, Singapore, Australia, and Japan have used FTAs as the cornerstone for building a security architecture; in other words, an FTA leads, and security follows.

The current challenges to the United States in the Asia Pacific are twofold: economic integration and military security. In trade and finance, the United States' share dwarfs all other extra regional players in Asian markets, but trade asymmetry has grown wider and become a contentious issue that could upset existing security relationships with traditional allies, and present security competitors with new opportunities to exploit. A full 40 per cent of the American trade deficit comes from four Asian countries: Japan, Korea, Taiwan, and China (CRS 2008b, p. 28). The first three are America's security partners while the last is its competitor and strategic rival. Also, the first three are high-income countries to which few American jobs were lost and where America's FDI has been welcome. China is another matter, however. A significant loss of U.S. jobs and a gaping trade surplus that finances the modernization of the People's Liberation Army (PLA) and its sister services, in addition to covering China's trade deficits with Southeast Asia, have become bones of contention with the American public and the U.S. Congress (CRS 2009b). There is a seed of discontent that has encouraged American politicians in Washington and anti-American hardliners in Beijing to take a confrontational stance.

For the past three years, China has ceased to introduce new reforms and fine tune its economy, in spite of its commitment to the WTO when it applied for full membership in 2000. The understanding at that time was that China would open up its economy by adopting a series of market-friendly measures such as lowering tariffs, privatizing state-owned enterprises, and removing investment restrictions for WTO members. China has only partially delivered on its commitment. In the May–June 2009 issue of *Foreign Affairs*, a Heritage Foundation fellow and a specialist on the Chinese economy wrote an intriguing article that could have an effect on America's foreign economic and security policy towards the region. The conservative think tank's economist began his pessimistic analysis (from the standpoint of a neoconservative or a plain free marketer) with the statement that "the U.S.-Chinese relationship...is the most important bilateral economic relationship in the world" (Scissors 2009, pp. 24–30).

The combined GDPs of the two behemoths in 2007 came to a staggering 30 per cent of world GDP. Furthermore, the bilateral trade between the United States and China in 2008, amounting to US$409 billion, dwarfed the Japan-U.S. trade of US$206 billion, but was a bit smaller than the U.S.-EU trade value of US$642.4 billion. An interesting picture of trade asymmetry and dependence emerges from these numbers. The combined two-way trade between the United States and China and between the United States and Japan in 2008 accounted for US$615 billion of the total U.S.-Asian trade of US$876.3 billion, or 70 per cent. The remaining US$261.3 billion was U.S. bilateral trade conducted primarily with Korea, Singapore, Malaysia, Thailand, Hong Kong, and Taiwan.

China is also the largest holder of foreign exchange (US$2.65 trillion as of September 2010) and is also the largest holder of United States Treasury bonds. The Heritage economist argues that China has been "recycling" its trade surplus in dollars (US$295 billion in 2008 alone) into U.S. Treasuries so that the excess funds could be kept out of China's capital account and hence its economy, thus protecting itself from inflation ("China Foreign" 2010).

China has reneged on its promise of economic reforms that it made to the WTO and its major trade and investment partners, as the following examples will illustrate. A series of new laws and administrative measures have been adopted since the advent of Hu Jintao as president. The People's National Congress empowered the Ministry of Commerce to vet all incoming FDI on "economic security" grounds and to reject any proposal that could potentially harm state assets. This has had the effect of "walling off" the state sector from foreign buyers. If the investment proposal is deemed inconvenient to national interests, or, more specifically, is challenging the interests of involved state-owned enterprises (SOEs), the ministry could reject the offer.

Another case comes from an American equity firm, the Carlyle Group, which is well connected to Chinese leaders. Its board of directors and officers included former U.S. president George Bush (father), former secretary of state James Baker, former secretary of defence Frank Carlucci, and other high-ranking officials from the Reagan and Bush administrations. The Carlyle Group has also been the American investment manager for the Saudi royals (Briody 2003, pp. 51–55). The group agreed to acquire Xuzhou Construction Machinery Group, an SOE, in October 2005. The Central Committee of the Chinese Communist Party found the project unacceptable and vetoed it (Scissors 2009, pp. 30–31).

There were other administrative measures as well that deliberately locked out FDI. A new labour law discriminates against multinationals, whose labour-management practices have been closely monitored by the All China Federation of Trade Unions, an arm of the Chinese Communist Party. An antimonopoly law prohibits firms with dominant market positions from selling "at unreasonable prices", presumably judged by government standards. The law exempts SOEs for national security reasons, however. New export taxes have also been introduced and taxes on FDI now make China less attractive to foreign investment. The European Union is already reporting that its investment flows into China have been falling (Scissors 2009, p. 28). The European Union's investment in China was down from US$7.9 billion in 2006 to US$1.5 billion in 2007, while China's overall inflow of FDI was up by 55 per cent in this period, according to its Ministry of Commerce (Scissors 2009, p. 30). Also in 2006 and 2007, the Chinese Government suspended trading in SOE stocks, thus keeping those corporations out of China's bourse. SOEs were allowed to list themselves in overseas stock markets, however. Private Chinese firms were allowed to operate, thus expanding their space within China, while SOEs raised funds in Europe, the United States, and elsewhere. Eager bankers around the world raised money for Chinese SOEs for hefty fees. The Heritage economist argues that as many as 75 per cent of the 1,500 Chinese companies listed in overseas markets (with government authorization) were SOEs.

Behind this picture, the weakest link is between China's trade dependency on the United States and the future well-being of its domestic economy. Of the US$409 billion in two-way trade, over half represents a trade surplus in China's favour (or trade deficit, for the United States). China's working population is 808 million, of whom 120 million are migrant workers, who have the highest unemployment rate. Officially, only 4 per cent of these workers are unemployed, although others place the figure closer to 16 per cent, or some 20 million individuals looking for jobs (*Time*,

"Back to" 2009, p. 10). The Chinese authorities are painfully aware of the double edged sword effect of this trade asymmetry.

China needs unencumbered access to the American market to pay for its own trade deficits with Japan and some Southeast Asian countries, as well as for energy. Its oil reserves represent a paltry 2.1 per cent of the world's total, so it must import 90 per cent of the petroleum it consumes: 6.2 million barrels per day in 2004, which is projected to increase to 12.7 million barrels by 2010. In 1997, China spent US$3.3 billion for oil imports; by 2006, that figure had increased to US$7.4 billion (CRS 2008a, p. 11). Much of this oil comes via sea and generally travels through Southeast Asia's four choke points: the Straits of Malacca/Singapore, Sunda, Lombok, and Makassar, none of which the PLA Navy can secure at the moment.

For security reasons, China has been working to build seaports in Myanmar, thereby avoiding the world's most dangerous choke point (at the Malacca and Singapore Straits). There are also two pipeline projects that China has been pushing: one across the Malaysian peninsula, linking the Andaman Sea to the Gulf of Thailand, and another from Sittwe or Bhamo on the Irrawaddy River (hit by a major typhoon in the summer of 2008) to Kunming. In addition, China is contemplating building a railroad parallel to the pipeline route. To secure the support of the Burmese military junta, China has been pumping billions of dollars in military aid into the country as well as cancelling its past debts (CRS 2006, pp. 23–24). When the naval port, railroad, and pipeline projects are completed, China's navy will have an Indian Ocean base. In turn, this will reduce its risk of relying solely on sea lanes to import oil, particularly if China cannot build its blue water naval capacity fast enough to secure the maritime transport routes.

China's appetite for, and consumption of, for non-energy raw materials are equally voracious: in addition to being the world' second largest oil importer, the country consumes 50 per cent of the world's cement, 30 per cent of its steel, 25 per cent of its copper, and 20 per cent of its aluminum, all of which constitute the core of China's seaborne trade (CRS 2006, pp. 19–21). An interesting point about China's raw material dependency is that it must develop sufficient "blue water" naval capabilities to protect the sea lanes. At the moment, China's rationale for building up its naval power is to subdue Taiwan. Once the PLA Navy becomes a formidable force in its own right, its impact will inevitably be felt throughout Southeast Asia, and the real test of *how* and *for what purpose* China will deploy its naval capabilities and personnel is yet to be seen (see Conclusion). Once these infrastructure projects are completed, China's temptation to explore and exploit underwater hydrocarbon resources in the South China Sea will increase, and so will the tension between the ASEAN claimants to those waters and China.

Several key points have emerged from the Heritage study that will affect U.S. foreign policy towards Asia. First, China is turning back the clock to its own model in which SOEs and state finances drive growth. Private firms are allowed to operate, but cannot aspire to dominate the national economy. In order to achieve this steeply state-favoured and -dominated economy, China needs a strong centralized government. What will happen to the considerable decentralized economic decision making power that it has adopted and granted provinces and cities? My prediction is that as long as the Chinese Communist Party remains in control of the provinces, the system will be allowed. But as in the case of FDI, the minute Beijing detects that decentralized economic decision making is hurting national "economic security", the government will clamp down on it. So far, the Chinese model has worked, so there is no need to embrace a market economy and introduce greater liberalization, deregulation, and privatization measures. Leaders think that China has perfected the balance between the state's role and the market. It has learnt to use, and has needed, the capitalist ethos to grow to its own advantage by opening just enough space for FDI to rush in. However, once its economy is modernized and booming, it is likely to impose restrictions on foreign control of the economy by walling off key sectors, beefing up SOEs to compete against FDI, and keeping private firms in the chain as suppliers of advanced technologies and providers of services. The Chinese seem to have zeroed in on the crucial distinction between FDI and investment in SOEs: state-owned banks must dominate national credit, the key to controlling the economy.

The Heritage study shows that the SOE banks lent out US$5 trillion (the outstanding cumulative loan value at the end of 2008) and that their annual lending grew at a brisk pace of 19 per cent (Scissors 2009, p. 29). In terms of FDI, investors can conceive of projects that they want to implant in China, or invest in those projects that investors can control, but all these projects require government authorization. Selling SOE stocks on foreign exchanges means that buyers recognize the value and management of the companies as they are packaged — with implicit guarantees of moral hazard — future state help in times of distress and often enjoying state patronage and even monopoly and monopsony status as favoured contractors, buyers, and sellers. There are plenty of investment bankers in Europe, Asia, and the United States eager to take on SOEs and sell their stocks and bonds for profit. China has learnt to play the capitalist game well. Concurrently, China's SOEs have been investing heavily in natural resources in Africa, Latin America, and Central Asia; keeping dollars, euros, and yen out of the domestic economy; instead, these currencies are used to acquire stakes and access natural resources around the world.

6.7 ASIA'S PREFERENCES, AMERICA'S CHOICES

The fundamental difference between the Asia that Richard Nixon had to deal with and the one that Barack Obama will have to contend with is not just two radically different eras, but rather the closing of the wealth and power gap between Asia and America. For half a century, the United States has been investing and engaging in the region to make Asia (and itself) secure and prosperous. America did this in two ways: by providing a security umbrella, albeit on its own terms (the propagation of democracy and opposition to communism, sharing America's bounty with Asia, and urging its allies to adopt American-style free market system); and by expanding trade and finance. The result of such a policy has been better in some countries than others. At times, the United States was more driven by, and focused on, security matters than it was on forging trans-Pacific economic integration. Obama has been moving away from these obsessive security concerns and focusing more on expanding economic links. His trip to Asia in November 2010 was all about economics: creating more trade opportunities in India and Indonesia, and fine-tuning the Korea-U.S. Free Trade Agreement which Bush had signed before he left office, but which was not approved by Congress. And in the process, Obama wanted to create jobs at home.

When it was still poor and undeveloped, Asia had little latitude in choosing a political economy model. Survival was at stake most of the time. Market capitalism, communism-socialism, and statist developmentalism were the three options available. The latter two became the preferred models, including for Singapore. It was the prevailing political wind, driven by Cold War rivalries and hostilities, which caused Asia's choices to be limited. It could either stand with America or with the Soviet Union and China. Once fully developed (as in the case of Korea, Singapore, Taiwan, and Japan, once it was fully recovered from the ravages of war),

Asian nations could then make their own choices about how to sustain their hard-earned wealth and power. Having done so has also put them at odds with America's choices at times. For instance, a more assertive Korea prefers to impose restrictions on how the United States can use its military stationed in the peninsula. A prosperous Japan would prefer to confine the United States to the role of the regional military watch dog while it exercises unbridled economic hegemony. An ever-suspicious and paternalistic China prefers its "rightful place" in history: to be restored as the region's economic and military centre.

A confident, wealthy, but vigilant Singapore prefers to look out for ways to accumulate more wealth and through it fortify its security with great powers, both Asian and non-Asian. Each key player in the international political economy and international security relations of the Asia Pacific sees its role in a different light when it comes to dealing with the rising China and a sunset America that is seemingly strapped in by its own internal political decay and growing economic inefficiency. Some have argued that America has entered an irreversible phase of decline. Others have insisted that a rejuvenated and reinvented America is not just a possibility, but is indeed the next phase of its history. U.S. presidents before Obama spent more time, resources, and energy for seemingly unending crises, or firefighting on a global scale. Committing its resources and manpower beyond the country's means, the George W. Bush administration squandered a valuable opportunity to reconstruct America. Obama was elected because a majority of America's 300 million people wanted a fundamental change that will arrest and reverse its decline, but also bring about a new dawn for its future. This new trajectory means that a new foreign economic and security policy must also be fashioned that can accommodate Asia's preferences and America's choices at the same time — not an easy task, but one that can be accomplished.

What is clear is that cultural values and economic interests will supersede ideology and will have to become the new foundation for America's twenty-first century foreign policy. The Palmerstonian perspective that a nation has no permanent alliances, just permanent interests, will have to be the guiding light. Asia's high-income countries will be focused on how to extend their current prosperity, and the poor, how to overtake the rich. As wealth is earned and accumulated, how to keep it and expand it will require a carefully choreographed security strategy, and Asia will need a comprehensive security architecture in the region that is realistically formatted. The core of economic growth and development strategy will remain national priorities.

Only a regionalized, comprehensive security architecture can sustain Asia's economic prosperity as globalized trade and investment continue to flow into the region. Europe's success can be emulated, but it will require strong political will to discard history and turn a new page. The denizens of the Asia Pacific have not achieved this momentous goal, but have made valiant efforts in that direction. In this, ASEAN and its institutions dedicated to free trade, security, and integration have been in the driver's seat, while Asia's great powers have remained obtrusive passengers. This configuration of relationships is also changing as the rivalry between China and Japan one the one hand, and between China and the United States on the other, heats up. At the moment, the trilateral relationship is fragile at best. In addition, India and Russia will contribute to this power realignment as they become more viable players in the region. It is the responsibility of the political elites of the region to manage this change in peaceful and mutually accommodating ways. So far, cementing FTAs that build bridges through economic partnerships has been one way to meet this challenge. This makes Obama's strong support for the completion of the Trans-Pacific Partnership Agreement more compelling in view of this reality. Certainly, his policy is aimed in the right direction.

A forecast based on this change in the Asia-Pacific's international political economy is that there will be rivalry, competition, and even conflict between the American neoliberal model on the one hand, and three distinct Asian political economy models (the more open market economies of Japan, Korea, Singapore, Taiwan; the mildly statist economies of Malaysia, Indonesia, and the Philippines; and the transitional economies of Vietnam, Myanmar, Cambodia, Laos) on the other. The United States needs to craft carefully policies that accommodate the peculiarities of the various Asian models, instead of pushing a one-size-fits-all neoliberal model. The modified Cold War model of the common defence of democratic ideals, while sharing the fruits of a free market system, cannot work.

For America and Asia to prosper and to engage China as a constructive stakeholder in the international political economy and security in the region as well as around the world, the Obama administration needs to produce a policy that will not only reflect the convergence of economic interests and security exigencies, but also a model that will be flexible enough to allow the globalization of finance and investment, as well as the regionalization of trade and production to continue and thrive. This means that no single multilateral trade and security system for the region will work. Rather, the U.S. administration should retain a mixed bag of bilateral arrangements in trade and investment until the region can develop a viable, collective system of its own. The eventual goal must be an arrangement of overarching economic integration with a multilateral system of security, but short of a security community. This can be achieved by economic integration among high-income countries in the Asia-Pacific region. They must lead the way. This will allow flexibility in the Asian political economies, where securing an individual country's economic needs and material prosperity still remains the core objective.

It is true that material prosperity has prolonged the rule of authoritarian governments in the region. It may be prudent to accept this reality because it has been the case for every government which has brought about economic miracles. Many Asians assume that the political payoff for material well-being is to keep the government, or the ruling party, in power. Here is the foundation for the Asian social contract. For the near future, a dual approach — bilateral economic and security engagement, while laying a cornerstone for collective security — will not diminish America's power. On the contrary, it will make the indigenous great powers such as China, Japan, and India more attuned to group demands that no single great power can satisfy, thus letting it dominate the Asian commons. Let the ARF lead. Bolster ASEAN's centrality. In this scenario of preserving ASEAN's systemic integrity as an impartial agent, the United States is likely to enjoy the luxury of being an external power, as well as a resident player of the Western Pacific.

In a collective or multilateral system, great power tends to lose its leverage; hence, the United States has been reluctant to support multilateralism in Asia. For the Europeans, who have shared a common history of good and bad times, multilateralism is an anodyne. Portugal has as much voice in the councils of Europe and NATO as Germany does. How Germany flexes its muscle is through its ability to set the rules for the majority in economic and financial decisions, but its moral high ground helps sell the collective economic agenda. Common security then follows.

In the Asia Pacific, the opposite approach should be introduced and put in place for another five decades or so, given the depth of the region's historical and cultural experiences as defined by the dynamics between the three indigenous great powers (Japan, India and China) and the rest. The need for an external great power(s) is more real than apparent. But this state of affairs will pass in another generation or two. For this reason, bilateral FTA arrangements *cum* multilateral security cornerstones may best serve the interests of the region, as well as those of America. The question then becomes: what happens to the bilateral FTAs that the United States, Japan, and other high-income countries have been building? In Asia, they can be pulled into a multilateral system since there has been greater economic integration than security cooperation.

So far, Asia's three disparate systems of political economy have prevented the region from creating a cohesive interstate system, whether for trade or for security. This reality has posed enormous challenges for external powers such as the United States and the European Union, which have to deal with individual countries bilaterally, and regional multilateral organizations such as ASEAN, ASEAN Plus Three, the East Asia Summit, the ASEAN Free Trade Area, and the ASEAN Regional Forum. On the issue of security, these entities are not effective and even dysfunctional. On the issue of economic integration, they have made impressive progress. But it has taken over forty years for ASEAN to produce even a charter, and the current one still lacks enforcement power and leaves room for its members to flout group decisions without fear of rebuke.

Thus, it is incumbent upon the Obama administration to appreciate these nuances and devise a strategy that will result in success, both in security and economic universes by accepting these Asian values and practices and without disturbing the existing power correlates. This will reinforce the nature of the regional political economy models. Also, bilateral FTAs such as the USSFTA, KORUSFTA, and USAFTA, as well as a minilateral RTA like the Trans-Pacific Partnership, can reinforce them. But for the multitude of the bilaterals to thrive, a comprehensive regional security arrangement is needed so that the rules for security and economic engagements can converge. Even at a superficial level, attempts to forge a multilateral security system can be beneficial. This issue will be dealt with in the conclusion of this book.

Conclusion

The 2010 report by the Congressional Research Service, examining the first five-year performance of the USSFTA, concludes that it has been a win-win situation for both parties. The United States exported US$16.6 billion worth of goods to Singapore in 2003, US$27.9 billion in 2008, and US$22.3 billion in 2009 (see Table 2.2). The Bush recession was most likely the cause of the decline in 2009. The Untied States has gained much from the FTA, which has produced a consistent trade surplus for it: US$6.6 billion in 2009, although this was down from US$12 billion the previous year. Interestingly enough, the American share of Singapore's total trade has declined from 16 per cent in 2003 (before the FTA went into effect) to 12 per cent in 2009. Singapore's international trade has expanded, but it has also diversified, which explains the relative decline of trade with the United States. But Singapore's imports from the United States in 2009 (US$28.5 billion) was slightly larger than from China (US$26 billion) (CRS 2010, pp. 1–2).

On the investment side, the United States has done well. In 2001, American firms invested a total of US$40.8 billion, increasing the amount to US$51.1 billion in 2003 (the year the FTA was signed) and US$81.9 billion in 2006, the third year of the FTA. The U.S. Department of Commerce reported that at the end of 2008, the total stock of American investment in Singapore reached US$106 billion, the largest in the Asia Pacific, surpassing Australia (US$89 billion) and Japan (US$79 billion), the top three destinations. U.S. investment in China that year was US$45.8 billion, while Hong Kong hosted more than the mainland at US$51.5 billion. In 2005, exports of U.S. multinationals in Singapore accounted for 15 per cent of Singapore's GDP, compared with 13.2 per cent in the first year of the FTA. Only Ireland surpassed Singapore in terms of American exports as a share of GDP (18.5 per cent). U.S. non-banking firms in the city state held US$150.7 billion worth of assets, accounted for US$162.7 billion in sales, and created jobs for 123,600 Singaporeans. The net income of US$18.7 billion from this U.S. FDI in the city state surpassed that from Japan (US$15 billion), Australia (US$13 billion), and China (US$7.9 billion) (CRS 2010, pp. 10–11).

Singapore's multiple FTAs and its adoption of a slew of IPR reforms since 2004 have made the city state a prime choice for high-tech multinationals. By the middle of the first year of the FTA, the Government of Singapore had introduced these reforms. The result has been both the arrival of new MNCs and the expansion of existing ones: Microsoft, Pfizer, Motorola, ISIS Pharmaceuticals, Genentech, Lucas Films, Abbott Laboratories, and several others from Europe, Korea, and Japan. In order to attract biomedical investment, Singapore set up Tuas Medical Park. In addition to the above medical-related corporations, Merck Sharp and Dohme, GlaxoSmithKlein, Schering-Plough, Wyeth, and Eli Lilly operate there as well (CRS 2010, p. 13).

Thus, the United States-Singapore Free Trade Agreement is not about trade in merchandise. It is about two high-income countries accessing each other's financial markets, investment in high-tech industries, and upgrading IPR laws and enforcement. This has had salutary effects on domestic firms as well. The USSFTA has taken higher standards than the WTO requirements for the provisions for capital controls, competition rules, and state monopolies, to mention a few non-trade concerns. But it also reinforces existing security ties between the United States and Singapore, promotes political reform, and enhances mutual cooperation in regional and international systems. Trade was never the main agenda of the neoconservative advisers who dominated the Bush administration. For them, the USFFTA was a *political tool* to reinforce further the complementary security interests of the two countries by other means. The FTA has established the highest "gold standard" for all trade agreements that the United States may enter into with the objective of security underpinning trade relations.

American diplomatic historians have observed that the core foundation of U.S. foreign policy has always been economic interests since the times of the Founding Fathers, with the sole exception being the Nixon-Ford-Kissinger era. There were historical periods when America's foreign policy was driven by non-economic forces, but they were brief and more an exception than the rule. Diplomatic pressures may not always work. Frequent use of sanctions (denying access to trade and finance), supplemented by occasional blockades and inspections on the high seas, is an economic act. When unilateral sanctions fail to produce a desired result, Washington often seeks allies to adopt a similar stance. In the post-World War II era, the United States has gone to the United Nations and other multilateral organizations to internationalize its sanctions, but has not been always successful. War is the last resort. This tradition has gone through several renditions and modifications through the last two centuries, but the fundamental aspect of linking economic interests to security interests at the bilateral, regional, and global levels has survived the test of time.

In the early years of the Franklin D. Roosevelt administration, when the United States was in a deep slumber of self-imposed isolationism, its leaders were preoccupied with the assertive rise of Japanese militarism and German Nazism. Security considerations were at the forefront of the American foreign policy debate. Thus, the strategy of embedding security concerns into trade negotiations was devised, and Americans insisted on inserting free trade demands into the Lend Lease agreement with Britain. Subsequently, the notion was enshrined by Roosevelt and Churchill in the Atlantic Charter (Art. 4) of August 1941, only a few months before the Pearl Harbor attack.

The Cold War further hardened America's resolve to refine this convergence approach. The reconstruction of war-torn Europe and Japan became Washington's primary preoccupation in the immediate aftermath of the Second World War. The assertive Soviet Union and its designs on Europe had to be addressed. The continent was easy prey for a communist takeover: a poor Europe could not be a bulwark against expanding Soviet communism. This American reasoning was built on the assumption that a stronger economy could afford a better military, or, conversely, better security could bring stability, which in turn lays the groundwork for economic growth and development. Hence, the Truman administration introduced the Marshall Plan and encouraged Europe to establish the North Atlantic Treaty Organization. By then, the security policy against the communist bloc advocated a two-prong strategy: *economic and military containment*. The United States, its Western European allies, and others in Asia refused to trade with the Soviet bloc. Economic isolation would slow or even deprive the Soviet bloc's growth and hence would result in it having few resources to build a strong military. This economic containment was neatly complemented by military encirclement. The policy worked.

Those eager to build economic ties with the United States and the capitalist west found reasons to bolt from the Soviet bloc: Yugoslavia in the early 1960s; China and Romania by the mid-1970s; and Poland, Hungary, and Czechoslovakia in the 1980s. The collapse of the Soviet Union was *economically driven*, as it reeled from its inability to grow from its autarkic model, as well as its lack of trade integration with the outside world. It did not have the economic resources to match America's massive arms build-up under Ronald Reagan. Faced with this reality, Moscow chose *détente* and accommodation. It is a prevalent American thinking that good security could be bought.

By the 1990s, the continued logic of the convergence model was driven by globalized trade and was further reinforced by the events of 9/11 and its aftermath. From the World Bank to the World Trade Organization, and everything in between, the gospel was that trade contributes to economic growth, and the more free trade, the better. China, India, Mexico, Chile, and other one-time tightly closed economies were swift in embracing this message. In order to sustain the current momentum of economic growth and expansion, the world needs peace and stability. But without economic resources, good security could not be had. Where there is no indigenous power to provide stability and defence, great powers intervene to establish their order. Once security is restored, stability follows; then economic exploitation can proceed and growth can begin. The century of the Pax Americana in the western hemisphere from the 1880s to the 1980s assured Latin America's incorporation into the North American economy. The history of the modern-day Middle East, especially the relationship between Saudi Arabia and the United States since the late 1930s and 1940s, can also be understood through the prism of the convergence model. Japan's attempt to create a similar hegemony through the region under the Greater East Asian Co-Prosperity Sphere Policy in the 1930s and 1940s descended into a tragic war with China, the United States, and European colonial powers in the Pacific.

In this vein, the USSFTA can have wider regional ramifications than what it offers at first glance. On the economic side, bilateral trade went from US$38 billion in 2003 to $50 billion in 2008. The city state's imports from the United States almost equaled France's or Taiwan's and were three-fourths of what China bought from the United States. Singapore has emerged as the largest host for American investment in the Asia Pacific region, trailed by Australia and Japan. Hong Kong and China are fourth and fifth, respectively. Singapore should receive much credit for bringing Indonesia into the FTA by securing "Made in Singapore" status for products manufactured on Bintan and Batam by its firms. Over time, there will be others in the ASEAN region to walk the Singapore road. By using the Singapore FTA model of including integrated sourcing initiatives, the web of FTAs could reach other ASEAN countries which, for reasons of their own, may not be ready or wish to enter comprehensive FTA relations. Such indirect economic lassos could lead to formal relationships, precisely because ASEAN rules do not prevent its members from developing bilateral *economic* and *security* ties with non-member countries.

The FTA negotiations and talks about FTAs with Malaysia, Thailand, the Philippines, and Vietnam have been replaced by a new strategy. In 2009 the Obama administration enthusiastically embraced American participation in the Trans-Pacific Partnership (TPP), originally known as the Trans-Pacific Strategic Economic Partnership agreement among Singapore, Brunei, New Zealand, and Chile. This participation also brought Vietnam, Australia, and Peru into the group to make a total of eight countries. In August 2010 Malaysia chose to join the TPP negotiations at their third round, held in Lima, instead of pursing a bilateral agreement with Washington. Japan is considering joining, but as of November 2010, the Kano government has decided not to join the TPP negotiations, but to consult TPP countries for further information. In September, the Philippine Government informed the USTR of its intent to join the negotiations. Canada and South Korea are also said to be interested in signing on. In the October 2010 EAS meeting in Hanoi, the TPP group briefed China and other ASEAN members on the initiative's progress (Cahiles-Magkilat 2010; "Malaysian cabinet" 2010; "Ohata says" 2010; Barkley 2010; "Editorial" 2010). When the TPP concluded its third round of negotiations in Peru in August, the prevailing mood was that the overlapping FTAs among the negotiating parties must be replaced by higher standard, or "gold standard" rules for the TPP agreement. This is an important endorsement for the USSFTA. The member countries hope to launch the regional trade agreement (RTA) by November 2011 when APEC holds its summit in Honolulu. If Japan, South Korea, Canada, and possibly Mexico join down the road, the group will contain more than half of the twenty-one members of APEC and will emerge as the core of an Asia Pacific free trade area, effectively replacing the non-binding Bogor plan (Fukue 2010). These cascading effects of the USSFTA must be recognized, and much credit should be given to Singapore and its role as the untiring promoter of Asia-Pacific economic integration.

On the security side, the United States has gained much more with the present terms. The Bush administration could not have waged its two wars simultaneously in Iraq and Afghanistan without access to Changi and Paya Lebar, and, more importantly, the seasoned counsel of Singapore's leaders has had a moderating effect in Washington. Singapore's access to America's first-class military hardware and bases in Texas, Arizona, and Idaho would not have been easily realizable without the *quid pro quo*. The FTA strengthened elite relations at the military-to-military, as well as civilian leaders' level. More critically, the two sets of state elites have had opportunities to share their world views and synchronize their cooperation in regional and international arenas when and where possible. The Bush administration's appointment of an ambassador to ASEAN was no doubt instigated by the positive effects of the USSFTA. And Singapore strongly supported America's full membership in the East Asia Summit organization.

Barack Obama, who was born in Hawaii and grew up in Indonesia in the 1960s, has claimed the title of "America's first Pacific president". When there had been a pervasive feeling in the region that America has diverted its attention to the Middle East and Afghanistan, Obama has revalidated his claim that America is back in the region and here to stay. He became the first American president to meet with his counterparts in the ASEAN-10. The second summit took place in New York in September 2010. After two unpalatable cancellations, Obama finally made his trip to Indonesia in November 2010, adding further credence to his commitment to the region. It is more than a trip of obeisance. The United States signed ASEAN's Treaty of Amity and Cooperation, a key step towards the next phase of deepening the bilateral relationship. Hillary Clinton has made at least six trips to the region, and Robert Gates has met with his Northeast and Southeast Asian counterparts a dozen times. In late October and early November 2010, the president, secretary of state, and secretary of defense, were all out in the Asia Pacific. Also, it must be recognized that the quiet diplomacy of Singapore has netted a seat for the United States as a member of the East Asia Summit, consistent with the city state diplomacy of engaging the United States in the region.

For the time being, the United States should proceed with the current stratagem of two-track security diplomacy: holding annual multilateral meetings of heads of state and defence chiefs while retaining bilateral and multilateral military-to-military relationships, with regular bilateral or multilateral naval and air exercises in the Pacific and Indian Oceans, and a greater opening of America's military warehouse to trading partners with which it has FTAs. The lesson from the Bush years of neglect has been that it was American military diplomacy — joint exercises, exchange visits by high-ranking officials, training programmes stateside, and a transfer of American hardware — that was holding U.S.-Asian relations intact. Obama must push for more American economic expansion throughout the region. The ultimate goal of Obama's strategy must be what Kissinger has said about the enduring American foreign policy objective: no one hegemonic power should dominate a region, especially Southeast Asia, *economically and militarily*.

America's future strategies in the Pacific-Indian system will have to take into account continued economic growth for Southeast Asia as the cornerstone. America must not forget its own dictum: without good economic prosperity, there is no good security, and *vice versa*. The geostrategic centrality of Southeast Asia (and therefore ASEAN) — straddled between the Pacific Ocean to the east and the Indian Ocean to the west and buffering China and India — will become indispensable to its external great power-trading partners. A stronger and more prosperous Southeast Asia can become a better endowed facilitator, interlocutor, and burden sharer for its external partners. A security conflict between China and the United States can disrupt the future economic prosperity of the region, but one between China and Japan, and another between China and India could wreak havoc just as well. For this reason, incipient ASEAN institutions need to be built up, and its centrality must be preserved and strengthened so that its geostrategic value can be maximized for all.

List of Abbreviations

AFL-CIO	American Federation of Labor and Congress of Industrial Organizations
ACTPN	Advisory Committee for Trade Policy and Negotiations
AFTA	Association of Southeast Asian Nations (ASEAN) Free Trade Area
AmCham	American Chamber of Commerce
ANZUS	Australia - New Zealand - United States security treaty
APEC	Asia Pacific Economic Cooperation
ARF	ASEAN Regional Forum
ASEAN	Association of Southeast Asian Nations
ASEAN-10	The original ten members of ASEAN
BRIC	Brazil, Russia, India, and China
CAFTA-DR	Central America - Dominican Republic - United States Free Trade Agreement
CCS	Competition Commission of Singapore
CIEL	Center for International Environmental Law
CRS	Congressional Research Service (United States)
CU	Customs Union
CUSFTA	Canada - United States Free Trade Area
DBS	Development Bank of Singapore
DPJ	Democratic Party of Japan
EAS	East Asia Summit
EDS	express delivery service
EIA	economic integration area
EPA	economic partnership agreement
EPI	export-promoting industrialization

EU	European Union
FDI	foreign direct investment
FPI	foreign portfolio investment
FTA	free trade agreement
FTAA	Free Trade Agreement of the Americas
GAO	Government Accountability Office (United States)
GATS	General Agreement on Trade in Services
GATT	General Agreement on Tariffs and Trade
GDP	gross domestic product
GLC	government-linked corporation
GNI	gross national income
GOS	Government of Singapore
GSP	Generalized System of Preferences
HLOG	Honest Leadership and Open Government
IBRD	International Bank for Reconstruction and Development
IMF	International Monetary Fund
IPE	International Political Economy
IPR	intellectual property rights
IR	International Relations
ISI (1)	import substitution industrialization or import substituting development
ISI (2)	integrated sourcing initiative
IT	information technology
ITC	International Trade Commission (United States)
ITO	International Trade Organization
KORUS	Korea - United States Free Trade Agreement
LAC	Labor Advisory Committee
MAS	Monetary Authority of Singapore
MERCOSUR	Mercado Común del Sur (Argentina, Brazil, Paraguay, and Uruguay)
MFA	Ministry of Foreign Affairs (Singapore)
MNC	multinational corporation
MTI	Ministry of Trade and Industry (Singapore)
NAFTA	North American Free Trade Agreement (Canada, Mexico, and the United States)
NAS	National Archives of Singapore
NATO	North Atlantic Treaty Organization
NTB	non-tariff trade barrier

OAS	Organization of American States
PAC	political action committee (United States)
PAP	People's Action Party (Singapore)
PL	Public Law
PLA	People's Liberation Army
PS	partial scope
R&D	research and development
RTA	regional trade agreement, regional trade area
SACU	Southern African Customs Union
SCO	Shanghai Cooperation Organization
SEATO	Southeast Asian Treaty Organization
SEP	strategic economic partnership
SOE	state-owned enterprise
STR	Special Trade Representative (United States)
TAA	Trade Adjustment Assistance (United States)
TPA (1)	Trade Promotion Authority of 2002 (United States)
TPA (2)	trade promotion authority (United States)
TPP	Trans-Pacific Partnership
TRIPS	trade-related aspects of intellectual property rights
TVA	Tennessee Valley Authority
UN	United Nations
UNCTAD	United Nations Conference on Trade and Development
USAFTA	United States - Australia Free Trade Agreement
USC	U.S. Congress
USDoA	U.S. Department of Agriculture
USDoC	U.S. Department of Commerce
USDoD	U.S. Department of Defense
USDoS	U.S. Department of State
USGAO	U.S. Government Accountability Office (formerly Government Accounting Office)
USITC	U.S. International Trade Commission
USNIC	U.S. National Intelligence Council
USSFTA	United States - Singapore Free Trade Agreement
USTR	U.S. Trade Representative; U.S. Office of Trade Representative
WASP	White Anglo-Saxon Protestant
WB	World Bank
WTO	World Trade Organization

References

BOOKS AND ARTICLES

Abbott United States. 2009 (20 January). "Abbott Opens New Pharmaceutical Research Laboratory in Singapore". <http://www.abbott.us/us/url/pressRelease> (accessed 5 May 2009).

Abernethy, David B. 2000. *The Dynamics of Global Dominance: European Overseas Empires 1415–1980*. New Haven: Yale University Press.

Abramowitz, Morton, and Stephen Bosworth. 2006. *Chasing the Sun: Rethinking East Asian Policy*. New York: The Century Foundation Press.

Abu-Lughod, Janet L. 1989. *Before European Hegemony: The World System A.D. 1250–1350*. New York: Oxford University Press.

Acharya, Amitav. 2001. *Constructing a Security Community in Southeast Asia: ASEAN and the Problem of Regional Order*. London: Routledge.

AFL-CIO. 2008 (11 September). "Immigration Laws, U.S. Trade Policy Hurts All Workers". <http:/blog.aflcio.org/2008/09/page/9/> (accessed 5 May 2009).

———. 2009 (18 March). "Trade Experts: Renegotiate NAFTA". <http://blog.aflcio.org/2009/03/page/6/> (accessed 5 May 2009).

American Chamber of Commerce in Japan (ACCJ). 2006. "Working Together, Winning Together". Tokyo.

American Chamber of Commerce in Singapore. 2007 (April). "United States – Singapore Free Trade Agreement: 2007 Review". Singapore.

Amin, Samir. 2003. *Obsolescent Capitalism: Contemporary Politics and Global Disorder*. London: Zed Books.

Amsden, Alice H. 2001. *The Rise of "The Rest": Challenges to the West from Late Industrializing Economies*. New York: Oxford University Press.

———. 2007. *Escape from Empire: The Developing World's Journey through Heaven and Hell*. Cambridge, MA: The MIT Press.

Anderson, Lisa, ed. 1999. *Transition to Democracy*. New York: Columbia University Press.

Armacost, Michael H. 1996. *Friends or Rivals? The Insider's Account of U.S.-Japan Relations*. New York: Columbia University Press.

Bacevich, Andrew J. 2002. *American Empire: The Realities and Consequences of U.S. Diplomacy*. Cambridge, MA: Harvard University Press.

"Back to the Countryside". 2009 (16 February). *Time*.

Baker, Jim. 2005. *The Eagle in the Lion City: America, Americans and Singapore*. Singapore: Landmark Books.

Balaam, David, and Michael Veseth. 1996. *Introduction to International Political Economy*. Upper Saddle River, NJ: Prentice Hall.

Baldwin, Robert, and Christopher Magee. 2000. *Congressional Trade Votes: From NAFTA Approval to Fast-Track Defeat*. Washington, DC. Institute for International Economics.

Barkley, Tom. 2010 (June 23). "US Trade official: Ready to draft for Pacific trade deal". *The Wall Street Journal*. <http://bilaterals.org> (accessed 3 November 2010).

Barr, Michael D. 2002. *Cultural Politics and Asian Values: The Tepid War*. London: Routledge/Curzon.

Barro, Robert J. 1996. *Getting It Right: Markets and Choices in a Free Society*. Cambridge, MA: The MIT Press.

Barry, Ellen. 2009 (27 November). "Russia Seeks Naval Upgrade, to Neighbors' Dismay". *The New York Times*.

Bates, Robert H. 2001. *Prosperity & Violence: The Political Economy of Development*. New York: W.W. Norton.

Behrman, Greg. 2007. *The Most Noble Adventure: The Marshall Plan and the Time When America Helped Save Europe*. New York: Free Press.

Bello, Walden. 2004 (14 December). "ASEAN Is Sadly Lacking in Relevance". *The Bangkok Post*.

Bercuson, David, and Holger Herwig. 2005. *One Christmas in Washington: The Secret Meeting between Roosevelt and Churchill That Changed the World*. Woodstock, NY: The Overlook Press.

Bergsten, C. Fred, ed. 1997. *Whither APEC? The Progress to Date and Agenda for the Future*. Washington, DC: Institute for International Economics.

Bernstein, William J. 2008. *A Splendid Exchange: How Trade Shaped the World*. New York: Atlantic Monthly Press.

Bhagwati, Jagdish. 2004. *In Defense of Globalization*. New York: Oxford University Press.

Biers, Dan. 1998. *Crash of '97: How the Financial Crisis Is Reshaping Asia*. Hong Kong: Review Publishing Company.

Bobbitt, Philip. 2002. *The Shield of Achilles: War, Peace, and the Course of History*. New York: Alfred A. Knopf.

Briody, Dan. 2003. *The Iron Triangle: Inside the Secret World of the Carlyle Group*. New York: John Wiley & Sons.

Brooks, Stephen G. 2005. *Producing Security: Multinational Corporations, Globalization, and the Changing Calculus of Conflict*. Princeton: Princeton University Press.

Brown, Drusilla K., Alan V. Deardorff, and Robert M. Stern. 2002. *Multilateral, Regional, and Bilateral Trade-Policy Options of the United States and Japan*. Ann Arbor, MI: University of Michigan.

Brown, Raj. 2006. "The Emergence and Development of Singapore as a Regional/ International Financial Center". A paper presented at the XIV International Economic History Congress, Helsinki.

Brzezinski, Zbigniew. 1983. *Power and Principle: Memoirs of the National Security Advisor 1977–1981*. London: Weidenfeld and Nicholson.

Bumiller, Elizabeth. 2002 (7 August). "Bush Signs Trade Bill, Restoring Broad Presidential Authority". *The New York Times*.

Burks, Ardath W. 1961. *The Government of Japan*. New York: Cromwell.

Cahiles-Magkilat, Bernie. 2010 (29 September). "RP Notifies US of Intention to Join TPP". *Bilaterals.org*. <http://www.bilaterals.org> (accessed 3 November 2010).

"Capital Controls Will Not Affect Trade: Rafidah". 1998 (4 September). *Business Times* (Singapore).

Center for International Environmental Law. 2003 (9 July). "Chile and Singapore Free Trade Agreements Are Wrong Models for the Environment". Washington, DC.

Center for Responsive Politics. N.d.[a]. "Annual Lobbying by Covington & Burling: Total Lobbying Income". <http://www.opensecrets.org> (accessed 7 May 2009).

———. N.d.[b]. "Client (Organization Paying for Lobbying) Lookup". <http://www.opensecrets.org> (accessed 7 May 2009).

———. N.d.[c]. "Reelection Rates Over the Years". <http://www.opensecrets.org> (accessed 7 May 2009).

———. 2008. "2008 Overview: Most Expensive Races". <http://www.opensecrets.org> (accessed 7 May 2009).

———. 2009. "Top Spenders: All Years (1998–2009)". <http://www.opensecrets.org> (accessed 1 December 2009).

Chan, Heng Chee. 2004. "Lobbying for the United States-Singapore Free Trade Agreement". In *The United States Singapore Free Trade Agreement: Highlights and Insights*. Edited by Tommy Koh and Chang Li Lin, pp. 163–76. Singapore: Institute of Policy Studies.

Chang, Ha-Joon. 2002. *Kicking Away the Ladder: Development Strategy in Historical Perspective*. London: Anthem Press.

Chang, Ha-Joon, and Ilene Grabel. 2004. *Reclaiming Development: An Alternative Economic Policy Manuel*. London: Zed Books.

Chang, Li Lin. 2005. "Eight Lessons from the United States-Singapore Free Trade Agreement". Unpublished paper.

Chhon, Keat, and Aun Porn Moniruth. 1999. *Cambodia's Economic Development: Policies, Strategies and Implementation*. London: ASEAN Academic Press.

"China dismisses resumption of talks". 2010 (30 October). *Xinhua News.* <http://news.xinhuanet.com> (accessed 3 November 2010).

"China Foreign-Exchange Reserves Jump to $2.65 Trillion". 2010 (13 October). *Bloomberg News* <http://www.bloomberg.com> (accessed 12 March 2011).

"Chinese premier wants immediate, unconditional release of boat captain". 2010 (22 September). *CNN.com* <http://edition.cnn.com> (accessed 1 October 2010).

"Citibank Offers First Travel Card in Region". 2007 (18 August). *The Straits Times.*

Clarke, Richard A. 2004. *Against All Enemies: Inside America's War on Terror.* New York: Free Press.

Clarkson, Stephen. 2008. *Does North America Exist? Governing the Continent after NAFTA and 9/11.* Toronto: University of Toronto Press.

Clines, Francis X. 1998 (29 January). "The President's Trial. The Scene: Some Friendly Mingling in the Chamber Despite a Day of Hard Party Division". *The New York Times.*

Collins, Alan. 2003. *Security and Southeast Asia: Domestic, Regional, and Global Issues.* Singapore: Institute of Southeast Asian Studies.

Covington & Burling, LLP. 2008. "Lobbying Report". Filed by Mark E. Plotkin, Partner, 21 April 2008, 17 July 2008, 17 October 2008, and 21 November 2008 (amending the October report).

Dallek, Robert. 2007. *Nixon and Kissinger: Partnership in Power.* New York: HarperCollins.

Dam, Kenneth W. 2001. *The Rules of the Global Game: A New Look at US International Economic Policymaking.* Chicago: University of Chicago Press.

Daquila, Teoflilio C., and Le Huu Huy. 2003. "Singapore and ASEAN in the Global Economy". *Asian Survey* (Nov./Dec.): 908–28.

Das, Bhagirath Lal. 2004. *The WTO and the Multilateral Trading System: Past, Present and Future.* London: Zed Books.

Davis, Kenneth S. 2000. *FDR: The War President 1940–1943: A History.* New York: Oxford University Press.

De Castro, Renato Cruz. 2004. "The Revitalized Philippine-U.S. Security Relations: The Triumph of Bilateralism over Multilateralism in Philippine Foreign Policy". In *Asia-Pacific Security Cooperation: National Interests and Regional Order.* Eds. See Seng Tan and Amitav Acharya. Amonk NY: M.E. Sharpe. pp. 154–71.

"Democrats question U.S. Chamber of Commerce money spent on Buck". 2010 (9 October). *The Denver Post* <http://www.denverpost.com> (accessed 3 November 2010).

Dent, Christopher. 2008. *East Asian Regionalism.* London: Routledge.

———. 2006. *New Free Trade Agreements in the Asia-Pacific.* Basingstoke, Eng: PalgraveMacmillan.

————, ed. 2003. *Asia-Pacific Economic and Security Cooperation: New Regionalism Agendas*. Basingstoke, Eng.: PalgraveMacmillan.

Destler, I.M. 1995. *American Trade Politics*. 4th ed. Washington, DC: Institute for International Economics.

Dicken, Peter. 2007. *Global Shift: Mapping the Changing Contours of the World Economy*. 5th ed. London. Sage Publications.

Dieter, Heribery. 2009. "Bilateral Economic Arrangements in the Asia-Pacific: Implications for Competitiveness". In *Southeast Asia in the Global Economy: Securing Competitiveness and Social Protection*. Edited by Helen E. S. Nesadurai and J. Soedradjad Djwandono, pp. 89–113. Singapore: Institute of Southeast Asian Studies.

"Don't internationalise South China Sea issue". 2010 (31 July). *The Straits Times*.

East-West Center. 2008. "U.S. Exports to Asia (Merchandise Exports 2008)". <http://www.asiamattersforamerica.org> (accessed 6 May 2009).

Economist Intelligence Unit. 1999. *Country Report. Indonesia: 1st Quarter 1998*. London: EIU.

"Editorial: Pacific Free Trade Pact". 2010 (5 October). *The Asahi Shimbun*. <http://wwww.bilaterals.org> (accessed 3 November 2010).

"Election Spending Sets Record: No Recession Here", 2010 (7 September). *The Huffington Post*. <http://www.huffingtonpost.com> (accessed 8 September 2010).

Emmott, Bill. 2003. *20:21 Vision: Twentieth-Century Lessons for the Twenty-First Century*. New York: Farr Strauss Giroux.

————. 2008. *Rivals: How the Power Struggle between China, India, and Japan Will Shape Our Next Decade*. New York: Harcourt.

Evans, Peter, and Dietrich Rueschemeyer, and Theda Skocpol, eds. [1985] 1987. *Bringing the State Back In*. New York: Cambridge University Press.

Fackler, Martin. 2010 (29 May). "Attack Bares South Korea's Complex Links to North". *The New York Times* <http://www.nytimes.com> (accessed 2 June 2010).

Fallows, James. 1994. *Looking at the Sun: The Rise of the New East Asian Economic and Political System*. New York: Pantheon Books.

Feinberg, Richard E., ed. 2003. *APEC as an Institution: Multilateral Governance in the Asia-Pacific*. Singapore: Institute for Southeast Asian Studies.

Felsenthal, Carol. 2008. *Clinton in Exile: A President Out of the White House*. New York: William Morrow.

Fforde, Adam. 2009. *Coping with Facts: A Skeptic's Guide to the Problem of Development*. Sterling, VA: Kumarian Press.

Finkel, Caroline. 2005. *Osman's Dream: The History of the Ottoman Empire*. New York: Basic Books.

Frankel, Jeffrey A. 1997. *Regional Trading Blocs in the World Economic System*. Washington, DC: Institute for International Economics.

Frieden, Jeffrey A. 2006. *Global Capitalism: Its Fall and Rise in the Twentieth Century*. New York: W.W. Norton.

Fukue, Natsuko. 2010. (14 November). "Foreign media search for signs future stance on TPP". *The Japan Times online*. <http://search.japantimes.co.jp> (accessed 14 November 2010).

Fukuyama, Francis. 2006. *After the Neocons: America at the Crossroads*. London: Profile Books.

Gaddis, John Lewis. 1997. *We Know Now: Rethinking Cold War History*. New York: Oxford University Press.

Gelb, Leslie. 2009. *Power Rules: How Common Sense Can Rescue American Foreign Policy*. New York: Harper.

Gereffi, Gary and Donald L. Wyman, eds. 1990. *Manufacturing Miracles: Paths of Industrialization in Latin America and East Asia*. Princeton: Princeton University Press.

Gill, Stephen, and David Law. 1988. *The Global Political Economy: Perspectives, Problems and Politics*. Baltimore: Johns Hopkins University Press.

"Global 500". 2005 (18 July). *Fortune*.

Goldman Sachs. 2003 (1 October). "Dreaming with BRIC: The Path to 2050". Global Economics Paper No. 99. New York.

Goldsmith, Sir James. 1994. *The Trap*. New York: Caroll & Graf Publishers.

Gordon, Beate Sirota. 1997. *The Only Woman in the Room*. Tokyo: Kodansha International.

Haacke, Jurgen. 1999. "The Concept of Flexible Engagement and the Practice of Enhanced Interaction Intramural Challenges to the 'ASEAN Way'". *The Pacific Review*: pp. 581–611.

Hardt, Michael, and Antonio Negri. 2000. *Empire*. Cambridge, MA: Harvard University Press.

Harrison, Lawrence E. 1985. *Underdevelopment Is a State of Mind: The Latin American Case*. Lantham, MD: Madison Books.

Hart, Natasha Hamilton. 2002. *Asian States, Asian Banks: Central Banking in South East Asia*. Ithaca, NY: Cornell University Press.

Herring, George C. 2008. *From Colony to Superpower: U.S. Foreign Relations since 1776*. New York: Oxford University Press.

Hertz, Noreen. 2001. *The Silent Takeover: Global Capitalism and the Death of Democracy*. New York: Free Press.

Hettne, Bjorn. 2000. "The New Regionalism: A Prologue". In *The New Regionalism and the Future of Security and Development*. Edited by Bjorn Hettne, Andras Inota, and Osvaldo Sunkel, vii–xxvi . New York: St. Martin's Press.

Hinds, Michael Decoure. 1994 (23 June). "Teen-Ager Caned in Singapore Returns Home". *New York Times*.

Hirschman, Albert. 1963. *Journeys toward Progress: Studies of Economic Policy Making in Latin America*. New York: The Twentieth Century Fund.

———. 1971. *Bias for Hope: Essays on Development and Latin America.* New Haven: Yale University Press.

Hoadley, Stephen. 2002. *Negotiating Free Trade: The New Zealand-Singapore CEP Agreement.* Wellington: New Zealand Institute of International Affairs.

Hong, Mark. 2006. "East Asian Integration: FTAs and Policy Implications". Paper presented at the Conference on Regional Cooperation Experience in Europe and Practices in East Asia, Beijing.

Huntington, Samuel P. 2004. *Who Are We? The Challenges to America's National Identity.* New York: Simon & Schuster.

Ikenberry, G. John, and Michael Mastanduno, eds. 2001. *International Relations Theory and the Asia-Pacific.* New York: Columbia University Press.

"Japan faces dilemma over civilian nuke pact with India" 2009 (25 October). *The Mainichi Daily News* <http://mdn.mainichi.jp> (accessed 3 November 2010).

"Japan's PM announces resignation". 2010 (20 June). *Politico.com* <http://www.politico.com> (accessed 20 June 2010).

"Japanese comments torpedo meeting". 2010 (30 October). *People's Daily Online* <http://enlgish.people.com.cn> (accessed 3 November 2010).

Joffe, Josef. 2009. "The Default Power". *Foreign Affairs* (September/October): pp. 21–35.

Johnson, Chalmers. 1995. *Japan: Who Governs? The Rise of the Developmental State.* New York: W.W. Norton.

———. 2000. *Blowback: The Costs and Consequences of American Empire.* New York: Metropolitan Books.

Jomo, K.S, ed. 1998. *Tigers in Trouble: Financial Governance, Liberalisation and Crisis in East Asia.* London: Zed Books.

Kang, David. 2003. "Hierarchy and Stability in Asian International Relations". In *International Relations Theory and the Asia-Pacific.* Edited by G. John Ikenberry and Michael Mastanduno, 164–89. New York: Columbia University Press.

Kaplan, Robert D. 2009. "Center Stage for the Twenty-first Century: Power Plays in the Indian Ocean". *Foreign Affairs* (March/April): pp. 16–32.

Katzenstein, Peter J. 2005. *A World Region: Asia and Europe in the American Imperium.* Ithaca, NY: Cornell University Press.

Kesavapany, K. 2001a (27 June). "Singapore FTA Initiatives Not a Backdoor to AFTA". *Business Times.*

———. 2001b (11 July). "Singapore's FTAs Can Benefit All". *New Straits Times.*

Khanna, Parag. 2008. *The Second World: Empires and Influence in the New Global Order.* New York: Random House.

Kim Dae Jung. 1994. "Is Culture Destiny? The Myth of Asia's Anti-Democratic Values". *Foreign Affairs* (November/December): pp. 189–194.

Kim, Eun Mee. 1997. *Big Business, Strong State: Collusion and Conflict in South Korean Development 1960–1990.* Albany, NY: State University of New York Press.

Kisluik, Bill. "The Who, When, and How Much of Hiring a Lobbyist". <http://www.lobbysearch.com> (accessed 7 May 2009).

Kissinger, Henry. 1979. *White House Years*. New York: Little, Brown.

Kissinger, Henry A. 2001. *Does America Need a Foreign Policy? Towards a Diplomacy for the 21ˢᵗ Century*. New York: Simon and Schuster.

Koh, Tommy. 1998. *The Quest for World Order: Perspectives of a Pragmatic Idealist*. Singapore: Times Academic Press.

———. 2004. "The USSFTA: A Personal Perspective". In *The United States-Singapore Free Trade Agreement: Highlights and Insights*. Edited by Tommy Koh and Chang Li Lin. pp. 3–22. Singapore: Institute of Policy Studies.

Kohli, Atul. 2004. *State-Directed Development: Political Power and Industrialization in the Global Periphery*. New York: Cambridge University Press.

Kollmorgen, Walter M. 1945. "Crucial Deficiencies of Regionalism". *The American Economic Review* (May): pp. 377–389.

Krugman, Paul R. 1990. *Rethinking International Trade*. Cambridge, MA: The MIT Press.

Krugman, Paul R., ed. 1993. *Strategic Trade Policy and the New International Economics*. Cambridge, MA: The MIT Press.

LaVine, Dom, and Kathleen Conners. 2006. "Public Submission for the Proposed U.S.-Malaysia Free Trade Agreement (USMFTA)". Kuala Lumpur: American Chamber of Commerce in Malaysia and U.S. Chamber of Commerce.

Lee, Kuan Yew. 2000. *From Third World to First: The Singapore Story: 1965-2000: Memoir of Lee Kuan Yew*. Singapore: Singapore Press Holdings.

Lim, Jessica. 2009 (1 August). "More Land for Growing Food". *The Straits Times*.

Lincoln, Edward J. 2004. *East Asian Economic Regionalism*. Washington, DC: Brookings Institution.

Lipset, Seymour Martin, and Jason M. Lakin. 2004. *The Democratic Century*. Norman: University of Oklahoma Press.

List, Friedrich. 1983. *The Natural System of Political Economy 1837*. Translated by W.O. Henderson. London: Frank Cass.

———. 1991. *The National System of Political Economy*. Translated by Sampson S. Lloyd. Fairfield, NJ: Augustus M. Kelley Publishers.

Macmillan, Margaret. 2001. *Paris 1919: Six Months That Changed the World*. New York: Random House.

McNamara, Robert S., and James G. Blight. 2001. *Wilson's Ghost: Reducing the Risk of Conflict, Killing, and Catastrophe in the 21ˢᵗ Century*. New York: Public Affairs.

Mahan, A. T. 1987. *The Influence of Sea Power upon History, 1660–1783*. New York: Dover Press.

Mahathir, Mohamad. 2000. *Politics, Democracy and the New Asia*. Subang Jaya, Malaysia. Pelanduk Publications.

Mahbubani, Kishore. 2008. *The New Asian Hemisphere: The Irresistible Shift of Global Power to the East*. New York: Public Affairs.

"Malaysian cabinet gives green light to join TPP". 2010 (2 August). *TWN FTA Info* <http://www.bilaterals.org> (accessed 3 November 2010).

"Malaysia's Controls May Not Delay Reforms, says IMF". 1998 (29 October). *New Straits Times*.

Malone, David M., and Yuen Foong Khong, eds. 2003. *Unilateralism and U.S. Foreign Policy: International Perspectives*. Boulder, CO: Lynne Rienner.

Mann, James. 2004. *Rise of the Vulcans: The History of Bush's War Cabinet*. New York: Vikings.

Margariti, Roxani Eleni. 2007. *Aden & the Indian Ocean Trade: 150 Years in the Life of a Medieval Arabian Port*. Chapel Hill: University of North Carolina Press.

Martin, Peter-Hans, and Harald Schuman. 1997. *The Global Trap: Globalization and the Assault on Democracy and Prosperity*. New York: Zed Books.

Mauzy, Diane, and R. S. Milne. 2002. *Singapore Politics under the People's Action Party*. London: Routledge.

Mearsheimer, John J. 2001. *The Tragedy of Great Power Politics*. New York: W.W. Norton.

Mearsheimer, John, and Stephen M. Walt. 2008. *The Israel Lobby and U.S. Foreign Policy*. New York: Farrar, Straus, and Giroux.

"Media Spending Surges toward Record". 2010 (6 October). *Politico.com*. <http://www.politico.com> (accessed 10 October 2010).

"Mild-mannered American Takes the Market by Surprise". 2009 (7 February). *Financial Times*.

Mitchell, Alison. 1998 (20 December). "Impeachment: The Overview, Clinton Impeached". *The New York Times*.

———. 1999 (13 February). "The President's Acquittal: The Overview: Clinton Acquitted Decisively: No Majority for Either Charge". *The New York Times*.

Moghadam, Mashaallah Rahnama, Hedayeh Smavati, and David A. Ditz. 2002. "An Analysis of Capital Flight from East Asian Emerging Economies". In *2002 Proceedings of Midwest Business Economics Association*, 14–17.

Mohan, C. Raja. 2009 (16 April). "Sino-India Naval Engagement". Singapore: Institute of South Asian Studies.

Moller, Jorgen Orstrom. 2008. *European Integration: Sharing of Experiences*. Singapore: Institute of Southeast Asian Studies.

Myrdal, Gunnar. 1968. *Asian Drama: An Inquiry into the Poverty of Nations*. 3 vols. New York: Pantheon.

Nathan, S. R. 1994 (31 March). "Caning in Singapore: Letters to the Editor". *International Herald Tribune*.

Nau, Henry. 1990. *The Myth of America's Decline: Leading the World Economy into the 1990s*. New York: Oxford University Press.

North, Douglass C. 2005. *Understanding the Process of Economic Change*. Princeton: Princeton University Press.

Nye, Jr., Joseph S. 2004. *Power in the Global Information Age: From Realism to Globalization*. New York: Routledge.

O'Brien, Robert, and Marc Williams. 2004. *Global Political Economy: Evolution and Dynamics*. New York: PalgraveMacmillan.

"Ohata eyes multilateral Asia FTA". 2010 (22 September). *Kyodo News*. <http://www.bilaterals.org> (accessed 3 November 2010).

Ohmae, Kenichi. 1995. *The End of the Nation State: The Rise of Regional Economies*. New York: Free Press.

Ostry, Sylvia. 1997. *The Post-War Trading System: Who's on First?* Chicago: The University of Chicago Press.

Pang, Eul-Soo. 2000. "The Financial Crisis of 1997–98 and the End of the Asian Developmental State". *Contemporary Southeast Asia* (December): pp. 570–93.

————. 2002. *The International Political Economy of Transformation in Argentina, Brazil, and Chile since 1960*. Basingstoke, Eng.: PalgraveMacmillan.

————. 2007. "Embedding Security into Free Trade: The Case of the United States–Singapore Free Trade Agreement". *Contemporary Southeast Asia* (April): pp. 1–32.

Pang, Eul-Soo, and Laura Jarnagin. 2009. "MERCOSUR: The Elusive Quest for Regional Integration". In *MERCOSUR Economic Integration: Lessons for ASEAN*. Edited by ASEAN Studies Center. pp. 87–130. Singapore: Institute of Southeast Asian Studies.

Passavant, Paul A., and Jodi Dean, eds. 2004. *Empire's New Clothes: Reading Hardt and Negri*. New York: Routledge.

Paus, Eva. 2005. *Foreign Investment, Development, and Globalization: Can Costa Rica Become Ireland?* New York: PalgraveMacmillan.

Peebles, Gavin, and Peter Wilson. 2002. *Economic Growth and Development in Singapore: Past and Future*. Cheltenham, UK: Edward Elgar.

Pei, Minxin. 2009. "Asia's Rise". *Foreign Policy* (July/August): pp. 32–36.

Pempel, T. J. 2005. "Emerging Webs of Regional Connectedness". In *Remapping East Asia: The Construction of a Region*. Edited by T.J. Pempel, 1–28. Ithaca, NY: Cornell University Press.

————. 2006. "Challenges to Bilateralism: Changing Foes, Capital Flows, and Complex Forums". In *Beyond Bilateralism: U.S.-Japan Relations in the New Asia-Pacific*. Edited by Ellis S. Krauss and T. J. Pempel. pp. 1–28. Stanford: Stanford University Press.

Perlstein, Rick. 2008. *Nixonland: The Rise of a President and the Fracturing of America*. New York: Scribner.

Peterson Institute for International Economics. 2008. "A Report to the President-Elect and the 111th Congress from the Trade Policy Study Group, December 2008". Washington, DC: 2008.

Petras, James. 2003. *The New Development Politics: The Age of Empire Building and New Social Movements.* Burlington, VT: Ashgate.

Petras, James, and Henry Veltmeyer. 2001. *Globalization Unmasked: Imperialism in the 21ˢᵗ Century.* New York: Zed Books.

Phillips, Nicola. 2005. "State Debates in International Political Economy". In *Globalizing International Political Economy.* Edited by Nicola Phillips, pp. 82–84. Basingstoke, Eng.: PalgraveMacmillan.

Powell, Colin. 2004. "A Strategy of Partnership". *Foreign Affairs* (January/February): pp. 22–34.

Quilan, Joseph. 2000. *Global Engagement: How American Companies Really Compete in the Global Economy.* New York: Contemporary Books.

Quinlan, Joseph, and Marc Chandler. 2001. "The U.S. Trade Deficit: A Dangerous Obsession". *Foreign Affairs* (May/June): pp. 87–97.

"Rafidah: Asean Members Not Permitted to Enter into FTA". 2001 (10 June). *New Straits Times.*

"Rafidah: New Controls Won't Drive Away Investment". 1994 (4 September). *New Straits Times.*

Ravenhill, John. 2001. *APEC and the Construction of Pacific Rim Regionalism.* Cambridge: Cambridge University Press.

Reyes, Alejandro. 1994 (25 May). "Rough Justice". *Asia Week.*

Ricks, Thomas E. 2006. *The Fiasco: The American Military Adventure in Iraq.* New York: Penguin.

———. 2009. *The Gamble: General David Petraeus and the American Military Adventure in Iraq 2006–2008.* New York: Penguin.

Rosenberg, Justin. 2000. *The Follies of Globalization Theory.* London: Verso.

Rothkopf, David. 2008. *Superclass: The Global Power Elite and the World They Are Making.* New York: Farrar, Straus, and Giroux, 2008.

Rubin, Robert E, and Jacob Weisberg. 2003. *In an Uncertain World: Tough Choices from Wall Street to Washington.* New York: Random House.

Sachs, Jeffrey. 1998. "International Economics: Unlocking the Mysteries of Globalization". *Foreign Policy* (Spring): pp. 97–111.

Safire, William. 1994 (19 May). "President Doormat". *The New York Times.*

Sally, Razeen. 2004. *Southeast Asia in the WTO: From Hanging Together to Bowling Alone.* Singapore: Institute of Southeast Asian Studies.

———. 2006. "FTAs and the Prospects for Regional integration in Asia". Brussels: European Center for International Political Economy.

Sassen, Saskia. 2001. *The Global City: New York, London, Tokyo.* 2nd ed. Princeton: Princeton University Press.

Schott, Jeffrey. 2003. "Unlocking the Benefits of World Trade". *The Economist* (30 Oct.). <http://www.economist.com> (accessed 5 May 2009).

Schott, Jeffrey J. 2004. *Free Trade Agreements: US Strategies and Priorities.* Washington, DC: Institute for International Economics.

Schultz, Michael, Fredrik Soderbaum, and Joakim Ojendal, eds. 2001. *Regionalization in a Globalizing World: A Comparative Perspective on Forms, Actors and Processes.* London: Zed Books.

Scissors, Derek. 2009. "Deng Undone: The Cost of Halting Market Reform in China". *Foreign Affairs* (May/June): pp. 24–30.

Scott, Alan J. 2003. *Regions and the World Economy: The Coming Shape of Global Production, Competition, and Political Order.* New York: Oxford University Press.

Seagrave, Sterling. 1995. *Lords of the Rim: The Invisible Empire of the Overseas Chinese.* New York: C.P. Putnam's Sons.

Serra, Jaime, Guillermo Aguilar, Jose Cordoba, Gene Grossman, Carla Hills, John Jackson, Julius Katz, Pedro Noyola, and Michael Wilson. 1997. *Reflections on Regionalism: Report of the Study Group on International Trade.* Washington, DC: Carnegie Endowment for International Peace.

Severino, Rodolfo C. 2006. *Southeast Asia in Search of an ASEAN Community.* Singapore: Institute of Southeast Asian Studies.

———. 2010. *The ASEAN Regional Forum.* Singapore: Institute of Southeast Asian Studies.

Shamshul, Amri Baharuddin. 2004. "Creating an ASEAN Identity". In *Towards Building an ASEAN Community.* Edited by Ilango Karuppannan, Rahmat Mohamad, and Umminajah Salleh. pp. 111–21. Shah Alam, Selangor, Malaysia: Universiti Teknologi MARA.

Sideri, S. 1970. *Trade and Power: Informal Colonialism in Anglo-Portuguese Relations.* Rotterdam: Rotterdam University Press.

Skidelsky, Robert. 2000. *John Maynard Keynes: Fight for Freedom, 1937–1946.* New York: Viking.

Soderberg, Nancy. 2005. *The Superpower Myth: The Use and Misuse of American Might.* New York: Wiley & Sons.

Srisamorn, Komsa Tontermvasana. 2006 (30 January). "More Questions than Answers at Shin". *The Bangkok Post.*

Stallings, Barbara, and Robert Kaufman, eds. 1989. *Debt and Democracy in Latin America.* Boulder, CO: Westview Press.

Staples, Anthony J. 2006. "Japanese Foreign Direct Investment and the Transformation of the East Asian Political Economy: Comparative Strategy in the Automotive Sector". In *Emerging Multiplicity: Integration and Responsiveness in Asian Business Development.* Edited by Sten Soderbaum. pp. 89–115. Basingstoke, Eng.: PalgraveMacmillan.

Stein, Peter, and Kostas Paris. 2009 (21 July). "Goodyear Won't Be Temasek CEO," *The Wall Street Journal.*

Stott, David Adam. 2008. "The Japan-Indonesia Economic Partnership: Agreement between Equals?" *Bilaterals.org.* (25 July). <http://www.bilaterals.org> (accessed 7 May 2009).

Strange, Susan. 1996. *The Retreat of the State: The Diffusion of Power in the World Economy*. New York: Cambridge University Press.

Talbott, Strobe. 2008. *The Great Experiment: The History of Ancient Empires, Modern States, and the Quest for a Global Nation*. New York. Simon & Schuster.

Thatcher, Margaret. 1993. *The Downing Street Years*. New York: HarperCollins.

"The China Blog: Unemployment Numbers: II". 2009 (3 February). *Time*.

"Three GOP candidates spend $243 million". 2010 (24 October). *Politico.com*. <http://www.politico.com> (accessed 2 November 2010).

Tsuchiyama, Jitsuo. 2007. "War Renunciation, Article 9, and Security Policy". In *Japan in International Politics: The Foreign Policies of an Adaptive State*. Edited by Thomas U. Berger, Mike E. Mochizuki, and Jitsuo Tuschiyama. pp. 47–73. Boulder, CO: Lynn Rienner.

"2010 Election Spending Makes It the Most Expensive Mid-term Election Ever". 2010. <http://www.savings.com> (accessed 20 November 2010).

"Unleashing the Trade Winds: Achieving Free Trade across the Globe Is a Daunting Task. But America is Committed, says Robert Zoellick". 2003 (5 December). *The Economist* <http://www.economist.com> (accessed 7 May 2009).

"US praises Japan for FTA plan". 2010 (25 October). *Reuters*. <http://www.bilaterals. org> (accessed 3 November 2010).

"U.S. Presence Necessary for Korean Security, Officials Say". 2010 (16 September). *American Forces Press Service*. <http://www.defense.gov/news> (accessed 10 October 2010).

Volcker, Paul A., and Toyoo Gyohten. 1992. *Changing Fortunes: The World's Money and the Threat to American Leadership*. New York: TimesBooks.

Wade, Robert. 1990. *Governing the Market: Economic Theory and the Role of Government in East Asian Industrialization*. Princeton: Princeton University Press.

Wallerstein, Immanuel. 1974. *The Modern World-System I: Capitalist Agriculture and the Origin of the European World-Economy in the Sixteenth Century*. New York: The Academic Press.

Weidenbaum, Murray, and Samuel Hughes. 1996. *The Bamboo Network: How Expatriate Chinese Entrepreneurs Are Creating a New Economic Superpower in Asia*. New York: Free Press.

Weintraub, Stanley. 2007. *15 Stars: Eisenhower, MacArthur, Marshall: Three Generals Who Saved the American Century*. New York: Free Press.

Weiseman, Alan. 2007. *Prince of Darkness: Richard Perle: The Kingdom, the Power and the End of Empire in America*. New York: Union Square Press.

Weiss, Linda. 1998. *The Myth of the Powerless State*. Ithaca: Cornell University Press.

Wolf, Martin. 2004. *Why Globalization Works*. New Haven: Yale University Press.

Woo, Jung-En. 1991. *Race to the Swift: State and Finance in Korean Industrialization*. New York: Columbia University Press.

Yahuda, Michael. 2003. *The International Politics of the Asia Pacific*. London: RoutledgeCurzon.

Yergin, Daniel, and Joseph Stanislaw. 1998. *The Commanding Heights: The Battle between Government and the Marketplace That Is Remaking the Modern World*. New York: Simon & Schuster.

Zakaria, Fareed. 1994. "Culture Is Destiny: A Conversation with Lee Kuan Yew". *Foreign Affairs* (March/April): pp. 109–126.

Zoellick, Robert. 2002 (14 April). "Falling Behind on Free Trade". *The New York Times*.

———. "Letters: Free Trade". 2003 (4 December). *The Economist*. <http://www.economist.com> (accessed 7 May 2009).

INTERNATIONAL ORGANIZATIONS

International Monetary Fund (IMF)

International Monetary Fund. 2006. *Integrating Poor Countries into the World Trading System*. Washington, DC: IMF.

Organization of American States (OAS)

Organization of American States. Sistema de Información para Comércio Exterior. 2000. "Joint Statement by the United States and Singapore on the US-Singapore Free Trade Agreement Negotiations, 21 December 2000". <http//www.oas.org/sice> (accessed 5 May 2009).

———. 2001a (25 May). "Joint Statement by Singapore and the United States on the US-Singapore Free Trade Agreement, 25 May 2001". <http//www.oas.org/sice> (accessed 5 May 2009).

———. 2001b (20 Jul.) "Joint Statement of Singapore and the United States on the US-Singapore Free Trade Agreement, 20 July 2001". <http//www.oas.org/sice> (accessed 5 May 2009).

———. 2001c (26 Oct.). "Joint Statement of Singapore and the United States on the US-Singapore Free Trade Agreement, 26 October 2001". <http//www.oas.org/sice> (accessed 5 May 2009).

United Nations (UN)

United Nations Conference on Trade and Development (UNCTAD). 2006. *World Investment Report 2006: Transnational Corporations and the Internationalization of R&D*. New York: United Nations.

United Nations Development Programme (UNDP). 2007. *Human Development Report 2007/2008: Fighting Climate Change: Human Solidarity in a Divided World*. New York: PalgraveMacmillan.

World Bank (WB)

World Bank. 1998. *1998 World Development Indicators*. Washington, DC.

———. 2002. *Globalization: Growth and Poverty: Building on Inclusive World Economy*. New York: Oxford University Press.

———. 2003. *Regional Integration and Development*. Washington, DC.

———. 2007. *2007 World Development Indicators*. Washington, DC.

———. 2008. *2008 World Development Indicators*. Washington, DC.

World Trade Organization (WTO)

World Trade Organization. N.d. "List of All RTAs in Force, by Date of Entry into Force. Regional Trade Agreements Notified to the GATT/WTO and in Force by Date of Entry and into Force". <http://www.wto.org/english/tratop_e/region_e/region_e.htm> (accessed 14 May 2007).

———. 1997 (17 April). "WTO Director-General's Address to the Korean Business Association." <www.wto.org/English/news_e/pres97_e/seoul.htm> (accessed 14 May 2007).

———. 2007. *International Trade Statistics 2007*. Geneva.

———. 2009. *International Trade Statistics 2009*. Geneva.

INTERVIEWS

Koh, Tommy, Ambassador at Large, Ministry of Foreign Affairs, Singapore. 2008. Interview by author. 22 July. Singapore.

Loh, Derek K.Y., Hunton & Williams International Law Firm, Singapore. Interview by author. 14 July. Singapore.

Overmyer, Phillip, Chief Executive, Singapore International Chamber of Commerce. 2008. Interview by author. 23 July. Singapore.

Simmons, Dana, Supervisory Archivist, William J. Clinton Presidential Library. 2008. Interview by author. 8 October Little Rock, Arkansas.

Tietjen, Jim, Colonel, U.S. Air Force, Ret., Military *Attaché*, U.S. Embassy, Singapore. 2008. Interview by author. 12 July. Singapore.

LETTERS

(N.B.: Entries arranged alphabetically by surname of letter's author.)

Abrams, Elliott, Richard L. Armitage, William J. Bennett, Jeffrey Bergner, John Bolton, Paula Dobriansky, Francis Fukuyama, Robert Kagan, Zalmay Khalilzad, William Kristol, Richard Perle, Peter W. Rodman, Donald Rumsfeld, William

Schneider Jr., Vin Weber, Paul Wolfowitz, R. James Woosley, and Robert B. Zoellick to The Honorable William J. Clinton, President of the United States. 1998 (26 January). <http://www.newamericancentury.org/Iraqclintonletter.htm> (accessed 4 December 2009).

Gladden, Brian T., Vice President and General Manager, GE Plastics Global LEXAN Business to Barbara Weisel, Assistant U.S. Trade Representative. 2006 (14 September). <http://www.ustr.gov> (accessed 15 February 2008).

Janisnowski, Jerry to George W. Bush, Jr. 2003 (27 February). With a document, "The U.S.-Singapore Free Trade Agreement (FTA): The Report of the Advisory Committee for Trade Policy and Negotiations (ACTPN)".

Morris, Armond (Chairman, Georgia Peanut Commission), Carl Sanders (President, Alabama Peanut Producers Association), Michael Davis (President, Florida Peanut Producers Association), and Joe Morgan (President, Mississippi Peanut Growers association) to Susan C. Schwab, United States Trade Representative. 2006 (24 August). <http://www.americanpeanuts.com/082406trade.pdf> (accessed 15 February 2008).

Murray, Sean T., Miller & Company to Joni Jensen, Office of the U.S. Trade Representative. 2006 (20 September). <http://www.ustr.gov> (accessed 15 February 2008).

Rumer, Roger,Vice President, Bayer-Makrolon Polycarbonates to Barbara Weisel, Assistant U.S. Trade Representative. 2006 (15 September). <http://www.ustr.gov> (accessed 15 February 2008).

Schwab, Susan C., U.S. Trade Representative, and Carmen C. Suro-Bredie, Assistant U.S. Trade Representative to Daniel R. Pearson, Chairman, U.S. International Trade Commission, Washington DC. 2006 (23 October). <http://www.usitc.gov/publications/docs/pubs/332/singapore_request_letter.pdf> (accessed 15 February 2009).

Suro-Bredie, Carmen C., Assistant U.S. Trade Representative for Policy Coordination to Lyn Schlitt, Director, Office of External Relations, International Trade Commission. 2006 (7 November). <http://www.ustr.gov> (accessed 15 February 2008).

Walker, Robert C., Vice President and Site Operation, Texas Operations, The Dow Chemical Company to Barbara Weisel, Assistant U.S. Trade Representative. 2006 (13 September). <http://www.ustr.gov> (accessed 15 February 2008).

Yeo, George, Minister for Trade and Industry, Singapore, to Robert B. Zoellick, United States Trade Representative. 2003 (6 May). <http://www.ustr.gov> (accessed 15 February 2008).

PUBLIC DOCUMENTS: SINGAPORE

Competition Commission of Singapore (CCS)

Competition Commission of Singapore. N.d. "Competition Act (Chapter 50B):

Background". <http://www.ccs.gov.sg/Legislation/CompetitionAct/index. html> (accessed 25 May 2009).

Government of Singapore (GOS)
Government of Singapore. 2001 (2 January). "Joint Press Statement by the Ministry of Foreign Affairs and Ministry of Trade and Industry".

Ministry of Foreign Affairs (MFA)
Ministry of Foreign Affairs. 2007. "Speech by George Yeo, Minister for Foreign Affairs, at the OAV Liebesmahl Dinner in Hamburg on 13 March 2007". Media Resources Center, Ministry of Foreign Affairs. <http://www.mfa.gov.sg> (accessed 22 May 2009).

Ministry of Trade and Industry (MTI)
Ministry of Trade and Industry. N.d. "Integrated Sourcing Initiative." <http://www. fta.gov.sg> (accessed 1 August 2008).
———. 2003. "Speech by George Yeo, Minister for Trade and Industry, Singapore. 'At the Bintan Industrial Estate-Expanding for Growth' Event in Bintan, Indonesia on 29 January 2003 at 11:00am".
———. 2004. "Competition Bill".

Monetary Authority of Singapore (MAS)
Monetary Authority of Singapore. 2003. "Singapore and US Reach Agreement on the Issue of Free Transfer of Capital, 16 January 2003". <http://www.mas.gov. sg> (accessed 1 August 2008).

National Archives of Singapore (NAS)
Goh, Chok Tong. 2001. At the Reception of the WTO Informal Ministerial Meeting on Saturday, 13 October 2001, at 12 Noon at the Shangri-La Hotel. National Archives of Singapore. Singapore Government Press Release. Media Relations Division. Ministry of Information and the Arts.
———. 2003a. "Challenges for Asia". Speech by Singapore Prime Minister Goh Chok Tong at the Research Institute for Economy, Trade and Industry (RIETI) in Tokyo, Japan, on Friday, 28 March 2003". National Archives of Singapore. Singapore Government Press Release. Media Relations Division. Ministry of Information and the Arts.
———. 2003b. "East Asia in 2025". Key note Address by Prime Minister Goh Chok Tong at the World Economic Forum East Asia Economic Summit Opening Dinner on Sunday, 12 October 2003, 7:30PM, at Shangri-La." National Archives of Singapore. Singapore Government Press Release. Media Relations Division. Ministry of Information and the Arts.
———. 2003c. "ASEAN Economic Community", Keynote Address by Singapore Prime Minister Goh Chok Tong at the APEC CEO Summit on 18 October 2003,

Sunday, at 2:30PM (Thailand Time), in Bangkok, Thailand. National Archives of Singapore. Singapore Government Press Release. Media Relations Division. Ministry of Information and the Arts.

PUBLIC DOCUMENTS: UNITED STATES

Congressional Research Service (CRS)

Congressional Research Service. 1997 (13 June). "CRS Report for Congress. NAFTA: Economic Effects on the United States after Three Years". By Arlene Wilson. Washington, DC.

————. 2002a (13 May). "CRS Report for Congress. The U.S.-Singapore Free Trade Agreement". By Dick K. Nanto. Washington, DC.

————. 2002b (June). "CRS Report for Congress. NAFTA Labor Side Agreement: Lessons for the Workers Rights and Fast-Track Debate". By Mary Jane Bolle. Washington, DC.

————. 2003a (2 April) "CRS Report for Congress. Trade Promotion Authority (Fast-Track Authority for Trade Agreements): Background and Developments in the 107th Congress". By Lenore Sek. Washington, DC.

————. 2003b (22 May). "CRS Report for Congress. The U.S.-Singapore Free Trade Agreement". By Dick K. Nanto. Washington DC: CRS.

————. 2005a (12 January) "CRS Report for Congress. The U.S.-Australian Free Trade Agreement: Provisions and Implications". By William H. Cooper. Washington, DC.

————. 2005b (8 February) "CRS Report for Congress. Why Certain Trade Agreements Are Approved as Congressional-Executive Agreements Rather than as Treaties". By Jeanne J. Grimmett. Washington, DC.

————. 2005c (7 October) "CRS Report for Congress. Uzbekistan's Closure of the Airbase at Karshi-Khanabad: Context and Implications". By Jim Nichol. Washington, DC.

————. 2006 (4 April) "CRS Report for Congress. China-Southeast Asia Relations: Trends, Issues, and Implications for the United States". By Bruce Vaughn and Wayne M. Morrison. Washington, DC.

————. 2007a (22 January) "CRS Report for Congress. U.S. Strategic and Defense Relationship in the Asia-Pacific Region". By Bruce Vaughn. Washington, DC.

————. 2007b (15 March). "CRS Report for Congress. Trade Agreements: Impact on the U.S. Economy". By James K. Jackson. Washington, DC.

————. 2007c (18 July). "CRS Report for Congress. The Proposed South Korea – U.S. Free Trade Agreement (KORUS FTA)". Updated. By William H. Cooper and Mark E. Manyin. Washington, DC.

————. 2007d (12 December). "CRS Report for Congress. The U.S.-Australia Treaty on Defense Trade Cooperation". By Bruce Vaughn. Washington, DC.

————. 2008a (4 January). "CRS Report for Congress. China's Soft Power in Southeast Asia". By Thomas Lum, Wayne M. Morrison, and Bruce Vaughn. Washington, DC.

————. 2008b (4 January). "CRS Report for Congress. East Asian Regional Architecture: New Economic and Security Arrangements and U.S. Policy". By Nick K. Nanto. Washington, DC.

————. 2008c (7 January). "CRS Report for Congress. Emerging Trends in the Security Architecture in Asia: Bilateral and Multilateral Ties Among the United States, Japan, Australia, and India". By Emma Chanlett-Avery and Bruce Vaughn. Washington, DC.

————. 2008d (7 January). "CRS Report for Congress. The U.S.-Singapore Free Trade Agreement: Effects after Three Years". By Dick K. Nanto. Washington, DC.

————. 2008e (30 January). "CRS Report for Congress. Agriculture in U.S. Free Trade Agreements: Trade with Current and Prospective Partners, Impact, and Issues". By Remy Jurenas. Washington, DC.

————. 2008f (26 February). "CRS Report for Congress. Guam: U.S. Defense Deployment". By Shirley A. Kan and Larry A. Niksch. Washington, DC.

————. 2008g (28 April). "CRS Report for Congress. Korea – U.S. Relations: Issues for Congress". By Larry A. Niksch. Washington, DC.

————. 2008h (26 November). "U.S. - International Trade: Trends and Forecasts". By Dick K. Nanto, Shayerah Dias, and J. Michael Donnelly. Washington, DC.

————. 2008i (18 December). "Singapore Background and U.S. Relations". By Emma Chanlett-Avery. Washington, DC.

————. 2008j (31 December). "CRS Report for Congress. Membership of the 111th Congress: A Profile". By Mildred Amer and Jennifer E. Manning. Washington, DC.

————. 2009a (3 June). "Agriculture in Pending U.S. Free Trade Agreements with Colombia, Panama, and South Korea". By Remy Jurenas. Washington, DC.

————. 2009b (17 June). "CRS Report for Congress. China's Currency: A Summary of the Economic Issues". By Wayne M. Morrison and Marc Labonte. Washington, DC.

————. 2010 (26 March). "The U.S.-Singapore Free Trade Agreement: Effects After Five Years". By Dick N. Nanto. Washington, DC.

U.S. Congress (USC)

(N.B.: Entries for USC/H/CWM 2003 [10 June] are arranged alphabetically by testifier's surname.)

U.S. Congress. House. Committee on Ways and Means (USC/H/CWM). 2003a (10 June). "Statement of Thomas J. Donohue, President and Chief Executive Officer, U.S. Chamber of Commerce. Free Trade Deals".

————. 2003b (10 June). "Statement of Selina E. Jackson, UPS. Free Trade Deals".

———. 2003c (10 June). "Statement of Gawin Kripke, Senior Policy Advisor, Oxfam America: Testimony before the Subcommittee on Trade of the House Committee on Ways and Means".

———. 2003d (10 June). "Statement of L. Maury, President, Business Round Table. Free Trade Deals".

———. 2003e (10 June). "Statement of Harold McGraw III, Chairman and Chief Executive Officer, McGraw-Hill Companies, New York and Chairman, Emergency Committee for American Trade. Free Trade Deals".

———. 2003f (10 June). "Statement of Kristin E. Paulson, American Chamber of Commerce in Singapore. Free Trade Deals".

———. 2003g (10 June). "Statement of the Honorable Pete Sessions, a Representative in Congress from the State of Texas. Testimony before the Subcommittee on Trade of the House Committee on Ways and Means".

———. 2003h (10 June). "Statement of Daniel K. Tarullo, Professor, Georgetown University Law Center. Free Trade Deals".

———. 2003i (10 June). "Statement of William Weiler, Chairman of the Board and Chief Executive Officer, Purafil, Inc., Atlanta, Georgia. Free Trade Deals".

———. 2008[?] "Statement of Charles D. Lake II, American Chamber of Commerce in Japan".

U.S. Congress. House. Subcommittee on Commerce, Trade, and Consumer Protection on Trade in Services and E-Commerce (USC/H/SCTCPTSE). 2003 (14 May). "Testimony of Thea M. Lee, Chief International Economist, AFL-CIO. The Significance of the Singapore and Chile Free Trade Agreements".

U.S. Department of Agriculture (USDoA)

U.S. Department of Agriculture. FAS Online. 2000. "Singapore: Destination and Gateway for U.S. Exports to Southeast Asia. By Dale Good. <http://www.fas.usda/gov/info/agexporter/2000/September/singapo.htm> (accessed 5 April 2009).

U.S. Department of Commerce (USDoC)

U.S. Department of Commerce. 2009 (August). "Survey of Current Business". <http://www.bea.gov/scb/pdf/2009/08%20August/D-Pages/0809dpg_g.pdf> (accessed 15 September 2009).

U.S. Department of Defense (USDoD)

U.S. Department of Defense. 1998. *The United States Security Strategy for the East Asia-Pacific Region 1998*.

———. 2004. "2004 Statistical Compendium on Allied Contributions to the Common Defense Covers Allied Contributions in 2003". Washington, DC.

———. 2007 (27 September). "Admiral Details Tenets for New Maritime Strategy".

American Forces Press Service. By Jim Garamone. <http://www.defenselink. gov> (accessed 1 August 2008).

———. Office of the Assistant Secretary of Defense. 1998 (23 January). "Secretary Cohen's Remarks at the Navy Flag Officers Conference".

U.S. Department of State (DoS)

U.S. Department of State. 2005 (25 May). "U.S. to Resume Military Education Training with Indonesia". <http://www.usinfo.state.gov> (accessed 1 August 2008).

U.S. Embassy, Singapore

U.S. Embassy, Singapore. 1998 (September). "Singapore's Banking Industry Report (September 1998)". <http://singapore.usembassy.gov> (accessed 1 August 2008).

———. 1999 (May). "Reforming Singapore's Financial Services Sector: A Background & Progress Report (May 1999)". http://singapore.usembassy.gov (accessed 1 August 2008).

———. 2000 (June). "State-led Creative Destruction: Singapore Plans for a New Knowledge-Based Economy". June 2000. <http://singapore.usembasy.gov> (accessed (accessed 1 August 2008).

———. 2005. "U.S. Singapore Relations: U.S. Singapore Trade Highlights 2005". <http://singapore.usembassy.gov/trade_2005.html> (accessed 1 August 2008).

———. 2008. "Singapore: Trade Summary 2008". <http://singapore.usembassy. gov> (accessed 1 August 2008).

U.S. Government Accountability Office (USGAO; formerly Government Accounting Office)

U.S. Government Accountability Office. 1989 (23 February). "Testimony. Statement by Joseph. E. Keller, National Security and International Affairs Division before Subcommittee on Commerce, Consumer Protection and Competition, Committee on Energy and Commerce, House of Representatives. U.S. Military Aircraft Coproduction with Japan".

———. 1994 (July). "Report to the Congress. The General Agreement on Tariffs and Trade: Uruguay Round Final Act Should Produce Overall U.S. Economic Gains". Vol. 1.

———. 1995. "Report to the Congress. U.S.-Japan Cooperative Development Progress on the FS-X Program Enhances Japanese Aerospace Capabilities".

———. 2004 (January). "Report to Congressional Requesters. International Trade: Intensifying Free Trade Negotiating Agenda Calls for Better Allocation of Staff and Resources".

———. 2007a (June). "Report to Congressional Requesters. Trade Adjustment Assistance. Industry Certification Would Likely Make More Workers Eligible, but Design and Implementation Challenges Exist".

———. 2007b (14 June). "Testimony before the Committee on Ways and Means, House of Representatives. Trade Adjustment Assistance. Changes Needed to Improve States' Ability to Provide Benefits and Services to Trade-Affected Workers. Statement of Sigurd R. Nilsen, Director, Education, Workforce, and Income Security Issues".

———. 2007c (November). "Report to the Chairman, Committee on Finance, U.S. Senate: International Trade. An Analysis of Free Trade Agreements and Congressional and Private Sector Consultations under Trade Promotion Authority".

———. 2008a (12 June). "Testimony before the Committee on Finance, United States Senate. International Trade. The United States Needs an Integrated Approach to Trade Preference Programmes".

———. 2008b (August). "Report to the Committee on Finance, U.S. Senate. U.S. Multinational Corporations. Effective Tax Rates Are Correlated with Where Income Is Reported".

———. 2009a (17 March). "Testimony before the Subcommittee on Commerce, Trade, and Consumer Protection, Committee on Energy and Commerce, House of Representatives. International Trade. Effective Export Programmes Can Help in Achieving U.S. Economic Goals. Statement of Loren Yager, Director, International Affairs and Trade.

———. 2009b (April). "Report to Congressional Committees. 2008 Lobbying Disclosure. Observations on Lobbyists' Compliance with Disclosure Requirements".

U.S. International Trade Commission (USITC)
U.S. International Trade Commission. 2007. "U.S.-Chile Free Trade Agreement: Key Market Access Results and Benefits". http://www.usitc.gov (accessed 11 February 2007).

———. 2008 (October). "Probable Economic Effect of Certain Modifications to the United States-Chile Free Trade Agreement Rules of Origin".

U.S. National Intelligence Council (USNIC)
U.S. National Intelligence Council. 2008 (November). "Global Trends 2025: A Transformed World". NIC 2008-003. Washington, DC.

U.S. Office of Trade Representative (USTR)
U.S. Office of Trade Representative. 2002 (13 December). "Trade Facts: Free Trade Agreement with Singapore: America's First Free Trade Agreement in Asia". <http://www.ustr.gov> (accessed 1 August 2008).

———. 2003a (February). "Report of the Agricultural Technical Advisory Committee of Cotton, Peanuts, Planting Seeds and Tobacco". <http://www.ustr.gov> (accessed 1 August 2008).

———. 2003b (27 February). "Dissenting Views of James P. Hoffa, General President, International Brotherhood of Teamsters". In "The U.S.-Singapore Free Trade Agreement (FTA): The Report of the Advisory Committee for Trade Policy and Negotiations (ACTPN)". <http://www.ustr.gov> (accessed 1 August 2008).

———. 2003c (28 February) "Report of the Labor Advisory Committee (LAC) for Free Trade Negotiations and Trade Policy. The U.S.-Chile and U.S.-Singapore Free Trade Agreements". <http://www.ustr.gov> (accessed 1 August 2008).

———. 2003d (6 May). "Quick Facts: U.S.-Singapore Free Trade Agreement, 05/06/2003". <http://www.ustr.gov> (accessed 1 August 2008).

———. 2003e (6 May) "United States-Singapore Free Trade Agreement". <http://www.ustr.gov> (accessed 1 August 2008).

———. 2005 (31 March). "USTR Issues 2005 "1377" Review of Telecommunications Agreements. Renewed Focus on Identifying, Dismantling Tellecommunications Trade Barriers around the World.

———. 2006 (March). "Goods Issues to Be Raised by Singapore at the 2nd USSFTA Review".

———. 2008. (8 April). "Schwab Announces Results of Annual 1377 Review".

The White House

The White House. Office of the Press Secretary. 2000 (16 November). "Joint Statement by President Bill Clinton and Prime Minister Goh Chok Tong on a United States-Singapore Free Trade Agreement". <http://clinton6.nara.gov> (accessed 2 April 2008).

———. 2003 (6 May). "President Signed U.S.-Singapore Free Trade Agreement, 6 May 2003 East Room". <http://www.thewhitehouse.gov> (accessed 2 April 2008).

———. 2009a (14 November). "In Tokyo, Our Common Future". <http://www.thewhitehouse.gov> (accessed 5 December 2009).

———. 2009b (15 November). "Remarks by President Obama and Prime Minister Abhist of Thailand after ASEAN-10 Meeting". <http://www.thewhitehouse.gov> (accessed 5 December 2009).

———. 2010 (May). *National Security Strategy*. Washington DC. <http://www.thewhitehouse.gov> (accessed 30 May 2010).

Index

About the Author

Eul-Soo Pang is a Visiting Professorial Fellow at the Institute of Southeast Asian Studies, Singapore. He is Professor Emeritus in international political economy and history, Colorado School of Mines, Golden, Colorado. Receiving his Ph.D. in Latin American history (Berkeley), his interests have branched out into comparative political economy, in particular, trade and security issues for Latin America and East Asia. He has held several research fellowships (the Doherty Foundation, Social Science Research Council, National Endowment for the Humanities, and the American Philosophical Society). He also received two Fulbright visiting professorships (to Brazil and Malaysia) and on several occasions worked with a Department of State speakers' program on international political economy and security issues, touring Argentina, Brazil, Chile, Guyana, Honduras, Paraguay, Suriname, and Trinidad and Tobago. Between 2000 and 2007 (eight consecutive summers), Pang was a visiting professor at the Institute of Diplomacy and Foreign Relations in Kuala Lumpur, then a department of Malaysia's Office of the Prime Minister, teaching international political economy. He has published four books and some sixty book chapters and articles. His current research interest is the power shift and newly emerging paradigm of economy and security in the greater Asia-Pacific world-system in the Indian Ocean, South China Sea, and Western Pacific. He is currently completing a book on United States foreign policy toward Southeast Asia since the end of the Vietnam War.